Early Praise for **T**.

"Moran's survival is a cinematically grand story, bigger than life but not fantastical, dramatically gripping as well as emotionally stirring. An extraordinary, moving account of survival and endurance."

—*Kirkus Reviews*

"A survival story that bridges generations, told with heart-rending poignancy. *Tailspin* unveils the twin stories of two remarkable, resilient men facing the biggest trials of their lives. More than a war story, it's a universal story of family. I highly recommend this book filled with truth and compassion."

—Heather Shumaker, author of *Saving Arcadia*

"*Tailspin* is a survival story you'll never forget. While it centers on the vivid and harrowing tale of Gene Moran's ordeal as a German POW in WWII—and the trauma that followed him home—the book is more than a tribute to Armbruster's courageous friend and neighbor. By including the stories of how he worked with Gene to unearth his painful past all while supporting his young wife in her battle with Stage IV cancer and then grieving her death, Armbruster transcends the genre in powerful, surprising ways. What you're left with, at the end of this incredible reading experience, is a richer appreciation of all the ways we're connected in our suffering—and the everyday courage it takes to fight, heal, and soldier on."

—Mark Rader, author of *The Wanting Life*

"Armbruster actually tells three stories in this book. The first is about sensitively getting to know Gene Moran and enlisting his trust; then facilitating the therapeutic sharing of Gene's traumatic ordeal; and last but not least, the painful telling of his own wife's battle with cancer. It is three carefully interwoven journeys, well told. Think of *Tuesdays With Morrie*, *Unbroken*, and *Steel Magnolias* all in one."

—Edward Krall MD, MS, LFAPA, Assistant Professor of Psychiatry, Medical College of Wisconsin

"*Tailspin* is one of the most engaging books I have ever read. Like his mentor Ben Logan, John carefully and reverently tells a story which was buried in Eugene Moran's emotional bedrock for years. With patience and respect, the story of a survivor and survival is evoked and intersects with the story of the author. The story is human and humanizing; there is dignity and strength in sacrifice and suffering. These truths are known but seldom spoken with such compassion and competence. Eugene and John invite us to explore our lives of sorrow and joy, triumph and tragedy, by humbling sharing their lives and love with each of their readers and fellow human beings."

—Thomas Thibodeau, Distinguished Professor of Servant Leadership at Viterbo University

"*Tailspin* is a compelling story that transcends genre. It is about the struggles of two individuals: one surviving horrific wartime events, the other dealing with devastating family tragedy. This narrative demonstrates the power of resilience when confronting the 'tailspins' of life."

—Kathleen Hendrickson, Reading Specialist, Westby Area Schools

"Once I started reading *Tailspin*, I couldn't put it down for the better part of two long nights. But beyond being simply gripping, this story of Gene Moran's life, and how he came to share it with author John Armbruster, is deeply human. An indomitable spirit, sustained through bonds of love and companionship, kept Gene alive through unspeakable horrors of war, then kept at bay the shadows of trauma that followed him home. In bringing Gene's story to light, *Tailspin* brings a dark chapter of history into the present and ultimately offers hope that although it may take generations, sharing our stories can help even the deepest wounds to heal."

—Keefe Keeley, co-author of *The Driftless Reader*

"I have been recommending *Tailspin* since I read the first draft. The interviews and interactions with Gene later in his life intertwined with the story of his incredible survival make you feel like you're slipping back into those memories with Gene. *Tailspin* tells the story of young Gene Moran, tail gunner. It also gives us John and Gene and how they became part of each other's lives and supported each other through happy and difficult times. Thank you, Gene, for sharing your story. Thank you, John, for sharing with us."

—Joelle Clark, Elementary and Dance Educator

"The story of how these two men's lives dovetail in unexpected ways makes for a powerful story that should be on the shelves of not just World War II collections, but men's relationship literature and any library collection where stories of friendship and connection are valued."

—D. Donovan, Senior Reviewer, *Midwest Book Review*

TAILSPIN

JOHN ARMBRUSTER

www.ten16press.com - Waukesha, WI

Dedication

To Gene, and those whose lives were cut short by cancer or war: especially Carmen and the crew of *Rikki Tikki Tavi*.

TABLE OF CONTENTS

INTRODUCTION

For those of you who knew Eugene Paul Moran and waited for so long to learn his story, you won't find it *all* here in this book. Most of it, yes.

Oh, I tried to learn every detail of the most incredible survival story I'd ever heard. In three years of off-again, on-again recorded interviews, I pushed Gene as far as he'd let me. When we came to a difficult scene, he'd stop talking, fill his cheeks with air, and then slowly exhale. Sometimes he'd go on. Sometimes he would not.

Once, when I'd prodded Gene to describe sights and sounds from his journey on the infamous hell ship, he slapped his hands on the tabletop and flatly stated, "John, that is as far as we are going today." He quickly ended the interview. I hurriedly packed up my legal pad and voice recorder and scurried out the mobile home side entry door.

When he later spoke of his trek on the death march, he'd often fall silent and stare at the tabletop. I'd wait. I guessed whom he was seeing in his mind's eye. A Polish girl with sunken cheekbones clinging to her mother's hand in a crowd of terrified refugees? An emaciated prisoner lying dead in a ditch, staring back at Gene with lifeless eyes? These would be images Gene took to his grave. They are his stories, not ours.

Two other questions may arise for the reader, one of which

haunted Gene his entire life: why did his Flying Fortress bomber fall back? Why did *Rikki Tikki Tavi* retreat from the protective embrace of its squadron to be hunted down by a pack of German fighter planes? The reams of narrative operation reports from the National Archives that I pored over only say that Gene's plane, bomber AC 42-30359, went missing after dropping its bombs on Bremen, Germany, on November 29, 1943. I'm certain when Gene left this world and arrived at his heaven in 2014, it would be the first question he'd pose to St. Peter . . . followed by, "Do you guys have Blatz beer up here?"

The other question is one I've been asked again and again: how did Gene survive a four-mile free fall in a severed tail section that slammed into a forest? I will give the same answer I told a German television crew when I visited the crash site on the seventy-fifth anniversary of Gene's fall: I have no idea.

Tailspin is a work of narrative nonfiction. I chose this form because Gene's story could only be told as a story. No characters have been invented or names changed. No events have been fabricated. Some may question the accuracy of scenes that happened decades ago described by a man in his late eighties. I don't. I saw Gene's eyes widen when he talked about his Army Air Force comrades, his "brothers." I felt the kitchen table shudder from his fist pounding, bitter about how military brass asked young airmen to do the impossible. Gene knew exactly what he was talking about.

It wasn't always so clear. There were times I'd press Gene, asking him for the exact words at a critical moment, only to have him growl at me, "I don't know, John. It's been damn near seventy years. Just write it the best you can."

Whenever possible, dialogue and quotations by Gene (and other interacting persons) are directly supported by combat records, letters, recorded recollection, phone interviews with relatives of the characters, and all available sources concerning his service in the 96th Bomb Group and his time as a prisoner of war. When information was lacking, I supplied likely dialogue for completing the narrative and conveying, to the best of his knowledge, the most faithful portrayal of the events as they happened. This is particularly true of the conversations Gene had with his beloved bomber crewmates and the lifelong friends he made as a prisoner of war.

Whenever I came to a crossroads in writing *Tailspin*, I remembered the advice of author Ben Logan. Ben wrote *The Land Remembers*, a book I judge to be one of the two most important books to ever come out of Wisconsin, along with Aldo Leopold's *A Sand County Almanac*. I had the incredibly good fortune to become friends with Ben late in his life. He often visited my social studies classes and would give this advice to my students interested in writing:

When you have to decide between facts and legend, choose the legend. The truth is too important to be left to facts.

I hope you, the reader, enjoy the legend of Gene Moran.

1. SNETTERTON HEATH: Home to the 96th Bomb Group, Gene arrived in England in late October, 1943 to begin his combat tour.

2. KNABEN, NORWAY: Gene didn't know it at the time, but his mission here was part of an effort to destroy the Nazi atomic bomb project.

3. BREMEN, GERMANY: On Nov. 29, 1943, Gene and his plane, *Rikki Tikki Tavi*, were shot down over this industrial city. Gene lay trapped in the severed tail section of his plane without a parachute.

4. SANDBOSTEL POW CAMP: Jammed with prisoners from all over Nazi-occupied Europe, two Serbian doctors put Gene back together after he miraculously survived his fall.

5. DULAG LUFT: Two months after being shot down, Gene was sent by the Germans to this interrogation center in Frankfurt, Germany, where he met "Shorty" Cyr. It was here that he learned that one other member of his crew survived, Jesse Orrison.

6. STALAG LUFT VI: After interrogation at Dulag Luft, Gene was sent to this POW camp where he met an old Wisconsin friend, Bill Dorgan. The Germans evacuated the camp in July 1944 as the Soviet Army approached.

7. THE HELL SHIP: On a scorching midsummer day in 1944, the Germans jammed Gene and a thousand other prisoners into the dark hold of a rusty ship with no food, water, or toilets. For three days and two nights on the Baltic Sea, Gene suffered on this ship on his way to his next prison camp.

8. STALAG LUFT IV: Often described as the worst of the German POW camps for Allied prisoners, Gene was imprisoned here until he was moved out again ahead of the oncoming Soviets in February 1945.

9. THE DEATH MARCH: Also known as the Black March, an estimated one thousand Allied prisoners died on this six-hundred-mile forced march in late winter/early spring in 1945. American forces liberated Gene at Bitterfeld, Germany, in late April.

Map design by Charles Angell

GENE'S WAR

The crew of
RIKKI TIKKI TAVI

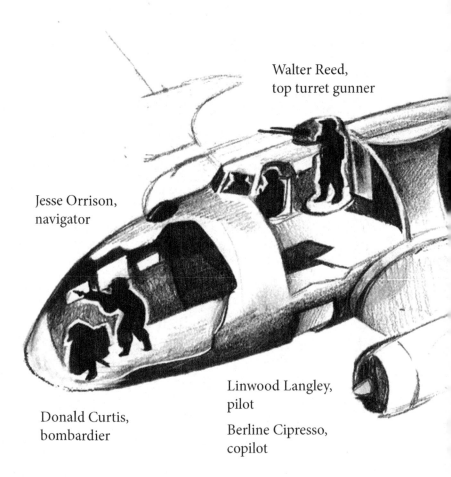

Walter Reed,
top turret gunner

Jesse Orrison,
navigator

Linwood Langley,
pilot

Donald Curtis,
bombardier

Berline Cipresso,
copilot

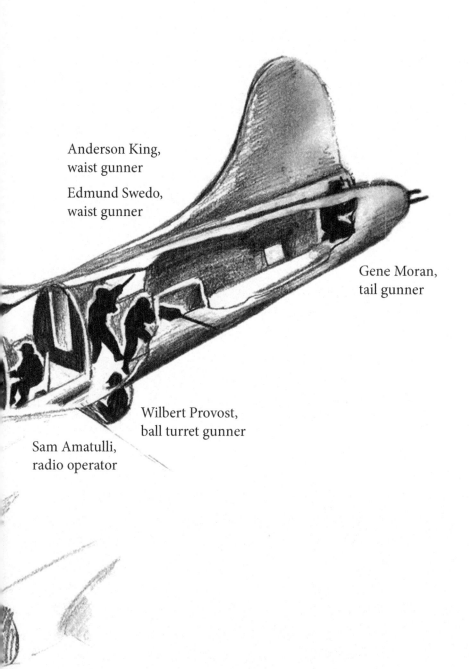

Anderson King,
waist gunner

Edmund Swedo,
waist gunner

Gene Moran,
tail gunner

Wilbert Provost,
ball turret gunner

Sam Amatulli,
radio operator

*Diagram of *Rikki Tikki Tavi* illustrated by Jayden Ellsworth

CHAPTER 1

The Secret Story

November 29, 1943

Tail gunner Gene Moran sat in his flight suit, his silk undershirt soaked with sweat. Outside, the air temperature measured nearly forty-five degrees below zero. His battle station was unheated, yet sweat beads streaked down his back, tickling his spine. His B-17 Flying Fortress bomber, the *Rikki Tikki Tavi,* had just flown through a gauntlet of German fighter plane attacks and anti-aircraft gunfire.

Squatting behind twin fifty-caliber machine guns in the rear of the four-engine airplane, the nineteen-year-old Wisconsin farm kid sucked in a deep breath and blew out his cheeks. He relaxed his body into his bicycle-seat chair and let his shoulders slump. They'd made it, his fifth bombing run.

Pillars of coal black smoke spiraled up from the industrial city of Bremen. During their attack, enemy anti-aircraft gunners on the ground had pumped so much exploding flak into the sky that Gene believed he could have stepped out of his plane and walked on it. But despite the intense fire, *Rikki Tikki Tavi* flew level and her bombs dropped cleanly from the belly of the plane. No hang-ups.

Looking out his window, Gene watched strings of five-hundred-pound bombs fall from one hundred and fifty Flying Fortresses. In the nose of the plane, bombardier Donald Curtis flicked the switch to close the bomb bay doors. Relieved of the weight of its bomb load, *Rikki Tikki Tavi* leapt upward and banked sharply right in unison with the other bombers, turning a wide arc west back toward its home base in England. Gene exhaled. *By God, we're gonna make it.*

Then the sweat on Gene's back chilled. From a distance off to his side, he spotted dozens of black specks growing larger. The German Air Force—the Luftwaffe—had returned. Sleek, single-engine Messerschmitt 109 and Focke-Wulf 190 fighter planes along with stub-nosed, twin-engine Messerschmitt 410 fighters hovered above the American bombers. The Flying Fortresses, stacked in three separate formations, flew straight into the ambush. Gene watched several of the dark enemy planes peel off from their groups and barrel straight for his plane.

This couldn't be happening. It hadn't happened to Gene in any of his previous missions. He leaned into the steel chest plate mounted above his twin machine guns. He lowered his gloved hands to finger both triggers and waited for a Nazi fighter to fill his gun sight.

Co-pilot Berline "Benny" Cipresso called out the incoming fighters closing in on *Rikki Tikki Tavi*.

"Bandits! Two o'clock high!"

Seconds later, every machine gun on the bomber opened fire. Gun turrets whined as they spun around, tracking German planes that swept in from every angle. Gene's eardrums ached. The stink of spent gunpowder seeped under his oxygen mask and tinged his nostrils. The voices of his comrades crackled in the speakers of his headset as they shouted out the location of the attackers. Someone blurted out, "Jesus! They're everywhere!"

A Nazi fighter flashed above Gene, heading in the opposite direction of his tail guns after sweeping his bomber with a head-on attack. Another enemy plane zipped past the tail and snapped a roll to the right.

Suddenly, the hum of *Rikki Tikki Tavi*'s engines slackened. The bomber slowed and fell behind the rest of the squadron. Gene's stomach tightened. He yelled into his throat microphone.

"What's going on? Why are we falling back?"

"Don't know," another gunner crackled back. "Something's pushing us back."

Gene looked left, then right. No smoke or fire trailed from any of the engines. The bomber stayed level; they were flying straight. No one on the plane called out any damage. This didn't make any sense. If the plane hadn't been harmed, why were they falling back?

From the cockpit, pilot Linwood "Woody" Langley said nothing. The plane's propellers cut into the cold air, trying to catch up to the other Flying Fortresses. Still *Rikki Tikki Tavi* fell back. They were losing altitude. Gene's teeth rattled as the plane shuddered against the labored groans of the engines. From a side window, he could see the rest of the American bomber squadron flying on, leaving his plane all alone.

From the bottom of the bomber, ball turret gunner Wilbert "Pee Wee" Provost, Gene's best friend, screamed. "Mo! There's a son of a bitch coming at us! He's coming right up our ass! Buddy, I'm done!" Gene heard the enemy bullets and cannon shells tear into Pee Wee's aluminum and Plexiglas cocoon.

Shouting voices overlapped on the radio. Some screamed out in pain.

"Pee Wee! Are you hit?!"

"Who's hit?!"

"What's going on up front?! Lieutenant? Benny? Anybody?"

A twin-engine Messerschmitt fighter flew up and passed the rear of the bomber right in front of Gene's guns. *Don't think about Pee Wee. See the enemy fighter. Shoot. Shoot now.*

Gene squeezed hard both triggers. His guns barked in rhythmic vengeance. Fifty-caliber bullets arced out toward the fleeing German fighter and found their mark. Oily smoke belched from the enemy aircraft. Chunks of metal hurtled into the air. The twin-engine fighter abruptly dove out of sight.

From every neck-twisting direction, more Luftwaffe fighter planes swept over *Rikki Tikki Tavi*, riddling the bomber with machine gun bullets and cannon shells. The plane stayed level, but continued to lose airspeed and altitude. Gene stole quick glances out his side windows. He could no longer see the other American bombers. They were alone, separated from the protective cluster of the squadron, every airman's worst nightmare.

And then waist gunner Edmund Swedo began to sing.

"I'm gonna buy a paper doll that I can call my own.
A doll that other fellows cannot steal.
And then the flirty, flirty guys with their flirty, flirty eyes . . ."

Gene always thought Swedo had a swell voice.

"Goddammit, Swedo, get the hell off the mike!" a crewmate roared.

In the rear of the bomber, Gene kept firing as enemy planes pressed their attack. Soon he noticed an eerie quiet. The panicked chatter on the intercom ceased. Not a gunner spoke. No gun fired except his own. *Where is everybody? Did they bail out? Are they all dead? Am I alone?*

And then Gene's eyes widened. He stared. A lone Messerschmitt 109 slowly approached the tail of *Rikki Tikki Tavi*, slightly to Gene's right. Gene slammed his guns to the side to shoot him, but the German pilot stayed just outside the range of the tail guns. The cigar-shaped plane pulled up next to the wounded American bomber. There he was, the enemy, just twenty feet away. The jet-black German cross on the fuselage contrasted sharply with its white background, the Nazi swastika emblazoned on the tail.

For a moment, Gene stared at the white scarf of the Luftwaffe fighter pilot. The German pilot looked back at him. Gene watched as the pilot slowly raised his gloved hand above his head. He extended his index finger and jabbed his hand in a downward motion. Gene sat transfixed. Again, but more quickly and sharply, the fighter pilot repeated the gesture.

Gene's mind raced. *What do you want? What do you want?! I don't understand!* And then he guessed: *Is he giving me a chance to get out, a chance to jump?*

The enemy fighter pilot waited. His Messerschmitt 109 fighter kept pace with Gene's plane. Except for the drone of the bomber's engines, all was quiet. Gene stared back at the pilot. He thought of his parachute strapped safely on his back. He wondered if his crewmates had jumped. He didn't move.

At that moment, a machine gun on *Rikki Tikki Tavi* fired. Someone was still alive and fighting! Was it Swedo or Andy King on the waist guns? Maybe it was Walter Reed, the quiet one, from the top turret. In an instant, the German pilot jerked his Messerschmitt up, flipped it onto its back, and banked sharply away.

Waiting German fighter planes moved in for the kill. Gene leaned forward again on his chest plate, lowered his arms, and began firing. There would be no second chance to parachute.

Wham! Wham! Wham! German fighters methodically pumped twenty-millimeter cannon fire into the dying bomber. A cannon shell exploded below Gene's tail guns. The concussion of the blast threw him up out of his seat and jerked his twin machine guns sideways. He bent back down, squeezed his triggers, but the guns didn't fire. *I'm jammed. I'm jammed!* Gene backed off his chest plate and squeezed himself down the side of it. He lowered his arms to fix the crooked guns.

As he fumbled with his broken weapon, a hailstorm of bullets punctured the tail section and snapped both his forearms. Glass shattered overhead and clanged off the metal sides of the plane.

Gene looked up to see two orange-sized holes in each side window. Enemy gunfire shot through the space occupied by his head a few seconds earlier. Bitterly cold air poured into the tail of the plane.

Gene sat up and lifted both arms in front of his face. His left forearm bent at an awkward angle. From his right forearm, a bloodied and jagged bone stuck out of a torn sleeve of his leather flight jacket. For a second, he marveled at how quickly blood coagulated in sub-zero air.

Frigid air whooshed through the shattered windowpanes and frosted Gene's eyebrows. Again, he lowered his arms to his guns. He squeezed the triggers. The left gun remained silent, but the right one fired.

Another explosion slammed Gene into his chest plate, snapping every rib on his left side. Still sitting upright, he then noticed something as pretty as his right arm was repulsive. Translucent strings of silk swirled through the air like apple blossoms caught in a spring breeze. It was his parachute, now a torn mess upon his back. Gene muttered to himself, "It's over." *Rikki Tikki Tavi's* nose dropped. The plane began to spiral earthward.

The spare chute! Gene remembered the extra parachute set just a few feet behind him next to the plane's retracted tail wheel. He turned his body off his chair, lay on his stomach, and crawled on his elbows, trying to keep his broken forearms off the floor. He squirmed forward, but barely moved toward the parachute. Centrifugal force pinned him to the floor. The whine and moan of his plane deafened him as *Rikki Tikki Tavi* cried out her death rattle. Agonizingly slow, he inched forward. *Almost there. Almost there!* He could see the spare parachute just a few feet away. He also spotted Swedo and Andy, lying still, sprawled out on the plane floor amidst a heap of empty shell casings. Cold air whistling in from dozens of bullet holes in the fuselage poured over their broken and bloodied bodies.

Suddenly, the bomber lurched forward. The big plane groaned as its aluminum skeleton tore apart at the tail wheel. Blue sky opened up from every direction around Gene's head. The tail section, with Gene in it, fell away from the rest of the plane.

Gene's hands shot out and grabbed the aluminum ribbing of the fuselage floor. His broken forearms pushed back as he tried not to slide past the jagged edge and into the open air just inches from his face. The tailless bomber floated aimlessly out into space. With it went Pee Wee, Swedo, the rest of the crew, and the spare parachute. For a brief moment, Gene watched his plane drift away. No one bailed out.

The severed tail of *Rikki Tikki Tavi* began its four-mile free fall toward enemy soil. The force which had pinned Gene to the plane's floor vanished. He could move. He jerked his torso around and crawled away from the open end of the wreckage.

Gene was all alone, severely wounded with a shredded parachute. He pulled the torn silk around him. Lying on his back with his feet inches from the ripped edge of the tail wreckage, he waited for the end. The icy wind rushed across his face as he plunged toward the ground.

He clumsily yanked off his fur-lined gloves and fumbled through the chest pockets of his flight jacket, searching for his rosary. His grandmother had given him the chain of holy beads before he left for Europe. His fingers touched the crucifix. Gripping the rosary, he pulled it out of his jacket pocket and pinched hard the sharp-edged, pea-sized beads. Skin scraped from his thumb and fingertips as he rolled and ground the rosary beads into his flesh.

He softened his hold on the rosary and repeated, "Hail Mary, full of grace. The Lord is with thee. Hail Mary, full of grace. The Lord is with thee. Hail Mary, full of grace . . ."

October 1994

The story of the man who fell four miles without a parachute and lived dropped into my life during a routine teacher training class.

It was an in-service day, no students, at North Crawford Schools. I was two months into my rookie year as a middle and high school social studies teacher. I loved teaching history, but on that sunny late-October day, I sat trapped in a molded plastic chair inside a windowless auditorium, daydreaming about escaping to a deer hunting stand or a cornfield goose blind.

Our small K-12 public school sat next to the Kickapoo River, a crooked stream that twisted through a forested valley dotted with dairy farms just a few miles south of the town of Soldiers Grove, Wisconsin. Ahead of me sat two men, visiting educators from another district. At break time, most of the teachers drifted out to the hall to head to the restroom or sip coffee. Not feeling like making small talk with strangers, I stayed in my seat and overheard the conversation in front of me.

"Isn't this the school with the art teacher whose dad was shot down without a parachute and lived?" one of the men said to the other.

I leaned forward.

"Yeah, Joni Peterson," the other replied. "Her dad was a tail gunner during World War II. He was shot down over Germany. I guess he fell some four miles or so before he hit the ground."

"Incredible. It doesn't make any sense."

"He came down in a chunk of the plane, from what I know, and the Germans captured him."

It took a moment for my dulled brain to make sense of the words I had just heard. Shot down without a parachute . . . and lived? Four miles? I could only catch snippets of the conversation as teachers shuffled back into the auditorium to take their seats. But I knew just where to go to get this story. Joni Peterson's art room sat right next to my classroom.

Joni's art room was a kaleidoscope without the symmetry. Partially completed clay sculptures of every shape and color cluttered the tops of her art tables. Models of Leonardo da Vinci's flying machine hung from fishing line tied to the exposed steel ceiling rafters. More than forty images of the *Mona Lisa* were taped on the walls. The creative chaos was familiar to me. I often hung out in Joni's room during free moments. The art room functioned both as a student classroom and an unofficial teacher lounge. Conversation flowed easily there. But I was about to find out that one topic was taboo.

I found Joni setting out construction paper and glue for the next school day, hurrying so she could get home.

"Is it true, the story I heard about your dad?" I asked.

She paused, chuckled, and continued laying out construction paper.

"Yes, it's true," she said. "Ole 'Lean Gene the Fightin' Machine.'"

I quickly shared with Joni the conversation I'd overheard a few hours earlier.

"I heard his plane went down over Germany. How was he shot down? When? Where did he land? He was a tail gunner, right? On what kind of plane? Flying Fortress? Liberator? How badly was he hurt? Did the Germans capture him right away? How long was he a prisoner?"

Joni continued working, but offered few answers. She did identify his plane as a Flying Fortress bomber. As a lifelong World War II airplane buff, the B-17 Flying Fortress bomber topped my list of favorite aircraft.

"So when can your dad visit my classroom?" I asked.

Joni dropped a ream of construction paper on a table. She glared at me. "That's not happening. We don't go there."

I should have known better. Many veterans don't share their war stories. On top of that, Joni had just lost her husband, a paralyzed Vietnam War veteran, to a heart attack a few months before I was hired at North Crawford. I muttered apologies and sank into silence. Joni shrugged. "It's all right," she said. "We just don't talk about it."

She finished setting out the last glue bottle. We stepped out of her classroom and walked down the hall to leave for the day. She buttoned her long coat, tossed her scarf around her neck.

"Maybe someday I could arrange for the two of you to get together and talk," she said before we walked outside into the crisp autumn evening, heading for our cars. "If you learn anything, you'll know more than I do."

A few days later, Joni handed me a copy of a regional newspaper with a front-page picture of Gene standing next to the tail gun of a Flying Fortress bomber. I scanned the headline: "Bomber Brings Back Memories of Tail Gunner's Four-Mile Free Fall." Two years earlier in the summer of 1992, a vintage Flying Fortress bomber had visited the airport in La Crosse, Wisconsin. La Crosse was about an hour's drive north from Gene's home in Soldiers Grove. Gene had driven up to see the old warbird, and he allowed a reporter there to snap a picture and ask a few questions. The article was the result. I eagerly scanned the story, but there were few details. An eyewitness had watched Gene's fall. Gene had suffered a skull fracture.

"As far as I know, this is the only time Dad spoke to the press about it," Joni explained. "Now you know as much as my sisters and brothers know."

For the next thirteen years, that article was my only source of information about Gene's war. His story receded to the back of my mind as teaching, coaching, and becoming a father to two boys filled out my life. But each year when my lesson plans turned toward the Second World War, I craved to know the full story of the local tail gunner and his death-defying fall.

During those years, my wife, Carmen, a graphic artist, became good friends with Joni. The two creative souls traded books, recipes, and attended every *Harry Potter* movie premiere together.

In 2002, Carmen sat up from her computer after a long night of designing an ad for a client. She stretched her arms into the air and then placed her hands underneath her armpits, wrapping her torso. The fingers of her left hand grazed against a golf ball-sized lump in her right breast. She sprinted upstairs from her office, lifted her t-shirt, and placed my hand on her side. I recoiled in horror. I gathered myself and speculated that it could be anything. She was only thirty-five. Two days later, I met Carmen in the driveway where I anxiously awaited her return from her mammogram appointment. She stepped out of the car and gave me a blank stare. She said nothing. While Carmen suffered through chemotherapy and radiation treatments the next four months, Joni dropped off homemade meals. She often stayed at our home, watching our two preschool-aged sons, Matthew and Joe, while Carmen and I were away at hospitals.

Carmen's cancer went into remission at the same time Joni lost her mother after a long illness. After fifty-seven years of marriage, and with all nine of his children grown, Gene was alone for the first time since the end of World War II. Joni, who lived just a mile from Gene, now cooked for her dad.

In November 2004, Joni invited Carmen, the boys, and me for Sunday supper. Ten years after telling me she would someday introduce me to her dad, Gene and I would finally get to talk for the first time.

When we walked into Joni's living room that afternoon, Gene got up from watching a Green Bay Packers game and walked over to my family. He grabbed Carmen's hands and said, "So this is the beautiful woman I pray so hard for." Carmen gave Gene a long hug. She then joined Joni in the kitchen. Gene and I settled into a sofa to watch the Packers game. Our first conversation included cheering for Brett Favre's touchdown passes and groaning at his interceptions. But soon, my mind drifted from the game. I sat in silent awe, glancing at Gene's fingers wrapped around a can of Blatz beer, knowing those same digits fired on Nazi fighter pilots. I had a thousand questions for him, but I didn't dare ask a one. Joni's warning replayed in my mind: "We don't go there."

Over the next few years, Gene became a fixture in my family. Joni brought him to campfires, birthday parties, and the First Communions of my sons. He became a surrogate grandfather to my boys as Carmen and I had both lost our fathers a few years earlier. My youngest son, Joe, wore denim overalls whenever he could, insisting, "I want to be like Gene." Despite the many get-togethers and my growing friendship with Gene, I never asked him about the war. It seemed his secret story would remain hidden.

Then in July 2007, I received a breathless phone call from Joni.

"John. Dad agreed to do an interview with Ron Kind at the La Crosse airport. And a Flying Fortress is being flown in to give him a ride after the interview!"

Ron Kind was the U.S. House representative for southwest Wisconsin who conducted oral interviews with American war veterans for his Veterans History Project.

"Bring Carmen and the boys!" she added.

On the day of the interview, I sat on the edge of my seat in an airport hangar. At last, I'd finally hear some of the story that was not to be told. The news media set up cameras and microphones in front of a growing crowd of family, friends, and veterans. Gene sat up front wearing his black "U.S. Army Air Corps" baseball cap. He was stone-faced, except for his tongue which constantly darted in and out of his mouth, licking his lips.

The questions began. Ron Kind eased into the interview, asking about Gene's birthday and home. Then talk moved toward the air war over Europe. Gene gave short, perfunctory answers.

"They just swarmed us," Gene said, referring to enemy fighter planes. "The flak. It was just . . ." Gene's voice trailed off.

Kind waited. Gene continued.

"The ball turret guy called me, and . . ." Suddenly, Gene waved his hands in front of his face. "Let's just leave that alone."

Kind moved on to Gene's fall. Gene briefly explained how he became trapped in the tail after it tore away from the rest of the bomber. He raised his arms and explained how bullets from German fighter planes shattered both his forearms. His right index finger traced the seven-to-eight-inch skull fracture he suffered when the severed tail section crashed into a forest.

"What was it like in the POW camp?" Kind asked.

"It wasn't good. It wasn't good," Gene answered, shaking his head.

Kind pressed further. "How so?"

"Well . . ." Gene paused a moment. "It just wasn't good."

Gene mentioned a ship he rode for three days on the Baltic Sea while being transferred from one prison camp to another. I sat riveted and hung on Gene's every word.

"We were put down this hold," Gene added, now leaning forward, head down. The brim of his cap covered his eyes. He spoke at the floor. "Thank God for the chaplain. He finally got them to open up the top, so we at least could get some fresh air."

Gene leaned back and revealed his closed eyes. He exhaled. Opening his eyelids, he turned toward Kind. "You know. This is kind of hard."

Kind replied quietly, "I know. We're almost done."

After the interview, Gene and a television crew walked outside to the rumble of four idling propeller-driven engines and boarded the Flying Fortress bomber. "This time there will be no one shooting at us," Gene quipped. Landing after a twenty-minute ride over the Mississippi River Valley, Gene added that he would never do it again. I had a feeling he wasn't just talking about the plane ride.

But that day only brought more attention to Gene and his remarkable story. Later that year, the Wisconsin Board of Veterans Affairs bestowed on Gene its first ever lifetime achievement award at a gala in Madison, Wisconsin. In 2008, Gene's hometown of Soldiers Grove held a street-naming ceremony in his honor, two days after he married again at age eighty-four. Under a gazebo in the town park, Gene held hands with his new bride, Pauline, and led a crowd of politicians, media, family, and friends down the road to a wrapped street sign that read "Eugene P. Moran Park Drive."

As Gene passed his mid-eighties, his children, friends, and fellow veterans at the Soldiers Grove Legion Hall pressed him to say more. A few people suggested a book. Joni had experience creating a war memoir. Just before her husband died in 1994, she'd helped him finish the account of his days in Vietnam as an infantry grunt. I urged Joni to convince her father to also record his story, soon.

"You've got to find an author and get your dad to talk before he takes his story to the grave," I pleaded.

"Why don't you write it?" she asked.

Me?! The suggestion was preposterous. In a former life, before I became a teacher, I'd earned a journalism degree and written for radio and newspapers for two years. Twenty years removed from typing high school basketball stories hardly seemed the experience needed for recording one of the most amazing survival stories of World War II. I explained to Joni that I had read many historical narratives before, and the best ones always had two elements: an indomitable character and a great writer. "You're halfway there," I told her.

A few weeks later, Joni stopped by my classroom at the end of the school day. She said she broached the idea of a book with her dad.

"Well, John. He'll do it," she stated excitedly.

I was elated. "Do you have a writer in mind who could help?" I asked. I figured she had a few contacts after publishing her husband's Vietnam story.

But I sensed she was withholding something from me. "He doesn't want to work on this with a stranger. He'll do it, but only if you write it."

The notion of me writing Gene's story didn't seem any less ridiculous than when she first suggested it. How could I possibly pull this off? When would I find the time? My teaching career consumed me. I was raising two young sons. And then there was Carmen. The cancer had returned. Six months earlier, I had driven my wife to Mayo Clinic Hospital in Rochester, Minnesota, where surgeons cut out a grape-sized tumor from her brain. There was no time for book writing in a life like this.

Joni persisted. "He won't talk to me or my brothers and sisters. He knows you and trusts you, yet you have some distance from him because you're not one of his kids."

I left Joni without giving her an answer. I needed time to think. Gene's story had enthralled me from the moment I first heard it. But I was a teacher, not a writer. Carmen and the boys needed me now more than ever. Yet, if I didn't write it, who would? It was time to talk to Ben.

Ben Logan was a real author, a local celebrity. He'd written the best-selling *The Land Remembers*, a story about growing up on a remote dairy farm in southwestern Wisconsin during the Depression. This land that molded Ben lay just fifteen miles east of Gene's home farm. First published in 1975, *The Land Remembers* saw eight editions printed over a thirty-year period. I had the good fortune to teach in the same district where Ben lived. Ben had bought his home farm back after retiring from a writing career in New York. Each spring, I assigned the book in my history class, and Ben graciously toured my students and me around the farm and the land he'd immortalized.

It had been a while since I'd last visited Ben. A few years before turning ninety, he'd moved into an assisted-living home just a few miles from my house. A mutual acquaintance warned me his mind was fading. A nurse at Bethel Homes led me down a carpeted hallway and softly knocked on the door of his room. "Ben? You have a visitor," she said.

Ben sat in a reclining chair with a blanket draped over his lap.

"You seem like someone I'm supposed to know," he said in a voice much quieter than I remembered.

"Ben. It's . . . it's John Armbruster." My voice raised an octave. "The North Crawford teacher that used to bring my students to your farm." I paused. "Every spring? My history students?"

Ben smiled and motioned for me to come in. I exhaled and picked up a chair in the small living room and set it next to him. Looking out a large window on that sunny August day, we made small talk. Each sentence seemed to bring him back closer to the vibrant, wise man my students and I revered.

When I moved to the subject of writing Gene's story, Ben's head nodded. He was also a combat veteran of World War II, commanding a landing craft for the U.S. Navy during the invasion of Italy in 1943. Ben had met Gene at various veterans functions and other civic meetings over the years. Like many in southwestern Wisconsin, he knew the basics of Gene's war saga.

"It's a sensational story," he stated. "It really deserves a book."

My confidence to write this story grew exponentially at that moment. I suppressed the urge to leave and drive straight to Gene's house.

"Be careful," Ben added. "Rural people don't like to give up their stories. Start with his farm years, and then work your way toward the war. When you see him backing away, then you back away. He may give you what you want later if you give him some time."

We talked for an hour. Before I got up to leave, Ben sat staring at the bright sunshine pouring into the living room window. I wondered if his mind had put him back at the helm of his landing craft as it cut through Mediterranean waves on its way to an Italian beach. I knew Ben wrestled with his own war demons. During the fighting in Italy, Ben had landed in sick bay with a stomach ailment. A replacement officer temporarily took over his landing craft and crew. On the first mission without Ben, the vessel struck a German mine. The explosion obliterated the landing craft, killing the stand-in officer and Ben's entire twelve-man crew. Sixty-six years later, the former naval officer reached over and grabbed my arm. "You know, this whole thing could blow up in your face."

My head was spinning as I drove away from Bethel Homes. Ben's stamp of approval that Gene's story warranted a book thrilled me. But his warning checked my excitement. What if after weeks, months, years of work Gene suddenly said no?

When I spilled the details of my visit with Ben to Joni, she confided in me that her father was having second thoughts. I didn't know what to expect when Joni called a week later.

"I told Dad all about your visit with Ben. He said, 'If Ben Logan thinks it needs to be written, then dammit, let's do it now before I change my mind.'"

CHAPTER 2

Fibbing Flyboy

October 2010

Sixty-five years after World War II ended, the story of the tail gunner who fell four miles without a parachute and lived would finally be told. I bought a voice recorder, a new laptop computer, and a stack of legal pads. But I wasn't able to hear it, at least not yet.

Soon after Joni told me her dad was ready to share his story, Carmen and I sat in a windowless examination room at Gundersen Lutheran Hospital in La Crosse. We both fingered through the pages of magazines we weren't reading and waited for results of a CT scan of Carmen's brain. It was the same routine we'd endured every few months for the last eight years: CT scan in the morning, quiet lunch at the hospital cafeteria, and then the interminable wait in the afternoon for the oncologist to bring us results.

Both scans in the past year were clean, but the moment the oncologist stepped into the examining room this time, we knew the winning streak was over. The doctor forced a smile and sank down by the computer. She brought up the CT images on the monitor and tilted the screen toward us. A new grape-sized tumor appeared in the same location where the tumor had been removed the previous November.

"Okay. There will be no pity parties this time," Carmen said on the drive home. "We're just not going to make this a big deal. Let's get over to Rochester, yank this sucker out, and get back home."

Her attitude didn't surprise me. She was adamant that cancer not define her life. Since the beginning of her fight, she politely declined invitations to cancer support groups and refused to wear pink t-shirts. She was all about wearing brash-colored headscarves after she lost her hair—twice—to chemotherapy and radiation. She pinned Rosie the Riveter "We can do it!" buttons on the bulletin board in her office.

Back home after the appointment, we prepared supper and told Matthew and Joe the news after we ate. Carmen spoke as if she were making plans for a root canal.

"This isn't a big deal, guys. We got it out last year, and we'll do it again," she assured.

"So which grandma is coming to watch us?" Matthew asked.

Matthew's matter-of-fact attitude put me at ease. The boys were twelve and nine years old. They'd been through this before. They would be fine. The next day at school, I prepared lessons for a substitute teacher while Carmen called her mother and packed for a second trip to Mayo Clinic Hospitals.

The knot in my stomach tightened as each mile brought us closer to the place where doctors would again cut open my wife's skull. Carmen could recall little from her operation last year. I remembered everything: sitting next to her bedside for a week in her intensive care room, my eyes glued to the blinking monitor lights signaling her proximity to life or death, the white gauze encasing her head, the doctors fretting over her brain swelling, the moment when Carmen slowly opened her eyes and mumbled, "Please . . . let . . . me die." Would that happen again?

The surgery took nine hours. The knot in my stomach grew

tighter and tenser. Then the neurosurgeon appeared, with a broad smile. He'd removed the tumor without any complications. Her brain was not swelling. My innards slowly unraveled. Carmen only spent a single day in intensive care. Relieved and amazed, I joked with the neurosurgeon as he made his rounds. "Why don't you just stitch a zipper on her skull, and I can take care of this myself next time." If the cancer held its pattern of returning to the same spot, and we detected it early, we might be able to contain this disease.

We were home a week later, the air crisp with October radiance. I drove past our freshly picked apple trees and turned onto our gravel driveway to reunite my boys with their mother. Carmen quickly reopened her at-home graphic design business. She joined a friend for Pilates classes, whipped together a vampire Halloween costume for Joe, and helped me clean and package the last of the season's apples. By early December, family life was back to normal. It had been four months since Joni had said her dad was ready to talk. I broached the topic of starting Gene's book. To my relief, Carmen was enthusiastic.

"You need to get going on it," she insisted. "He's not going to live forever, and when you see him, let him know his prayers worked."

I returned to work in December eager to find Joni to let her know the book project was back on. Walking near Joni's room, I saw construction paper creations hanging on the painted block walls: rows of black-and-white cows wearing Santa hats and riding motorcycles. Two weeks before Christmas break, the hallways buzzed with holiday excitement. The students' mood reflected my own. Carmen was healthy again. She'd given me the go-ahead to finally pursue the story I'd waited so long to hear . . . and on the walls across from my classroom, Holstein cows cruised on Harley-Davidson motorcycles. I read the title on the artwork: "Deck the Walls with Cows on Harleys."

Joni and I arranged to meet Gene for a Friday night fish fry dinner. Joni suggested the Country Gardens tavern in Soldiers Grove, which Gene said served the best seafood chowder in the state. We met after school: Gene, Joni, Gene's new wife Pauline, and me.

I drove straight from work and parked in front of the tavern. I sat in my dark vehicle. The car thermometer registered a mere ten degrees. The last shards of pink sky faded to night. I hadn't eaten in hours, but I had no appetite. Of course, I'd shared meals with Gene before, but this time the stakes were so high. I stared at the red-and-white neon Budweiser sign in the tavern window and wrestled with my self-doubt. I'm not a writer. I spend fifty-plus hours a week at my school. I have two growing sons. And the question that shadowed everything, as it had for eight years: would Carmen's cancer return?

But if I didn't write Gene's story, who would?

I headed into the tavern. The place was full. Men nursing cans of Bud Light and Coors Light sat on barstools that ringed the oval bar. Couples stood along the walls sipping Brandy Old Fashioned cocktails and glasses of white zinfandel wine while they waited to be called to their tables.

Joni and her family had already staked out a table in the rear of the dining room. Gene wore his usual bib overalls and Army Air Corps baseball cap. He sat across the table from me, next to Pauline, his wife now of two years. Joni kept the conversation light, but I said little. The waitress jotted down our orders for beer and soda; Gene asked for a can of Blatz. The smell of fried cod and steaming baked potatoes arriving at our table helped settle my nerves a bit. It was time to talk book. I looked at Gene, swallowed a forkful of fish, and began.

"I was thinking about starting after Christmas, on Thursdays, after school, for an hour or so. Will that work?" I asked.

Gene kept eating, not looking up.

"That would be fine," he replied, nodding his head, eyes riveted on his fish.

"I'd like to get in as many interviews as we can before spring," I added. Gene knew I operated a side business to supplement my teaching income. I raised apples, cherries, and raspberries on the five acres at my rural home. "But as soon as school is out, we can pick back up with the interviews."

Gene nodded.

"I want to start talking mostly about your growing up on the farm and move to the war later," I said. I hoped talk of his childhood instead of the war would put Gene at ease. But I could sense Joni was getting restless.

"Dad!" she burst out. "There's so much you haven't told anybody." She rushed on. "You need to talk about your prisoner-of-war days and the ship ride, the ship ride when the Germans transferred you. We know nothing about that."

Gene stopped eating and slowly set his fork down. He set both his arms on the table, looked up, and sat back in his chair. I didn't like what was happening. Joni's mention of the ship had stirred something in Gene. I closed my eyes and said to myself, *Jesus Christ, Joni. Shut up! You're moving too fast!* But she pressed on, firing questions, rapidly talking, oblivious to her father's change in mood. Gene turned toward his daughter and roared.

"There are some things that are NEVER going to go into any book!"

Everyone at the table froze. Nearby diners stopped talking. I didn't know what to say or do. I thought about Ben Logan's warning to me. Just five minutes into this project, and it was already blowing up in my face.

"Gene," I said at last. "This is your story. We don't need to do this."

Gene quietly picked up his can of Blatz and took a sip. He studied me for a moment. Then his face softened.

"John," he said, his voice much quieter. "If we don't do it now, it will never happen."

July 1936 – July 1942

When the pilot waved back, something in Gene stirred.

Gene was following the mud-rutted trails, bringing the cows back for milking. He was eleven, maybe twelve, trudging up the craggy hills of the Moran family farm. *These hills!* He was sweating bullets. His shins ached. Gene's home farm sat firmly in the middle of rugged terrain known as the "Driftless Area," an area of Wisconsin unlike any land in the Midwest. Massive glaciers from the last Ice Age had flattened most of Wisconsin, Minnesota, and Iowa, but had given Southwest Wisconsin a wide berth. Those walls of ice and stone never tamed the craggy Kickapoo Valley or straightened the crooked Kickapoo River. All this was lost on Gene every time he tromped along the rough ridges or when a loaded hay wagon tipped over on a steep hill. *Of all the flat land in the Midwest, why did Grandpa Moran choose the Kickapoo Valley to start a farm?!*

Gene heard a strange droning and looked up. All thoughts of farm chores vanished. The cows, heavy with milk, bellowed and stamped their feet, but Gene deserted them. He sprinted, leaping over fallen trees in his excitement.

Where was that sound? There it was! He stared up into the dazzling summer sky and cupped his hands over his eyes to shield the sun. An airplane. The first Gene had ever seen fly over the farm. He ran after it, wildly waving both arms. The plane banked. Did it see him? An arm waved back. The pilot had seen him! Gene stopped and stared at the magnificent machine soaring over the ridge top.

Standing in the rutted pasture, Gene made a solemn vow: *Someday, I'm gonna be up there. I'm going to fly.*

Five years later in the summer of 1941, Gene still walked the hills of the Kickapoo Valley chasing dairy cows for his dad. His high school report cards had run heavy with Cs and Ds, and after graduation, there were no other job prospects in the Kickapoo Valley. So here he was, still wearing bib overalls and stepping over cattle manure. He wasn't leaving cow country.

Gene found employment with a local farmer who also hauled milk to cheese factories. The work was grueling. He labored from dawn until midnight, hauling eighty-pound steel milk cans, feeding pigs and cows, and driving the milk route. He hardly took a break to eat and lost twenty pounds in a month. Some days he'd park the milk truck by the fields on his home farm and rip immature cobs off cornstalks to eat.

He also got a bite of extra food from his new friend Bill Dorgan. Bill was a few years older than Gene, and he also labored on a dairy farm. Gene's milk routes brought him to Bill's farm daily, and the two young men took water breaks together. They'd flop under a shade tree, crunch apples, and wolf down any spare sandwiches Bill happened to bring along. The two talked about hitchhiking together to Madison or Milwaukee, somewhere, anywhere away from farm life.

By fall, nothing had changed for Gene, only the location of his work. Now working at his Uncle Paul's farm, he still milked cows every morning and evening. He fed the horses and pigs and shoveled their manure. During the rest of the daylight hours, he picked and husked the ripened corn by hand.

One Sunday afternoon in December, after finishing chores in the barn, Gene tramped into the farmhouse and shook snow off his clothes. He stepped into the kitchen. The smell of coffee and fried meat hung in the air. His aunt and uncle sat at the kitchen table, listening intently to the radio.

"What's going on?" Gene asked. They both waved their arms to shush him. Voices crackled on the radio with details of attacking planes and burning ships. Uncle Paul looked over at Gene. "The Japs bombed Hawaii," he said.

Gene tried to make sense of the news. Why would Japan do

such a thing? Hawaii? What had America done to anger Japan? For months, all the war talk at the Rolling Ground Store and Tavern had been about the possibility of fighting Germany.

Then his mood changed. A wave of excitement washed over him. America was now in a world war. Soon, the government would be screaming for new recruits, including flyboys. The pilots of the Imperial Japanese Navy who attacked Pearl Harbor that day had just punched his ticket off the farm.

Gene looked at the calendar. He made a quick calculation: seven months until he turned eighteen, the minimum age to join the military. Though a high school graduate, Gene was still only seventeen. He'd started school early as a four-year-old first grader— no kindergarten at the one-room schoolhouse that sat about a mile from the home farm. Gene Moran had always been the runt of his class.

Seven more months of heaping cow dung. But once Gene turned eighteen, there would still be one more obstacle in his way of making good on the promise he had made years earlier to join the wild blue yonder: his mother.

In the summer of 1942, Gene counted the days until July 17— his eighteenth birthday. Then he would go to Madison and sign up with the Army Air Force. No more staring at a horse's ass in a dirt field.

Gene was determined to fly. He would not stay on the farm like his older brother, Byron. Both his father and Byron were farmer-exempted from military service. Dad had actually been drafted. At age forty and a father of five children, he held the first draft number in Crawford County drawn from the bowl in the national lottery held in Washington, D.C. almost two years earlier. The local draft board gave Dad an exemption to stay on the farm, and Gene knew his mother prayed that he'd be farmer-exempted too. Mom had enough on her mind being pregnant again. She'd simply order Gene not to enlist. If he had to go to war, let the government draft him.

"There's no need for you to go and get killed when you can serve your country right here on the farm," his mother told him. "Soldiers need beef and milk to fight just as much as they need tanks and airplanes."

His mother's logic meant nothing to Gene. He would go to war. If he joined the Army or Navy once he turned eighteen, there was nothing Mom could do to stop him. But Gene wanted to fly. However, the Air Corps was an all-volunteer force that required parent permission for anyone under the age of twenty-one. Gene knew there was no chance of getting his mother's signature on enlistment papers, and Dad would have to live in the barn if Mom caught him signing anything that would send one of her boys to war. But the thought of shoveling cow manure for three more years waiting for his twenty-first birthday sent Gene into agony.

Gene boiled inside. He had to find his wings. What he needed was a plan. He fumed as he sweated through scorching days pitching hay onto an endless caravan of wagons. But under the glaring summer sun, he hatched a scheme to get him off the farm and into an Air Corps uniform.

A few days after turning eighteen, Gene told everyone he wanted to celebrate by visiting cousins in Madison. Madison was where his cousin Imogene worked as a nanny and his cousin Ruth went to nursing school. Madison was also where the nearest Army Air Force recruiting station was located.

Gene hitched a ride with Ruth's boyfriend, who was home on leave. He got dropped off near the capitol. Gene waited until his car was out of sight and then walked straight to the post office.

The post office was a block away from the state capitol building and housed the Army Air Force recruiting station. Gene strode into the recruiting office, approached the sergeant on duty, and asked him for enlistment papers.

"How old are you, son?" the sergeant asked.

"I turned eighteen a week ago," Gene answered with complete honesty. After that, he'd engage his web of lies. Would this sergeant buy it?

"You do know that I need your parents to sign for you to enlist in the Air Corps," the sergeant added.

"I'm in Madison with my parents visiting some family. I can have the signatures here tomorrow."

That evening, with a delicate hand, Gene slowly wrote his mother's signature onto the papers. He knew faking a second signature for his father might look too similar to the first forgery, so he decided on a plausible scheme. He would tell the recruiting sergeant that his father couldn't read or write. After all, that wasn't uncommon for a lifelong Wisconsin dairy farmer. He laughed at the irony of his ruse. His dad was not only literate, he served as clerk for the Soldiers Grove school board.

The next day, Gene returned to the recruiting office. The same sergeant sat behind the desk. Rats! He'd been hoping for a new man. Gene handed over the papers, trying not to look nervous as the sergeant looked them over.

"Where's your father's signature?"

"My dad can't read or write," said Gene promptly. He'd been expecting the question. "He's been a farmer his whole life. He didn't have much education."

The sergeant handed Gene a blank piece of paper. Gene looked at it, perplexed.

"Mr. Moran, I want you to sign this piece of paper for me," the sergeant ordered.

This guy was no fool. Gene reluctantly took the paper, signed it, and handed it back. The sergeant's eyes flicked back and forth between the blank paper and Gene's enlistment papers. Then he looked up at Gene.

"Young man," the sergeant said, "I don't want to see you again unless I have an honest signature from your mother. And if your dad can't read and write, then you need to have him sign with an 'X' and have a witness sign next to it." The sergeant threw down a new set of enlistment papers in front of Gene.

Gene was not dispirited. He guessed he might need a backup plan, and he had one ready. He would get Imogene to write the signatures. She was Gene's favorite cousin. The two had won first place at a jitterbug contest a year earlier. Gene knew she would do anything for him.

He set off for the home where Imogene worked as a nanny and explained his predicament. Imogene smiled and wrote a beautiful signature that Gene swore was a dead ringer for his mother's handwriting. Then she marked out a bold 'X' for her "illiterate" uncle and then signed as a witness with a signature just a bit different than the one she'd forged for Ethel Moran. Perfect!

The next day, Gene retraced the path into the recruiter's office, hoping that maybe a different recruiter would be working that day. His confidence slipped when he saw the same sergeant sitting behind the desk.

Gene handed the papers over. He watched as the sergeant's eyes scrutinized the new signatures. The sergeant set the papers down and, with a decidedly softer look on his face, leaned back in his chair.

"Son, I really admire your desire to serve your country. But if you come back with any more of these forged papers, you won't need to worry about ever getting into the Air Corps. You'll be going to jail."

The sergeant again set a new set of enlistment papers in front of Gene.

"Now I want you to go back home and get signatures from both of your parents, and I don't want to hear any more bullshit about your dad being illiterate."

"Yes, sir," Gene sheepishly replied.

Gene hitchhiked the two hours back to his home. Sitting in the passenger seat across from a stranger, Gene went over his options. His first two schemes had failed. His mother would never sign his papers no matter how much he begged. He desperately needed a Plan C.

The driver of the car dropped Gene off at the Rolling Ground Store and Tavern located about five miles south of Soldiers Grove. The flyboy wannabe walked the last two and a half miles back to the farm.

His father was in the barn when he arrived, so he decided to confront his mother first. Gene found her in the kitchen preparing supper, holding his two-week-old baby brother, Marty. Gene steadied himself and ran through his plan in his head. Plan C. More lies. He hadn't fooled the recruiting sergeant. He had to dupe his mother. He cleared his throat.

"Mom, I'm in the service now. I've signed up with the Air Corps."

His mother wheeled from the stove.

"We didn't sign for you!" she shouted.

"I forged yours and Dad's names to the papers," Gene replied as calmly as he could. "I'm in."

"Well, we can all take a trip down to Madison and get that fixed!" his mother shot right back.

But Gene was ready with another arrow in his quiver of lies.

"It's too late, Mom," he said. "I've already taken the oath. I'm sworn in. I can't get out of it now."

His mother stood as still as a tree trunk, livid.

Gene kept his cool and went on. "It won't make any difference now if you sign or not." He went on about the legalities and solemnity of the oath, an oath he had not taken. His mother glared back at him, saying nothing.

Gene set his enlistment papers on the kitchen table and piled on more nonsense.

"Mom, it would just make everything easier if you and Dad would sign these papers so the Army doesn't come looking for me."

"Go get your father," she cried.

Gene headed to the barn. He found his dad shoveling manure out of the gutters. He explained the situation.

"You could still get a deferment," his father reasoned. "Or at least wait until you're drafted."

Gene said nothing.

They walked back into the house. Gene's ten-year-old sister, JoAnn, stood near the kitchen table where their mother was seated. Without saying another word, his father grabbed a pen from the tabletop. Gene held his breath. He was going to do it! Joe Moran quickly signed the form and set the pen next to his wife. No one spoke. Then his mother burst out.

"You know you just signed his death warrant!"

Her eyes welled with tears when she finally grasped the pen.

"Well, if you're that determined to get yourself killed, then you go right ahead."

Gene stared at his parents' signatures on the enlistment forms. They'd signed. He'd done it!

Dad went back to the barn. Mom sat silently at the table. Gene didn't dare make eye contact with his mother. He didn't speak, but inside his head, he was already hitchhiking back to Madison.

CHAPTER 3

Gunner Gene

January 2011

Soldiers Grove, Population 624. The sign flashed past. A common green road sign with white lettering mounted on a pair of metal posts. I'd passed this sign hundreds of times on my daily commute, but today it made my stomach churn. In minutes, I'd be knocking on the door of a man who didn't want to talk to me.

It was Thursday. The day of my first interview with Gene.

It had been sixteen years since I'd first heard his story. Sixteen! I was married now, a veteran history teacher. My kids were twelve and nine years old. Hearing Gene's saga was what I'd longed for all those years. But now I fought the urge to yank the steering wheel in the opposite direction and head home to my family. The boys would be home from school. There might still be enough light left to play football in the snow.

I'd left work right after school with a stack of yellow legal pads and my new digital voice recorder stashed inside my book bag. Already, the winter sky was darkening on that January Thursday. Short, cut stalks of harvested corn poked through the snow-covered crop fields surrounding the crooked Kickapoo River.

Up ahead was another road marker I knew well: Eugene P. Moran Drive. I swallowed hard. Gene didn't want me to interview him. The outburst at the fish fry with Joni proved that. What was I doing thinking I could write this story? A small-town history teacher and part-time apple grower who'd never seen combat? A former beat reporter whose writing credentials didn't boast much more than high school basketball game summaries? What if he blew up again? Who was I to pry open a vault stashed with dark memories when he wouldn't even talk to his own children? War was war. And that war ended almost seven decades ago. Leave it alone.

My car turned onto a single-entry road bisected by two rows of mobile home trailers. Baker Creek Homes. Gene's home was the fifth unit on the left. Hanging from the mailbox was a wooden sign announcing "Eugene Moran – Fire Warden." Gene's days as a volunteer firefighting chief were over. But if anyone wanted to raze a brush pile in Soldiers Grove, they needed a permit from the town's fire steward, age eighty-six. Parked in the driveway was Gene's "throaty Dodge," his coal-black pickup truck, sporting a commemorative license plate that read "POW – 85C."

I stood in Gene's driveway. There was no turning back. It was time to climb the steps of the cedar deck and knock on the door. Breathe. Seize the day.

On the deck was his bait stash: a snow-encrusted refrigerator propped up against the vinyl siding of the mobile home. Joni had warned me about this eyesore. Gene needed a place to keep his live bait cool in the summer, and Pauline refused to allow worms in the house. I paused a moment by the refrigerator, begging my stomach to settle. Live bait. Fishing. These were things I knew. Why didn't I just ask Gene to go fishing? This summer. Mississippi River. Northern Wisconsin. Canada. We'd clean crappies and drink beer. That's how I wanted to hang with Gene. Not this. What the hell was I doing here?

I opened the creaky storm door and knocked.

"Come in, John."

A raspy voice answered me, distinctly Gene. A voice that sounded as if he'd spent nearly nine decades gargling gravel.

There was Gene, sitting at his kitchen table dressed in his usual bib overalls, his eyes glued on a game of solitaire.

"Could I interest you in a beer, John?" Gene asked. His eyes never left the cards that he flipped softly onto the rectangular aluminum table. "I've got Coors Light and Busch Light."

I settled on Coors Light and hung my coat on the back of a chair on the short side of the table.

On the edge of the table sat a pile of mail, the latest edition of the *Crawford County Independent* newspaper, and an *American Legion* magazine. A magnifying glass rested on top of a tin of Copenhagen chewing tobacco. Above the table, a bookshelf was mounted on the wall. On it sat a black-and-white picture of a middle-aged couple I assumed to be Gene's parents. A six-inch white porcelain statue of the Virgin Mary stood next to the portrait, keeping watch. To the right of the statue was a poem framed in a clear, acrylic frame. I leaned forward to read it. Gene's youngest daughter, Bridget, had written the poem. She bragged about finally beating her father at euchre.

Gene popped the top of the Coors Light and pushed the cold, silver can into a Styrofoam can cooler with the faded logo of a Soldiers Grove tavern. He did the same to his can, Busch Light. No Blatz? Gene followed my quizzical gaze.

"Well, John, my stomach has been giving me problems lately, and the doc said it's time for me to knock off the hard stuff," Gene said.

I nodded and thought about my own queasy stomach. Gene gathered up the cards and slid a rubber band over the deck. He was ready to talk. I rummaged in my bag, pulled out my legal pad, pen, list of questions, and digital voice recorder.

My eyes stole glances at Gene's head. The Busch Light wasn't the only thing different. Gene's bald head wasn't covered with a hat.

I couldn't recall him not wearing some type of baseball cap. And then I saw it: a seven-inch scar that carved through the right side of his scalp about three inches above the ear. It was a dark, angry pink color, sickle-shaped. Carmen's skull scar had a darker maroon color and was more L-shaped. Surgeons had just dug into her skull three months ago. I should be with her. I shouldn't be here. Why did Gene choose me? I can't do this.

We both stared at the recorder. I looked up at Gene. My eyes drifted again to the sickle curve of his head scar. Gene saw where my eyes landed but said nothing, waiting for me to begin. I gripped my pen and looked over at Gene. I wouldn't ask about his scar. Not today.

"Okay," I said, pressing the record button. "Today is January 13th, 2011."

July 1942

With signed enlistment papers burning hot in his hand, the night couldn't pass fast enough for Gene. He thought about driving his Model A to Madison, but he couldn't trust the rusty, dented car, and he didn't have enough gas ration stamps in any case. So, it was another walk to Rolling Ground Store and Tavern along Highway 61 for a chance to hitchhike.

A trucker picked him up, and in a few hours, he arrived in Madison and marched straight to the post office. This time, he was delighted to see the same stubborn recruiting sergeant facing him. He triumphantly laid the enlistment forms on the sergeant's desk. The sergeant looked them over. He nodded. The signatures looked authentic. He did not get out another set of papers. The sergeant signed his name and then looked up at a grinning Gene.

He was in! Mission accomplished. It was time to celebrate. In such high spirits, he decided to keep his promise to spend time with his cousins. Imogene couldn't leave her nanny job, so he called his cousin Ruth and invited her out to dinner. Ruth asked Gene if her roommate, also a nursing student, could tag along. Her name was Margaret Finley. Friends and family called her Peg.

Gene treated both young women to a restaurant just outside of Madison. His head buzzed with visions of flying, but despite the day's excitement, he could not stop staring at Peg's dark, curly hair. And her eyes. She had hazel-green eyes which sparkled with gold flecks, plus an enchanting, delicate face highlighted by dark lipstick. Peg said she'd grown up on a dairy farm on the northern edge of Crawford County, just twenty-five miles from Gene's home. She was also Catholic and, like Gene, had five siblings. There had been a seventh child once, a baby girl, but the girl was killed in a tornado before Peg was born. The cyclone snatched the baby from Peg's mother's arms, and the baby was found dead in a tree two miles from her home. The conversation between the two went deep into the evening. Gene wondered how he had never heard of her before.

Gene saw Peg and Ruth back to St. Mary's Nursing School in time for curfew. Wishing that the evening could go on longer, he politely wished Peg good night. She promised to write. Gene wondered if he should ask for a second date. But the next time he'd see Peg, he'd be heading to basic training. He thought better of it. No time for romance. His mind was spinning. In one heady day, he had signed up for war and had a new crush.

Gene spent his final weeks of civilian life picking up milk cans again for a local milk hauler. It was the perfect job. The long hours on his route meant he could avoid the wrath of his mother. When it was time for Gene to leave for basic training in October, she couldn't stop crying. Dad was stone-faced when he drove Gene to Boscobel, a town fifteen miles south of the home farm to catch a ride with a local boy heading to Madison for a date with Imogene. The date was

October 19, 1942. In a few hours, Gene returned to the Army Air Force recruiting office to swear in.

Soon he was on a bus to Milwaukee for an Army physical. He stood in line naked with dozens of men of all shapes and sizes, holding his clothes, waiting to be poked and prodded by medical examiners checking hearts and hernias. When he approached a doctor seated on a stool, he heard the orders repeated tens of millions of times in America during World War II: "Bend over and spread your cheeks" and "Turn your head and cough." Height: 5 feet, 6 inches. Weight: 168 pounds. Gene passed.

The next stop was Fort Sheridan, Illinois, just north of Chicago. Low-ranking noncommissioned officers ordered Gene and the other bewildered recruits to march from building to building where they watched training films and received their shots. The marching itself was tricky. Gene noticed he wasn't the only one who stumbled to keep in step. At Fort Sheridan, Gene took a series of demanding physical and mental tests which measured his eyesight, motor coordination, psychological stability, and general intelligence. Then he received his dog tags, duffel bag, haircut, and a uniform. He wondered the next time when he'd wear bib overalls. Gene wasn't on the farm anymore. Now he was enlistee #161732701.

A day after his testing, Gene spotted a sign-up sheet for aerial gunners on bomber planes. The air war in Europe was heating up. Hundreds of B-17 Flying Fortress and twin-tailed B-24 Liberator bombers were flying over the Atlantic and flocking into newly constructed airfields in eastern England. The Army Air Force needed gunners for these aircraft, immediately.

Gene scribbled his name on the sign-up sheet right away. He wasn't confident his test scores would get him in the cockpit of an airplane. He might not make it as a pilot, but if he volunteered for a dangerous job like bomber gunner, at least he'd get into the air. He couldn't stand the thought of possibly spending the war as a desk jockey pushing papers.

A few days later, Gene squirmed in his seat on a jammed troop train headed for Jefferson Barracks, Missouri, for basic training. Two hours into basic, Gene realized he wouldn't be able to play the class clown like he did at Soldiers Grove High. The drill sergeants roared at him when he smirked or tripped up on a march, but he quickly saw these instructors were just doing their job. It was the second lieutenants Gene resented. He hated biting his tongue when a twenty-two-year-old, fresh out of officer candidate school, got in his face.

After years of sharing a room with only his brother Byron in a farmhouse nestled in a tranquil rural valley, Gene had trouble falling asleep in the barracks. Here he slept in a room with fifty other men snoring and farting. But he wasn't homesick. He'd already spent more than a year living away from home working on other farms. A lifetime of milking cows prepared him for getting up at the crack of dawn to begin a day of physical labor. But where were the guns? What a shame there were no guns in basic training. He was eager to show off his marksmanship skills. A childhood of sniping squirrels from tree branches should count for something.

Just before Christmas, the Army sent Gene straight from basic training to Air Corps Gunnery School outside Las Vegas. Here he second-guessed his decision for the first time. The desolation of the base rattled him. It was all treeless hills and gray-black rock. Nothing like Wisconsin. In December, the trees that covered the slopes of the Kickapoo Valley would be coated in frost. JoAnn and Rosemary had probably hung the blue and green plastic Christmas wreaths from the windows. Dad would soon fill the candy sacks he always gave to each of his children. Gene tried not to think about it: his first Christmas away from home out in this barren land.

One day, when he crossed the highway that split his barracks from the gunnery range, Gene spotted a Greyhound bus stopping to take on passengers. He stared. A quick jaunt over to the waiting passengers was all that it would take. He'd slip into line, mount the bus steps, the doors would close, and *snap*, he'd be whisked out of this wasteland.

All thoughts of deserting the desert vanished though the moment the Army put a gun in Gene's hands. Now he felt like a soldier. The feel and heft of a gun was familiar to him. He started with rifle marksmanship. Then he got to shred small plane silhouettes with a toy gun that spurted streams of pellets. Next came skeet shooting. Blasting clay pigeons with a shotgun developed the skill of leading a target. Gene loved "super skeet," when the Army put the trainees in the backs of moving trucks to fire at unexpected clay pigeons. He couldn't believe he was getting paid for something that would have landed him in jail back home.

Next came the "fifty cal." The trainees sat inside a mock-up of a turret similar to what they would later see on actual bombers. They fired a fifty-caliber machine gun at a model of an airplane set on a miniature rail car that traveled along a triangular track. From a bird's eye view, the shape of the track resembled a "hanger without its hook" and was laid out over an area Gene thought could enclose a good-sized hayfield.

The fifty cal was heavy. Some new gunners struggled to handle it, but all those years of pulling cow teats had thickened Gene's forearms, and he easily mastered the pulsating gun. Gene was taking a shine to Army life. Outside of a few math classes and calisthenics, gunnery school basically consisted of shooting guns all day and eating three square meals. Gene began to think about making a career in the military.

In the last two weeks of the five-week gunnery training, Gene finally made good on his boyhood pledge to reach the wild blue yonder. It was the moment all the enlistees looked forward to: the day they marched to the flight line to hop aboard AT-6 airplanes. Nicknamed "The Texan," the AT-6 was a single-engine monoplane the Army Air Force used for training pilots and for gunner training. Gene had never been on a plane before. The first time he sat strapped in the seat behind the cockpit, Gene leaned forward and tapped the pilot on the shoulder. "Wanna trade seats?" he asked. The pilot smiled back.

Once in the air, however, Gene reached his hand down to massage a soreness emanating from an area to the right of his groin. The pain became worse the higher the plane flew. And then it popped out, a bulging hernia. Gene said nothing to the pilot. Once on the ground and back in the barracks, he dropped his pants and showed the lump to his fellow gunners. They speculated that the change in air pressure at high altitude caused the injury. Gene's blood ran cold. America's four-engine bombers, the B-17 Flying Fortress and the B-24 Liberator, flew as high as thirty thousand feet. If he couldn't hide his hernia injury, he'd wash out of gunnery school. That couldn't happen! If it did, Gene might become a desk jockey. Or worse. The Army could send him home back to cows and manure.

His buddies came up with a plan. They fashioned a homemade girdle made out of canvas straps to keep the hernia from bulging. During the next two weeks, Gene hid the contraption under his clothes as he walked out to the flight line. Once inside the plane, he tied himself into his seat and tightly wrapped one of the straps around his upper right thigh. In the air, Gene turned his body to face another plane towing a three-by-six-foot rectangular target attached to a cable that stretched about a hundred feet behind the towing plane. Shock waves of pain radiated through the lower half of his body each time he made a move in his seat. Above the firing of his gun and the drone of the airplane engine, Gene prayed the pilot didn't hear him grunting and swearing. He was grateful that the machine gun for this target practice was a single-barreled thirty caliber "pea shooter" and not a double-barreled fifty caliber. Shooting with the hernia was agony, but the smaller gun made it possible.

When the day for Gene's qualifying test arrived, his hernia had become unbearable. The exam required that a gunner shoot five hundred holes into the target. Since the targets were used for more than one test, every gunner dipped his belt of bullets into a bucket of paint to identify his bullet holes. Gene was assigned the color orange. His comrades rallied to help. Two men who had already qualified and were only shooting practice rounds that day dipped half their bullets in orange paint.

After Gene strapped himself in and wrapped his protruding hernia, he looked up to see the pilot watching him.

"What's been wrong with you the last couple of days?" the pilot asked.

Gene had a hunch the pilot might be sympathetic, so he decided to come clean. "It's my hernia," he replied. "It popped out a couple weeks ago."

"Is that what those funny-looking straps are for?" the pilot asked. Gene nodded.

The pilot shook his head. "What do you need to qualify?"

"Five hundred," Gene answered.

"I'll get you in close," the pilot said. "Just don't let that target surprise you and knock you out of your seat. If you start feeling weak, let me know, and I'll make another pass."

After the test, Gene waited for the scoring sergeant to go over his results. The sergeant approached Gene and the two other gunners who had dipped their bullets in orange paint. He looked at them all quizzically and said, "I'd like to know why the target I just counted has seven hundred orange holes when the guy testing on it didn't have seven hundred rounds."

The sergeant waited. "Anybody care to explain?"

The two gunners standing next to Gene looked at each other and then shrugged their shoulders. "I thought I was supposed to be orange today," said one of the men, barely hiding his smirk. The other swore that it was his turn for orange. The sergeant rolled his eyes and walked away. Later, the sergeant told Gene he qualified.

In a few days, Gene pinned silver wings onto his flight jacket and had three stripes sewn on his uniform sleeve. He had graduated with "scholastic honors with complete knowledge of gunnery" and was promoted from private to sergeant.

The jubilation of graduating gunnery school was short-lived. Gene arrived at his next stop, Lowry Field near Denver, Colorado. The untreated hernia blinded Gene with pain. He passed out soon after reporting to his barracks. Gene awoke in a hospital where a nurse told him he was being prepped for surgery. The surgery went well, but Gene contracted pneumonia while recovering. He spent four weeks flat on his back in a hospital bed. His agony was compounded by his fear that any day someone might walk to his bedside and tell him that he'd be losing his wings and sergeant stripes.

If he didn't get better, the Army might classify him as a medical discharge and send him home. He'd be a reject.

The Army would send Gene home. He was to be put on a train and sent back to Wisconsin. A sergeant stood by Gene's bedside reading an order. But what was that? The sergeant gave him a report-back date to Lowry Field. Gene sighed with relief. It was only a twenty-day sick leave. As long as he got better, he'd get to keep his wings.

Back home, Mom bear-hugged him and then looked him up and down. "You look worse now than when you left," she said. Gene had lost a lot of weight during his month in bed back at Lowry Field, but nothing a few weeks of home cooking couldn't cure.

It snowed and rained often that early March of 1943 in southwestern Wisconsin, but the mood in the Moran home was much brighter than when Gene first left the previous autumn. Mom had come to terms with her "Little Revy" becoming a soldier. She had clipped out the local newspaper articles announcing Gene's graduation from gunnery school for her scrapbook and had a bounce in her step when the whole family walked into St. Philip's for Sunday Mass with Sergeant Moran dressed in his military uniform.

One afternoon, Gene drove the family's green 1928 Chevy sedan to pick up his kid brother and sister, Michael and JoAnn, from

Upper West Fork School. He hopped out of the car to help Michael take down the United States flag, while JoAnn and her classmates peered out the schoolhouse window. Gene made a show out of it and smartly saluted the flag on its way down. But on the way home, Gene pulled into the Rolling Ground Store and Tavern, parked the car, and left his young siblings there while he strode inside to down a few beers. The children scowled when he returned, beer on his breath. Gene paid no attention. He was a man now, a soldier.

When Gene returned to Lowry Field for armorers' school, he'd gained back some of his lost weight and his hernia wasn't bothering him at all. He spent much of the next four weeks in a classroom reviewing how to identify the silhouettes of enemy and friendly planes. Over and over again, he disassembled and reassembled a fifty-caliber machine gun. He also studied the various gun turrets used on American bombers, but had no idea what turret or even what plane he'd be assigned.

At Lowry, Gene received a letter from the local draft board back home. The letter warned him that if he didn't register for the draft soon, they would find him and turn him over to the proper authorities. Gene wrote back: "I'd be tickled to death if you came to visit me. You can find me at Lowry Field in Denver, Colorado, where I'm currently attending armorers' school for aerial gunnery." He signed the letter "Sergeant Eugene P. Moran, United States Army Air Force."

After completing his education at Lowry Field, Gene traveled to an air base outside Salt Lake City. The base served as a staging area where hundreds of enlisted gunners, aerial radio operators, and flight engineers gathered to wait for their assignment to specific planes and bomber squadrons.

On the troop trains, some of the gunners were annoyed that as newly minted sergeants they had to pull kitchen duty, but Gene enjoyed KP. He even volunteered for it. He knew the kitchen was the place to sneak the best food, especially the choicest cuts of meat.

At Salt Lake City, Gene was cutting cheese during one kitchen shift when someone set a large wheel of cheese on the table in front of him. He read the stamp on it: "Schneider Cheese – Rolling Ground, Wisconsin." The cheese factory sat just a stone's throw from Rolling Ground Store and Tavern. For a moment, Gene was home again.

One week went by at the staging area. Two weeks. Three.

Without much to do, the airmen sat around and speculated about whether they would be fighting the Germans or the Japanese and what plane they would be flying. Like Gene, most wished for the B-17 Flying Fortress. Gene loved the curved lines of the bomber. The plane was "sexy" as compared to its "ugly sister," the capable but boxy-looking B-24 Liberator. The slab-sided, blunt-nosed B-24 had greater range and carried a heavier bomb load. Range and bomb load meant nothing to Gene. He knew the glamorous B-17 wasn't just pretty. It had a reputation for durability in combat. Gene wanted to be in a plane that could take punishment and get him back to safety.

CHAPTER 4

Closer Than Brothers

February 2011

"Still thirsty?" asked Gene.

I'd just pressed the stop button on my voice recorder and drained the remainder of my Coors Light. Our weekly meetings always wrapped up after one beer and roughly an hour and a half of talking. I yearned to go on, get closer to the war story, but I knew I had to let Gene set the pace.

"Yeah, I'll have another," I replied, my voice jumping an octave in surprise. Today, he was offering me a second beer. Gene gave me a wink and headed to the refrigerator.

In more than a month of "Thursdays with Gene," our conversations centered on his home farm and childhood escapades. He'd had a pet, a buck sheep named Benny, that charged his father and butted him into the air. Gene saw the attack coming, but said nothing. Dad gave him a good paddling after he got up from the ground and saw his son laughing at him. There was the explanation of Gene's squirrel hunting method. He'd set fires to the base of trees and smoke them out. One day, his squirrel "hunt" started a small forest fire. After the neighbors rushed over to extinguish the blaze, Dad grabbed Gene for another meeting with his son's backside.

We took a quick break between beers, and I headed to the bathroom.

This was a rare opportunity. Gene was opening up. What would my next questions be? Was Gene ready to talk about the war? For the first time, I spotted a framed sepia-shaded photograph hanging on the wall. It was the crew of *Rikki Tikki Tavi*, all ten members posing in front of a B-17 Flying Fortress bomber. The six sergeant gunners stood behind the four kneeling officers. There was Gene, standing furthest on the left. Of the ten young men, only Gene was still alive. The other nine men looked back at me with unsmiling faces, perhaps unimpressed that I was the one who would tell their story. I returned the stern gaze of the officers. *Today, I'm going to start asking about you guys. Today I'm going to hear the tale of* Rikki Tikki Tavi.

Back in the kitchen, my beer, in its Styrofoam cooler, sat waiting for me next to my legal pad. I swallowed hard. Was Gene ready? I was about to open wounds scarred over for more than six decades.

I pressed the red button on my voice recorder to continue my first two-beer interview.

"We were tighter than tight," Gene began. "They were closer than my brothers and sisters. We got along very well, officers and enlisted." He took a swig of beer and exhaled. I said nothing. "Except for Langley," he continued. "We never grew close with Langley."

"Langley was your pilot, correct?" I asked.

"Yes, but he wasn't our original pilot," Gene explained. "With our old pilot, Winters, the distinction between officers and enlisted didn't exist. We generally treated each other as equals. But when Langley came later, everybody got their ass chewed out for not saluting him. He thought he was King Shit."

Gene stopped talking. I waited and scribbled on my legal pad. He took a swig from his can.

"You know, maybe you better not write that down about Langley," Gene said.

My shoulders slumped the second he made his request. I was new at writing war memoirs, but I knew I needed the raw truth. If Gene wouldn't come clean on his dislike of his pilot, what else would he hold from me? I flashed back to my journalism days when I hated getting close to a good story only to have my subject tell me that it was off the record.

"Um. You know . . . I think . . . well," I stammered. How could I tell Gene I didn't want to pull any punches on this story? But it was his story, and it was just the first day of "war talk." I'd come back to Langley another time.

To my surprise, Gene continued without prompting. "While I was prisoner, my parents wrote me that Langley's parents came out to visit them. This was during the war, and they drove from out East, which was a big deal because gas was rationed. They stayed the night at the farm. Langley's dad wanted to run up and down the hills. Oh, he liked our hills. My parents said they were very nice people, just the nicest people."

April 1943

After three weeks of KP, Gene finally received his orders to report to Pyote, Texas. He learned that Pyote was a training base for B-17 bombers. The Flying Fortress! He'd get to fly in the rugged yet sultry queen of American air power.

But his heart sank when he stepped off the military bus and looked around at the flat, West Texas landscape. Not a single tree, just rocks, scattered bushes, and gray dirt. The air was summer hot even though it was early April. The blazing sun combined with the wind-blown dust made his skin feel like sandpaper. Gunnery school in Las Vegas seemed like an oasis compared to this place.

Airmen there called it "The Asshole of the Universe," or sometimes "Rattlesnake Air Base."

They weren't kidding. Gene spotted twenty rattlesnakes his first day there. The base PX store sold stationery with "Rattlesnake Army Air Base" as the letterhead. Some airmen carried forty-five-caliber pistols in case they encountered rattlers on the way to the latrine.

Gene reported to a barracks covered in tarpaper and tied down with steel cables. He called it his shack. That humble hovel would be home for the next six weeks. At least he'd lucked out to get a barracks room. Other guys were stuck in tents. All around him, Gene could see tents of all sizes and colors flapping noisily in the hot Texas wind.

Inside his home sweet shack, Gene met his bomber brothers, the six young men who would make up the enlisted crew. The kid he spotted first was a twenty-year-old, dark-haired Texan named Wilbert Provost. He was shorter than Gene, in fact, shorter than everybody, which soon earned him the nickname "Pee Wee." Gene took an immediate liking to the small, tanned Texan, the son of a shipyard worker.

Gene and Pee Wee buddied up quickly with a fair-skinned nineteen-year-old from Chicago, Edmund Swedo. With that name and his white-blond hair, Gene figured he was Scandinavian. But Swedo—the only name anyone would ever call him—was a Polish kid and, like Gene, was raised Catholic. Swedo was quiet. Shy, perhaps. Some called him the Dumb Polack, but Gene figured he just wasn't much of a talker. Sometimes after lights-out in the barracks, Swedo would sing himself to sleep. No one minded. The Chicago kid had the voice of an angel that sent shivers down Gene's spine.

"How about meeting someone from a real city?" said a taller, grinning man who approached Gene with an outstretched hand. It was Samuel Amatulli, the radio operator for the crew. He grew up in the Bronx, from an Italian family. The twenty-two-year-old Catholic joined Gene, Pee Wee, and Swedo each Sunday as they headed to Mass. Amatulli was the jokester of the bunch. Gene found him to be borderline crazy. Of course, he was nicknamed "Sparky," like hundreds of other bomber plane radio operators. Sparky loved a good prank, but he was all business in the air. Sending and understanding complicated radio codes and keeping the pilot informed of the progress of a mission was critical work. Sparky was the "ears" of the crew.

The crew's other technical specialist was flight engineer Walter Reed, whom everyone just called "Reed." At twenty-three, he was the oldest of the enlisted crew. Reed grew up on a farm outside of Broken Bow, Nebraska, where he raised and sold chickens to help support his parents and six siblings. His father suffered from severe arthritis and didn't work, and his mother helped make ends meet by taking in laundry and sewing clothes for others. Reed was even quieter than Swedo, and he never drank alcohol. He stayed back at the base reading books and writing letters when Gene and the others got a weekend pass and went looking for a party. On the plane, Reed sat behind the pilot and co-pilot and kept a close eye on every dial and gauge on the plane's control panel. He also operated the twin fifty-caliber machine guns in the bomber's top turret. Reed loved his work, and Gene admired his competence.

Anderson King, the last of the enlisted crew, reported a few days after Gene arrived after his release from military lockup. Like Gene, Andy was only eighteen, and the hard-partying Oklahoman respected Army curfew the way a cow's behind respects a barn gutter. All of the enlisted crew had made sergeant, but Andy was demoted to corporal before he arrived at Pyote. He explained that he was absent without leave after a night of drinking. It wouldn't be the last time.

Names and nicknames quickly got sorted during Gene's first few days in the barracks. Sergeant Eugene P. Moran received the shortest moniker: everyone simply called him "Mo."

During their first week together, talk turned to what gunner spot each would take on a Flying Fortress. Reed and Sparky had their positions set as trained technicians. But Gene, Pee Wee, Swedo, and Andy had not been assigned specific battle stations.

"Well, who wants what spot?" Gene asked.

"I suppose I got ball turret," said Pee Wee, and everyone whooped. It made sense. The short, small-bodied Texan was certainly the best fit. The cramped ball turret was an electronically powered rotating sphere that protected the underbelly of the plane. It was also the most dangerous spot on the Flying Fortress. There was no room for a parachute. If the plane was hit, getting out of the steel and Plexiglas ball with the plane in a spin or a dive with enough time to grab a parachute was next to impossible.

The laughter died down. Gene spoke into the grim silence. "I'll take the tail."

"But, Mo, you sure?" Pee Wee asked. "It's so lonely back there."

Gene didn't mind. He'd spent many solitary hours in hayfields on a mower or rake with no one to talk to other than the horses pulling him. But loneliness wasn't the main problem, and everyone knew it. The tail spot was also dangerous. Many pilots and crewmen conceded the tail gunner was the most important shooter on the airplane since he protected the vulnerable rear of the bomber. Enemy fighter pilots knew a dead or wounded tail gunner meant the plane was easy pickings for a quick kill. Gene was volunteering to be a bull's-eye.

Andy and Swedo would take the waist guns. It was an odd team: a hell-raiser from Oklahoma paired with the silent Catholic boy from Chicago. They would protect the midsection of the plane.

All of this positioning had to meet the approval of their pilot, of course. They'd meet him soon, along with their three other officers: the co-pilot, navigator, and bombardier.

Gene couldn't wait to get started. The heat, dust, and rattlesnakes didn't matter so much when he walked toward the flight line and spotted the majestic sweep of a Flying Fortress tail. Gene's chest swelled when he heard the husky snarl of the twelve-hundred-horsepower propeller engines revving.

Gene scrutinized a tall, skinny first lieutenant walking up to meet his crew and shake their hands. It was Jim Winters, their pilot. Winters' skin was light brown, and the crew later learned that his mother was native Hawaiian. Gene grinned and gave him a firm handshake. Already, he couldn't help laughing to himself. His pilot's name was Winters, who had grown up in Hawaii. In a short time, the crew teased him and called him "Summers."

Not every officer would tolerate such needling from his enlisted subordinates, but Winters didn't mind. This pilot was laid-back: he preferred that his crew not salute him, and they didn't address him as "sir" or "lieutenant." But Winters made it clear to everyone that in the air, he was in charge. Gene thought he was a perfect fit for this bunch.

The other three officers, coincidentally, all came from Michigan: co-pilot Berline Cipresso, bombardier Donald Curtis, and navigator Jesse Orrison. At twenty-seven, Berline, known as "Benny," was the oldest of the crew. The burly co-pilot was an unassuming fellow who shared Winters' disdain for military formality. Benny had a serious girlfriend back home, and he couldn't wait to marry her on his next leave.

Curtis, the bombardier, had taught Sunday school. The twenty-four-year-old was a quiet teetotaler, and Gene respected his piety. Curtis planned to become a minister after the war.

Jesse Orrison was twenty-six and the only married member of the crew. Everyone called him "Orrison," or sometimes just "Orson." A soon-to-be father, Orrison exuded maturity and quiet leadership. Gene liked him immediately and came to think of his navigator as the big brother of the group. He and the others liked their pilot, but they went to Orrison first if they had a problem.

Training began immediately to mold these farm boys and city kids into a team. Gene quickly learned his way around the tail gun compartment. In this aluminum cocoon, he sat on a padded bicycle-style seat squeezed between two wooden ammunition boxes. His lower legs rested on padded knee supports. In front of his stomach sat two gray-black fifty-caliber machine guns that swung and tilted on their own. Gene's guns were not motorized like the ball and top turrets. From a squatting position, he tracked imaginary targets through a simple ring and bead sighting system mounted outside his back window. He extended his index finger and pushed the lightweight aluminum skin of the airplane. He figured he could easily poke a screwdriver through it. That thin veneer was all that would separate him from enemy bullets and exploding anti-aircraft shells.

Over Texas, the crew flew simulated missions. The gunners didn't fire their weapons, but they practiced calling out imaginary enemy planes using a clock system. Twelve o'clock was front, the tail was six, and the wings pointed at three and nine. With nothing real to shoot at, Gene struggled at times to stay focused. The officers, however, could never take a mental break, especially flying in close formation with other Flying Fortresses. Despite the intense concentration of pilots, co-pilots, and navigators, training crashes and midair collisions were common. During World War II, some 15,000 airmen died at training bases in the United States and overseas. Gene's plane never had a close call during training. Winters handled the Flying Fortress smoothly, rarely bouncing a landing. And not once did they get lost thanks to Orrison's precise navigating.

When Gene's plane glided over the Gulf of Mexico for the first time, he soaked in the magnificent cobalt-blue ocean water below him. Less than a year ago, he'd been stuck on the farm. Now, instead of squatting a foot above a barn floor on a milk stool, he was perched ten thousand feet in the air in an iconic airplane, flying with men he considered his brothers. Gene loved this new life. The flying. His crew. His officers who didn't mind first names or nicknames. He thought about the arguments he'd had with his father and brother. Here he never had a single disagreement with his fellow gunners despite spending every waking and sleeping minute with them.

Training was going well. One day, after a long flight, the squadron commander, a major, walked up to the gunners. "You boys got any money?"

Then to Gene's surprise, the major handed them all a two-day pass and fifty bucks to share. "Why don't you guys see if you can find some refreshments," he said with a wink.

With fifty dollars and a bounce in their step, the enlisted crew headed for Odessa, about sixty miles east. Pyote was off-limits to the four thousand servicemembers on the air base. That was okay with Gene. Pyote wasn't much bigger than Soldiers Grove, two blocks long and no night life. Reed politely declined to go, but Gene, Pee Wee, Sparky, Swedo, and Andy started walking the highway, thumbing for a ride. They didn't have to wait long. It was the war years, and drivers gladly picked up hitchhikers wearing a uniform. They arrived in Odessa in good spirits, checked into a hotel, and then spent the rest of their two days out looking for bars and girls.

Gene and his merry group lost track of time. They had planned to take a bus back to base the evening of the second day, but they arrived late at the station and missed the only bus going to Pyote. It was well past midnight. They had no choice but to hitchhike, but at this time of night, rides were few and far between. Gene figured there was no way they could make it back before their morning training flight.

The sun was just coming up over the arid Pyote air base when the five sleepless, still-drunk airmen hustled to their plane to beat Winters and the other officers. When Gene saw his normally easygoing pilot walking toward them with a scowl, he knew the gig was up. The stench of liquor hung in the air, thick as the drink itself. "You sons . . . of . . . bitches," roared Winters. "You had two days and you couldn't get back here on time? And you're still piss drunk!"

"Uh, sir," Andy replied, hoping that addressing their commander formally might soften him up. "We missed the bus, and no one would pick us up on the way . . ."

Winters cut him off. "I don't give a shit!" It was minutes before takeoff. He glared at his drunken crew.

"All of you get your asses back to the barracks, now," Winters ordered.

Gene and the others looked at each other. They didn't move.

"I'll make some excuse. None of you ain't in any shape to fly," Winters added. "And don't come out of there until we're done flying."

Winters glanced down at Gene. His eyes landed on a bulge in his tail gunner's flight pants. Gene shifted uneasily. He had hoped Winters wouldn't notice. He had stashed a half pint of whiskey in one of his pockets.

"For Christ's sakes, Mo, I can see the bottle in your pants," Winters said. "Now all of you get the hell out of here, except for you, Sparky."

Sparky would have to fly drunk. It needed no explaining. A B-17 flying over Texas didn't have to worry about enemy fighters, but it did have to have its radio operator, even a hungover one. Gene slunk back to the barracks with the others. He didn't seem so drunk anymore. Now he was feeling guilty. They'd let their pilot down, let their team down.

Winters covered for them. He flew his plane half-empty with a drunk radio operator. When he landed, he filed a report saying all had flown without incident. Gene said a short prayer of gratitude.

Winters got a chance to get Gene's goat not long after. At the end of his six-week training at Pyote, Gene's throat became very sore. A doctor at the base hospital took one look at Gene's throat and ordered his swollen tonsils be cut out, immediately. After the surgery, nurses wheeled Gene into a ward for men suffering from venereal disease. There were no beds available anywhere else in the hospital.

Winters led the entire crew into the ward for a visit. Winters stood at the foot of the bed and crossed his arms.

"Tonsillitis, my ass!" he said. "How does it feel to have the clap?"

Gene's throat ached. Amidst the laughter and teasing of his crew, he could say nothing in his defense.

The next stop was Dyersburg Army Air Base in Tennessee for the final phase of training. Another six-week assignment before Gene went to war.

An unexpected surprise awaited him when he and the rest of his crew arrived at the crowded post. Bomber crews ahead of Gene had not yet finished their training, so the Army Air Force was forced to give Gene and his buddies time off.

Hot dog! Six days of leave.

Benny, the co-pilot, wasted no time heading to Michigan to marry his sweetheart. Gene also decided to go back home to Wisconsin. It might be his last chance to see his family before heading to combat. He made the calculation: a two-day train ride to reach Madison, then two days to get back to Tennessee. It would be tight, but he could get two days at home.

Gene arrived in Madison after two days of sweating it out on packed troop trains. From there, he hitchhiked ninety miles to the Rolling Ground Store and Tavern, then walked the last two miles to the home farm. He saw his father outside the barn the minute he entered the barnyard. Dad's face broke into a wide grin.

"I have never been so tickled to see anyone in my life," he said, his smile growing wider.

Gene grinned back. It wasn't like Dad to be so affectionate. It felt good. As his father talked about ripe oats and a new colt and explained how his stomach ailment had flared up again, Gene quickly understood. The oats needed to be harvested. Now. And the son who was good with horses had arrived just in time.

Gene followed his dad to the new colt. "She's only been harnessed once before," he said. "Do you think you can handle her?"

In no hurry, Gene walked to the house to change out of his uniform. He pulled his bib overalls out of his dresser drawer for the first time in almost a year. Barely home one hour, Gene guided the colt pulling the cutter out to the fields. Under a blistering August sun, the Flying Fortress tail gunner cut ten acres of oats, and then helped his father bundle the fresh-cut crop before nightfall.

At sunset, Gene walked out alone to the spring-fed creek, which gurgled out of a hillside about a hundred yards downhill from the farmhouse. The creek was where the family had always stored the steel cans full of fresh milk to keep them chilled. As a boy, Gene had to go to the creek to yank the milk cans out of the cold water. Then he'd haul six or eight of the sloshing cans in a two-wheel handcart and push it uphill along a dirt trail where the milk truck waited.

Gene grabbed a tin cup hooked on a forked tree branch that hung over the creek. He bent down and thrust the shiny cup into the dabbling brook. He gulped the clear liquid, whose cold magic shot through his sweaty, tired body. Still the best water in all of Crawford County. It was good to be home.

Gene leaned back and watched the last of the sunlight disappear over the ridge. This would be his last time home before he went to war. He wouldn't tell his family, but he sensed they knew. He slid the cup back onto the forked tree branch and headed back for the house.

They knew. The next day, the entire family dressed in their Sunday best to pose in front of the house for a picture. Wearing his uniform, Gene stood next to Byron. His mother sat next to Dad holding baby brother Marty, now a year old. Michael and JoAnn filled the middle next to Rosemary. The whole family together, one last time.

A few hours later, Gene waved out the window from the passenger seat of his Uncle Jack's car. Dad was a little low on gas ration stamps, so Uncle Jack had offered to drive Gene to the train station in Boscobel. Gene looked back and saw his mother standing next to his father as the car rattled down the gravel road. He could see Mom was crying. But he couldn't know what she was saying to his father: "Joe. We'll never see him again."

Back at Dyersburg Army Air Base, training became more rigorous. They grunted out more push-ups during morning calisthenics. They huffed through miles-long cross-country runs. It wasn't all physical preparation, however. Gene logged many hours in the classroom studying shooting patterns in formation flying so he wouldn't punch holes into friendly planes. He straightened in his chair and listened intently when instructors described how to survive a crash landing, how to get out of a ditched plane in the water, and how to use a parachute.

The days began to blur together. Gene crawled out of bed at 5:00 a.m. and flew missions eight to ten hours long, sometimes as far as over the Gulf of Mexico. Winters and Benny practiced touch-and-go landings over and over again. They made several high-altitude flights to become accustomed to using oxygen masks. Flying Fortresses were not pressurized airplanes, so airmen had to don masks on flights higher than ten thousand feet. Gene hated wearing the bulky, molded rubber mask. But he diligently plugged in the rubber tube connected to an oxygen regulator mounted on the plane's aluminum wall. To ignore wearing the mask meant a flier could die from anoxia, a common, hidden killer. Airmen who got caught up in combat wouldn't notice anoxia symptoms sneaking up on them. Winters constantly told Gene to check his mask for frozen saliva that might cut off life-giving oxygen. It was especially important for Gene. An isolated tail gunner could pass out without any of his crewmates noticing.

Not only were Flying Fortresses unpressurized, the bomber was also unheated. A balmy day on the ground belied the double-digit below-zero temperatures that existed five miles above the earth.

Gene and his fellow bomber boys wore "bunny suits": electrically heated, woolen jumpsuits designed to plug into an outlet on the plane. With the heating wire and another electrical line which connected the throat microphone to the interphone system, Gene was beginning to feel like a creation by Dr. Frankenstein. All the wires and tubes made it difficult for him to move around.

The next unexpected break for the crew was due to sabotage. Mechanics found cotton balls shoved into the fuel lines of several bombers. Gene never learned who did it, but the act gave Gene and his buddies a chance to have some fun in Memphis, a popular destination for servicemen with free time. The fun was short-lived. Gene, Pee Wee, Sparky, Swedo, and Andy ran into a dozen Navy sailors who had already been thoroughly enjoying Memphis' nightlife. One of the sailors spotted the five airmen and yelled out, "Hey, look at the pretty flyboys. You guys really think you're hot shit, don't you?"

"Did I hear you say you have a problem with the Air Corps?" countered Gene.

Someone threw a punch, and Gene didn't wait to see who started it. Gene knew how to use his fists. Back home at St. Philip's, Father Mathieu taught boxing lessons to the teenage boys after Sunday school. Gene had also boxed on his high school team, often stepping into a ring with boys two to three years older than him. The brawl became a whirling pile of olive drab and navy-blue uniforms. Out of nowhere, Swedo leapt on top of the heap of snarling men and flailed away. Swedo's aggressiveness shocked his buddies. Despite Gene's boxing experience and Swedo's ferocity, the Navy boys were getting the best of them. The bomber boys were outnumbered. Soon, other uniformed men pulled them apart before the military police showed up. The fight was over.

The bruised men returned to Dyersburg on time, but when they got back, Andy was missing. Gene couldn't remember when they'd lost contact with him in Memphis. Word came the next day. The military police had Andy in lockup again. His comrades went to fetch him out of the base jail. Andy had just earned back his sergeant stripes, but Gene knew the incorrigible gunner would soon be busted back down to corporal.

Because of the intense training at Dyersburg, the airmen rarely enjoyed an unscheduled evening, let alone a chance to leave the base. When they did, they played fast-pitch softball. Lieutenant Winters' bomber crew made a formidable team, and Gene was the team's catcher. During one game, Gene leapt from his squatting position to throw out a runner stealing second base. But when he made his throw, the batter took a late swing at a pitch. The bat crashed into Gene's right arm. For the third time that year, Gene was in a hospital, this time for a wrist fracture. But he didn't worry about the injury washing him out of flying. If Andy could keep his wings after being in and out of jail, Gene guessed the Army Air Force desperately wanted to keep its gunners.

But Winters wouldn't be so lucky during another ball game. He and his crew were just a few days from finishing their training. As Gene sat on a dugout bench with his arm wrapped in a cast, he watched his pilot leaning off first base, eyeing up a chance to steal second. Winters took off and slid hard into second base. He let out a yell. Gene sprung from his bench seat and joined the rest of his team running to second base. One of Winters' legs lay bent at a funny angle.

Everyone knew what this meant. The crew was scheduled to ship out in just a few days, and they'd lost their revered leader. A replacement pilot would be coming.

The next day, Gene and the crew—minus their pilot—huddled under the nose of their Flying Fortress shooting quick glances in every direction, looking for their new commander. A small man with a gold bar on his military cap approached them.

"What the hell is going on here?" the diminutive officer asked. "Line up."

Gene and the others froze.

"Line up!" the second lieutenant repeated.

In shock, the men shuffled into a line in front of their plane and stood shoulder to shoulder. Satisfied, the lieutenant continued. "I'm Lieutenant Langley, your new pilot. And from now on, when I come to this plane, you will all be at attention with your hands at your heads saluting. Is that clear?"

"Yes, sir," mumbled Gene and the other men.

Linwood Langley, just twenty-one years old from Pittsfield, Massachusetts, had entered their lives. He had a nickname, "Woody," but Gene wouldn't dare call him that to his face. From now on, Langley insisted that the enlisted crew refer to officers as "lieutenant" or "sir." The days of yelling out "Benny," "Orson," or "Curtis" were over. Langley demanded the enlisted men salute their officers. Benny, Orrison, and Curtis awkwardly returned the gesture when Gene and the others obeyed the order.

When Langley was out of sight, sympathetic pilots and officers from other planes shared stories with Gene and the others about Langley being bounced from one crew to the next because of his insufferable attitude. One airman said Langley was a "fighter pilot wannabe" who grew a chip on his shoulder when the Army assigned him to fly plodding four-engine bombers instead of speedy and sleek single-engine fighter planes.

Later that week, with Lieutenant Langley occupying the pilot's seat, Gene and his crewmates sat in a Flying Fortress which lifted them away from the Dyersburg Air Base for the last time. Langley and Benny turned the bomber west for Grand Island Air Base in Nebraska. The base at Grand Island served as a staging area for checking out for overseas duty. The men arrived among a hornets' nest of activity. Grand Island was buzzing as Flying Fortress and Liberator bombers arrived from U.S. training fields and took off for Europe or the Pacific.

The Army had no duties for the crew other than final checkout

and waiting for the order to go to war. For the next two weeks, Gene
went with Pee Wee, Swedo, Andy, Sparky, and Reed every morning
to check the assignment board. No orders, yet.

It was October. Just a year earlier, Gene had left for basic training. After a year of training and countless practice flights, Staff
Sergeant Eugene P. Moran was now a highly skilled Flying Fortress
tail gunner. With nothing to do at Grand Island, Gene had plenty
of time to think. This was it. Next stop was war. He was anxious to
do his job.

But sometimes he wasn't.

Gene and the others guessed they would be sent to join the
Eighth Air Force, which was based in England. In 1943, the German Air Force—the Luftwaffe—still controlled the skies over Western Europe. Its fighter planes punched massive holes into American
bomber formations trying to bomb Nazi industrial targets.

Gene had read newspaper accounts of one mission known as
"Black Tuesday," the raid on the German industrial cities of Schweinfurt and Regensburg. Of the three hundred bombers sent up
by the Eighth Air Force on August 17, 1943, German fighter planes
along with anti-aircraft cannons on the ground gunned down sixty
American bombers. Six hundred men lost in a single mission.

While Gene waited in Grand Island, the "Mighty Eighth" went
after Schweinfurt again on October 14. Another sixty bombers
lost to the Germans. *That's sixty dead or missing tail gunners,* Gene
thought. He added to that number by estimating the dead and
wounded airmen that lay in riddled, charred bombers that limped
back to England . . . he stopped doing the math.

During his down time, Gene checked out America's other big
bomber, the B-24 Liberator. He crawled into the tail gun position.
The tail turret on the Liberator was hydraulically operated. Gene
didn't like the setup. The turret had sliding doors behind the gunner
that he would have to open in the event of an emergency. Gene fa-
vored the more open structure of the tail gun position on the Flying

Fortress. With so many bombers falling from the skies over Europe, he wanted to be in a plane that provided a quick escape.

After waiting two weeks, Gene spotted Langley's name on the assignment board. They were flying out the next day . . . to England. Gene would fight the Luftwaffe.

On the morning of departure, Gene and the others paced back and forth on the tarmac next to their Flying Fortress, checking their watches. Andy was missing again. No one had seen him that morning, but nobody wanted to tell Langley. Their pilot was already on the plane with the other officers firing up the four engines. When they could wait no more, everyone climbed into the plane. As the plane's engines idled, Gene clambered up to the cockpit. "Lieutenant, sir," he said to Langley, "Sergeant King isn't on board yet."

"What? Where the hell is he?!" Langley snapped back.

"We don't know," Gene replied.

Just then, they spotted him.

Everyone looked out a window to see their once-again AWOL gunner running toward the parked plane. Above the rumbling of the engines, Gene heard sirens coming closer.

Were the sirens coming for Andy? Orrison didn't want to wait to find out. "Lieutenant, we're all warmed up and ready to go," he said. "Let's get him on board and get out of here."

"Let him on and lock up," Langley ordered.

Gene opened the entry door by the tail wheel, and Andy clambered onto the plane. Langley taxied the Flying Fortress to the runway. The sirens faded in the distance. The bomber shot down the runway and soared into the air. They were off! Out of earshot of Langley, Andy admitted to the other gunners that he'd sneaked into the city of Grand Island the night before for one final drink, which became many. Gene sighed. Andy was sure to be knocked down to private.

Once in the air, Langley opened a sealed order which outlined the direction he and his crew would take to England. The Army assigned one of two paths to England: a southern or northern route. Before they left Nebraska, supply personnel took away the crew's heavy coats and pants and issued everyone lightweight clothing. Gene assumed this meant they'd be flying the route that would take them through the Caribbean to Brazil and on to northern Africa before a final flight to England.

Langley pressed his throat microphone to talk to his crew. "Everyone, listen up. We're heading to Presque Isle, Maine, and from there we're flying to Newfoundland."

It would be the northern route. Gene shuddered in his thin summer flight suit. *We're gonna freeze our asses off.*

The crew spent one night in Maine before shivering through the second leg of the flight to Newfoundland. A sympathetic supply sergeant at that air base rounded up winter jackets for everyone after they landed. The sergeant then turned Gene's plane into a delivery truck. He and his men loaded up the Flying Fortress with canned food, cartons of cigarettes, boxes of Hershey bars, and bathroom supplies. Langley ordered the enlisted gunners to take turns pulling guard duty outside the plane overnight to watch over the cache of groceries.

What? Lose a night's sleep over a supply of Spam and canned beans? What sort of Canadian crime wave would attack a remote air base? Gene fumed when it was his turn to get out of bed and stand watch. This was another pointless order from Langley. While Gene was guarding soap and toilet paper, Langley slept snugly in a warm cot.

The groceries and bathroom supplies survived the night without incident. The next morning, it was time to fly again, edging Gene closer to war. Next stop: Greenland. The flight to the American air base on the east coast of Greenland was long: eight hours. Some of the crew slept while others played cards. Langley engaged the plane's autopilot so that he and co-pilot Benny could get some sleep. With autopilot on, every crewman took his turn sitting in the cockpit ready to wake the pilots in case of a problem. Gene and the enlisted guys didn't mind pulling "pilot duty." They enjoyed sitting up front and soaking in the warmth of the cockpit heater.

When it was Gene's turn, he eagerly sat in the pilot's seat. Looking at the dials and gauges, he listened to Langley's instructions.

"And don't mess anything up," Langley added. "Think you can handle that, farm boy?"

Farm boy? Maybe it was the loss of sleep from pulling guard duty in the cold the night before. Or maybe it was that Gene had never walked away from an insult his whole life. He wasn't about to start when it came from an East Coast city boy.

"Yes, I think I can handle it, Lieutenant," Gene retorted. Then he continued, "And may I politely add that I think you're nothing but a HORSE'S ASS!"

The dam had broken, and not just for Gene. The other men backed him up. Throughout the plane, the other men sounded off before Langley had a chance to reply.

"We're sick of your bullshit!"

"Why are you such an asshole?"

"What are ya gonna do? Send the whole crew to the brig when we get to England?"

"Everybody, SHUT UP!" came the order, but not from the cockpit. It was Orrison's voice on the intercom. The enlisted crew immediately quieted for their "big brother." They awaited his tongue-lashing. But instead, Orrison reprimanded his pilot. "Lieutenant, we're about to go to war. If you want this crew to like you, you're gonna have to get off your high horse and show some respect for these guys."

Hardly a word passed on the intercom the rest of the flight to Greenland. Gene always liked Orrison, but now he revered him.

The approach to Greenland would be tricky. Langley and Benny would have to guide their Flying Fortress through a narrow, glacier-cut fjord on their approach to a one-way landing strip. The pilots had to nail the landing the first time. There was no room for a "go-around." The bomber slowly descended through the pass. Steep mountains towered over the plane on both sides. Below lay a small bay dotted with icebergs and a few ships. Several wrecked airplanes that had not made successful landings littered the west end of the bay. Sitting in the radio room with Sparky and the other gunners, Gene peered out a window and watched the steep mountainsides covered with ice and snow pass by the plane. One wrong move by Langley and Benny and their Flying Fortress would cartwheel across the jagged slopes. In the radio room, no one said a word. They listened to the engines wind down on the approach. They ached to feel the jolt of the wheels touching down. Finally, the plane's wheels squeaked on the steel-planked runway. Gene exhaled. Everyone in the radio room started gabbing. Gene hated Langley's arrogance, but maybe he wasn't too bad of a pilot.

They waited five days in Greenland. Langley and the crew had reached a tentative peace, or at least a grudging respect for each other. Each night, Gene and the other enlisted men shared guard duty watching over the plane. It wasn't just about canned Spam anymore. An officer at the air base told Gene and the others to shoot on sight anyone who came near the plane. Earlier that year, a couple of guys on the base had snuck onto the flight line, siphoned the alcohol-based de-icing fluid from a plane's wings, and then ran off with the fluid to have a party. They poisoned themselves. Gene wondered what officer would write home to the parents saying their son died stealing vital fluids from a plane and getting shit-faced.

While waiting for the next leg of their trip, Gene became bored playing poker and blackjack. He learned that shotguns were available for checkout and that some edible critters roamed the barren landscape of Greenland. He grabbed Pee Wee and told him they were going hunting. The two airmen hiked across the icy terrain. They joked about feeling like intrepid Arctic explorers. They looked for ptarmigan, a partridge-like bird with white feathers that blended in perfectly with their snowy habitat. Soon, two birds flushed in a flurry of wing-whipped snow. Gene and Pee Wee fired and missed. But after a few hours of trekking across glaciers and rocky streambeds, they managed to bag three birds. The two sportsmen presented their trophies to a mess hall cook, who agreed to cook them up in a stew. It was delicious, even better than squirrel stew back home.

Gene's short, Nordic vacation ended when Langley's crew flew to the next stepping-stone in their transatlantic journey—Iceland. Gene saw nothing of the island nation. His plane landed in the early evening darkness and took off the next morning before sunrise. The only memorable incident there happened during the landing. The runway had iced up. Langley put the Flying Fortress down perfectly onto the runway, but the bomber skidded sideways on the ice-glazed airstrip. Langley screamed at everyone to assume crash positions. He regained control of the plane, but couldn't prevent it from sliding off the end of the runway. The plane plowed through ice and snow, finally lurching to a stop. The only damage suffered was the confidence of Gene and his comrades, who had not experienced a single close call in all of their training.

Gene finished his trip across the ocean at an airfield near Belfast in Northern Ireland. It was the last stopover of the journey. From Belfast, they'd fly directly to their permanent base in England. The transatlantic trip had taken nine days, five stops, and two gut-churning landings. The war was still ahead. But here in Belfast, they got a brush of it. Here Gene met airmen who'd completed their combat tours and were heading the other way back to America. He and the other rookies peppered the veteran crews with questions. From what direction do German fighter planes attack a bomber? What's the German flak like? Where can you meet English girls?

After just a few days in Northern Ireland, the bigger picture of the battle over Europe was beginning to emerge for Gene. Early in the air war, the Army Air Force required that a bomber crewman must complete twenty-five missions before finishing his combat tour. In 1943, only one in three bomber boys reached that magical number. The majority could expect death or serious injury from Luftwaffe machine gun bullets, exploding flak shells, midair collisions, or crash landings. Others wasted away in German prison camps. In the summer and autumn of 1943, the average airman survived fewer than ten missions. Gene noticed the number of bomber crewmen going home was paltry compared to the new arrivals headed to air bases in England. As one lucky returnee informed him about the odds of being shot down: "For most of you guys, it's not a matter of if, but when."

One morning at breakfast, there was a mix-up in the chow line. British fliers filed through the line with bacon and eggs. Gene and his crew stood before cooks who ladled heaps of stewed kidneys and beans onto his tray. Everyone got to taste another nation's breakfast.

"Hey, Mo. What farm animal did these come from?" asked one of Gene's friends.

Gene stabbed one of the kidneys with his fork and held it up to his eyes. "I have no idea," he replied. He grabbed a condiment bottle filled with vinegar and poured liberally over his breakfast. A lifelong coffee drinker, Gene wolfed down his foreign meal between gulps of tea.

Breakfast food wasn't the only area where British and American fliers differed.

"I can't believe you Yanks keep trying to fly in the day," said one British airman. "You're sitting ducks for 'Jerry' fighters."

"I think you guys are nuts flying at night," Gene shot back. "At least in the day, you can see and not crash into one another."

"Well, Jerry doesn't get much sleep, does he?" said a British flier, bringing the two sides together. "With you bombing in the day and us at night."

The day before he left for his base in England, Gene stepped into a shower room where another airman stood under a flowing showerhead. Gene gasped when he looked at the flier gently cleaning a gaping wound in his upper thigh. A roast-sized chunk of flesh was missing from his leg. The man looked up and caught Gene staring.

"What happened?" Gene asked apologetically.

"Schweinfurt," the man replied, continuing to massage the wound. He turned off the shower valve. "I don't envy you new guys one bit."

CHAPTER 5

"It's Just a Job."

March 2011

Just a trace of melting snow capped the top of Gene's bait fridge. "Come in, John."

I hadn't even knocked. Gene recognized my footsteps the moment I passed his deck refrigerator. Now that it was spring, I knew he'd have it packed soon with plastic containers thick with night crawlers and red worms. Come June, there'd be extra beer chilling next to the worms, ready for deck parties with his fishing buddies, and Gene's gang would be headed "up nort" for their annual trek chasing walleyes in Canada.

Two months ago, I didn't think Gene wanted me and my voice recorder in his house. Now we both looked forward to our Thursdays. Would he still now that we were getting to the hard stuff?

Today would be different. I would ask my first questions about shooting people and blowing up buildings. I had a surprise for Gene that I thought might ease his anxiety.

"I've got something to show you," I said, pulling out my laptop.

"Did I tell you that I used a computer for the first time about a month ago?" Gene asked, a touch of pride in his voice. "I had an appointment at the Madison VA. I just had to press a few buttons. I think I did all right for the first time."

He leaned in as I brought up the image on my screen. There was the *Rikki Tikki Tavi.*

One of Gene's relatives had discovered it online. The photo captured only the nose and cockpit on the pilot's side of the plane, but you could see the nose art, a naked woman riding a bomb, and just make out the name painted above a side window. Gene brought up his magnifying glass.

"Yeah, that's the dolly," he said matter-of-factly. Confirmed! We'd found Gene's plane. The history buff in me was elated. But reality set in.

We were headed into untold memories of the war today. Gene first shared a story about wartime England.

"I only got one twenty-four-hour pass. I went to a college town, Cambridge," said Gene. "I went to this fancy restaurant, and I ordered rabbit. The waiter brought me burnt toast with cheese on it. I asked him, 'Where's the rabbit?' He laughed and said, 'If you really want meat, all you will get is *meow-meow.*'"

On the train ride back, he'd stared out the window, looking at blackened shells of yellow-brick terrace houses and stucco cottages bombed by German air raids. Gene had heard the terrifying *thump, thump, thump* of Luftwaffe bombs that had smashed these very dwellings. Barely more than a week after his arrival at Snetterton Heath, the Germans had bombed Norwich, just twenty miles north of the 96th air base. Airmen listened to the attack from inside their bomb shelters. Blazing anti-aircraft fire from British air defense men streaked up through the black sky. Falling bombs screamed in the distance. When they exploded, fiery geysers shot into the air and lit up the night like a summer thunderstorm. People died. Now he watched the charred remains of a city street pass by his train window.

When Gene returned to his base, he was eager to get back in the air.

"After seeing that, I knew we had a job to do," Gene told me once. "And we did it."

October 1943

Gene was stationed at Snetterton Heath, England, home of the 96th Bomb Group. The 96th was just one of forty bomb groups that made up the Eighth Air Force. Each bomb group had its own airport which maintained roughly forty bombers.

The forty air bases were scattered throughout East Anglia, a peninsula north of London that jutted into the North Sea. Before the war, farmers tilled the land, a landscape of grazing cows and farmhouses surrounded by lush, green fields. But in 1942, the British government was so pleased the Yanks had joined the war that they practically ceded the entire area to the American Eighth Air Force. Flying Fortress and Liberator bombers now roared onto the runways that crisscrossed the once green pastures, turning East Anglia into history's largest airport.

Upon arrival, Gene walked with Pee Wee, Swedo, Andy, Reed, and Sparky through a heavy mist toward a dull, gray airplane hangar shrouded by thick fog. Greasy mud sucked at their boots. Gene swore English fog was wetter than Wisconsin fog. Not even his leather flight jacket and uniform shirt could keep the drizzling rain from soaking all the way through to his t-shirt. A first sergeant marched them to their living quarters. The sodden bomber crew stopped in front of a half-round structure known as a Nissen hut. Each of the metallic half-domes housed the enlisted crews of two bombers. When Gene and his buddies went inside, the other six airmen who lived there greeted them with icy silence.

"You guys are replacing a crew lost this morning," the first sergeant explained. He gave no other details. Gene looked around and saw photos and other personal belongings of the missing men still sitting on shelves and foot lockers.

"You do your business outside in the slit trench," the first sergeant added before he left, pointing to the back of the Nissen hut where the Army Air Force had provided an open pit toilet.

Gene set his duffel bag on a metal bunk occupied the night before by a man who was now missing or dead. A foot locker sat at the base of each bed. He waited patiently to stack his clothes into the locker while base staffers cleared out the personal items of the lost men. Were they dead? Or hiding in a forest with broken limbs and burned faces, watching enemy soldiers search for them?

In the hut, blackout curtains shaded the windows. The two light bulbs strung from the ceiling struggled to light the dark cave. A potbellied charcoal stove sat in the middle of the hut, separating the living areas of the two six-man air crews. On a shelf near the stove, Gene was surprised to see a radio. The radio could only pick up two channels: BBC and a German broadcast called *Axis Sally*. This "Sally" was an American citizen who had renounced her citizenship and broadcast English-language Nazi propaganda from Berlin. Later, all the men in the hut would sit around the radio and laugh at her programs. They were intended to make Allied servicemen lonely and scared, but had just the opposite effect. No one cared she was a gabby traitor so long as she also played American jazz and big band music.

Gene spent his first week at Snetterton Heath sitting on benches in briefing rooms listening to training lectures. Marching to class, Gene spotted African American soldiers unloading trucks. It was a common sight at Snetterton Heath, but he and all the other white airmen never talked to the Black troops.

Inside the briefing rooms, Gene sat in rapt attention, hanging on every word coming from the instructors, so different from snoozing through English grammar class at Soldiers Grove High School.

The information he was getting now could soon mean the differ-ence between seeing his parents once more or lying in a common German grave. The instructors advised Jewish fliers to get a second set of dog tags with different, more Gentile-sounding names. If shot down, they were to rip the real tags from their necks as soon as their parachute hit the ground.

Gene learned the Army Air Force expected downed fliers who were not injured to get to France and contact the Underground. Agents there would lead the escape back to Great Britain. All the men received phony identification papers. Later, the new bomber boys dressed in civilian shirts and posed for a photograph to add to their escape documents. Gene admired his headshot photo. He believed his thin, new mustache growing above his lip gave him a certain *je ne sais quoi.*

Gene was reunited with Orrison, Curtis, Benny, and Langley when the enlisted gunners and their officers met on a runway hardstand to look over their assigned Flying Fortress. It was a used, battle-weary plane dubbed *Rikki Tikki Tavi*. The men hooted and catcalled when they spotted the nose art: a painted blonde lady not wearing a stitch of clothing. She was a busty woman straddling a bomb with her hands locked behind her head, exposing her perfectly rounded breasts. Gene laughed, thinking what his mother would say. He was perplexed by the name of his plane, though. He knew Rikki-tikki-tavi was a fictional mongoose in a Rudyard Kipling story. Mongoose? Naked woman riding a bomb? It made no sense.

Gene counted more than a dozen bomb symbols painted on the plane's nose, which indicated the number of missions the B-17 had already flown. There were also other signs of previous battles: pieces of metal slabbed over repaired bullet holes. *Rikki Tikki Tavi*. In this plane, he would fight. In this plane, he would protect his comrades from Nazi fighter planes. Would the plane protect him? For now, they rapped the aluminum sides and joked with the crews nearby, flyboys from *Ramblin' Wreck, G-String,* and *Dear Mom.*

Of the four squadrons in the 96th Bomb Group, Gene was assigned to the 339th Squadron. Their commanders placed him and his crew "on alert." Airmen on alert were restricted to the base. New bomber crews generally flew practice missions over England for a week or two before beginning their combat tour. But after a month of heavy losses, the Eighth Air Force needed replacements—immediately.

November 3, 1943 – First mission

Putter-putt-putt-putt-putter-putt-putt-putt . . . Gene couldn't sleep. It was early morning on his first mission day. Small generators sputtering outside on the airplane hardstands kept him awake. The generators provided dim light to the ground crewmen, who cautiously loaded bombs with hand-operated winches into the bomb bays of the Flying Fortresses. Such low-light conditions were a must in late 1943. German planes still roared across the English Channel at night occasionally to bomb cities and air bases.

At 4:00 a.m., an orderly rapped loudly on the door. "Time to get up, boys."

Gene rolled out of his bunk. He pulled on his silk long underwear, wool shirt, and pants and headed to the mess hall with the others. In the chow line, Gene watched cooks dump real fried eggs onto the trays, not the usual square-cut powdered eggs. Everyone went back to the hut to finish dressing after breakfast. Gene put on his electrically heated "bunny suit," then layered on another one-piece jumpsuit, followed by fleece-lined leather pants and boots. Everyone grabbed their insulated flight jackets and gloves and hustled to the briefing shack to gather with the officers to receive their first mission orders.

Dozens of enlisted men and officers of the 96th Bomb Group piled into the cold, unheated briefing room and sat on wooden benches. Some of the fliers took long drags on cigarettes, others talked in a low murmur. Gene took it all in. And then it hit him. *Oooooh, boy. This is it!* He settled himself by trying to think of it as just doing a job.

The briefing officer strode onto the stage in front of the men. The room fell silent in anticipation. It was the moment of awe and dread when the curtain opened to reveal a map of western Europe and the target for the day. Gene watched the experienced fliers lean forward, eyes glued to the curtain. When the black draping was finally pulled back, it revealed a red string with a dogleg-right bend in it that ran from Snetterton Heath to the target: Wilhelmshaven, Germany. The red string was not long. Wilhelmshaven was a port city located in northwestern Germany on the coast of the North Sea. Gene looked around at the other fliers breathing sighs of relief. This would not be a deep raid to such heavily defended cities like Schweinfurt or Bremen.

"You'll have P-47 fighter escort to the target," the officer added. Gene watched veteran fliers clap their hands and pump their fists. There was more excitement. He learned that his first bombing run would be mission number fifty for the 96th.

Another officer stepped on the stage to give weather reports and altitude assignments for the squadrons. He warned where the bombers could expect to meet "Goering's Boys," the elite German fighter squadrons named for Hermann Goering, Luftwaffe chief and Hitler's right-hand Nazi. A "flak report" was read, explaining that the bombers should expect most anti-aircraft fire from the area just around the target.

Gene hung on every word he heard. He thought, *This is good . . . shorter raid, fighter planes escorting all the way to the target. My first mission might be easy, a "milk run."*

"Are there any questions?" the officer asked tersely. No one raised a hand. He continued, "Anyone who's sick report to the flight surgeon now. The chaplain is also available."

Gene stood up and looked to the back of the briefing room

where many fliers gathered around an officer with crucifix symbols on his uniform jacket lapels. Gene walked over with his crew and bowed his head. He was surprised to see Andy, who had never joined Gene at Sunday Mass, lowering his head too. The chaplain raised his right hand and read a prayer of general absolution for all. The entire group responded, "Amen." In unison, Catholic fliers like Gene, Pee Wee, Swedo, and Sparky crossed themselves.

Langley, Benny, Orrison, and Curtis stayed back for final instructions for officers. Gene joined other gunners at a nearby equipment building to pick up extra belts of machine gun bullets, parachutes, flak mats, and their yellow "Mae West" life jackets, named after the well-endowed female film star. The life jacket gave Gene a measure of comfort. He'd be fine in case of a water landing, having Mae West's bulky bosoms pressed to his chest. With ammunition belts slung around his neck, Gene piled into the back of a three-axled 6x6 truck waiting to take fliers to their planes. It was still drizzling when the transport truck rumbled through the gray early-morning fog. The good news back at the briefing of a possible milk run had steadied Gene's nerves, but he couldn't believe they'd be taking off in this fog. Midair collisions were common when squadrons formed up in bad weather. Gene knew his rookie pilots, Langley and Benny, would have to fly blind through the soupy weather until they got above the clouds.

The truck jolted to a stop at the hardstand of *Rikki Tikki Tavi*. Gene could still smell the exhaust fumes of the generators that had run all night. The crew hopped off the tailgate and headed for their positions. Reed pulled himself up chin-up style through a hatch in the nose of the plane and checked his guns in the top turret. Sparky sat in the radio room reviewing his frequencies. Gene, Swedo, Andy, and Pee Wee entered their bomber through the fuselage door in the rear. Swedo and Andy mounted their single-barrel machine guns inside the open waist windows. Pee Wee gave the ball turret a final power check.

Gene hauled all his equipment back to his lonely battle station. He lay the flak mat on the floor. He shuddered, wondering how the thin apron lined with metal panels would stop an exploding anti-aircraft shell. He shook off the thought. Time to get to work. Next came plugging in his intercom microphone, his oxygen hose, and his electrically heated suit. The warmth soon radiated over his buttocks, but he sensed nothing near his feet. He set a coffee can on the floor, his personal toilet. There was a "piss tube" in the radio room, but he wanted no part of unhooking everything and then having to waddle through the fuselage to get to Sparky's compartment. He checked his guns and the ammunition belts that flowed to it. He checked them again, and then a third time, anything to keep his mind occupied.

Langley, Benny, Orrison, and Curtis arrived and pulled themselves up through the nose hatch and into the plane to begin their lengthy pre-flight checklists.

"Intercom check," Langley called out.

"Tail gun, okay," Gene replied. Everyone else repeated in order from back to front.

Gene stepped out of the plane once he finished his pre-flight duties. He was soon joined by the rest of the crew, except Langley, who stayed in the cockpit. They all huddled up under the nose of *Rikki Tikki Tavi*. Each man clasped the fleece-lined jacket collar of the man next to him. The nine intertwined men stared quietly at the ground. Nobody spoke. In a moment, they would take off for the first time to take on the Luftwaffe's best fighter pilots. They would fly over hundreds of German anti-aircraft cannons zeroed in to shred American metal and flesh. Orrison, the crew's big brother, broke the silence. "Well. This is it," he said. Everyone softly chuckled. A few quiet seconds passed. "Okay. Let's get back on board," Orrison said.

After everybody else entered the plane, Gene snuck back behind the tail. He needed to take a final "nervous pee." He unzipped and fished through five layers of clothing before he could finally grab his crumpled penis. If peeing outside standing on solid ground was such a chore, Gene figured his piss can would be useless inside a rollicking bomber at twenty-five thousand feet in sub-zero air. He decided if he had to go in the air, he'd just wet his pants.

Back in the plane, Gene clambered up to the radio room to join Pee Wee, Andy, and Swedo already seated on the floor next to Sparky, who sat in his chair behind the radio table. On takeoff, the five men filled the radio room, serving as the center of gravity to a bomb-filled Flying Fortress. They had to sit farther back if the plane carried a maximum bomb load. They knew to take their positions only once *Rikki Tikki Tavi* was airborne.

A flare burst from the control tower and arced through the air, signaling Langley and Benny to start the plane's four engines. Sitting in the waiting room with Sparky, Pee Wee, Swedo, and Andy, Gene listened to each engine cough, spat, and then settle into a steady roar. Cyclones of mist and dirt blew out the back of the bomber. A ground crewman removed the wheel chocks. *Rikki Tikki Tavi* lurched forward and joined a line of lumbering Flying Fortresses taxiing to the runway. Each was filled with five thousand pounds of bombs. Everyone in the radio room stared blankly, avoiding eye contact. Gene thought it took forever for his plane to get to the runway. Then Langley centered himself for takeoff.

"Tail wheel locked, light on, light out," Benny reported. The plane was ready to go. Gene looked out the radio room window— still foggy. On clear days, planes took off in thirty-second intervals. In this weather, Langley and Benny would have to wait a full minute. Seconds ticked by. Nobody talked. When Langley revved the engines and released the wheel brakes, Gene's heart leapt into his throat. He reached for his rosary inside his flight jacket. He'd sat through dozens of takeoffs, but never before had his plane flown into such weather stuffed with a full load of fuel and bombs. He stroked the crucifix with his fingers, and the Flying Fortress raced down the runway. The roar of the four engines and the drone of the plane's tires on the steel-matted runway were deafening. The plane

reached 110 mph. It lifted. Brakes off, landing gear up, flaps up . . .
Rikki Tikki Tavi was airborne.

As the bomber flew straight ahead, gaining altitude, Gene left
the radio room and took his position. Sitting on his bicycle-seat
chair, he stared out the back window and saw nothing but a white
haze. He couldn't get out of his mind the thought of a propeller
from another plane suddenly appearing and churning toward him.

And then *Rikki Tikki Tavi* topped the clouds. The sun was just
rising. It splashed all shades of pink, orange, red, and purple color
across cloud tops. Gene thought it looked like some imperial city
from a fairy tale. He had a sudden urge to step out of the plane and
walk out onto the puffy clouds. *Is this what heaven looks like?*

The view improved. One by one, other Flying Fortresses rose
out of the cloud deck like tiny, newborn trout rising from a stream-
bed. The bombers leveled off at assigned altitudes and circled, looking for their spot in formation. Tail gunners in lead planes fired
colored flares, directing the turning bombers to form up with their
squadrons. Gene watched the red, blue, and yellow smoke of the
flares loop across the turquoise sky.

Once above the clouds, bombers formed into three levels: a
top, middle, and bottom. The top tier led the middle and bottom
groups, which were spaced behind it. Each level included a dozen
or more planes divided into groups of three planes. The bombers
flew closely together for better protection against fighter attacks.
Gene watched other Flying Fortresses from the 96th pull up just a
hundred feet behind his tail gun position.

The bombers headed east to link up with bomb groups rising
from bases all across East Anglia. From the back of his plane, Gene
watched more than five hundred Flying Fortresses and Liberators
come together above England. He had never seen so many airplanes. His chest swelled at being part of such a grand first mission.

"Oxygen check. Tail gunner, do you hear me?" Langley asked
from the cockpit.

Gene snapped out of his momentary daydream. He lifted the oxygen mask slung around his neck and tightened it to his face. "Tail gunner, okay," he answered.

Rikki Tikki Tavi and the bombers in her group climbed to twenty-three thousand feet. Gene saw the comforting sight of Flying Fortresses on both sides of him. The formation would be his plane's refuge. He was especially glad to see the other Flying Fortresses tightening up behind him. No one wanted to be the last plane. Nazi fighter planes liked to target "Tail-end Charlie."

The attacking force headed northeast out over the English Channel. When there was a break in the clouds, Gene could see the churning November waters below. This was the point of no return. Bombers experiencing mechanical problems or other maladies had already aborted their missions and turned back.

A half hour into the flight, Langley ordered everyone to check their guns. Gene couldn't wait to press his two triggers. It seemed like a year since he last fired his guns back during his stateside training. Up front, Curtis and Orrison fired their small thirty-caliber guns sticking out the Plexiglas nose. Reed opened up with his double fifty calibers in the top turret, as did Pee Wee in the ball turret. With the sliding windows open at the waist position, Swedo and Andy fired their single-barreled guns. Sub-zero air blasted their faces. Everyone shot three or four bursts simultaneously. The vibrations rattled every bone in Gene's body.

"Tail gunner, okay," Gene reported. He kept his voice steady. Around him, the other gunners reported back to the cockpit in calm, dispassionate voices, masking their inner terror.

Rikki Tikki Tavi flew over the North Sea. Soon, more than three hundred American fighter planes flew up to meet the Flying Fortresses and Liberators. Gene watched chubby P-47 Thunderbolts pulling up near his squadron. Off in the distance, he recognized the box-tails of twin-engine P-38 Lightning fighters.

After a few hours of flight over the North Sea, the air armada crossed over the coastline of western Europe. Below them was Hitler's Germany. For the first time, Gene was in enemy airspace. He heard a new sound. *Whump, Whump, Whump.* He looked down. Above the cloud deck, he spotted scattered bursts of black clouds—flak, the hidden enemy. From the ground, long-barreled 88mm anti-aircraft cannons were firing shells filled with metal pellets that would detonate as high as thirty-five thousand feet. Gene's oxygen breathing bag below his mask expanded and contracted more rapidly. But there was nothing he could do other than pray that the exploding shells stayed low. This time, they did.

"Fighters! Nine o'clock," someone on *Rikki Tikki Tavi* yelled. Gene snapped his head to the right. Off in the distance, slender, dark planes charged into a group of bombers. Lightning and Thunderbolt fighter planes banked to meet the enemy. A few moments later, Gene saw a burning Flying Fortress trailing ugly, dark smoke. The plane nosed up and, like a wounded beast, flipped on its backside and dove away out of sight.

He spotted no parachutes.

Gene turned back to his guns and scanned the sky behind his plane. *Focus. Just do your job. Nothing else matters.*

The bombers approached their target: Wilhelmshaven. Before the war, the coastal resort city was famous for its mud baths. The Eighth Air Force came to lay waste to its submarine and ship construction centers. Gene looked below and saw nothing but clouds. With an overcast sky covering the target, he feared they'd turn back. Everything had gone well so far. No flak bursts near his plane, and the American fighter escort had kept enemy fighters on the fringe. First mission flown, but would they get credit?

"Pilot to bombardier," Langley said to Curtis. "I'm switching the plane over to you."

Curtis sat over his Norden bombsight, a mechanical gyroscope system that computed the correct release point for the bombs. It was also connected to the autopilot, which ensured steady flight as the bombardier found his aiming point. Curtis now controlled *Rikki Tikki Tavi* as it began its bomb run. He guided the plane using the controls of his aiming device. More flak bursts lit up the sky. Closer. Curtis held snug behind the lead bombers. He had to fly straight and stay in formation. The planes up front were equipped with a new technology, an air-to-ground radar that could locate targets through an overcast sky. Curtis would release his bombs soon when the lead planes dropped theirs.

"Bomb bay doors open," Curtis reported over the intercom. He fingered the bomb release toggle switch. Everyone held their breath. Gene felt like a sitting duck flying straight and level as flak bursts peppered the sky around the squadron, though none of the oily, black plumes came close to their plane.

"Bombs away!" Curtis yelled. They were the sweetest two words Gene had ever heard. Four general-purpose bombs and thirty-one fire-igniting incendiaries fell from the belly of *Rikki Tikki Tavi*. His heart leapt just as the plane jumped too. *Rikki Tikki Tavi* vaulted skyward, suddenly relieved of her two and a half tons of bombs.

Langley banked the plane and followed the other bombers to begin the trip home. Just minutes after the bombing run, Gene smiled. Out his windows, he could see Lightning fighter planes returning. He spotted a "dogfight" out on the edge of the formation— German fighters taking revenge.

They were back over the North Sea now. German fighter attacks dropped away. Gene's eyes scanned the skies still. That was his job. Failing to see incoming fighters coming back for one last lick could exact a terrible price on his crewmates. But as carefully as Gene watched for the black pinprick of a German aircraft, no more enemy fighters appeared. His first mission, and he hadn't fired a single shot. *If only they could all be this easy.*

In a few hours, the English coast appeared. The weather had cleared. Flying over land once again, Gene looked down and saw how many bombed-out buildings had been destroyed earlier in the war. *We just did that to the Germans.*

Rikki Tikki Tavi approached Snetterton Heath and circled the base. Langley landed the plane smoothly and taxied to its assigned hardstand. Gene stepped out and saw the propellers from other planes spinning to a stop: *Ramblin' Wreck, G-String,* and *Dear Mom.* It seemed that everybody made it back. Gene joined his smiling crew, looking for damage. Not a single hole from a German bullet or flak shell had punctured their plane.

All ten of the crew marched to a briefing room for the post-mission interview. There were shots of whiskey, and it loosened the tongues of the keyed-up fliers. In monotone voices, officers questioned them about enemy fighters, flak, shot-down bombers, and parachuting survivors. Gene's debriefing was short; no firing on any enemy planes. The interrogation officer informed them they were restricted to base. They'd be flying again in a day or two.

After a welcome hot meal of ham and eggs in the cafeteria, Gene and the crew returned to their Nissen hut. The others played cards and wrote letters to family and friends. But Gene didn't feel like letter writing or poker playing. He flopped on his bunk and stared at the ceiling. *One down . . . twenty-four to go.*

November 5, 1943 – Second mission

Gene stroked his thin mustache with his thumb and index finger, waiting for the briefing officer to begin. It was two days after his first mission. Sitting again in the packed briefing room, he hoped this second mission would go as well as the first. When the black curtain was drawn back, his optimism faded. The red string stretched further south this time to Gelsenkirchen, located in the heart of Germany's industrial Ruhr Valley.

"Flak Valley" it was called because of the thousands of anti-aircraft guns that protected the factories that churned out war material.

Gene swallowed. No way would his bomber return scratch-free this time.

Back in the air for the second time in three days, *Rikki Tikki Tavi* climbed to twenty-eight thousand feet and joined the thirty-two other Flying Fortresses of the 96th. More bomber groups joined the 96th's planes, and soon, Gene looked out over another five hundred bomber raid. The feeling of awe that had overwhelmed him during the last mission was replaced by anxiety. "Flak Valley." He shuddered.

Out over the English Channel, Thunderbolt and Lightning fighter planes pulled up to provide their protective shield. Gene found it ironic that the "Little Friends" protected the big boys, like baby chicks chasing the fox away from the mother hen back at the farm.

The vast fleet of four-engine bombers approached Nazi territory. "Bandits, twelve o'clock!" someone cried out on the intercom. In the nose, Curtis and Orrison steadied their machine guns. Reed spun his top turret toward the front. German fighter planes often made head-on attacks, not just to kill the pilots, but because the nose of a Flying Fortress was a weak spot in its defensive shield. Several slender Messerschmitt 109 fighter planes zipped under Gene's guns, heading toward a group of Fortresses farther back.

Reed yelled from the top turret. "Mo, another 109 is coming your way at ten o'clock high. I can't get 'em." Gene swung his guns to his right. In a millisecond, the fighter flashed by and dove low in front of Gene. He had no time to square the enemy plane in his sights. He fired at the fleeing attacker anyway. Not even close to hitting him. Several other enemy fighters made passes near Gene's squadron. Each time, Gene let go with short three- or four-second bursts, resisting the urge to hold in his triggers too long. Must not waste bullets.

Above and to the side of Gene's plane, enemy fighters zeroed in on the lead Flying Fortress from another bomber group flying adjacent to the 96th's aircraft. The wings of the German planes blinked fire as they swept past the bomber. The nose of the doomed Fortress started to rise. *Rikki Tikki Tavi*'s intercom erupted.

"Look out!"

"Jeez-us Christ!"

"Holy shit!"

In the rear of the plane, Gene yelled out, "What's going on?"

Flaming debris swept past his window. The stricken lead plane had flipped backward and crashed into another bomber. Gene watched in horror as the damaged second plane spun out of control and slammed into a third Fortress, which collided with a fourth plane. The sky was a conflagration of smoking wreckage, wildly spinning propellers, and falling bodies. Gene looked for parachutes. He saw none. *Four planes, forty men. Gone in seconds.*

The bomber armada—minus four planes—flew through the smoke and fire and continued toward Gelsenkirchen.

Just before the bomb run, flak bursts erupted from below. The German gunners had found their range. A flak shell exploded near *Rikki Tikki Tavi*. The concussion jolted the bomber, followed by a sound like someone hurling a bucket of gravel. Gene saw flak exploding behind him. Some shells were so close he could see the orange burst in the middle of the black puffs. His crewmates uttered a string of "goddammits" and "son of a bitches" over the intercom after each blast. Gene seethed with useless rage.

Gene ached for revenge after flying through the flak storm. So unfair that he couldn't fight back! This time, when *Rikki Tikki Tavi* dropped her payload, he willed for the bombs to find their mark, smashing machine shops and factory floors, demolishing anything that produced flak.

After Curtis yelled, "Bombs away," *Rikki Tikki Tavi* banked west and headed back for England. It was a cloudless day. For the first time, Gene could see the effects of strategic bombing. He looked down at fires that boiled red. *Take that, you Nazi bastards!*

Gene kept staring at the factories blazing below his plane. There were people in those buildings. What had *Rikki Tikki Tavi* just done? Men scorched in that cauldron. Intense heat, like a barn fire he once saw as a kid. Dad had battled the blaze with neighbors. Gene sat in the car, well back on the road, waves of heat rolling over him from the inferno. Cows trapped in the barn bawled in otherworldly screams. Men fired lever-action rifles at them, pumping bullets into the barn to put the cattle out of their misery. Gene shut out the sound of those screaming cows, the cries of people below.

Those people made flak. They made German fighter planes. To hell with them.

The Eighth Air Force lost fifteen Flying Fortresses on the raid on Gelsenkirchen. None from Gene's bomb group. The 96th brought all thirty-two planes back to Snetterton Heath Air Base. But this time, many of the bombers had holes in them. Flak Valley had lived up to its name. One damaged bomber crashed on landing. Another landed with a dead top-turret gunner who died from a lack of oxygen. Other planes had wounded men aboard.

Langley circled the base, waiting for his signal to land. Planes with wounded men landed first. Gene saw a couple of bombers shooting one or two flares to alert the ambulance trucks to the number of broken and bleeding men on board.

Back on the hardstand, Gene and the others inspected their plane and tallied its wounds. *Rikki Tikki Tavi* was lucky: just a few holes and jagged cuts.

This debriefing took longer than the first interrogation. The Army Air Force particularly wanted details about the four-plane crash. The interviewing officer peppered Gene with questions since tail gunners always had the best view of the aftermath of such disasters.

Back in his Nissen hut, Gene collapsed onto his bed. So much had happened. His mind conducted its own debriefing, replaying the four-plane collision in endless cycles. Reed, Andy, and Swedo sat on the edges of their beds, describing how it all began. They moved their flattened hands at intersecting angles to mimic the stricken bombers.

Gene also replayed his first strike against the enemy. He'd shot many squirrels and rabbits to fill the family soup kettle as a boy. But today he'd fired bullets at another human being. *Just a job,* he repeated to himself. *It's just a job.*

CHAPTER 6

A Thousand Ways to Die

April 2011

Gene hadn't seen me yet. He wandered along the bank of Baker Creek behind his home. Towering, leafless oaks and maples rose up from the opposite bank of the creek. No leaves would come for a few weeks, but their buds were swelling. Spring took its time coming to Wisconsin.

"Here, duckies! Where are you?" His gruff, grating voice held a sweetness in it. "It's suppertime. Here, ducks. Come on, ducks."

The sudden whoosh of flapping wings heralded the arrival of a dozen mallards. They landed around Gene. I watched as the tail gunner who'd fought in history's greatest air war led a parade of quacking waterfowl toward the patio deck where I stood. He spotted me and nodded.

"I've got to feed my girls before we start."

He headed for the plastic resin bins on the patio deck. Lifting off the light-brown cover, he took a milk jug with a cut-off bottom and plunged it into the crushed dried corn. He leaned over the patio railing. Careful not to hit the United States flag mounted on the deck railing, he flung out the grain. The ducks quacked their approval.

"How often do you feed them?"

"Every day."

He gave me a quizzical side glance as if I just asked a dumb question. Not a good way to start an interview where I'd be asking some tough questions about the war.

I watched the ducks charge at the scattered corn. Gene tossed out another scoop. The grain arced and fell on top of the ducks. They quacked and scrambled away, startled by the sudden bounty. I leaned my elbows on the deck railing next to Gene. For a few minutes, we watched the mallards eat.

"Did you get a chance to look over the questions I sent you?"

Two weeks earlier, I'd dropped off a list of typed questions asking about Gene's final missions. I wanted to give him a heads-up on the difficult topics we'd be discussing today.

"Didn't we talk about some of those already?" Gene tossed the milk jug scoop back in the bin.

"We did." I shuffled my feet and stared at the deck planks. "I need a few more details about those last couple of missions."

I'd sent the list to prepare Gene. Would he take me where I wanted to go? Would he go deeper into his war memories? It all seemed wrong leaning on that deck railing. After a long winter cooped up in his mobile home, Gene was soaking in the warmth of a spring breeze. He was watching his ducks, his "girls." He was at peace. But I wanted to take him back inside and talk about bombing people.

With neither of us saying a word, we left the quacking ducks and went inside. I slid my coat over the back of the kitchen chair, accepted my ritual Coors Light, and pressed the recorder button.

"November of '43 was a busy time for me. It seemed like we were flying every day. I think I got up to fly nineteen times that month," Gene said.

Nineteen? I stopped taking notes. I had all of Gene's mission records. The 96th Bomb Group never gave him credit for that many missions. Most bomber crewmen never made nineteen, much less the twenty-five required in 1943. Nineteen times in less than a month? I'd never heard of such an intense combat tour.

"Wait. I don't understand. I have your mission records," I said. "You weren't credited with nineteen."

"If you didn't drop those bombs where you were supposed to, you got no credit." Gene banged his index finger down on the kitchen table, his gravelly voice shifted to a growl. "You'd go up, and maybe you'd be gone three or four hours, and then you'd find out your target and secondary target were covered by bad weather. One time we were only an hour from the target. We fought all the way in and all the way out and got no credit. Boy, that sure pissed me off, scrubbed missions."

Gene stopped and took a swig from his can. He stared straight ahead and said nothing. I sensed bitterness. What memories did I trigger? I remembered Ben Logan's advice to back off from the war if I thought I'd touched a nerve. Maybe we should take a break, just go outside. Put our arms on the deck railing, drink beer, and throw more corn to the ducks.

I could hear the mallards still quacking outside. Inside, Gene's demons were rising.

November 1943

November 16, 1943 – Third mission

Sitting on the rows of wooden benches in the chilly briefing room, airmen stretched and rubbed their eyes. Gene couldn't stop yawning. It was only 3:00 a.m. The "wake-up sergeant" had banged on the Nissen hut door at 1:30 a.m. Why so early?

Soon, the briefing officer strode earnestly onto the stage. The curtain opened. The room hushed. Today, the red string was different: vertical. Stretched north instead of the usual eastbound, horizontal line. Gene's eyes followed the string to its end point. His jaw dropped.

Norway?!

It was the longest red string Gene had ever seen on the map. Now it made sense why they'd been roused so early. The 96th Bomb Group was supposed to fly more than four hundred miles over the North Sea to bomb the Rjukan Dam in southern Norway. Gene shuddered. Four hundred miles of open ocean? If they had to ditch in that icy water, they'd never be found.

The airmen looked at the map and hung their heads. The briefing officer tried to rally them. He lectured about the special importance of the mission and about something called "heavy water" produced at the Rjukan Dam. The Germans were using this heavy water to develop a new type of bomb, a device more powerful than any explosive ever created. Gene had no idea what the officer was talking about.

The orders for *Rikki Tikki Tavi* were a bit different. Once they crossed the Norwegian coastline, Gene's plane and another 96th Flying Fortress were to merge with a separate attacking force assigned to bomb a molybdenum mine in Knaben, not far from the Rjukan Dam. The briefing officer explained the mine was also connected to the German effort to build a super bomb. Gene didn't like being split from the usual formation, but he saw on the map that Knaben was located about a hundred miles south of the Rjukan Dam. At least he'd have a shorter flight than the rest of the bomb group.

Loaded down with clothing and ammunition, the enlisted *Rikki Tikki Tavi* crew grumbled as a truck hauled them to their bomber. Gene figured this mission would be at least an eight-to-nine-hour round trip. God, how his backside would ache after sitting on his metal bicycle-seat chair for that long. Pee Wee would be scrunched in the ball turret for almost half a day. With no chairs at the waist gun positions, Swedo and Andy would have to stand the entire length of the flight.

The Norway mission worsened Gene's already sour mood. Since arriving at Snetterton Heath three weeks ago, he'd tallied only two completed missions. After *Rikki Tikki Tavi*'s raid on Gelsenkirchen, thick, wooly fog had blanketed the airfields of East Anglia for the next ten days. Each dark morning, wind-driven rain lashed at Gene when he headed to the briefing room. It seemed as if he was getting up to fly every day, but the missions were always canceled, usually because of bad weather. What was worse, the order to abort a mission could come at any time: waiting on the tarmac, taxiing to the runway, or forming up the bomb group above the clouds. Gene hated scrubbed missions. He'd get all psyched up wondering if this was going to be his last day on earth only to have all that mental stress spent for nothing.

Weather wasn't the only reason for aborted missions. Five days earlier, while flying to Munster, Germany, *Rikki Tikki Tavi* had to return to base with the entire bomb group when a fire broke out on the lead plane. Two days later on a different mission, Langley and four other bomber pilots got lost in the early-morning darkness above the English coastline searching for the formation. *Rikki Tikki Tavi* and the other disoriented bombers were forced to return to base after wasting too much precious fuel spent looking for the rest of the bomb group.

A week earlier, *Rikki Tikki Tavi* had sat third in line, waiting to take off. Above the roar of idling engines, Gene heard shouting from the cockpit. Looking out the radio room window, he spotted black, oily smoke wafting by. Reed hustled back to tell the gunners that the first plane had crashed at the end of the runway. The bomber had lifted off, but then dropped to the ground in a heap, obliterated in a flash of fire. The second plane had already started its takeoff and was forced to fly through the fire and smoke. Langley and Benny held *Rikki Tikki Tavi* in place and watched blood-red flames consume the Flying Fortress and its ten men.

Langley taxied back to the hardstand, but the crew was ordered to stay near the plane. The mission was still on. Outside the bomber, Gene watched a bulldozer shove the charred wreckage off the runway. Another bulldozer pushed dirt into the crater holed by exploding bombs. A team of men lay down steel mats over the fresh dirt. No one paused to honor the ten dead men. No prayer. No ceremony. Hurry up and get the runway ready. The mission must go on.

Rikki Tikki Tavi was the first to rumble down the repaired runway. Four engines roared as they headed straight for the crash site. Gene gasped when the plane sunk a bit rolling over the steel maps covering the repaired spot. Just an hour before, that soft spot had been scorched aluminum and melted rubber. He closed his eyes and envisioned the open sky. Above the clouds, he'd get to work and forget the runway disaster. But once *Rikki Tikki Tavi* broke through the cloud deck, Langley called out that the mission was canceled. Thick cloud cover over the target. The first bomber had crashed for nothing. They returned to the airfield where faint wisps of smoke still drifted from the wreckage of the crashed Flying Fortress.

Two missions in three weeks. At that rate, Gene figured he'd never complete his combat tour. The strain was getting to him. Get up at 3:00 a.m. March bleary-eyed to breakfast. Sweat out the unveiling of the target in the briefing room. Endure the nervous truck ride to the tarmac. Pray your overloaded bomber wouldn't crash in a fiery ball on takeoff. And then to have it all canceled because of lousy weather. No credit at all for day after day of internal agony.

Today, braced for the Norwegian mission, the group huddled together before takeoff. After Orrison's pep talk, Gene slipped behind the tail to take his customary "nervous pee." Weather looked good. Partly cloudy skies. Mission number three had to happen today.

At formation above the clouds, Langley and Benny settled *Rikki Tikki Tavi* at a cruising altitude of 21,500 feet. For the next five hours, Gene didn't have much to do. He couldn't talk with anyone on the intercom. The secrecy of this special mission required strict radio silence. Dutifully, he scanned the clear, intensely blue skies. Because of their limited range, friendly fighter planes were not expected to escort the bombers on such a long mission. But Gene didn't expect to see enemy fighters this far out from enemy territory. Occasionally, he glanced at the darker blue water below. Not since flying over the Gulf of Mexico while stationed in Texas had he spent this much time over the ocean.

When *Rikki Tikki Tavi* neared the mountainous coast of Norway, Langley dropped the plane down to 13,000 feet along with the other planes of the 96th Bomb Group. At the lower altitude, Gene looked out at some of the most gorgeous landscape he'd ever seen. The weather was clearer at the lower altitude, so he had an unobstructed view of the snowcapped, jagged mountains. There were lakes every-where, some round, others finger-shaped. He snapped his head back to the sky to look for enemy fighters. None. No flak either.

On the bomb run toward Knaben, there was still no enemy ac-tivity. Gene thought maybe they'd caught the Germans by surprise. Maybe this would be an easy "milk run." Curtis let the bombs go just before noon. *Rikki Tikki Tavi* turned south and headed back for the North Sea. All they had to do now was cruise the uneventful, but long, flight back to England, land safely, and Gene would finally get credited for that elusive third mission.

On the return trip, with no threat of enemy fighters, the Flying Fortresses of the 96th flew loosely apart from one another to save fuel. Tight formation flying required constant adjustments, which used additional fuel. Four hours after leaving Norway, *Rikki Tikki Tavi* touched down at Snetterton Heath.

The gunners climbed out of the airplane groaning with sore joints and aching muscles. Gene's lower back bothered him more than anything, but his spirits were high. The Norway flight had been long, but relatively safe. Three missions down. Twenty-two to go.

When they returned to their Nissen hut, Gene gingerly low-ered himself onto his bunk. He stared at the ceiling. In two weeks of canceled missions, Gene and his buddies had a lot of free time. They had no assigned duties other than to fly missions. The crew would hike over to the enlisted men's recreation center to play ping pong or shoot pool. Or they'd just hang out in the Nissen hut playing poker or blackjack and listening to the radio. Swedo would sing along to the pop and jazz tunes.

But after the long Norway mission, Gene wanted to do something different. Even with an aching back, he was restless. Lying on his bed, he turned toward Pee Wee's bunk.

"Hey, Pee Wee. Feel like celebrating?"

"What you got in mind, Mo?"

"Let's you and me find that pub at the end of the runway we've been hearing about," Gene said.

The crew of *Rikki Tikki Tavi* had learned about the pub from other airmen. But because they were restricted to base every day after their first mission, they hadn't had a chance to visit. The watering hole was technically just outside the air base. Gene wasn't sure if visiting it would be off-limits, but after his long day, he didn't care.

He and Pee Wee hopped on bicycles and raced each other down the runway to the establishment. A gallon-sized pail hung from each side of the handlebars. They'd been told customers had to bring their own containers if they wanted any take-out beer. The two steel pails clanged and banged against Gene's bike as he pumped his legs trying to catch Pee Wee. The pub was nothing more than a house run by an elderly couple. They ordered two beers, which arrived warm. Gene was used to cold Wisconsin beer. He hated the taste of warm beer. But he still asked the old man of the house to fill up the four pails they'd brought with them.

It was harder to pedal with full pails sloshing from the handlebars. When they returned, Gene couldn't stomach the idea of a party without cold beer. He ordered someone to get a large bowl from the kitchen while he went searching for a fire extinguisher.

When the necessary tools were procured, Pee Wee poured the beer from the four gallon-sized steel buckets into the kitchen bowl. Gene grabbed the fire extinguisher and pointed the hose.

"Stand back, everybody," he warned.

Gene fired on the bowl. He hoped the carbon dioxide cloud would cool the beer to his Wisconsin standards. Everyone in the Nissen hut hooted after Gene carefully picked up the heavy bowl, took a sip, and proudly stated, "It's ready!"

November 19, 1943 – Fourth mission

The briefing officer nodded and stepped back from his podium. The curtain covering the mission map was drawn back. Gene had seen this red string before: Gelsenkirchen.

His back still ached from the Norway mission three days before. This would be a shorter mission, but much more dangerous. He was returning to "Flak Valley."

Ground crewmen had worked through the night stashing a maximum load of incendiary bombs into the bellies of Flying Fortresses. The smaller, one-hundred-pound, napalm-filled bombs had one purpose: burn buildings.

It was a big force again. Flying Fortresses from seven other bomb groups joined the 96th over Germany's Ruhr Valley. Nearing Gelsenkirchen, Gene readied himself for the sure onslaught of German fighters. But none appeared, and like Norway, there was no flak. What? No anti-aircraft fire over "Flak Valley"? Gene couldn't believe his good fortune. But the thick cloud cover below *Rikki Tikki Tavi* worried him. If they couldn't find their target, the mission wouldn't count, again. Three of the 130 bombers sent on the raid were equipped with Pathfinder radar, which was supposed to find a target through the clouds. When those three planes dropped their bombs, Curtis would release the bomb load of *Rikki Tikki Tavi*. But that day, the Pathfinder equipment failed, unable to penetrate the thick clouds above Gelsenkirchen. Would they all return and receive no mission credit after coming so far?

Some bombers flew through gaps in the overcast weather searching for their target. Langley turned his bomber and followed other Flying Fortresses speeding toward the assigned secondary target: Arnhem, Netherlands, just fifty miles to the northwest.

Gene didn't like the change of plans. German fighter plane bases dotted the Netherlands. But dropping the bombs on a secondary target would mean he'd get credit for the mission. In fifteen minutes, *Rikki Tikki Tavi* went into her bomb run above Arnhem.

"Bombs away!" Curtis yelled, and then he paused. "Hang on . . . Mo, get up here! Reed!"

The order from Curtis for Gene and Reed could mean only one thing: the bombs were stuck. Every gunner was trained for a secondary job, and Gene had studied bomb maintenance in his armorer classes. He scrambled past Sparky in the radio room. Reed was already in the bomb bay when he got there. Cold air pouring in from the open bomb bay doors blasted Gene's face. But his spine turned to ice water when he saw the problem. An incendiary bomb was jammed in one of the two bomb racks. On top of that bomb rested a stack of others. The nose spinners of each bomb twirled in the slipstream of air coming through the open bomb bay doors. The bombs were arming! If they didn't get the arming pins back into the nose spinners, which primed the bombs, the incendiaries would incinerate *Rikki Tikki Tavi*.

Reed carried a fistful of arming pins in one hand. He stepped onto the narrow catwalk between the bomb racks. Bitterly cold air roared through the open bomb bay. One slip and he'd be falling onto Arnhem. With an ungloved hand, Reed stopped the spinning primer of the first hung-up bomb. With his other hand, he gingerly slid the arming pin into the nose spinner and flipped the pin, locking it. One bomb defused. He slipped pins into two more bombs before his hands became too cold to work.

Gene took off his gloves. Reed slowly set several pins into his bare hands. For a second, Gene wondered if Reed had extras in case he dropped them. He couldn't think about that. And don't look down! Gene didn't panic. He'd been trained for this. He repeated Reed's careful procedure and defused three bombs before stepping aside to let Reed finish the job.

All bombs defused!

Gene and Reed then took turns wrestling the hundred-pound incendiaries to free them. They had to get rid of the bombs. *Rikki Tikki Tavi* did not have enough fuel to haul back the weight of a full bomb load. One by one, the bombs dropped through the bomb bay. With the arming pins in them, the bombs wouldn't explode when they hit the ground. With the last bomb out, Reed went back up front and called Curtis to close the bomb bay doors. Gene returned to his tail gun.

On the way out of the Netherlands, flak from enemy anti-aircraft batteries below rose up and exploded around *Rikki Tikki Tavi*, but nothing too close. Gene looked at the overcast sky below him. He marveled at how the Germans were able to accurately send up flak through cloud cover. The height was correct, but the range was off. None of the flak bursts hit *Rikki Tikki Tavi*. And best of all, no German fighter planes came up through the clouds.

Back at Snetterton Heath, Gene's post-mission debriefing was short since he fired on no fighter planes that day. In the Nissen hut, Swedo, Andy, Sparky, and Pee Wee peppered Gene and Reed with questions about the hung-up bombs. Gene didn't feel like talking. He did what he always did after a mission: he lay on his cot and stared at the ceiling.

November 26, 1943

A week later, at 5:00 a.m., Gene piled into the crowded briefing room with his crewmates. Looking for his four officers, he noticed

Langley was missing. Just before the mission briefing, Orrison explained.

"Langley's still in bed. He's sick. We aren't going up today, but get ready to fill in as replacements."

Replacements. This had never happened to the crew before. For the first time since they'd met back at Pyote Air Base in Texas, they were going to be split up. Being a replacement meant filling in for sick or injured crewmen from other bombers. It could be all of them. It might be none of them.

Sitting before the closed curtain covering the wall map, Gene rocked back and forth on the wooden bench, seething with the added tension. It worsened when the curtain drew back.

Bremen, Germany.

Bremen was the target they were supposed to hit the day *Rikki Tikki Tavi* got lost. They'd been told this industrial city was ringed with anti-aircraft guns, and northwest Germany was filled with air bases swarming with fighter planes.

"This will be a maximum effort, men," the briefing officer said. Gene listened to the officer explain that the Eighth Air Force was putting up six hundred Flying Fortress and Liberator bombers that day, its largest formation ever sent to battle.

Just before men gathered around the chaplain for the usual pre-flight prayer, an officer approached Gene and his gunner crew. The officer picked Pee Wee, Reed, and Sparky to fill in for missing men of other crews. Reed and Sparky would fly on the same bomber. Pee Wee was on his own. Gene, Swedo, and Andy got the day off. Outside the briefing room, Gene found Orrison. Orrison also didn't have to fly, but Benny and Curtis were going to Bremen.

Gene and the remaining crew stood outside near the control tower with men from the ground crew watching forty-three Flying Fortresses zip down the runway. Gene's guts twisted. He'd avoided the dangerous mission to Bremen. Yet every fiber of his being longed to be in the air. It was wrong to be on the ground while his buddies flew to one of the most heavily defended cities in Europe.

After the last of the bombers faded into distant dots in the sky, the left-out gunners returned to their Nissen hut. None of them were in the mood to talk. They spent the morning reading and writing letters. They went to the mess hall together for lunch. While eating, they hatched an idea: let's greet them with beer when they return.

Gene begged for three glass jugs from the kitchen staff. An hour before they guessed the 96th bombers would return, the three gunners hopped on bikes and pedaled to the small house at the edge of the air base. The elderly couple filled their jugs. Gene, Swedo, and Andy rode back to base carefully balancing the jugs on their handlebars and waited by the control tower.

Everyone heard the planes before they saw them. Gene looked out at the horizon and spotted the first Flying Fortress coming in. He'd never been on this side of a mission: the spectacle of an anxious air base awaiting the return of their flying comrades. Men excitedly pointed at the sky every time another plane was sighted and cheered when a bomber roared over the top of them. But Gene's enthusiasm stilled. Flares shot out of returning planes, indicating wounded airmen. Another Flying Fortress trailed smoke. Trucks with red crosses painted on them fired up their engines. *Dear God, not Pee Wee. Not Sparky and Reed or Benny and Curtis.*

When the last plane touched down, Gene, Swedo, and Andy grabbed the beer jugs and ran to the parked planes. Looking for their crewmates on the tarmac, they dashed to each cul-de-sac, careful to avoid revolving propellers slowly winding down. One by one, their comrades appeared. Pee Wee. Safe. Benny. Safe. Sparky and Reed. Safe, climbing out of the same bomber. Swedo and Andy immediately handed them the jugs.

But where was Curtis?

Gene was the one who found him. He ran to his bombardier, smiled widely, clutching the beer jug in one hand. He knew better than to offer it to Curtis. Curtis didn't drink. But Curtis grabbed the jug from Gene's hands. He lifted it above his mouth and chugged. Gene watched his Adam's apple thrusting in and out with each gulp. Curtis lowered the jug and wiped his mouth. He looked at Gene, sensing his shock.

"Bremen," Curtis said.

CHAPTER 7

Bremen

June 2011

Thursdays with Gene ended abruptly. Carmen's brain cancer returned . . . for the fourth time. I called Gene to let him know we'd again have to suspend interviews for a while.

"You tell my Blatz angel I'm praying for her," he said.

Carmen and Gene were close. Gene was a notorious flirt, and my wife had earned her nickname by dropping off Gene's favorite Blatz beer at an opportune time. He was in the middle of a card-playing party with his buddies when the beer ran out and Carmen opened the garage entry door, a halo of sunlight illuminating her hair.

"I'm telling you, John, it was the darnedest thing. The timing of it all," Gene said to me later. "With the sunset in the background, it was like my guardian angel had come to rescue me."

Now I sat with Gene's guardian angel in a small examination room at the Mayo Clinic Hospital. A single cancerous lump had formed in the exact spot where our neurosurgeon had already twice cut out a tumor.

We learned it was too risky to open up Carmen's skull a third time. We'd have to try lasers of radiation, a procedure known as Gamma Knife radiosurgery.

The radiosurgery shriveled the brain tumor. For the fourth time, Carmen had turned back brain cancer. Glory be! We beat it again. But how long could this winning streak go on?

It lasted five months.

By October, we were back. Brain scans found another tumor, lodged in the same place as the previous lumps. Again, we opted for radiosurgery, and the tumor shriveled.

Another victory. But when would cancer return? The cancer came back more quickly each time: three years, one year, six months, five months. It was no longer a question of if but when.

I waited until after the holidays to return to Gene's story. It had been more than six months since my last "Thursdays with Gene" because of Carmen's brain surgery. He agreed to meet twice a month, and we resumed our interviews in January.

Later that spring, Gene handed me an envelope when I arrived.

"I got a surprise for ya," he said.

I read the name on the return address: Gregory Swedo.

"Swedo?!" I blurted out, looking at Gene. He laughed.

"Go ahead, read it."

I fumbled with the already opened envelope, so excited to get at the letter inside. I unfolded the two-page typed note and read.

Gregory Swedo, M.D. He was a pathologist from Virginia, and a nephew of *Rikki Tikki Tavi*'s singing waist gunner, Edmund Swedo. Greg called him "Uncle Edwin." He'd been researching what he called "the family tragedy." He wrote that his grandmother never got over the death of her son, the youngest of three boys. Greg explained that Thanksgiving would forever be a sad holiday in the Swedo family because of what happened on November 29, 1943.

I continued reading:

My research on the internet has brought to me the incredible, dare I say, miraculous story of your personal survival and tribulations during WWII. It has all the makings of a Hollywood movie. If it hadn't actually happened, no one would believe it.

In the last paragraph, Greg wrote that he wanted to travel to Wisconsin and meet Gene. He wished to talk with the "only surviving crew member with knowledge of those times."

"Well, you gonna meet with him?" I asked.

"If he wants to talk, I suppose I can see him," Gene replied.

In May, Greg drove to Soldiers Grove with his wife, Susan, from their home in Virginia. They met Gene and Pauline at their mobile home. Joni was also there. Everyone sat down in the living room for introductions, but the group moved to the kitchen table when Greg brought out his laptop.

Sitting at the table, Greg showed Gene what he'd researched about his uncle's bomber. He brought up a picture of *Rikki Tikki Tavi*. Gene nodded. Greg also showed an image of a German pilot whom he believed was given credit for shooting down *Rikki Tikki Tavi*. Gene explained that so many enemy fighters attacked his bomber that he couldn't be sure what plane brought them down. He told Greg of the Messerschmitt 109 that had pulled up just off to the side of his tail gun. Gene said he could see the pilot's face. Greg showed Gene a picture of the German flier, Hans Ehlers.

"Do you think that's the pilot you saw?" Greg asked.

"It looks like him. I did see him up close when he motioned for me to bail out," Gene replied. "It's been almost seventy years. I just can't say for certain that he's the man who did the actual shooting."

Greg then moved to the question he drove half a country to find the answer to: how did his uncle die? He pulled up a letter Gene had written in 1946 as part of his Missing Air Crew Report filed after the war.

"You wrote that you remembered seeing the two waist gunners lying on the floor. So, they probably got shot up," Greg said.

"I think they were gone. I think the only . . ." Gene gulped and closed his eyes. "Ooooh."

No one spoke. Everyone waited for Gene to continue.

"Dad, do you want me to leave?" Joni asked.

"No, no," Gene answered.

"If you don't want to talk about it, that's fine too," Greg added.

Gene blew out a breath.

"I remember Pee Wee. He called me and said, 'Mo, get that son of a bitch that's coming up under you cause he's gonna pop up.' And I got him. And Pee Wee said, 'I'm gone.'"

Gene exhaled.

"My God, it was almost seventy years ago."

Gene stopped. Everyone else waited.

"You okay?" Greg asked.

Gene didn't answer. Silence filled the room.

"Dad, it's okay if it comes out," said Joni.

Tears streamed from Gene's eyes. No one moved or uttered a sound.

"Gene. I appreciate you talking to me, but you don't have to," Greg said.

"Greg. It's okay," Joni said. "He has to face his demons."

Everyone waited for Gene to cry it out. A few minutes later, he wiped his eyes and took a deep breath. He looked at Greg.

"You need to know," he said. "You need to know."

November 1943

Laughter echoed off the curved, corrugated steel ceiling of the Nissen hut. In the middle of the shelter next to the potbellied charcoal stove, Pee Wee, Andy, and Sparky sat at a blackjack game with other enlisted men who shared the hut with the crew of *Rikki Tikki Tavi*. Gene had been playing, but he retreated to his bunk after breaking even. Reed and Swedo also lounged on their cots.

Gene had just returned from the slit trench latrine. From the tarmac, he'd heard the *putt-putt* generators that provided light for the ground crew working underneath the planes. It wasn't raining or foggy outside. *Rikki Tikki Tavi* was probably going to war tomorrow.

Gene laid a book on his chest he'd been half reading. A month had passed since his arrival at Snetterton Heath Air Base. In that time, he'd seen Flying Fortresses cartwheel into one another and watched a boiling fire consume a crashed bomber with ten men trapped inside. His own plane had gotten lost. And a week earlier, he'd defused bombs jammed in a rack that were primed to atomize his plane.

All these near misses and only four missions down. Twenty-one left to go. Everyone knew their mission number, but no one talked about it. They'd discuss girls back home and reminisce about Mom's home cooking, but never did any of the enlisted gunners mention how close they were to twenty-five. Gene remembered his first day in the Nissen hut when the *Rikki Tikki Tavi* crew took over the empty bunks of a crew that had disappeared a day earlier. Six men, half a hut, gone. No funeral. No ceremony. Just a couple of base personnel men tossing letters and wallets into a box. Gene recalled what an airman had told him back at the Ireland air base when he first arrived in Europe: "For most of you guys, it's not a matter of if, but when."

Jazz music streamed from the radio. Swedo sang along. It was Axis Sally's program. The two bomber crews in the Nissen hut liked her show. As long as she played good music, they put up with her German propaganda.

The last song finished. Amid the guffaws coming from the blackjack game, Axis Sally came on the air.

"That song goes out to the boys of the 96th Bomb Group," she said.

96th?! Gene heard it. He immediately sat up on his bunk.

"Hey! Shut up!" Gene yelled at the card players. "She's talking about us."

He jumped up, ran toward the radio, and cranked the volume. Everyone froze.

"You new guys in the 96th are getting pretty cocky," Axis Sally broadcast. "But your turn is coming, really soon. Sleep tight, boys."

When the next song started playing, shouting, laughter, and backslapping ensued.

"We're famous!" yelled a man from the other crew.

But Gene turned his head away and listened to the generators running outside. Axis Sally's words mixed with the sputtering of the *putt-putts*. They would fly tomorrow.

November 29, 1943 – Fifth Mission

Gene got to sleep in a bit. The mission briefing was set for 7:00 a.m., a couple of hours later than usual. In line at the mess hall, he spotted a special treat: pineapple. Not since he'd arrived at Snetterton Heath had he seen such a delicacy in the chow line. He lifted his tray up.

"Load me up," he told the mess hall server.

In the briefing room, Gene looked over at his four officers. All were there. Langley was feeling better. The curtain pulled back.

Bremen.

It was the third time that month the 96th had been ordered to attack one of the most well-defended industrial cities in Germany. Gene's mind flashed back to Curtis chugging beer after he returned from Bremen three days earlier. He remembered Axis Sally's ominous warning the night before. Did the Germans already know they were coming?

The first group of planes would take off at 9:45. Gene figured the later-than-usual takeoff time was another bad sign. German fighter pilots and anti-aircraft gunners would be well rested.

Gene's innards churned. It didn't help that he'd eaten all that pineapple. His stomach wasn't used to acidic fruit. He bowed his head for the chaplain, focusing on the words of the prayer and trying to block out the target and his upset stomach. Gene reached into a pocket in his leather flight jacket and checked for the rosary his grandmother had given him before he left for Europe.

In the truck ride out to their bomber, none of the crew of *Rikki Tikki Tavi* talked. The air whipping through the back of the truck was colder than normal, a winter wind.

Once in the plane, Gene went through his normal routine. He checked his twin fifty-caliber machine guns, the ammunition belts, intercom, and oxygen mask. Everything looked good. Gene had a new item on his pre-flight checklist: a flare gun. Select tail gunners were instructed to fire colored flares—red, green, or blue—to guide planes to their positions in the complex, multi-layered formations. Gene was assigned to fire the red flare when the 96th formed up above the clouds.

After pre-flight checks, the crew headed to the nose to meet with Orrison. Langley stayed in the cockpit. The nine airmen formed their usual huddle, each arm draped over the man next to him. This time, Orrison didn't speak. Everyone just stared at the ground and clasped the shoulder of the man next to him, a little harder than usual. In the silence, Gene wondered if anyone could hear his queasy stomach growling. His nausea was getting worse. Finally, Orrison spoke up.

"Okay, guys. We can do this."

After a few slaps on the backs of leather flight jackets, everyone climbed back into the plane. As usual, Gene waited to be last. But when he snuck behind *Rikki Tikki Tavi*'s tail, he didn't have to urinate. He bent forward and vomited. It felt good to let go. Standing bent over with strings of vomit hanging from his mouth, he studied the mess on the ground in front of his feet: pineapple.

Gene climbed back in through the door by the tail. Hustling toward the radio room for takeoff, he wiped his mouth several times, making sure there was no evidence of his nervousness.

When it was their turn for takeoff, Langley throttled up the engines and released the brakes. *Rikki Tikki Tavi* lumbered down the runway and lifted into the overcast sky.

The 96th sent up forty-five Flying Fortresses in two separate groups. Five aborted after takeoff and headed back to base. Gene watched the bombers peel away from the group. This wasn't a good sign. If the Luftwaffe hit them hard above Bremen, then those departing planes would mean fifty fewer machine guns surrounding *Rikki Tikki Tavi.*

Once above the clouds, Gene opened a side window in his tail gun position and fired his flare gun. The red flare arced across the sky. The Flying Fortresses rising up to meet his plane reminded him of scattered ducklings looking for their mother.

Out over the North Sea, *Rikki Tikki Tavi* climbed to 28,000 feet and joined more than three hundred Flying Fortresses turning toward Germany. Crossing over the German coastline, Gene saw no enemy fighters and no flak. But he also didn't spot any American fighter planes sent to protect the bombers. Gene grew nervous. The fighters should have been here by now. *Come on, little friends. Where are you? It's Bremen.*

"Everybody, keep checking your oxygen masks for ice," Langley ordered from the cockpit. "I'm showing almost fifty below up here."

The brutally cold air mixing with hot engine exhaust caused another problem: contrails. The white vapor lines that trailed each airplane engine highlighted the bombers against the blue sky above them. German fighter planes often flew through the foggy contrails to sneak up on unsuspecting bombers. Gene cursed the situation. *No fighter protection and contrails? We're goddamn sitting ducks!*

American fighter planes finally found the bombers. Gene exhaled when chubby P-47 Thunderbolts moved in above *Rikki Tikki Tavi*. But they didn't stay long. They left a few minutes before the attacking force settled into its bombing run. Gene watched a P-47 wiggle its wings to say goodbye. *They just got here. Where are they going? Are they out of fuel already?* Gene's stomach sank. His bomber was heading to Bremen with no fighter protection.

Ten minutes from the target, the intercom erupted.

"Bandits, twelve o'clock!" Benny yelled from the co-pilot's seat.

More than a dozen twin-engine German fighter planes barreled into the 96th Bomb Group's formation from the front. Skinny contrails shot past Gene. The enemy planes were firing rockets. Gene had never seen this. A second later, the twin-engine planes that fired the rockets flashed by *Rikki Tikki Tavi*. Gene was ready. He squeezed both triggers.

"Mo, you got a bunch coming up behind you!" someone blurted out.

Gene saw so many single-engine Messerschmitt 109 and Focke-Wulf 190 fighter planes, he couldn't count them. A pair zeroed in on a bomber nearby *Rikki Tikki Tavi*. Gene squeezed off a long burst of fire. It felt good to fight back.

Benny continued to call out fighters from the cockpit. Everywhere Gene looked, he saw enemy planes. Everyone on *Rikki Tikki Tavi* was shooting. Empty shell casings piled up on the plane floor in front of Gene. In all his missions before, the enemy always seemed to attack planes from nearby bomb groups. Today was different. Gene swore there were a hundred German fighters coming after the 96th.

A burning Flying Fortress near *Rikki Tikki Tavi* fell back. Looking out his windows, Gene saw bombers on both sides of him trailing smoke and fire. He spotted a few parachutes.

More enemy fighters roared in. Gene fired left, right, high, and low. He saw planes he'd never seen before. Twin-engine planes that looked more like bombers than fighter planes. Below him, he spotted a plane with fixed landing gear. Gene remembered the type from all those airplane identification classes. It was a Ju 87 Stuka. He watched the slow, ungainly dive bomber fire rockets into another bomber group. *Stukas! Are you kidding me?!*

Then came the flak. The entire sky lit up with dirty, black explosions. Gene had never seen so much flak. *Rikki Tikki Tavi* pitched and rocked from the concussion of the blasts. Shrapnel from the flak raked the plane. Gene knew his bomber was getting hit. But none of the blasts were close. *Rikki Tikki Tavi* stayed level. No smoke or fire belched from its engines.

"Look out, Mo. 109s and 190s, five o'clock high!" someone yelled.

Gene looked up. What?! Enemy fighters? But there was flak in the skies! For the first time, Gene saw German planes flying through their own anti-aircraft fire. *They're nuts! This is it. Today we're gonna get it.* Gene spotted a pair of single-engine fighters sneaking through the contrails of a bomber above him. He aimed at the lead enemy fighter and let go a long stream of bullets. The Nazi plane flipped over and dove out of sight.

"Bomb doors open," Curtis said over the intercom. Gene had been so busy firing he'd forgotten about the bomb run. He looked out. Below him were clouds. *No! Drop the bombs! We fought too hard not to get credit for this mission.* Flak explosions continued to batter *Rikki Tikki Tavi*. But none were direct hits. Gene prayed for his bombardier to speak.

"Bombs away!" Curtis yelled.

"Thank you, God!" Gene whispered to himself.

Rikki Tikki Tavi lifted. Langley banked the plane to the right, following other bombers fleeing Bremen. Gene relaxed and looked at the pile of empty shell casings under his guns. He'd fired more bullets than on all of his other missions combined. The 96th bombers got hit hard, but none of the enemy fighters directly attacked Gene's plane.

"I want a damage report from everybody," Langley ordered.

Gene looked around him and found no holes or tears near him. Everybody else chimed in, reporting punctures of various sizes in the bomber's aluminum skin. But no gaping holes. No smoke from the plane's engines. All four purred smoothly.

It was almost 3:00 p.m. Gene scanned the skies. The flak had slackened. There were no enemy fighter planes. *By God, we're gonna make it.*

From his co-pilot seat, Benny stared out the window.

"Fighters, two o'clock high. They're coming right at us!"

In the nose of *Rikki Tikki Tavi*, Orrison and Curtis waited together at their single-barreled machine guns. Black dots appeared, two, then four, then twelve, maybe more. Black dots became silhouettes. Silhouettes became planes, their wings blinking yellow-orange flashes.

"Here they come!!!!"

Enemy fighters barreled in from every direction. Every gun on *Rikki Tikki Tavi* opened fire. The plane shuddered.

"There's more at three!" Gene barely heard the call from Benny above the din of machine gun fire.

Rikki Tikki Tavi started to fall back. Gene looked out both side windows. No smoke or fire coming from any of the engines. The bomber stayed level. But the surrounding Flying Fortresses were flying ahead, and a deadly gap was growing between *Rikki Tikki Tavi* and the last bomber.

"What's going on? Why are we falling back?" Gene shouted.

Langley said nothing. Or maybe Gene just couldn't hear him above the rattle of constant machine gun fire. But he thought he heard cries coming from the cockpit. It sounded like Benny.

The machine gun fire never let up. Everyone was screaming and calling out new fighter attacks. In the deafening noise, Gene could hear bullets and cannon fire puncturing *Rikki Tikki Tavi*.

On the intercom, Gene could hear crewmates hollering that they were wounded. He couldn't tell who was yelling. Andy was still calling out fighters and shooting back. More screaming. It was Sparky crying out unintelligible words. All throughout the plane, German steel shredded American flesh.

Above the tumultuous din, Gene heard Swedo singing.

"I'm gonna buy a paper doll that I can call my own.
A doll that other fellows cannot steal."

"Goddammit, Swedo, get the hell off the mike!" a crewmate roared.

Soon, voices fell silent. Outside of the hum of the bomber's engines, all was quiet when a Messerschmitt 109 pulled up alongside the plane's tail. The enemy pilot motioned for Gene to bail out. Machine gun fire from *Rikki Tikki Tavi* chased the fighter plane away.

The Germans moved in for the kill. Bullets ripped through the tail section, piercing both of Gene's forearms and shredding the parachute on his back. Cold air rushed in from the jagged tears in the plane's tail. An explosion slammed Gene into the chest plate above his guns, snapping his ribs on his left side.

It's over.

Gene turned and crawled forward. He spotted the spare parachute. Looking up, he saw Swedo's and Andy's mangled bodies lying together in a heap of bent limbs. Just inches from the spare parachute, the aluminum skin of the fuselage began to tear.

Hail Mary, full of grace. The Lord is with thee. Hail Mary, full of grace. The Lord is with thee. Hail Mary, full of grace . . .

In the front of the plane, Orrison and Curtis fired their single-barreled machine guns at more attacking fighter planes than they could count. A hailstorm of enemy bullets shot through the nose.

Curtis fell back into Orrison. Both men tumbled onto the nose floor littered with empty shell casings and jagged shards of Plexiglas. Blood smeared Curtis' stomach and legs. He didn't move. Orrison grabbed the bombardier and shoved him onto his chair. Curtis fell again. Orrison heaved Curtis back onto his chair. Curtis slumped into Orrison a third time. Curtis didn't have his parachute on, and his oxygen mask was missing.

Curtis' breathing was fading. Orrison grabbed the parachute lying on the floor and wrestled it onto Curtis' back. He lifted Curtis by the parachute straps and heaved him toward the nose hatch door. Orrison slipped on the floor pooling with blood. Curtis was limp. He made no sound. Orrison opened the hatch door. Fifty-below air blasted his face. Orrison pulled the rip cord on Curtis' parachute and yanked him toward the open hatch.

Boom!

The Plexiglas nose disintegrated. Orrison was sucked out through the nose. Jagged shards of Plexiglas tore through his flight pants. Hurtling through the air, he grabbed his rip cord. The parachute opened with a jerk. Orrison screamed out in pain. Looking down, he saw a bloody mess on his upper thighs and groin area. Then he looked down and off to his side.

The severed tail of *Rikki Tikki Tavi* was cartwheeling through the frigid air.

CHAPTER 8

Gangster

May 2012

Gene and I agreed it was time for a field trip. Seventeen months after my first "Thursdays with Gene," it was time to visit the farm that raised him. I'd never been there.

On an overcast and cool May afternoon, Carmen and I piled the boys into the car and picked up Gene. The home farm sat in a valley about five miles south of Soldiers Grove and two miles southeast of the Rolling Ground Tavern. Sleepy Hollow Road was still a gravel lane. It bisected the former Moran farm. Like many typical Wisconsin farms, the barnyard lay on one side, the house on the other.

The red, wooden barn where Gene last pulled a cow teat seventy years ago was still there. So was the house where he grew up. An absentee landowner owned the farm now. Renters occupied the house.

Gene was dressed in his normal outfit: bib overalls, a tan overshirt, and a black baseball cap. Walking with a cane, he led us to the barn. The red barn rested on a stone foundation. It still stood straight, not leaning like so many other abandoned farm buildings.

Peeking in, I saw there were no animals or farm machinery. Dusty cobwebs covered the wooden stanchions that used to hold dairy cows during milking time. A bent square piece of corrugated metal hanging from an open window flapped in the breeze. Two rusted fifty-five-gallon drums rested on their sides next to a pile of wooden boards. A few concrete blocks lay scattered on the dirt floor.

I stared at the faded wooden stanchions where Gene first milked cows when he was only six years old. Gene explained how each cow walked into the barn under the yellow-orange glow of a single kerosene lamp hung from the ceiling. He'd perch himself on a three-legged stool and sidle up to a half-ton Holstein, Jersey, or Brown Swiss. Grabbing the two left teats of the udder, he'd squirt milk into his steel pail and then move to the right two teats.

"Dad always crisscrossed his hands and squeezed a back and front teat," Gene said. "But I liked Mom's method better."

I jotted notes on my legal pad. Then we trooped after him across the gravel road toward the house. Across the yard from the house sat a small, orange Allis-Chalmers tractor surrounded by waist-high uncut grass. Near the tractor, briars and dried weeds surrounded a moss-covered camper. Gene pointed toward a meadow.

"In that direction is the spring-fed creek where we stored our milk cans. Damn, if that wasn't the best drinking water in all Wisconsin."

The tour continued. We didn't go into the green, wood-sided, two-story house. No one was home. Gene pointed to the bedroom he shared with Byron. He explained the area where a laundry shed used to sit.

"God, would you look at that," Gene said, facing the ridgeline.

"At what?" All I saw was a line of deep green trees resplendent with new spring leaves.

"It just disgusts me," Gene said.

I didn't understand. How could a beautiful, ridgetop woods be disgusting? Gene looked at me, perturbed.

"We chopped down every tree off that ridgeline, and I had to grub out every stump to clear that land for farming," Gene explained, his voice growling. "And now look at it. It all came back. Geez, all that work for nothing."

I remembered my dairy farmer grandfather also felt the same way about trees on a farm. They were a nuisance to be cleared.

We crossed the road again to pose for pictures in front of the barn. I snapped a photo of Carmen and Gene, her arms wrapped around Gene's shoulders, his left hand resting on her forearm. Then, I took a picture of the boys with Gene in the middle. Matthew, now thirteen and growing like a weed, towered over Gene.

On the way home, we stopped at Rolling Ground Tavern, the same place Gene had started his hitchhiking trips to Madison to join the Army Air Corps all those years ago. We ordered root beer for Carmen and the boys, beer for Gene and me. Before we left, Gene and I settled on an early-June date for the next interview. Summer break was just around the corner, and I was anxious to capture more of his story, maybe even start outlining some chapters.

The Sunday before that interview, Carmen, the boys, and I were working outside in the yard, finishing spring cleanup. I was kneeling by the campfire pit, scooping out the ashes, when Carmen, rake in her hand, walked earnestly toward me.

"Something's wrong," she said. "I feel faint."

I helped her into a lawn chair next to the fire pit. Kneeling beside her, I saw it: her left cheek was twitching. The throbbing came in sharp, rhythmic pulses.

"What day of the week is it, hon?" I asked.

"I . . . I . . . I don't, d-don't know," she stuttered.

Matthew and Joe ran up to us. Carmen looked at her sons with a blank stare. They knew.

"Mom. Who's the president?" Matthew asked.

Carmen didn't answer.

"What's my name, Mom?" Joe demanded. "What's my name?!"

I rushed Carmen to the emergency room a few miles away in nearby Viroqua. She'd had a seizure. I called Mayo Clinic, and her oncologist said, "Get her here. Now."

I dropped the boys at a neighbor's home. Drove two hours to Rochester. Beside me, Carmen's cheek throbbed and pulsed, more sharply than before. Her speech slurred.

Within a day at Mayo, her mind was clear again. She could speak without slurring. I was elated. The seizure was over. The worst had passed. It was June. Summer vacation was here. In a day or so, we'd be home, and I could work in the orchard and start my next round of interviews with Gene.

Later that morning, the neurosurgeon showed us a new brain scan. I braced for the probable return of that stubborn tumor that always showed up in the same spot. It was easy to find on the monitor. It would appear as a bright, white circle against the gray image of the brain.

This time, there was more than one bright circle, many of them, and now, thick, irregular bright lines. Everywhere.

No one moved. No one talked. I turned toward the neurosurgeon.

"We really don't need you anymore, do we?"

He didn't look at me. His eyes stayed fixated on the black-and-white brain scan.

"No. You don't."

November 29, 1943

"Hail Mary, full of grace. The Lord is with thee. Hail Mary, full of grace. The Lord is with thee," Gene chanted, clutching his rosary.

Trapped inside the severed tail of *Rikki Tikki Tavi*, Gene hurtled through the cold air toward German soil.

Down he plummeted in the mangled tail section, an aluminum coffin. The speed and air pressure popped the gold teeth fillings right out of his mouth. Blood pooled in his eye sockets. A red stain spread over his eyes. His own blood was blinding him. All was red, roar, and rush.

"Hail Mary, full of grace. The Lord is with thee," he prayed.

He could do nothing now. He breathed deeply. *Why fight it?* He relaxed his body.

Suddenly, vivid scenes from his nineteen-year-old life exploded in his head. He saw his mother sprinkling holy water down in the cellar. His family huddled together, terrified of the freight-train roar of a tornado bearing down. Then, his favorite cousin, Imogene Cummings, appeared dancing with Gene as they took first place at a jitterbug contest. There was brother Byron sneaking a smoke with Gene behind the barn as cows stood waiting, bawling with swollen udders. He saw his father, muscles flexed, pitching hay onto a wagon. *By God, it's true! Your life does flash before your eyes when you die.*

Twisting . . . hurtling . . . falling . . . . . . IMPACT!

The severed tail blasted into a forest, snapping limbs from trees. The crash spun Gene around in a half loop. His head slammed into the steel cables housed in the tail above him. The open end of the tail swung toward the ground and came to a screeching halt.

Silence.

Gene lay in the tail section. He heard nothing and could see even less except for the curtain of crimson draping his eyes. Lifting his broken arms, he turned onto his stomach. His sight was gone— or almost. No shapes, but his eyes could sense light.

Gene crawled toward the light. He grabbed at the torn wreckage and wiggled his hips forward. He crawled a little more, clawing at the ground and twisting his legs until he slid out of the tail section. He was out. Gene slowly rolled onto his back.

He clutched the ground beneath him. Soft, moist debris came loose in his hands. Dirt? Leaves? He sucked in the smell of the forest. *I'm alive!*

He lay on his back. He breathed in deeply the cold November air. *I'm alive! I'm alive! I'm alive!*

Gene started giggling, which turned to laughing out loud. He lay laughing with two broken arms, who knew how many busted ribs, barely any sight, and his buddies probably dead in a crashed plane. On top of that, he was lost in enemy territory. But he was alive. He'd cheated death!

Now he sensed an unusual numbness on the right side of his skull. Something was wrong. Gingerly, he shifted his broken right forearm up to his skull and gently stroked his leather flight helmet. It was wet and sticky. He ran his fingers along a sharp edge. His skull was cracked. His fingertips delicately explored the space between the gashed edges of the fissure. It felt like stiff gelatin. It was his brain. His giggling stopped.

Normally, a downed airman's duty was to hide his parachute and begin mapping out his getaway plan. Western European nations under the Nazi jackboot all ran highly sophisticated escape routes which helped thousands of American and British fliers get back to their home bases in England. Gene had his escape kit tucked away in his flight jacket. It included his phony identification photo, a compass, maps, several Hershey chocolate bars, and German and French money. He knew he was in northwestern Germany. All he had to do now was get up, read his maps, and begin walking west. After evading German police and occupying troops for hundreds of miles, he'd hook up with Dutch, Belgian, or French partisans who'd ferry him back across the English Channel.

Except he wasn't going anywhere. Gene mulled over his injuries. Oddly, he felt no pain. He knew his arms were broken and that he'd busted his ribs when he slammed into the chest plate during the air battle. And now his skull was split wide open, exposing his brain.

All he could do was lie on the forest floor and wait for someone to find him. But who the "someone" was would mean everything. He hoped for German soldiers. Soldiers, not civilians.

Gene's instructors in the classroom had never fully discussed the fate of downed bomber boys in enemy territory. He'd heard stories from veteran airmen, however, and remembered their advice: stay away from civilians. In England, Gene learned it was much better to be captured by enemy soldiers than by German citizens. The German government had signed on to the Geneva Convention regarding rules for properly treating prisoners, and its military generally followed those guidelines for American and British POWs. The Luftwaffe, who were in charge of downed airmen, were particularly committed to humane treatment of its prisoners in the hope that the Allies would protect its captured fliers.

But German civilians didn't read the fine print of the Geneva Convention accords. A wounded airman parachuting into a hayfield was more likely to be run through with a pitchfork than be rescued if a farmer found him first. Gene had heard stories of German mobs stringing up American fliers from trees and lampposts or clubbing them to death still attached to their parachutes. German women were the most vicious. Driven by images of their dead children, shredded by Allied bombings, and the destruction of their homes, women screamed "Hang the scoundrels!" with inhuman rage. Women attacked even the most pathetically wounded American airmen, raging, screaming, beating them to death.

Breezes brushed the tree limbs above him. Gene waited. *Please, God. No pitchfork-wielding farmers. No grieving mothers.*

His sight was improving, slightly. The red shade still partially blinded him, but he could see light and vague shapes. And then, the pain came.

His head began to throb. He moaned, but breathed deeply, trying to remain calm. His body begged for sleep, but the cold kept him awake. He tried not to shiver. Any movement would jiggle the head wound. Maybe he should eat. He remembered the Hershey bars tucked away in his flight suit with his survival kit. Despite everything, he was hungry, and sweet milk chocolate might distract him from his pain. But could his broken arms undo zippers and buttons? Would the agony be worth it?

In the distance, he heard a new sound: voices. Here they come. His rescuers or his murderers. He rubbed his fingers, expecting to feel the rosary beads, but his grandma's rosary was gone. Did God spare him from the fall from the sky only to be pitchforked here in the forest? Gene heaved another breath. It sounded like several people. He didn't move. He couldn't move. Who would it be? German soldiers or enraged civilians?

The crowd arrived in a buzz of excited chatter. Gene didn't recognize the language, but it didn't sound German. He heard twigs and branches snapping. Gene sensed a blur of movement, then saw hazy figures surrounding him. He closed his eyes and waited.

Fingers worked his clothes. He sensed a person kneel beside him and start rifling through his leather jacket. Hands snatched his survival kit, including the Hershey bars. These scavengers knew exactly what they were looking for.

Fingers pried at his throat, trying to rip off his microphone. Gene opened his eyes and lifted his head slightly.

"Doctor, doctor," Gene pleaded.

The hands around his throat let go. Gene heard gasps from the person next to him, who scrambled to get away from him. Shouts and loud chatter followed. Gene guessed the group to be about four men.

"Oui, oui!" one of the men shouted at Gene. "Oui, oui. Doctor."

Now Gene recognized the language. What the hell were Frenchmen doing here?

Through his red haze, Gene could see blurry figures standing around him trying to figure out what to do next. One of them came back to his side and yanked off his leather flight helmet, sending shock waves of pain throughout his head.

And as quickly as they came, the Frenchmen disappeared, snapping twigs as they ran out of the forest. Where? Why? This didn't make sense to Gene. Wasn't he in Germany? He bitterly regretted not eating his Hershey bars. And the pain from his head. God, the throbbing! He passed out.

Voices again, more than before. The words sounded different, more guttural. Someone was barking commands. When the group arrived, several people surrounded him. Each picked up a limb. Gene couldn't see uniforms through his red-shaded eyesight, but he guessed these were German soldiers. He was in luck.

The men carried him clumsily through the forest. Branches brushed up against his flight jacket and pants, but thankfully, nothing scraped his exposed brain. The twigs stopped snapping, and Gene's vision lifted a little more. He sensed light. He figured they'd come to a field or clearing. Gene smelled cattle. He'd milked enough cows to know that smell, even when he couldn't see. The soldiers set him on a horizontal surface a foot or two above the ground. It lurched forward.

The sound of creaking wheels and heavy hoofs squishing in mud made Gene realize he'd been set on an ox cart. He was going for a ride. His gashed head and broken body rocked back and forth on the rickety cart. He passed out again. The wooden cart struck a rut in the dirt path, and he jerked awake.

Coming in and out of consciousness and being partially blind, Gene had no sense of time or place. But he could hear. A new sound rose above the creaking of the ox cart. Voices. Lots of them. A crowd, coming closer. The cart drew nearer. The voices gained volume and passion. Gene could hear angry voices. One word stood out. It was repeated over and over.

"Gangster! Gangster!"

Thwack!

Something hit the side of the cart.

Thwack! Thwack!

They were throwing rocks. Gene shrank into the cart's wooden boards. If a hurtling stone hit his exposed brain, it would kill him. *What the hell?* he raged. *I've made it this far, and now they're gonna kill me right here?*

The mob closed in around the cart. "*Schwein! Schwein! Schwein!*" the crowd screamed.

Gene recognized the German word for "pig."

Gene could see human shapes. A sticky liquid splashed on his face. It hit him again. People were spitting at him.

The cart rocked. Soldiers started yelling. Everyone was screaming. Gene could hear one soldier shouting loudly above all others. His words sounded ominous, threatening. The crowd quieted a bit. The cart kept rolling and swaying. The voices faded: *Schwein, schwein.* He passed out.

Gene whirled in the blackness of semiconsciousness. German soldiers carried him into a dark, concrete room and lay him on the dirt floor. Men milled about him. They spoke English. Soon after, the Germans shoved a new downed American airman into the room, a bomber pilot named Carl Fyler.

Fyler had also been flying above Bremen that afternoon, his twenty-fifth mission. He commanded a Flying Fortress named *Dark Horse* of the 303rd Bomb Group. After dropping its bombs, two flak bursts struck. German fighter planes finished off his damaged bomber. Unlike Gene, Fyler successfully bailed out by parachute, along with other men from his crew.

There were eleven men in the room, including Fyler and Gene. All of them were sergeant gunners shot down that day in the raid on Bremen. They looked rough, shaken. They peppered Fyler with questions and angry stories.

"Calm down!" Fyler ordered. "Or things are going to get bad."

The pilot knelt down next to Gene. Fyler studied Gene's head. It looked like a squashed watermelon.

"Anybody know who this guy is?" Fyler asked.

"Don't know for sure," answered a gunner. "Somebody said he's from Minnesota, and that he rode a tail section all the way down to the ground."

Fyler stared at Gene's dented head. He approached the German guard at the door and, using his hands and two years of high school German, asked the guard for first aid supplies. The guard returned with a small pan of water, strips of paper bandages, and a pair of scissors.

Fyler bent over Gene and turned him to examine his head wound. The stirring awoke Gene.

"Somebody, come over here and help hold him," Fyler ordered.

Gene sat up as best he could. One of the other sergeant gunners sat next to him and propped him up as Fyler cut off the matted, bloodied hair and dabbed at the gashed wound with a wet bandage. In the darkened room, Fyler couldn't see the injury well. But even in the dim light, it was clear he didn't have enough bandages to cover the gaping head fracture. He eyed a cot in the corner of the room and told two sergeants to carry Gene and lay him out on the bed.

Shortly after his makeshift first aid job on Gene, Fyler stretched himself out on the floor near Gene's cot. His rest was short-lived. German guards returned, ordering Fyler to get up and leave the room. He'd spend the rest of the night by himself in a nearby single-cell room. Fyler would never learn the fate of the gunner with the "squashed head."

CHAPTER 9

Celebrity

July 2012

I saw Gene for one more interview that summer. Carmen urged me to go, and her friends volunteered to do the driving to radiation treatments.

We had one last shot to turn back cancer. It was the devil's dilemma. Whole-brain radiation. Radiation might extend her life by a year, maybe more. But would she spend her final year on her back? Last time we'd used whole-brain radiation, she'd lost all desire to eat, drink, or get out of bed. It had destroyed two cancerous lumps, but her weight and blood pressure plummeted. And this time, there were many tumors instead of just two.

Carmen shaved her head before the radiation took her hair. The shock of her suddenly being bald again took me by surprise.

"I don't want it coming out in clumps and freaking out the boys," she answered. Then she faced the month ahead: a brutal regimen of blasting her brain with radiation five times a week for four weeks.

On a hot, muggy July afternoon, one of Carmen's friends pulled up in her gray Chevy Traverse. After I helped Carmen settle into the front passenger seat, I waved at the departing car and yelled a thank-you to the driver.

Guilt overwhelmed me the minute the car disappeared over the hill beyond our property. They were only going to La Crosse, a half hour away, but what was I doing? My wife was traveling to a vomit-inducing radiation treatment, and meanwhile, I was preparing to head in the opposite direction to swig beer and talk World War II with Gene. In that moment, it didn't matter that I'd been with her for all her other appointments. I shouldn't be reliving Gene's war. The battle I should be fighting was alongside my wife.

"You haven't seen Gene since spring, and I'm fine with Becky. It's going to be a 'Be'otch Day,'" she'd told me before she left. The "Be'otch" referred to her group of friends that took turns driving Carmen to her daily radiation blasts, followed by coffee and maybe some shopping.

I clutched my bag stuffed with my legal pad and recorder. It was just one interview. Just a few hours.

Gene was sitting on his couch in front of his television wearing a white undershirt and shorts. The baseball game was on, an afternoon contest between the Milwaukee Brewers and St. Louis Cardinals.

I tried not to think about Carmen's appointment. They'd have arrived by now. Waves of radiation would be penetrating her brain. I forced myself back to the room with Gene and the Brewers game. Maybe we could talk baseball. Gene loved baseball. It was his favorite sport growing up, but I wondered if his injuries ended his ball-playing days. He said he played for the Soldiers Grove team for fifteen years after the war and managed them for four years.

"I was in right field sometimes, but usually I pinch-hit. My right arm was awful bad then. I couldn't throw, but I could run."

With Gene talking about his war injuries, I seized the opportunity to ask about the wound I really wanted to know more about: his skull fracture. To broach the topic, I pulled out a large hardcover book entitled *One Last Look*, a sentimental retrospective about the

Eighth Air Force in England. I pointed to a page where a wounded Flying Fortress radioman described sharing a hospital recovery room at Sandbostel Prisoner-of-War Camp with a "strange roommate," a tail gunner who "had survived after coming down 24,000 feet in the shot-off tail of a B-17." The POW went on to describe how nightmares had sent Gene "into wild screaming delirium." The airman said Gene grabbed and threw anything movable in the room.

I leaned back in my chair to watch Gene's response to my research gem. He nodded but said nothing. I was disappointed, but I had a hunch as to his subdued reaction.

"Did your head wound bother you like that after the war?" I inquired.

"I'd rather you didn't ask," Gene replied.

I messed up. Too soon. But then, to my surprise, Gene went on.

"There were many, many, many of them," he said. "I self-medicated with alcohol. Sometimes it made it better. Sometimes it made it worse."

Gene praised a local physician, Dr. Sannes, who at any time would come to Gene's rescue with a sedative he'd inject whenever Gene had a meltdown.

"It sure put you out," he said. "I'd be out at Rolling Ground Tavern, and one of them spells would hit, and they'd call him right from the bar. He was a great man. He was great for the veterans, I'll tell you that."

The spells also haunted Gene at home when he and Peg were first married.

"So many times, I'd be on my back choking to death, and Peg would flop me over and slap me in the middle of the back to bring me around. Then she'd call Doc Sannes, and he'd . . ."

Suddenly, Gene stopped talking. I looked up from my notepad. His face was twisted. He bowed his head. And then, he let go.

The sobs came in heaps. He covered his eyes with his hands. He sucked in air between his weeping.

Gene kept crying. I didn't know what to do. I sat there like an idiot. Should I get up and hug him? Should I get out of the house? What had I done?

I just sat there and waited. Slowly, the crying stopped. He exhaled.

"What I put that poor woman through," he said.

December 1943

Gene still couldn't see. But his blood-covered eyes sensed daylight streaming into the concrete room he shared. He'd slept fitfully his first night in captivity, sharing a room with other captured bomber gunners. Lying still on his cot, his ribs ached. His head throbbed.

A door slammed open. Gene heard German soldiers shout. Then a group of men picked him up and carried him out of the building. They loaded him into the back of the truck and set him down, thankfully on a mattress. He could barely make out human forms through his crimson-shaded eyes, but he guessed about eight other men huddled around his mattress. Were they American prisoners or German soldiers?

"What's that smell?" Gene asked. "It smells like a wood fire."

"This damned truck has a wood burner attached to the front," someone said.

The men in the back of the truck laughed that the vehicle hauling them was powered by a wood stove. Gene relaxed when he heard everyone speaking English. He was with American prisoners.

"Goddamn Krauts are running out of gas," one of the men joked.

Gene smiled too. The smell of the wood burner reminded him of his first school bus that took him to Soldiers Grove High School. It was a flatbed truck with an empty chicken coop mounted on the back. A wood stove sat in the middle of the chicken coop. Kids took turns bringing wood to the heating stove during the winter. Occasionally, Gene's brother Byron got to drive the chicken coop bus when the regular bus driver was absent.

The wood-burning German truck wasn't any more comfortable than Gene's first school bus. Every bounce on the rutted road sent shock waves of pain through Gene's skull and chest.

"Hang in there, buddy," said one of the prisoners.

"Where are we going?" Gene asked. He wondered if the others in the back of the truck were looking at his mangled head.

"Hell if we know," another answered.

Another jolt of the truck sent Gene into delirium. He passed out.

Gene opened his eyes. He was lying on a bed. Voices spoke in different languages, but the words didn't seem German. He caught a few English words. Others sounded French. He knew he was in a large room.

The blood in his eyes was slowly clearing. He could make out a ceiling above him. He sensed people moving earnestly in the room. Turning his head ever so slightly, he could see the form of a man sitting next to him.

"Good morning," the man said.

Gene didn't answer. He was confused. There were strange smells.

"You are in the infirmary of Sandbostel Prison," the man said in soothing, accented English. "The doctors operated on your head yesterday. You have been sleeping for a long time."

Infirmary? Hospital. That explained the strange smells.

The man introduced himself as a prisoner of war from Belgium. He was the unofficial interpreter for the hospital. Gene learned he spoke eight different languages. He gave Gene a full report of his operation.

"Two doctors operated on your head one hour after you arrived," the Belgian explained. "The doctors are Serbs from Yugoslavia, also prisoners. One is a colonel, and one is a major."

The Belgian described how the two surgeons sewed a piece of human flesh into Gene's scalp to cover the crack in his skull. A muscle plate, he called it. They then packed the wound with three feet of gauze, which would serve as a drain for fluids fighting infection. Gene tried to make sense of the fact that another man's flesh was now part of his head.

"Where did they get the muscle plate?" Gene asked.

"I do not know," the interpreter answered.

The interpreter told Gene a story of how the two doctors had saved the wife of a German general. In gratitude, the general offered to allow the two men to return to their home in Yugoslavia. But the doctors would only agree to the kind gesture if their Serbian friends could return with them. This the general couldn't do. So, they both chose to remain at Sandbostel where they continued caring for wounded and sick prisoners.

"They are both very good doctors," the interpreter said.

Gene was glad to be in such capable hands. Looking down to assess his injuries, he noticed he wasn't wearing any of his flight clothes. His ribs were wrapped in cloth dressings. So was his head. He glanced at his bent and broken forearms. No bandages or casts on them. Through his blurry vision, he could barely make out the jagged bone that still stuck out of his right forearm.

"They will operate on your arms later," the interpreter said.

The Belgian was talkative, and he continued to describe Sandbostel Prison, officially known as Stalag XB. He explained that the main compound that housed most of the POWs was about one kilometer from the infirmary. The camp held 20,000 Polish, Belgian, French, English, Canadian, Serbian, Russian, and American prisoners. But the Russians, he explained, were segregated from the rest of the Allied prisoners. The Soviet Union had not signed the

Geneva Accords of 1929, an agreement by European nations outlining the treatment of prisoners of war. Add to that fact the brutality of the war on the Eastern Front between Germany and the Soviet Union meant that Russian prisoners were treated horribly. The Germans hardly fed the Russian captives and jammed them into overcrowded barracks. Two years earlier, a typhus outbreak killed three thousand malnourished Soviet POWs.

Soon after, the two Serb doctors stopped by Gene's bed for the first time. The interpreter stood up and greeted them. Gene listened to the three converse in a language he did not understand. One of the doctors appeared to be the leader, the other his assistant. The chief physician was Dr. Zoran Kamenkovic, the director of surgery. He oversaw the hospital and performed an average of forty operations a week at Sandbostel Prison. Kamenkovic was a thin man with dark, short hair. Gene guessed him to be about fifty years old.

The interpreter returned to Gene's side.

"They want to look at the back of your head and pull out some of the drain."

The doctors carefully lifted Gene up into a sitting position. They studied the back of his wrapped head.

"Your head wet. We clean drain. Okay?" said the assistant doctor.

Gene felt fingers working at the bandages. Kamenkovic gingerly pulled out an inch of cloth gauze from the head wound. A bolt of pain rocketed through his head. He moaned.

"If no infection, you walk soon," Dr. Kamenkovic said. "Three weeks."

With a cloth, the assistant gingerly dabbed off the wetness at the back of Gene's head. Gene was still dizzy. Both doctors slowly lowered him back onto his bed.

Gene mostly slept in the days after the surgery. He shared a recovery room with several other Americans and three British prisoners. His ribs ached anytime he turned his body in bed, so he stayed flat on his back. The blood in his eyes finally cleared. But there wasn't much to look at other than the rows of wooden, half-foot-wide boards that ran the length of the ceiling.

Now that he could see, Gene noticed a slender, inch-long piece of jagged aluminum sticking out of his left forearm near the elbow. He read the black letters printed on it: B-O-E . . . Boeing. The I-N-G was still lodged in his flesh. With his broken right arm, he gently reached across his midsection and grabbed the metal with his thumb and forefinger. He wiggled the jagged wreckage back and forth and pulled it out. He set this last remnant of his beloved *Rikki Tikki Tavi* alongside him on his bed cover. *That's going to make a hell of a souvenir when I get home.*

One night, he awoke to a rumble. It came from the sky.

"Lancasters," said one of his British roommates.

A British air raid. The four-engine Lancaster was Great Britain's primary long-range bomber plane. The roar grew louder. The hospital staff ignored the sound. Gene tried to assure himself that Allied bombers wouldn't target a POW camp. But bombs missed. Planes crashed. Flat on his back, Gene listened to the deep roar. Would an errant Allied bomb kill him after the Serbian doctors had just put him back together? His heartbeat slowed as the sound ebbed and then faded away.

Three days after the operation on his skull, the two Serb doctors returned, this time without the Belgian interpreter. They both smiled at him, but Gene knew what was coming: the daily pulling out of the gauze to check for infection. Gene swallowed hard when the doctors lifted him up. He scrunched his face and readied himself for the pain. Again, thankfully, no infection.

Kamenkovic gave an order to the assistant doctor. The assistant stepped over to Gene's side. His eyes moved over both arms. He studied the bone sticking out of Gene's right forearm. Gene scrutinized the doctor's furrowed eyebrows and pursed lips.

"Whew! A mess," the assistant said, shaking his head. "We must shoot you."

Gene's eyes immediately widened, his mouth agape.

"What?!"

Kamenkovic moved down the opposite side of the bed and looked at Gene's arms.

"Yes. We must shoot you." He nodded.

Gene cried out in terror, "Why did you bother saving me if you're just gonna shoot me?!"

The doctors exchanged perplexed glances, and then their faces softened and grew merry with laughter. Jolly laughs erupted from their bellies.

"No, no," the assistant answered, bent over with laughter. He straightened, held up his hand, and plunged his thumb toward his middle and index finger. "Shoot you with needle. For pain."

Gene exhaled. He was going to get an anesthetic before they worked on his arms. The Belgian interpreter later told Gene the doctors carefully discerned the need of each patient to be anesthetized. He said supplies of anesthesia and other medicines were so low that patients often endured surgery or other procedures without the benefit of a painkiller.

The assistant brought over two hypodermic needles.

"This one make you sleepy. This one for infection," he said.

Both doctors carefully swabbed and cleaned his bullet-ridden forearms. They cut off the exposed bone of his right forearm and fused the remaining length of bones, making Gene's right forearm forever shorter than his left. Gene appreciated the tender care the two doctors showed when bandaging his arms. He hadn't expected such treatment in a POW camp.

For the next three weeks, Gene didn't move from his bed. There was little to do other than stare at the ceiling or watch the hospital staff make their rounds. Sometimes the Belgian interpreter stopped by to talk. Gene was allowed to send a short note to his parents.

The only other pastime was killing lice and bedbugs. Vermin lurked everywhere at Sandbostel, even in the hospital. Gene would wait for bedbugs to crawl out from under his bandaged arms and then pinch them with the forefinger and thumb of his other arm. There was nothing he could do when he felt lice crawling under his chest bandages. Wiggling his torso to alleviate the itching of the crawling insects only brought stabs of pain to his mending ribs.

Sleep came in fits interrupted by nightmares. Being awake was just as bad. Then he replayed the final moments of *Rikki Tikki Tavi*. Did anyone else get out of the plane alive? He went through the list: he was sure Pee Wee had been killed in the ball turret. He remembered seeing Swedo's and Andy's bullet-ridden bodies lying motionless on the fuselage floor when he crawled forward to grab the spare parachute. He thought he'd heard Sparky screaming. Maybe it was Reed. Benny? Langley? Curtis? Orrison?

Orrison . . . Jesse.

Gene missed his "big brother." He wished for his leadership, his advice. Orrison was the officer all the enlisted men of *Rikki Tikki Tavi* sought when they had a problem. Gene had problems: a busted skull, broken bones, an aching back. He was lonely. Being a prisoner of war was worse than being a convict. At least a criminal knew the length of his prison sentence. Who knew how long the war would last. If Orrison were with him, he'd know the right thing to say. Gene longed to hear the soothing confidence of one of his pre-takeoff pep talks. He would never forget how Orrison backed him when Gene argued with Langley on the flight over the Atlantic.

The pain from Gene's ribs gradually lessened. He could now turn his body to look around the room. The caregivers moved quickly due to a shortage of nurses. He'd speak a few words to the Americans and British prisoners next to him, but no one said much. Every patient in that room was seriously wounded. Each day, Gene endured the agony of another inch of gauze being pulled from the back of his head. But the wound showed no sign of infection.

After three weeks of sleeping and staring at the ceiling, Dr. Kamenkovic came to Gene's bedside.

"Rest time done, Sergeant. You get up now."

Gene wasn't so sure. "I'll get up if you help me."

Putting his bandaged arm on the doctor's shoulder, Gene stood up. He took his first steps since climbing aboard *Rikki Tikki Tavi* three weeks ago. In the corridor between the rows of beds, the doctor stopped and motioned for Gene to keep going. He was a bit dizzy, but Gene kept his balance, walking about ten paces and then turning around.

"Gooooood. Gooooood," Kamenkovic said.

Gene made it back to his bed without any help.

"You walk every day," Kamenkovic ordered.

Each day, Gene gained a little strength, but the food at Sandbostel didn't speed his recovery. Just two camp kitchens supplied meals to all 20,000 prisoners, but the food was often spoiled and not very nutritious. In the morning, Gene munched on a slice of crusty bread. At noon, he sipped on a cup of rutabaga or potato soup. Sometimes, Gene could see tiny, white lice floating on the top of the broth. He learned to ignore it after a few weeks. At night, the prisoners ate a charcoaled potato.

When Gene was strong enough, the Belgian interpreter asked him if he would assist the Serb doctors in the operating room. Gene was glad to do something different. The operating area was the first place he'd seen outside his recovery room since arriving at Sandbostel. The facility looked clean, but Gene saw very little medical equipment.

Through the interpreter, the Serb doctors instructed Gene to sit up against the back of a wounded American pilot. He was in bad shape. Gene could see a lung expand and contract from an open wound on the side of his chest. Sitting behind the flier while holding him upright, Gene's nose twisted at the horrible smell coming from the wound. But he was glad to be up and out of bed. It felt good to help a fellow Air Corps comrade.

A few days later, Gene helped a Flying Fortress gunner who had a piece of shrapnel stuck in his skull right above an eye. The American airman was conscious and lying on a table.

"There will be no anesthetic for this procedure," the interpreter warned. "You must hold him and not let him move. The doctors say the metal is close to his brain. If he moves, he will die."

Gene recalled the anesthetic he received when the doctors repaired his busted arms. He wondered why this wounded gunner would have to take the pain.

With his bandaged arms and chest, Gene leaned over the patient's midsection. One doctor clasped the wounded man's head while the other slowly removed the jagged metal. The doctors left after bandaging the patient's head, but Gene decided to sit with him for a while.

"I saw you fall," the wounded gunner said.

Gene gasped.

"I saw your tail falling when I was coming down in my parachute."

The airman was George Fisher. The Germans shot down his Flying Fortress, *Dark Horse,* on the same afternoon Gene fell after the raid over Bremen. Fisher's pilot was Carl Fyler, the man who had tried to bind up Gene's head wound the night after both were shot down. Fisher had his own miraculous survival story. He and the other waist gunner lay bleeding on the fuselage floor, each with a broken arm. The tail gunner, who was also wounded, came to the rescue. The tail gunner was bleeding at his midsection and his left shoulder. His left arm was gone. But the one-armed airman managed to buckle a parachute on both Fisher and the other waist gunner and push them out of their crippled aircraft. The tail gunner himself never got out of the burning plane.

"I didn't know anyone was in your tail section. The Germans told me about finding you. Everyone here is talking about it."

Gene learned that Fisher spoke fluent German.

Fisher's story of Gene's notoriety was confirmed later that week on Christmas Eve. Gene was sleeping when four French prisoners burst into the room and picked up all four corners of his bed. They carried him to a nearby barracks where a Christmas party was well underway. The French sat Gene's bed down next to a Christmas tree.

A Christmas tree? Here in Sandbostel?

More French prisoners gathered around Gene. They knew his story. A few talked excitedly about his fall and motioned with their hands how Gene came down in the tail section. Others studied his head wound, which was now partially uncovered. They pointed at the stitches of the flesh plate sewn into Gene's scalp.

"Ah, you like vodka now?" one Frenchman joked. The others laughed heartily at the question. Gene didn't understand.

The English-speaking Frenchman explained. "That flesh in your head probably came from a dead Russian. There are many of them here."

Gene remembered the Belgian interpreter telling him how the Russians were segregated from the other prisoners and treated terribly. The Germans gave the Russian captives even fewer rations than the meager meals fed to prisoners from Western countries. The POWs from the Western Allies also received Red Cross parcels, which contained canned meats and dried fruit. The Russians got no such aid. Thousands of them died at Sandbostel from systemic malnutrition.

The English-speaking French prisoner told Gene he'd seen him come down in the tail section. Gene was shocked that someone else had seen his fall. The Frenchman said he and a group of French prisoners were sent to a work detail outside the city of Syke, Germany, about thirty miles southeast of Sandbostel Prison. On the afternoon of the American attack on nearby Bremen, he and others ran toward the tail section they saw hurtling through the sky. During air raids, the Germans allowed the French to run off and search the wreckage of downed Allied planes for food and clothing. With France under Nazi occupation, the guards didn't worry about French prisoners escaping. The scavengers looked for anything that would be useful to them, especially wires, which prisoners used to rig up homemade radios.

Gene remembered. *That's why they tried to rip the microphone wire from my neck.*

Another French prisoner thrust a metal cup into Gene's face.

"Cognac!" he exclaimed.

Cognac? In a POW camp? The French pointed to a clamped plastic tube attached to the Christmas tree that wound through the tree and ended at a secret still hidden behind a wall. Gene looked at the liquid. It was as clear as glass. With little food in his stomach, he drank it down.

And the food! The French prisoners handed Gene sweet breads and a plate of meat. He had no idea what kind of meat it was. It didn't matter. There was also cake. Gene gorged himself. Everyone in the room was eating, drinking, and singing.

It was Gene's second Christmas away from home. A year earlier, he'd eaten turkey and listened to carols sung in a cafeteria filled with American Air Corps trainees at the Las Vegas Gunnery School. Now he ate meat he couldn't identify and listened to Frenchmen belt out noels in tunes he recognized, but in a language he didn't understand.

Someone poured him more cognac. In a short time, Gene was very drunk.

He couldn't remember how he got back to his hospital room. He didn't eat for two days he was so hungover. But when his appetite returned, it was back to a small cup of bug-infested soup and a piece of crusty bread. Christmas was over.

In January, the Serb doctors deemed Gene healthy enough to move him to a prison barracks near the hospital. It was a crude shed, measuring about fifty feet long by fifteen feet wide, with a few windows. Gene shared the barracks with about twenty other American fliers, all of them recovering from wounds. It was crowded, but each man had his own cot.

The Americans were not allowed to leave the building. To pass the time, the prisoners played cards, picked bedbugs off their clothing, or wrote short letters, which the Germans heavily censored. A German soldier sat outside the only door to the barracks. The usual guard was a plump, jovial man whom Gene figured to be about sixty years old. When the old soldier became bored, he'd join the prisoners playing poker. He'd laugh and yell as loudly as any of the Americans.

Other German soldiers stopped by to visit. They'd step through the doorway and motion at Gene. "Ist das ihn?" they would ask. They wanted to meet the nineteen-year-old tail gunner who fell from the sky without a parachute and lived.

"Ja, ja. Das ist ihn," the old German guard nodded.

Gene enjoyed the attention. Except for the lack of food and not being able to go outside, it was nice to be famous, and prison life was tolerable.

French prisoners sometimes stopped by to chat a bit with the Americans. Gene didn't understand why the French were afforded the privilege to roam around outside when the Americans couldn't. Perhaps it was because they weren't airmen who would attempt an escape back to England. It seemed the French knew the chubby, old guard very well. One time, they offered him chocolate. Halfway through a card game, the old man suddenly stood up and yelled, "Schiessen! Schiessen!" He barreled out the door, sprinting to the latrine. Out of earshot of the old soldier, the French laughed uproariously. Gene learned they'd laced the chocolate with soap.

The French had special affection for Gene. They'd sneak him an extra piece of bread or a small piece of chocolate, without the soap. One evening, three French prisoners came into the barracks. One of them carried pants, a jacket, and a beret. Another spoke English and ordered Gene to change into the clothes. The third man jumped into Gene's cot. He would pretend to be Gene sleeping when the German guard came in for the nightly bed check.

Walking with the other two French prisoners, Gene was scared to be out of the barracks.

"You must walk," said one of the Frenchmen. "Dulag Luft is coming, and you must be strong."

Dulag Luft. Like all airmen, Gene knew what those words meant. It was the German Luftwaffe's interrogation center located in southern Germany outside of Frankfurt. All downed airmen captured in Nazi-occupied Europe passed through the camp before being sent to their assigned prison camp. Back at his air base in England, intelligence officers warned Gene that the Germans were very good at extracting information from scared, hungry fliers who were often wounded.

Gene wondered how the French knew he was leaving soon. Flanked by each of the French prisoners, the three walked on the open grounds in front of the barracks.

"If we are questioned by the guards, let us do the talking," the English-speaking Frenchman said. "You just nod your head and say, 'Oui, oui.'"

Each night after eating the potato ration, Gene changed his clothes, put on a beret, and walked out into the dark flanked by two French prisoners. Each night, the walk got a little longer. The Germans allowed the French to be outside until 10:00 p.m. Gene found it difficult to suppress a giggle whenever he said "oui, oui" to passing German soldiers. When he returned to his barracks, the French prisoner who covered for Gene during bed check jumped out of Gene's cot.

One night before the walk, the Belgian interpreter from the hospital visited the barracks. He gathered Gene and several other Americans in the barracks and informed them that he'd heard they'd be leaving for Dulag Luft in two weeks.

"You will wear civilian clothes," he said. "When you're on the train to Frankfurt, do not bring attention to yourself."

Gene understood the warning and the importance of civilian clothes. German citizens on those trains would not take kindly to prisoners in Air Corps uniforms. He wished he was leaving the next day. He was in no hurry to meet the Luftwaffe interrogators at Dulag Luft, but he was tired of worrying about it. He wanted to face it. He wanted the next dreaded step to be over.

CHAPTER 10

The Telegram

March 2014

In the banquet room of the American Legion Hall Post #220 in Soldiers Grove, a ceremony honoring Gene had just finished. Beer and conversation flowed freely in the after-party. I sat across from Gene's eighty-two-year-old sister, JoAnn, a nun and retired Catholic schoolteacher.

I hadn't expected to do "book work" that day. But when I'd been introduced to JoAnn, she suggested an interview after the speeches and accolades for her brother. It was hard to hear amid the scraping of folding chairs and laughter from the bar. But I begged a pen off a bartender to scribble notes onto bar napkins.

I had so much to discuss with JoAnn, and I wasn't sure where to begin. Then it came to me: Gene's *first* death-defying fall.

Gene had sheepishly told me about his infamous fall from a Minneapolis hotel balcony during his senior trip in the spring of 1941. Some of his roommates had sneaked past Old Man Krause, the high school principal and trip chaperone, cradling bottles of beer. Gene and the boys got tipsy. In the middle of the night, the girls started calling from a separate but adjacent tower of the hotel. The boys stepped out onto the balcony and looked longingly at the shouting girls, just a mere eight to ten feet away on their veranda. So near, yet so far away.

One of Gene's classmates stepped over the metal railing and leapt to the opposite balcony. He pulled himself up to the throng of squealing girls. More boys followed and jumped.

"What a bunch of idiots!" JoAnn exclaimed.

When it was Gene's turn, he clambered over the railing and steadied himself. He leapt. But midway through his jump, he knew his short frame had failed him. His hands missed the railing of the girls' balcony. He cartwheeled toward a lower level of rooms about ten feet below and blasted through a glass skylight.

Crash!

Gene landed on the bed of a sleeping woman. She wasn't hurt— neither, miraculously, was Gene—but she shrieked so loudly she woke the hotel management. The cops arrived and hauled Gene to a police station. At 3:00 a.m., Old Man Krause, dressed in his bathrobe, marched in to pick up his apprehended student.

"The hotel wrote back to the high school and said never, ever again will we welcome you back," JoAnn growled. I was startled that she was still mad. But Gene's notorious plunge had ruined her own future senior trip.

"Did your parents ever find out about it?"

"No. We didn't have a phone," said JoAnn. "So, Mom and Dad never found out anything from the principal. Even if Old Man Krause would have told them, Mom would've never believed it. We all knew he was her favorite. Her 'Little Revy.' He could do no wrong."

JoAnn threw her hands into the air. I chuckled: an eighty-two-year-old still bitter about her brother's high school mischief. But from what she told me, it didn't seem to matter whether Gene got in a fistfight or crashed a car. Mom loved that boy.

"She taught him how to waltz on the kitchen floor," said JoAnn, her face softening. "I can still see Eugene swinging Mom around and laughing."

I sensed the opportunity to ask about the war. I had no idea if she knew anything. The crowd at the bar had become louder. I slid my metal folding chair closer to JoAnn and leaned in.

"Do you remember when Gene left for the war?" I asked.

"Oh, yes. Mom was very against Eugene joining the service," JoAnn replied. "And when he became a tail gunner, I don't think she ever really understood how much danger he was in."

"Did you ever talk to him about the war when he came back?"

"Only once. We were by a lake watching the sun set. He said something about flying in the war, so I decided to finally ask him."

That was thirty years earlier. She'd been enjoying a weekend getaway with Gene, Peg, and two of her friends at a Minnesota lakeside cabin. After a supper of fried fresh-caught walleye and potato salad, Gene and JoAnn stayed at the lakeside picnic table while the others carried leftovers back to the cabin.

They watched the sun dip behind the evergreens. A blue evening sky with wispy clouds and bright streaks of orange slowly darkened. Neither spoke. Then something in the serenity of the scene gave JoAnn the courage to ask her brother what she'd never dared ask before.

"Eugene, when you were in the war, why did so many of the planes have trouble getting back?'"

Gene didn't say anything. He just kept staring at the lake. When JoAnn finally turned toward him, she saw tears trailing down his face.

"Why did we fall back?" he began repeating. "Why did we leave the formation? Why did we fall back?"

"I never talked to him about it again," JoAnn told me.

Another dead end. Joni had once told me, "We don't go there." I had very little from Gene's other children or siblings. A family of silence.

But there was more I needed from JoAnn. Joni had told me

that her aunt was the only living witness to the day the missing-in-action telegram came to the home farm.

"When did your family find out that Gene was missing?"

"It was a very snowy Saturday," JoAnn answered. "Mom was in the kitchen, and Dad was in the barn. An old car swung into the driveway, and . . ."

JoAnn abruptly stopped speaking. Her hand flew up to her mouth, and she closed her eyes. "My God, it's like it happened yesterday." Her voice quivered and broke.

I desperately looked for something to dry her tears, but all I had were my bar napkins which contained my just-written notes. I couldn't risk losing those.

"Someone please get this woman some tissue!" I hollered out to no one in particular.

December 1943

The snow falling in the late-afternoon winter air made it feel like Christmas when twelve-year-old JoAnn Moran sat at the living room table looking at a pile of ornaments. She couldn't decide what to hang up next. She'd already tied red and green tissue paper bells to the door handles. Now she moved on to the Christmas "tree."

It wasn't a real Christmas tree. Dad refused to spend the outrageous cost of seventy-nine cents on a cut tree. Instead, he sawed off cedar branches from trees in the woods, tied them up in a bundle, and set his mock-up in the corner of the living room. It looked almost like a genuine Christmas tree after JoAnn hung bulbs and sprinkled tinsel on the evergreen boughs.

Through the arched entryway that joined the living room with the kitchen dining area, Mom stood working over the kitchen sink. She wasn't in the mood for holiday decorating, scolding her daughter that it was too early.

But JoAnn knew the real reason for her mother's lack of holiday spirit. Each night since Gene had left for the war, Mom sat in the kitchen taking in the war reports airing from the Coronado radio that sat on the cupboard next to the dining table. From the boxy, wood-paneled radio set, the voice of newsman Gabriel Heatter would state, "There's good news tonight." But his trademark tagline was tempered by the melancholy voices of other reporters such as Eric Severeid or H.V. Kaltenborn. Their commentary detailed the horrendous losses the Eighth Air Force suffered in their deep raids over occupied Europe.

Mom usually sat alone taking in the war news. JoAnn avoided the kitchen whenever she heard her mother click on the radio dial. Dad refused to sit and listen to the radio after Gene was sent to England. He'd stay in the barn where he had to work alone now. Gene's older brother Byron still lived and helped out at home, but he kept a pillow at his Uncle Paul's house where he also farmed. Byron was engaged to Florence Murphy, and their wedding date was set just four days after Christmas. What a happy diversion to a season filled with dreary battlefront news.

When JoAnn went to hang the blue celluloid Christmas wreath on the living room window, she heard the dog barking. Looking out, she saw a rusty car she didn't recognize pull up in the driveway. It wasn't the mailman. And she couldn't identify the two men who got out of the vehicle.

"Why is the dog barking?" Mom hollered from the kitchen.

JoAnn didn't answer. She watched her father walk from the barn toward the two men. One of the visitors held a pale-yellow piece of paper in his hand. Her father took the paper and read it. His shoulders slumped.

"What's going on?" Mom yelled again.

"I don't know. You better come in here. Dad looks funny," JoAnn answered.

Mom walked over and peered out the window, drying her

hands with a towel. The moment she saw the pale-yellow paper in her husband's hand, she screamed.

"NOOOOOOOOO!!!!"

The shriek was primordial. Mom barreled through the living room to the kitchen. She burst out the side door and ran up the path cut in the snow, screaming, "Joe! Joe! Joe!" She snatched the paper from his hand and read it. It was a telegram. The War Department regretted to inform her that her "Little Revy" was missing in action.

She collapsed into her husband's arms. The two strangers helped Dad carry her back into the house. Gingerly, they set Mom in a chair at the kitchen table. Her head fell onto the table.

"No! No! No! No! What are we going to do, Joe?" she bawled at her husband, hardly drawing a breath between sobs. Then she disappeared into her bedroom, moaning.

Father Mathieu drove down from St. Philip's when he got the news. Byron came too. He'd been out furniture shopping with Florence. The priest talked to Dad and Byron in hushed tones at the kitchen table. Mom wouldn't come out of the bedroom.

Byron wasn't sure what to do. Should he postpone the wedding? Gene had written him several weeks earlier, congratulating Byron on his new bride. In the letter, Gene had also leveled with his older brother. Casualties were mounting in the Eighth Air Force that autumn; there was a good chance he'd never get to meet his new sister-in-law. Gene urged Byron to go on with the wedding even if the worst happened.

But had the worst happened? The War Department said Gene was missing, not dead. Father Mathieu studied Gene's letter to Byron. The priest knew this family. He'd taught Gene and his older brother how to box. He'd heard their confessions.

"Byron, it seems to me Eugene made it very clear that he wanted nothing to stop the wedding," Father Mathieu said. "I think you should go ahead with the ceremony as you and Florence planned."

On Christmas Day, the family attended Morning Mass at St.
Philip's, but no company came to call on the Moran farm. Mom had
made it clear she wouldn't entertain any visitors. Christmas that year
was like any other lonely winter day on the farm. Dad spent most of
the holiday in the barn. He did hand out the candy bags to JoAnn
and the other children, brown paper bags full of hard candies, peanuts, and chocolate drops, and before heading out to chores, Dad
knelt down by the bottom drawer of the bookcase standing in the
living room. He opened the drawer and set Gene's candy bag inside.

The somber mood in the Moran home only worsened the day
of the wedding. Michael sickened with measles. Dad also wasn't
feeling well. Mom disappeared when it was time to get dressed for
the ceremony. JoAnn found her mother crying alone in the laundry
shed, tears splashing on the cement floor.

The wedding ceremony was as somber as a funeral. Gene's sister, Rosemary, was a bridesmaid, looking radiant in pink taffeta.
Byron wore a blue suit. But Joe and Ethel received tears and condolences in the receiving line after the wedding instead of hugs and
congratulations.

Dad went home after the ceremony. Mom stayed on for the
wedding dinner, a spread of beef, chicken, mashed potatoes, and
jello salad. But when JoAnn complained about a sore throat, Mom
left the meal early to drive JoAnn home. Soon, she had two children
in bed with measles.

The winter trudged on: an unending cycle of snow, cold, sickness, and despair. On Wednesday nights, Mom and Dad drove up
to St. Philip's for a weekly service dedicated to area men serving
in uniform. Mom quarantined JoAnn and Michael upstairs. They
passed the time calling across the hall to each other from darkened

bedrooms. Mom disappeared regularly to cry in the laundry shed. Dad's migraine headaches came back, crippling his work and souring his mood.

The not knowing was torture. Mom wrote to Congress begging for information. Was her son dead or alive? The government had no updates on Gene. In January, a personal letter arrived from Wisconsin Senator Robert LaFollette Jr. No news, but polite, official regret that his office was unable to find any facts about Gene's fate.

But five other letters found their way to the farm. Mysterious envelopes from sympathetic strangers, simply addressed: Moran Family, Gays Mills, Wisconsin. Gays Mills was the nearest post office, seven miles from Soldiers Grove. Ethel Moran opened the letters at the kitchen table. Nothing could have prepared her for what was inside.

The first was from a man on the East Coast. He'd written that he picked up a German radio broadcast on a shortwave radio that told of a young Wisconsin tail gunner who'd fallen four miles through the sky without a parachute and lived. Lived? *Impossible!* And why would it be Gene, of all the gunners flying missions? This letter could only bring false hope.

Mom opened another letter. It gave the same story of overhearing a German radio broadcast, a report that told about an American airman falling through the sky and miraculously surviving. The airman was a sergeant gunner who had been seriously injured. Then shock! The letter named the gunner: Eugene Moran. Another letter gave more details. It stated the lucky airman had been saved by doctors at a prisoner-of-war camp in Germany.

Mom and Dad sat in stony silence. Did this mean Gene was alive? Did he really fall four miles without a parachute? That couldn't be! No one could survive those sorts of injuries. Dad wondered if the letter writers had misinterpreted the static-filled radio broadcasts. It would be easy to make a mistake about broadcasts in German sent across an entire ocean. But five letters with similar stories? He hardly dared to hope. Mom was cautiously optimistic. She said little, refusing to expose her hope to others.

That changed the first week of February. The Gays Mills post office contacted Joe Moran: come pick up a special letter from the War Department.

Dad waited until he got home to open the envelope. He read it to his wife.

Their son was alive!

The War Department reported that Gene had been found at a prisoner-of-war camp in Germany. The official announcement went on to state that "Eugene is suffering from a skull fracture . . ." It added that the injury came from bailing out over Germany. Nothing was said about a four-mile free fall without a parachute, but the facts added up. The mysterious letters describing the German radio reports could possibly be true.

Mom tried to make sense of the startling news. Prisoner of war? Skull fracture? She and Gene's father recalled the horrible reports in newspapers of the treatment of American POWs at the hands of their Japanese captors in the Philippines. She'd once told the family that she'd rather have her son dead than be taken prisoner. Now her "Little Revy" was a prisoner of war. How would the Germans treat their captives?

Later that month, an unusual off-white card arrived in the mail. It was stamped: "Postkarte" and "Kriegsgefangenenpost." German words. On the back, there was a simple message printed in pencil:

Dear Mom and all.—

I am in hospital, my wounds are not real serious, will be O.K. in a week. Your prayers saved me. Let all friends know I'm alright. Please try to write me often. Continue to pray for me. This is all the room, must close.

Your son, Eugene.

CHAPTER 11

Solitary

August 2012

We never told the boys about the brain scan that lit up like a Christmas tree. Summer was summer at our five-acre farm, which we'd named "Two Brothers' Orchard." The two brothers and I picked raspberries and cherries and sold them at the local farmers' market. We hand-thinned the apple trees, sprayed for bugs, and watched the apples turn from green to red. When Carmen cut off her hair and shaved her head, we simply explained to Matthew and Joe that some cancer had come back and we'd destroy it again with radiation.

"We've made a little progress," the oncologist said when we returned to Mayo Clinic in August.

"Progress?" My heart quivered. But what did she mean by "little"? The doctor pointed to images of Carmen's brain on a computer screen, which showed fewer glowing lines.

"But here," she added, pointing to the outer regions of the brain scan, "these bright areas indicate the cancer is still active." Those cancer cells had held their ground during the bombardment of radiation. No further explanation was needed. We knew. Soon, the cancer would spread again.

When we returned home, Carmen began dismantling her professional life. One by one, she closed the accounts of her graphic design business and recommended other graphic artists to her clients.

She'd lost weight again after enduring a month of radiation treatments. Her face had grown lean, her movements slow and thick. She spoke with short, simple sentences, trying not to stutter in front of the boys.

We still made it to our annual vacation spot, a rented cabin up in Door County, Wisconsin's peninsula paradise that jutted into Lake Michigan. The boys and I thrashed about in the shallow water, playing tackle football. Carmen watched.

One day, we visited the local art gallery, famous for its graffiti-covered shed. Carmen brought paint and brushes. She slowly painted "ARMBRUSTER" in powder-blue letters onto one of the brown siding boards and added our names and the date.

When summer was over, I did not return to work. I took a leave of absence from teaching for the fall semester to care for Carmen. Our neighbors pooled money and paid for a photographer to come and take family portraits. We all dressed in white t-shirts and jeans. Carmen put on her blonde wig. We posed on the front porch, the back porch, and next to our red barn. Carmen struggled to reach each spot. She couldn't walk in a straight line, so Matthew and I flanked each side of her and held her arms. It was the first time the boys had seen their mother unable to walk by herself. She had trouble standing up, so we propped her. We forced smiles for the photographer.

Then Joni called and said Greg Swedo was coming back to Soldiers Grove to visit Gene. He was due to arrive on Labor Day weekend, and this time, he was bringing his parents. Swedo! I was desperate to be there. Maybe with Greg's father, Swedo's own brother, Gene might give new details about the war and the crew of *Rikki Tikki Tavi*.

Could I do it? Should I leave Carmen? Would the boys be able to manage? Matthew was still only thirteen. I remembered the seizures that had struck Carmen just three months earlier. What if Carmen's face started twitching again and I wasn't home? But how could I miss this rare opportunity? What if Gene opened up to the Swedos and I wasn't there to hear his story?

I would go. Just make a quick visit to Gene's home. Joni was going to make her classic Italian dinner of cheese-filled tortellini and marinated tomatoes and cucumbers for everyone.

Carmen watched from the bed as I threw on a polo shirt and pulled on my cleanest pair of cargo shorts.

"I'll talk with them just an hour or so and come right back," I said. "I won't stay for dinner. The boys are here, and I'll have a phone in my pocket."

I could sense her staring at me as I dressed. Then she spoke in her strained and mumbled voice.

"You c-c-care more 'bout book than us."

I closed my eyes and felt the pit in my stomach. I became a statue. I'd always left for interviews with Gene with Carmen's blessing. She *wanted* me to write the book. She's the one who told me to go for it when I first had my doubts. Carmen believed in me, believed in the book. She'd always send me out the door with a hug and then joke "give Gene a big hug and kiss from me." Now she accused me of abandoning her, our family. Maybe I was.

Carmen pushed herself to a sitting position and waved her hands in front of her face. "No, no. I'm, I'm sorry. G-Go. You go."

She rolled over onto her side and shut her eyes.

The Swedo family was already gathered in the small living room with Gene, Pauline, and Joni. After introductions, I got out my legal pad and voice recorder. I had one hour. One hour. No more. Then back to Carmen.

I listened, distractedly, to Greg's ninety-three-year-old father. He'd served stateside during the war, but had been sent to Europe in 1945 the summer after Germany surrendered. He'd visited the Dachau concentration camp, just a few months after it was liberated. He'd seen the prisoner barracks, the ovens. He described a tree in the middle of the camp that looked like polished marble. Prisoners had stripped the bark and worn it smooth climbing it to avoid the guard dogs.

The talk turned to the final moments of *Rikki Tikki Tavi*. I braced for this conversation. Gene had sobbed earlier that spring when Greg had asked about his uncle's death. But this time, Gene's voice did not crack. He told about crawling forward, the frayed parachute on his back, Swedo singing on the mike, seeing Swedo and Andy lying dead on the fuselage floor.

Carmen was asleep when I returned home. I didn't bother unpacking the carrying bag with my interview notes and voice recorder. I set the bag in the office corner. I had no idea when I'd pick up Gene's story again.

February 1944

"Sergeant Eugene Moran. Tomorrow, you are going on train to Frankfurt." Without warning, a German officer had entered the barracks. "You will dress in civilian clothes."

Frankfurt. Gene knew what that meant. Dulag Luft.

The French had warned him. They prepared him. They made Gene take long walks with them each night to strengthen his wounded body. Now he must face the interrogation alone.

Before he was shot down, Gene had listened to briefings back in England which instructed captured fliers to reveal only name, rank, and serial number to enemy interrogators. He knew the basics of the Geneva Convention rules for treatment of prisoners of war.

He didn't expect torture. But how would the Germans try to break him? It didn't matter. Gene was confident he wouldn't give the enemy anything.

In the early-morning darkness, German soldiers piled Gene and seven other American prisoners into the back of a covered truck. The truck headed to a train station about six miles from Sandbostel.

It was still dark when the train pulled out of the railyard and headed south for the long journey to Frankfurt. Two German guards had crammed Gene and three other prisoners into a booth on the train. The compartment had its own door and was separated from the other passengers. Two benches faced each other. Curtains covered the windows so they would not be seen. Two guards sat down and squeezed in with a prisoner in a seat meant for only two people, not three.

The train car pitched and rolled. Gene was sleepy, but he couldn't rest. His lower back ached. A short time later, a German Luftwaffe officer opened the door and ordered the two guards to leave. He squeezed in next to Gene. Gene didn't know how to react.

"I'm Captain Wolfe," the officer said in perfect English. "I will escort you to Frankfurt."

This German officer seemed friendly enough. He was clearly middle-aged, but looked trim and youthful in his Luftwaffe uniform. The captain asked where they were from in the United States. Gene figured the war wouldn't be lost if he answered him.

"Wisconsin?" the officer said. "I lived in Wisconsin. After the war."

Captain Wolfe explained to Gene that he'd also been a prisoner of war. He'd been captured by Americans in the First World War. He liked his captors, and after the war, he'd moved to the United States where he lived near Oshkosh, Wisconsin, for fifteen years. He added that many German officers had lived and worked in America after World War I. Gene's suspicions lessened as Captain Wolfe described the dairy farms and named the state's lakes and rivers.

"Wisconsin was very beautiful. I didn't want to leave," Wolfe said. "But my parents became ill before this war, and I returned to care for them. When I wanted to return to America, the German government would not let me."

Captain Wolfe's English put Gene at ease. He and the other three American prisoners shared their stories from home. The Luftwaffe officer never discussed the war or asked Gene any questions about his military service. Gene was glad for the conversation. With curtains blocking the window, there was nothing else to do. As the train neared Frankfurt, Captain Wolfe's mood changed.

"When we leave the train at Frankfurt, do not look at the other passengers or anyone at the station. Bring no attention to yourselves," Captain Wolfe instructed. "You are gangsters. Terrorfliegers. They cannot know you are fliers."

It was midafternoon when the train pulled into a huge covered station. Shards of jagged glass framed blown-out window openings. Before getting up to leave the train, Captain Wolfe gave final instructions.

"You will follow me. Do not look at anyone. If we have to wait, don't even think about wandering around."

"Mister, I'm going to be right next to you," Gene said.

Wolfe had more advice. "If you have any cigarettes, smoke them up now. Eat your chocolate too. The German guards at Dulag Luft will take these from you."

Gene and the seven other American prisoners from Sandbostel followed Wolfe off the train. The two German guards walked behind the prisoners. They passed under a sign that read *Frankfurt am Main*. The station teemed with men in uniform as well as German civilians. Gene saw that the civilians were all young or middle-aged adults.

Wolfe had commanded his prisoners to look straight ahead, but Gene couldn't help gawking. Piles of rubble were everywhere. Buildings still standing had gaping holes and broken windows. Gene saw bent and twisted railroad tracks mounded in a maze of curled scrap metal. Yet he was stunned how the Germans, civilian and military, walked around oblivious to the destruction around them.

A few people in the train station shot inquisitive looks at Gene. He was grateful for the stocking cap he'd received back at Sandbostel. Not only did it keep his hairless skull warm, but it hid his head scar. Such a wound would have caught the attention of Germans at the train station and may have identified him as an airman.

Wolfe ordered the American prisoners to wait on a platform while he went looking for transportation that would take them to Dulag Luft. The captives lit cigarettes. Gene slowly dug the last of his chocolate bar out of his pocket, trying not to draw the attention of the two guards next to him. The guards were young and seemed much more interested in looking at German women walking by them. Gene quietly nibbled on his chocolate bar.

Captain Wolfe returned. They followed the captain for about a block from the train station where a truck waited for the prisoners. It was a large vehicle shaped like a bus. Gene spotted the wood burner attached to the side of the engine hood. He watched a soldier throw a log into the contraption. Before climbing aboard the back of the truck, Gene and the other Americans gave Wolfe their remaining cigarettes and chocolate. He thanked them and waved as they drove away.

Two guards sat in the back of the truck with the prisoners. Every bump in the road sent a jolt of pain through Gene's lower back. Except for occasional headaches, his head wound didn't bother him. He was bald now. In a few places on his skull, tiny hairs emerged.

It was dusk when Gene arrived at Dulag Luft. He saw a gate close behind the truck. The two guards ordered everyone off. In the fading evening light, the prisoners spotted a large wood sign with painted English words: *Welcome to Dulag Luft. We Have Been Expecting You.*

The guards directed Gene and the others into a room. A German officer sat at a table. Behind him towered three large soldiers. The Americans were ordered to strip to their underwear and set their clothing on the table. They also had to give up any personal items. Gene had nothing. He hadn't seen the rosary he clutched during his fall since the day he was shot down, and he'd lost the scrap metal imprinted with "Boeing" that he pulled from his arm. The German soldiers grabbed the clothing and carefully checked pockets and seams for compasses or other contraband that could be used in an escape.

The officer assigned new identification numbers. Gene was confused.

"I already have a number from Sandbostel. Why are you giving me a new . . ."

"Ve ask de questions here," the officer snapped.

Gene was assigned 108629. The officer continued filling out paperwork. "What air base did you come from?"

Gene was ready. "Eugene P. Moran. Staff Sergeant. 16132701," he said, dodging the question.

He knew better than to give his air base name. The officer asked more questions. Where was he shot down? When? How had it happened?

"Eugene P. Moran. Staff Sergeant. 16132701!" Gene shot back each time. "Eugene P. Moran. Staff Sergeant. 16132701."

The other Americans followed Gene's example, giving only name, rank, and serial number. The German officer and his soldiers smirked with each answer.

After being photographed, the prisoners were led down a hall lined with narrow doors on both sides. One of the soldiers unlocked a door and motioned for Gene to go inside. Gene could barely see in the unlit cell. He heard the door locking behind him. The only light came from a small opening up by the ceiling, too high to look through. Gene guessed the cell to be about eight feet long by four feet wide. Most of the width of the room was taken up by a cot.

There was no toilet, sink, or running water. Nothing but the bed and an electric heater mounted at the base of the wall.

Gene's world had changed. Gone were the days of celebrity treatment he'd enjoyed at Sandbostel. There were no French prisoners to entertain him, no jovial, card-playing German guards, no more visits from friend and enemy alike to shake hands with the man who'd fallen from the sky. No one at Dulag Luft knew the story of his fall and miraculous survival, and from the looks of it, they wouldn't care.

After he'd sat on the cot for a half hour, Gene noticed the room becoming warm, very warm. He took off his jacket. Still too hot. He stripped to his underwear and lay on his cot, sweat beads rolling off his body. About twenty minutes later, the heat subsided. The room became cool, very cool. Gene put his clothes back on. Then his jacket. Soon, he was shivering.

The Germans repeated the cycle of hot and cold. The heat reached 130 degrees before it was shut off and cold February air seeped back into the room. He couldn't sleep. The extreme temperatures and the constant dressing and undressing kept him awake. He listened to mice scurry under his bed. There were no books, writing paper, or any kind of diversion, not that he'd be able to see much in his dark tomb. Gene had no sense of time or whether it was night or day. From the hallway, he heard moaning, screaming, singing. He knew some men were breaking.

Someone opened a small sliding door at the bottom of the door and pushed in a tray. On it sat a slice of bread and a cup of coffee. Both were ersatz, substitute versions of the real thing. Sawdust made up more than half the small slice of bread. To Gene, the margarine-like spread tasted like axle grease. He had drunk ersatz coffee in Sandbostel. There were so many rumors about the vile drink he didn't know what to believe. Speculation about ingredients included tree leaves, tulip bulbs, acorns, and even coal. Sometimes the tray pushed under the door included a small cup of potato water with boiled cabbage.

Gene was always thirsty. The daily cup of ersatz coffee and soup ration didn't make up for all the sweat he lost from the heat torture. He tried to sneak water during bathroom breaks. Twice daily, Gene was allowed to pound on the door to signal a guard to escort him to a bathroom at the end of the hall. Gene quickly slurped water from the wash basin before the guard, armed with a bayoneted rifle, yelled at him that the break was over.

Time passed very slowly in solitary confinement. It baffled Gene that just months before he'd been an air warrior, fighting the enemy in the wild blue yonder with the finest friends he'd ever known. Now, he sat alone in a black box.

The solitude didn't bother Gene. He'd been alone often in his life: under a tree hunting squirrels, on a horse-pulled hay cutter taking down alfalfa, and in the tail of a Flying Fortress scanning the skies for enemy fighters. But in the eternity of that darkened cell, he couldn't stop thinking about the men of *Rikki Tikki Tavi*. He missed his comrades, his friends, his brothers. His mind went over the same questions from his final mission: *Why did we fall back? Did anyone get out of the plane?*

Gene wasn't sure how many days he spent in his cell before he heard hobnailed boots marching toward him.

Two soldiers led him down the hall and ushered him into a small, plain-looking room with a table and a chair. Gene peered through squinted eyes, not used to the light coming through the draped window. He was hungry and thirsty. Repeatedly yawning, he estimated it had been at least three days since he'd slept. He steeled himself for what was ahead. He was ready. No one would get anything out of him other than name, rank, and serial number.

A man in his mid-fifties, smartly dressed in a civilian suit, walked in with a five-inch stack of folders and papers under his arms. The interrogator set his pile of documents on the table, sat down, and lit a cigarette. He studied his young prisoner.

"So, you don't like pineapple?"

Gene stopped breathing. The interrogator continued in perfect English.

"It made you sick. Didn't it?"

Gene couldn't move. How? How could anyone know that before taking off on his final mission, he jumped out of the plane to puke up the pineapple he ate for breakfast? Gene knew the Germans ran spies everywhere in England. He and other gunners talked about how the enemy probably knew the targets before they did. But how could they know the contents of his vomit splashed on a concrete tarmac on a secured American air base?

The interrogator gave Gene a quizzical look, opened the top folder, and glanced at its papers. "Don't worry, Sergeant. You have been gone so long that I only have a few questions for you."

Gene wasn't fooled by the interrogator's friendly approach. He instantly hated him. His slickly combed hair. His dapper suit. The arrogant tone of his voice. The way the interrogator patiently waited for him to talk. Gene was ready. He stared at him and boldly proclaimed, "Eugene P. Moran. Staff Sergeant. 16132701."

The interrogator puffed on his cigarette, blew out smoke, and laughed at Gene.

"You can stop with that nonsense, Sergeant. So, you only want to give me name, rank, and serial number? I can tell you your mother's maiden name."

The interrogator lifted a document from the folder and smirked. "Ethel Powers."

Gene looked away, avoiding eye contact. The interrogator filed through other papers and read.

"Eugene P. Moran. Graduated from Soldiers Grove High School. Class of '41." The interrogator held up a newspaper and looked it over. "You were a boxer . . . and played baseball. Ah, American baseball. Many Germans like baseball. Were you a pitcher?"

"I was a catcher and played some right field. I could also play . . ." Gene caught himself. "Eugene P. Moran. Staff Sergeant. 16132701."

The interrogator ignored him and picked out another paper from his files.

"Your father is Joe, and your mother is Ethel. Brother Byron, sisters Rosemary and JoAnn, another brother, Michael." The interrogator paused for a moment and smiled at Gene. "And a baby brother, Marty. Do I have that correct?"

Gene tried to keep a poker face, but his breathing quickened. *They even know about Marty?*

The surprises didn't stop. The interrogator read off a list of Gene's high school girlfriends.

"Do you have a girl now?" the interrogator asked.

"Eugene P. Moran. Staff Sergeant. 16132701," he stated more loudly than before.

The interrogator also became bolder.

"Your mother was married once before she met your father. You have a half brother. Is that true?"

It was true. Gene's mother was a young widow with a baby boy before she met Gene's father. The baby went to live with relatives of his dead father. Gene's older half brother visited the Moran farm about once a year. But it was a story the family didn't share. Gene seethed with rage that the interrogator had such personal information about his mother. The interrogator was getting to him. He sensed the interrogator knew it too.

"Sergeant, you're obsolete. You were shot down almost three months ago. There really isn't anything new you can tell me."

"Then what the hell are you talking to me for? You already got everything," Gene replied.

"I just need you to verify that this information is correct," the interrogator shot back.

Gene was hungry, thirsty, and so tired. His back was killing him. He didn't care anymore. He glared at the interrogator.

"I ain't verifying shit!" Gene roared.

The interrogator took another drag on his cigarette and crossed his arms. Gene stole a quick glance at his face. The interrogator was smiling.

"Your navigator, Lieutenant Orrison, passed through here a few weeks ago."

Orrison! Jesse!

Orrison was alive! Gene closed his eyes. He breathed deeply, exhaled, opened his eyes, and looked straight ahead. Jesse. He wanted to cry. He wanted to shout. But he wasn't saying anything. He'd be damned if he was going to let this arrogant German know how much he admired his "big brother." But where was Orrison? How did he get out of the plane? Was he hurt? Did anybody else make it?

"The rest of your crew is dead," the interrogator coldly stated. "I'm sorry for that, but that is war. Isn't it?"

Gene shut his eyes again. *Everyone? Dead?* He figured Pee Wee, Swedo, and Andy had died in the air battle. But Sparky? Reed? Benny? Langley? Curtis? Gene squeezed his eyelids, vainly trying to fight back tears. His lips quivered. He gasped, but tried not to make a sound. How long could he hold it in?

The interrogator put his arms on the table and leaned in like a snake about to strike.

"You know, Sergeant. Let's stop with this name, rank, and serial number bullshit. You answer some questions for me, and then I can tell you something about Lieutenant Orrison."

The Germans at Dulag Luft knew very well the bond between the bomber boys. Gene was about to explode. The interrogator moved in for the kill.

"Did you like your navigator? Would you like to talk about him?"

Gene said nothing. The interrogator waited.

"Do you have anything to say, Sergeant?"

Gene breathed deeply and opened his eyes. He looked up and locked eyes with his interrogator.

"Yes. I do. Why don't you go fuck yourself and the horse you rode in on YOU NAZI PIECE OF SHIT!"

The last syllable of his sentence had barely left his lips before Gene realized he'd made a grave error. Both men stared at each other. The interrogator's face hardened.

"Listen, you American pig. We can let you go, or we can shoot you."

Gene's breathing had settled a bit. He cleared his throat.

"Eugene P. Moran. Staff Sergeant. 16132701."

The interrogator had had enough. He looked back and shouted at the soldier guarding the door. The soldier quickly entered the room and grabbed Gene from his chair.

"Maybe a few more days in solitary will get you to change your mind, Sergeant," the interrogator said.

The soldier led Gene back to his cell. Gene flopped onto his bunk. He rolled over. Mice scurried under his bed. The room was warming up again.

Maybe a day later, Gene heard the clicking of boots approaching his cell again. A soldier opened the door, and standing next to him was an officer Gene hadn't seen yet.

"You are now going to a prison camp," the officer announced.

Gene grabbed his stocking cap and coat and followed the officer down the hallway. It was night outside when Gene and several other prisoners hopped aboard a truck. The truck arrived at a large building not far from a train station in Frankfurt.

When Gene entered, he was surprised to see about forty other men milling around. The prisoners in the building were all American airmen, many of whom had just been released from solitary confinement. The guards stayed off to the sides of the building. The prisoners started shouting out their home states. Gene yelled a few times. He heard someone else call out "Wisconsin," and he worked his way through the crowd to find a short man with brown hair looking at him.

"Hey, Baldy," the man said, reaching out to shake Gene's hand. Gene had taken off his stocking cap. "Harold Cyr, Chippewa Falls. Everyone calls me 'Shorty.'"

"Eugene Moran. Soldiers Grove," Gene said, grabbing Shorty's outstretched hand.

"I know where Soldiers Grove is."

"How in the hell would you know that?"

Gene was suspicious. Airmen were told to trust no one if they became prisoners. Gene knew the Germans often planted spies among the prisoners who acted like Allied airmen.

"My family traveled down to the Westby ski jump competition every year," Shorty explained. Westby was a small town located about twenty-five miles north of Gene's home area. "We always camped out and stayed a few days. Sometimes we'd drive around. Yeah, I remember Soldiers Grove."

The warehouse was a part of the Dulag Luft complex. The building served as a transit camp between interrogation and the journey to prisoner-of-war camps. It was getting late in the evening, and it became apparent that the prisoners were going to spend the night there. There were no beds or blankets. The prisoners lay down on the floor.

Gene stayed with Shorty, and the two talked into the night. Baldy and Shorty. Gene knew at once he'd found a new friend. He'd forgotten his earlier suspicions about Shorty being a German plant. Both were relieved to be out of solitary confinement. Shorty was twenty-two years old and also Catholic. And like Gene, he was a Flying Fortress tail gunner. Shorty had been shot down ten days earlier over Germany when his plane was hit by anti-aircraft fire. He'd been filling in for a missing tail gunner of another crew that day. The Germans had captured him immediately and sent him straight to Dulag Luft. Unlike Gene, Shorty had no serious injuries, just cuts and bruises.

"How did you get that head wound?" Shorty asked.

Gene avoided any mention of his fall. He believed by now that Shorty wasn't a spy, but decided to wait before telling him his incredible story. Gene said tree limbs gashed his head when he parachuted into the forest.

The Germans woke the prisoners early the next morning. Gene heard some of the guards call the prisoners "kriegies," slang for *Kriegsgefangenen,* "prisoners of war." He and Shorty stayed together when all the prisoners were marched to railyards with waiting boxcars. He'd survived Sandbostel and then Dulag Luft. What was next? Gene and Shorty clambered aboard.

The wood sides of the boxcar were slotted. The floor was matted with straw. Gene thought it looked like a cattle car. About fifty more men joined them, pressed in with no room to sit. The prisoners were standing shoulder to shoulder by the time Gene heard the boxcar door slam shut.

In the dim light, Gene spotted a coal-burning stove. That and body heat kept everyone warm for a while until the train started moving and wind whistled through the slotted sides.

The prisoners huddled together to stay warm. This created room for a few men to sit down. Men took turns resting on the straw floor. A corner of the boxcar was quickly designated as the toilet area. Gene had no idea where the train was headed. All he knew was that he was on a long journey headed east.

The train stopped at a marshalling yard. Guards toting machine guns unlocked the boxcar doors and allowed the prisoners to jump out to relieve themselves by the side of the track. Women in Red Cross uniforms gave out a small piece of bread and a cup of foul-smelling soup. The bread was spread with the black, greasy substance. Gene called it "coal jam." He dabbed the rock-hard bread into the broth to make it edible. Then it was back on the train.

At a nighttime stop in another marshalling yard, Gene heard a distant rumble. He knew that faint sound. Air raid sirens began to wail. A few prisoners muttered, "Goddammit." Allied bombers often went after train yards. Gene knew with certain dread that their train could be a target.

Through the slotted cracks of the boxcar, he saw people running from the train yard. The Germans were heading for air raid shelters. No one came to fetch the prisoners and let them out of the boxcars. They were trapped.

The rumble became a roar. Gene heard muffled explosions in the distance. The blasts grew louder. The boxcar floor shook beneath his feet. He heard curses and prayers from the men around him. Gene did neither. He didn't care anymore. No rosary beads this time. He had nothing. Gene drew in a shaky breath, then relaxed and leaned against the side of the boxcar.

If I'm to die now, then let it be done.

CHAPTER 12

Kriegie

September 2012

Carmen had a string of good days in September. Her speech was clear. She even walked with me a quarter mile to visit a neighbor. The familiar days of the week had lost their significance now that we were dealing with late-stage cancer. There were no Sundays or Mondays. There were only good days or bad days.

One morning, Carmen stopped me after I rolled out of bed. It was 6:00 a.m. and time to get the boys off to school.

"You rest," Carmen said, not stuttering as she spoke. "I'll be darned if I can't even make the boys breakfast."

She boiled oatmeal on the stove. I watched her from the living room. More than once, she turned and braced her arms on the kitchen island. I sat on the couch, knowing she wouldn't want me to rescue her. She set out two glasses and poured orange juice. Then she pulled ham and cheese slices from the refrigerator to make sandwiches for the boys' lunch boxes. Before she opened the bread bag, she called for help. I sprang up and walked her back to the couch. She'd only been graced with a few good minutes.

A week later, though, Carmen had a string of good days. Her spunk got me thinking about Gene again, though I hadn't seen him since the Swedos' visit a month earlier. Could I possibly squeeze in an interview? I hesitated to ask. Her accusation a month earlier that I cared more about the book than my family still stung. But Gene was ready to talk these days, and the Swedo visit would still be fresh in his mind. I could only guess the vital information Gene may have shared with the Swedo family after I'd left. Carmen and I sat on the couch and folded laundry while I summoned the courage to ask.

"Any chance I could sneak down to visit Gene this week?"

"Give him a big hug and kiss from me," Carmen answered.

My heart leapt. Not just for the chance to visit Gene, but even more, for Carmen. The sweet, compassionate Carmen was back, at least for a moment. I almost said, "Just one more interview, promise," but I caught myself. What did one more interview mean? One more before what?

I'd only had one "Thursdays with Gene" since our spring visit to his home farm. We'd just started going over his time as a prisoner of war. I was anxious to get back to those stories. Now sitting again at Gene's kitchen table after such a long gap, I wondered if he'd open up again.

"You know," Gene added. "I don't remember our crew in all our time together having one argument, other than that time with Langley."

"Did you have that kind of camaraderie in the prison camps?"

"I tell you what. It was humanity at its best. When the new guys came, the old-timers made us feel welcome. They showed us our bunks, everyone threw in a couple of cigarettes or a little of something else. They made you feel welcome."

I made it a one-beer interview and dashed back home. Carmen was sleeping on the living room couch when I returned. We'd always discussed my talks with Gene. Waiting for her to wake, I had no idea when I'd share new Gene stories again.

We weren't the only ones fighting cancer. In early November, Chucky Herbst, a former student of mine, lost his battle to a rare form of skin cancer. He was twenty-eight. I asked a neighbor to stay with Carmen so I could attend the funeral.

Even a half hour before the funeral service, the only open seat was upstairs in the balcony of the Lutheran church. I squeezed in on the end of a wooden pew. I stared down at the slender, wood-grain cross mounted on the wall behind the altar. Its wooden silence matched the still body in the open casket.

It didn't make sense seeing Chucky lying there. He was an athlete, a sprinter, a leaper. In his school years, he ran track and played football, scoring the very first touchdown in my first game as a middle school coach. The play call was I-left, 47 Sweep. I remembered his eyes wide-open with delight and surprise when he darted around a tight end and saw nothing but open grass.

Nearby, a baby fussed. The child was dressed in a blue and gray Detroit Lions outfit, the blue lion prancing on his chest. I recognized the young mother, another former student and classmate of Chucky's. She was perched on the aisle steps. I offered her my seat.

"It's okay, Mr. A. He won't sit still there."

"He's grumpy because he knows he's in Packer country," said a gravelly voice. I turned to see it was the man next to me speaking. He was a thickset, gray-haired man about sixty years old. He stuck out his hand.

"Tom Moran," he said.

Moran? I thought I'd met all the Morans in Soldiers Grove.

"Do you know Gene Moran?"

"That would be my father."

Gene had four sons. How could I have not known Tom was one of them? He had that same rounded head and stocky build. Even the growl in his voice was similar to Gene's.

We talked in hushed tones as more friends and neighbors packed the church to standing room only. I mentioned the book and Carmen's cancer. How interviews had been called off. Tom gave me a sympathetic look and said Joni had been keeping him up to date.

"We left off this spring talking about his time as a prisoner. Do you know anything about his POW days?"

Tom leaned toward me and dropped his voice.

"Don't ask me. I hardly know anything. My whole life he only talked to me about the war twice, and both times he was drunk."

February 1944

Gene hated marshalling yards. Another train yard, another wait. Trains were easy targets for Allied planes when they sat waiting to hook up to a new engine. He'd already sweated through two British nighttime air raids. Luckily, no bomb had exploded near his boxcar.

In the morning, the train lumbered out of the station and continued its long journey east. It had been nearly a week since Gene left Frankfurt. Rolling through the countryside in the swaying boxcar, he guessed where he was. Geography was his favorite subject in school. He'd always liked studying maps, so he had some idea of their location. He figured they had to be through Germany and into Poland by now. This was mixed news. Traveling deep into the east of Nazi-occupied Europe put the train beyond the range of Allied bombers. Yet, it also made the chance for escape more out of reach. The further east they traveled, the further away from the air bases in England.

Discipline amongst the fifty POWs in the boxcar was good. There was no shoving or complaining despite being jammed into the boxcar shoulder to shoulder. The prisoners continued taking turns to sit. They all used the correct corner to urinate. The rhythmic clickity-clack of the boxcar wheels rolling over the tracks made Gene drowsy.

He dozed off leaning against Shorty's shoulder. Another man leaned against Gene. Most of the prisoners slept standing up.

When they weren't sleeping, Gene and Shorty discussed what lay ahead of them. They had no idea where they were going or how long it would take. Wherever they ended up, they guessed they'd be prisoners for at least a year, maybe two. Being tail gunners, they both knew the huge losses the Americans were suffering in the air war. Shorty said that before he was shot down, he'd heard the American army was having a tough time down in Italy.

The train ride stretched into its seventh day. The prisoners never left the boxcar other than for quick breaks at train yards to relieve themselves. Even if Gene didn't have to go, he jumped off the boxcar just for the chance to move around. No prisoner dared an escape attempt during these breaks. Guards toting machine guns watched their every move.

The train finally came to a stop at a town called Heydekrug. It was located in East Prussia, north of Poland, on the old Prussian-Lithuanian border about fifteen miles from the Baltic Sea. Immediately after stumbling off the boxcars, German soldiers formed the prisoners into a column for the three-mile march to their new prison: Stalag Luft 6.

Gene didn't mind the march in the cold, late-February weather. He was tickled to have solid ground under his feet, and it felt so good to be outside. When the column passed through Heydekrug, local inhabitants came out to gaze at the Americans. A few hurled the usual insults: "terrorfliegers," "luftgangsters." The prisoners marched to a forested area outside the town. Gene saw watchtowers, then a double row of barbed wire. They must be nearing his new home.

The column entered through the main gate. Prisoners in the compound gathered around the new arrivals. To Gene, the inmates appeared clean, but thin. He glanced around his new home. Two rows of barbed-wire fences surrounded three large compounds of barracks. The weathered, grayish-brown brick buildings looked as depressing as his barracks at Sandbostel. A water tower sat near the center of the camp. The only color within the compound was a red Nazi flag flying atop a tall pole.

The guards herded the prisoners onto a large parade ground. Gene noticed the soldiers in the camp were older, like those at Sandbostel. A middle-aged German soldier who spoke English read off names and numbers, assigning each prisoner to his quarters. Gene heard his name read out in the barracks list. And then—what luck!—he heard the guard read out, "Harold Cyr." Shorty would be in the same barracks! They'd be roommates.

Before heading to their rooms, the prisoners were marched to a large commons building with toilets and showers. The guards ordered the men to strip and moved them to the shower room. Cold water splashed over Gene's naked body. He noticed a smell in the water. It was delousing fluid.

Gene and Shorty's barracks was filled with about sixty prisoners. Bunks ringed the perimeter of the large, open room. On one end sat a potbellied stove. On the other end, a small room housed several buckets that the prisoners used for toilets at night. The room already looked full, but Gene and Shorty managed to find an empty double-decker bunk. Gene took the bottom bed. He looked at the mattress: a gunnysack filled with straw.

Gene and Shorty met the barracks chief their first day.

"So I hear you're the man who falls from the sky," the chief quipped.

How could his story have arrived at Stalag Luft 6 before he did? Gene was shocked and puzzled.

"This is George Fisher."

A prisoner put out his hand. Gene shook it, stunned. George Fisher! The man he'd met in the hospital at Sandbostel. The wounded waist gunner who'd actually witnessed Gene fall. That explained how the story got to Stalag Luft 6 before he did. Gene smiled, but averted his eyes. George's left eye socket was an ugly twist of scarred flesh. Gene remembered how he'd held George down while the Serbian doctors pulled metal shrapnel out of George's head. The operation had saved his life but left him disfigured. George also stuttered when he spoke, and bandages still wrapped his hands three months after he was shot down. Gene watched George's eyes to see if he peered at his bald head and jagged head scar.

"Roll call is twice a day, sometimes three," the barracks leader explained, going over the prison's rules. "Don't be late. There's a compound for British and Canadian prisoners. You can mingle with them during the day, but don't go into their barracks."

Each barracks had a chief and assistant to the chief. Both men were prisoners elected by their fellows to report to the MOC—Man of Confidence—who served as a liaison to the German commandant. No prisoner at Stalag Luft 6 was an officer. The camp had been built specifically to house noncommissioned Allied airmen. The Germans prized hierarchical order, even among their POWs, and kept the enlisted men separate from officers. The Man of Confidence himself was also an enlisted prisoner.

There was also an intelligence director, a secret position among prisoners. The intelligence director gathered war news and gave the prisoners a daily briefing. He got his news from many sources: clips of broadcasts gleaned from secret radios about the camp, snippets of overheard conversations, and barely audible whispers from German guards who had a fondness for American cigarettes.

"Be careful who you talk to," the intelligence director warned Gene and Shorty. "The goons plant snitches posing as kriegies to get information from you new guys."

Goons. The term used for the German guards. Gene also learned the prisoners called themselves "kriegies," the German slang for POWs. One group of kriegies Gene was told never to get near were the Russian prisoners housed in the back of the prison yard. "Worse than dogs" was how the barracks chief described their treatment by the goons.

Now that the rules and pecking order of the barracks had been explained, Gene and Shorty had a chance to meet other kriegies. Cliff Barker was one of the first to be introduced. Before the war, he played college basketball at Kentucky University before dropping out to join the Air Corps. Gene figured the lanky 6'2" aerial gunner would play basketball again if they all survived this war. Then there was Six-Toe Nigel, who had six toes on his left foot and didn't mind showing them off. Some of the "old-timers" who'd been POWs for a few months or more slipped cigarettes to Gene and Shorty or tossed over a tin of powdered milk from their Red Cross packages.

Life now settled into a routine of staving off hunger and boredom. Plus lice. In just a few days at Stalag Luft 6, the tiny parasites crawled underneath Gene's t-shirt. He hated lice and spent hours in his bunk picking them off his body.

"Hey, Shorty," Gene yelled up to the top bunk. "Between you and me, if we pick enough of them, we could make soup."

All the kriegies were hungry. In Gene's barracks, the men took turns each morning going to the "slop house" to bring back a twelve-quart pail of barley soup to be shared by sixty men. At noon, another kriegie would haul in a bucket of cabbage or rutabaga soup. In the evening, a loaf of bread would come with the soup ration. One loaf to be split by sixty men. It was the same black, sawdust-filled ersatz bread Gene had gnawed on at Sandbostel and Dulag Luft spread with the same black "coal jam." Food became an obsession. Prisoners fantasized about food far more often than they talked about women or sex.

Gene began losing weight. He cinched up the rope that held up his pants a little more each day. It would have been worse without the Red Cross parcels that were shipped into Germany by the Swiss Red Cross. The Germans distributed the food packages about once a week.

When Gene received his first Red Cross package, he went to his bunk and ripped open the cardboard box like an orphan on Christmas morning. Out spilled toothpaste, a toothbrush, toilet paper, a razor, shaving cream, cigarettes, and best of all, cans of food. The bounty included condensed milk, canned salmon, Spam, crackers, jam, and raisins. All the prisoners saved the condensed milk cans. Their rounded shape made them perfect for soup bowls or a shaving basin. The kriegies called them "Klim" cans.

The Red Cross also delivered packages and letters from home. Gene was thrilled when he opened a bundle from his mother that contained underwear, a sweatshirt, and tennis shoes. From his mother's own hands! And he sorely needed the clothes. The clothes on his back were all that he had, and they'd been issued back at Sandbostel. Gene knew he didn't receive everything his family or the Red Cross sent him. Sometimes his cigarette packs were opened or the bars of soap would be cut in half. At roll call, he'd look around wondering which German soldier it was who smelled like homemade soap from Soldiers Grove.

But what Gene and all the kriegies longed for as much as food were letters. Gene could endure sawdust-laced bread and watery rutabaga soup, but news from home was as sacred as a decent piece of bread. In one letter, Gene's mother wrote to tell him how the family had traveled to Madison to receive Gene's Air Corps Medal. The medal was presented to Gene's parents in a special ceremony at Truax Field. Hundreds of soldiers stood at attention when the officer in charge read out Staff Sergeant Eugene Moran's accomplishments and called him an "air raid hero."

Gene enjoyed hearing of his recognition, but another letter from his mother meant even more. Mom wrote about recent visitors they'd had. The parents of *Rikki Tikki Tavi*'s pilot, Linwood Langley, had driven all the way from Massachusetts to visit the Moran farm. Mom wrote that the Langleys had used up all their gas ration stamps to reach the Kickapoo Valley. "Oh, how Langley's father loved to climb the hills around the barn," she wrote.

Gene was stunned. He didn't like Langley. But he remembered

the skill his pilot had displayed getting their plane to land in a narrow pass in Greenland. He thought back to the raid on Bremen. Langley had said nothing when *Rikki Tikki Tavi* fell back. But somehow, he managed to keep the plane level during the chaos of screaming wounded and constant gunfire from German fighter planes. How did he do it? Did he expend his last breaths giving his men a chance to bail out?

Gene opened a notebook with a blue cover that his mother had included in one of her packages. Across the first two blank white pages, he sketched eight caskets. Above each casket, he drew a cross. Underneath each memorial, he printed the names of the dead of *Rikki Tikki Tavi*. Then in puffy balloon letters, he wrote "IN MEMORY OF MY BUDDIES." On the bottom, he finished with "THUS THY ART TO DUST RETURN, BUT THE GOAL IS NOT THE GRAVE."

Gene spent a lot of time writing in his notebook. He recorded the addresses of everyone in his barracks. The kriegies had already discussed plans for a reunion when the war was over. He meticulously sketched his barracks building, drawing the wooden crossbeams across the brick walls at precise angles and shading in each brick. He wrote poems, mostly from other prisoners: "A Burst of Flak," "Jerry Stew," "Dear Draft Dodger."

And "Mother."

When you didn't have a single thing
'Cept two small arms to play.
She nursed you into childhood
And taught you how to pray.

Writing and sketching helped Gene stave off "barbed wire disease." That's what prisoners called the overwhelming boredom of prison life. Combatting boredom was just as important as outsmarting starvation. Having grown up on a dairy farm where he worked from sunup to sundown, Gene never had so much free time. But here, besides cleaning his barracks area, there was little to do. The Germans left the kriegies to themselves. The camp commandant adhered to the rules of the Geneva Convention that forbade officers and noncommissioned officers to work as slave labor, so there was no work either.

Shorty drew pictures of airplanes. Gene played cards with his barracks mates. He taught them how to play euchre and cribbage, and he learned canasta and bridge. Marty Stachowiak, the other waist gunner on George Fisher's plane, tried to teach Gene how to speak Polish. Gene could only remember "dzienkuje," Polish for "thank you." Some of the men put on plays or variety shows in the barracks. Gene never participated, but he hooted and hollered at the actors playing female roles.

Gene believed rural kids could take prison life better. Most country boys like him had grown up without electricity, so they were used to long, dark nights. Many had also been raised on farms where monotony was a way of life, especially in the winter. Whenever Gene sensed one of his comrades getting edgy, close to losing it, he'd let the barracks chief know. The chief would put his arm around the shaky prisoner and head outside for a "walk and talk."

Sundays were the most depressing days, even for the country boys. Sunday was a day of rest back home. Gene missed riding horses with his cousins. He craved a Sunday dinner after Mass at St. Philip's. How nice it would be to sit next to Mom in clean clothes in a warm church. Gene wondered if his parents still got together with neighbors for Sunday night dances.

Gene did get to hear Mass sometimes. A mysterious priest known as Father Lynch would show up unannounced once or twice a month and perform Mass in the barracks. Some said he traveled with the Red Cross, but Gene noticed he always came to Stalag Luft 6 alone. Gene and Shorty both walked with Father Lynch along the perimeter fence to tell him their confessions. Father Lynch also took troubled prisoners for long walks, whether they were Catholic or not. The priest would discuss sports, movies, anything to get the men talking. Gene and Shorty enjoyed Father Lynch's company and always said yes when he asked, "One more lap, boys?" The next day, the priest would vanish as mysteriously as he'd arrived.

The highlight of Gene's day was the intelligence briefing. News from the battlefront was all-important. Any good news from the Allies meant one day closer to liberation. There were secret radios hidden in barracks all over Stalag Luft 6. Skilled radiomen patched together receivers using truck batteries and parts from German Army field radios. They secretly bartered for this equipment from German soldiers in exchange for cigarettes. Intelligence leaders met secretly to listen to BBC broadcasts from England. Then they'd scribble notes onto scrap paper and hurry back to their respective barracks.

Each evening, Gene and Shorty gathered with other prisoners around the center table where the intelligence leader sat. One prisoner stood by the door on the lookout for German guards. First the leader reviewed the air war: targets and airplane losses from both sides. Then he moved on to battlefronts in Italy and Russia. Gene's spirits soared when he heard the list of cities captured by the Allies.

Secret radios weren't the only source of news. New prisoners brought up-to-date war developments. The kriegies made a point to hang out by the main gate when the Germans brought in more prisoners. One day, Gene and Shorty stood with a throng of prisoners by the gate, all shouting out their home states. Someone yelled back, "Wisconsin!" Gene looked over and locked glances with a haggard-looking Air Corps gunner.

Bill Dorgan!

Bill Dorgan, the farmhand who'd once sat under a shade tree eating lunch with Gene on a break during Gene's milk truck delivery days. He staggered over to Gene.

"Moran! What the hell are you doing here?"

"I was about to ask you the same thing!" Gene yelled.

Bill couldn't conceal his limp. His cheeks were hollow, his face gaunt. Gene could feel Bill staring at his scarred head.

"We call him 'Baldy' around here," offered Shorty, and stuck out his hand.

But the next moment, soldiers were pushing them away, marching the new arrivals to the delousing showers.

"I'll find you later," Gene shouted as Bill limped away.

Gene hurried to his barracks to find the chief. He begged him to do whatever it took to get Bill assigned to their quarters.

"I'll see what I can do," the chief replied. "Go get your cigarettes, Baldy."

The next day in their barracks, Gene and Shorty showed Bill to his bunk, a spare bed they'd hauled over from another building. Gene didn't know for sure what the barracks leader had to do to get Bill assigned to the same quarters. But giving up his cigarettes for the chief to barter for Bill's new address was a small price to have a Wisconsin friend nearby. Bill sat on his bed and shared his story.

He was a waist gunner on a B-24 Liberator bomber that had been shot down March 18, 1944, in a raid over Friedrichshafen, Germany. He'd bailed out of the burning plane, but broke his right leg when he landed on a warehouse roof. Four other downed Americans found Bill and wrapped his leg with their shirts. The five airmen evaded capture for nearly a month.

"I was so damn hungry, I was kind of glad the Krauts caught us," Bill said.

But he didn't go straight to prison. After a doctor bound his leg in a brace, he was assigned to a work camp where he was sent out to gather dead bodies after air raids. The Germans once forced him to enter a bunker that had been hit by a bomb to pick up all the body parts. Then they sent him to Dulag Luft, where he survived solitary confinement for fifteen days. All this before he finally rode the boxcar on the long train ride to Stalag Luft 6.

Gene and Shorty gave Bill a few tins of canned food before leaving him to rest. Gene was worried about how skinny Bill was.

"He's in tough shape," Gene confided to Shorty. "We gotta do something."

For the next few weeks, Gene and Shorty always tore off part of their bread ration to give to Bill and poured some of their soup into his Klim can. Gene remembered Bill always sharing his sausage sandwich during those summertime lunch breaks back home three years ago. Munching on those sandwiches, the boys had wondered how they'd ever get off the farm. Now they were reunited. Would they ever see a red Wisconsin dairy barn again?

Some kriegies weren't willing to wait for the war to end to escape Stalag Luft 6. They took matters into their own hands. Tunnel digging had been going on since the moment Gene first arrived. He wasn't privy to it at first. The "old-timers" didn't share their tunneling scheme with the new guys until they trusted them. Gene was now part of that select committee.

Stalag Luft 6 was the farthest north and east Allied POW camp. Escape options were limited. One route had an escapee head east in the hope of reaching Russian lines. But that meant getting caught in the crossfire of the savage fighting on the Eastern Front, and there was no telling what the Russians would do with a prisoner lucky enough to get past the battlefront. The other choice was to head south and west searching for a boat ride to neutral Sweden. To many kriegies, the idea of trekking hundreds of miles through East Prussia and Poland while living on a few slices of sawdust bread and a can of Spam stuffed in a coat pocket seemed ludicrous. Even if an escapee somehow avoided capture, he'd still have to locate resistance fighters to ferry him across the Baltic Sea. Yet despite the odds, many prisoners wanted to try. Some felt it their duty to get back to the war.

The barracks leader and the tunneling committee determined the candidates for escape. Gene didn't make the list. He wasn't upset. His jagged head scar didn't help his case as a man healthy enough to hike hundreds of miles dodging German soldiers. His broken forearms, still on the mend, even kept him off the tunnel digging crew. But the tunneling committee had a job for Gene. He'd serve as a lookout for German guards.

Tunneling operations began underneath a latrine in a building located in the center of the prison camp. One toilet hole wasn't used by the prisoners. It was the entryway to a tunnel. On his first day at lookout, Gene ambled by the latrine, making small talk with Bill and Shorty. A pair of German guards marched around the corner of a barracks. Gene quickly stepped inside the latrine. "Goons up! Get a cover on that toilet."

Gene walked back outside, feigning zipping up his pants. The guards passed by. After a few days, Gene figured the Germans were getting suspicious, so he'd vary the timing of his visits to the latrine and walk different routes to get there. Gene loved the cat and mouse game. It passed the time.

One day, the tunnel committee sent Gene to the digging site with bed slats shoved into his pants. The wooden boards propped up the sides of the tunnel. They also attached bags with strings inside Gene's pants and gave him his instructions. After Gene dropped off the boards, tunnel diggers poured dirt into Gene's pants. He left the latrine building and strolled over to the makeshift basketball court. While walking, he slowly pulled the string on the sacks, letting the dirt slide down his lower legs.

The tunnels weren't the only escape route. Another method was to simply walk out the front gate dressed as a German soldier. Again, Gene stood guard. He'd keep a lookout at the door while other men tailored replicas of German Army uniforms. Gene couldn't believe how authentic they looked.

Three to four men made escape attempts every month. When a prisoner dressed in a fake uniform and strolled out the front gate, Gene prayed in his barracks. He strained his ears, hoping every passing second that he wouldn't hear the crack of a rifle.

When escapees took off, prisoners back at camp covered for them at roll call. Prisoners shouted out "here" when guards called the escapee's name and then ran to their own barracks group to step in line.

Runaways made it. The BBC reported a few successful escapes, but any news about escapees was usually bad. Once, a group of twelve left Stalag Luft 6 together. A few days later, Gene reported for a special roll call called by the camp commandant. German soldiers paraded six of the escapees, hands bound behind their backs in front of the assembled prisoners. All was quiet before the camp commandant spoke.

"The other six have been shot," the commandant said in English. He pointed to the six survivors. "How foolish of these men to even try."

The captured men were sentenced to solitary confinement. The commandant then walked back and forth, lecturing that anyone caught escaping would be shot on the spot. Gene couldn't understand why the six survivors had been spared. Then the commandant ordered the entire camp to be locked down with no food for two days. No one was to leave their barracks, not even to use the latrine.

Violating a lockdown, even accidentally, could be deadly. One morning in May, a prisoner assumed a lockdown was finished. With a towel slung over his head, he strolled across the open ground of the compound, headed toward the latrine. From a guard tower, without warning or an order to halt, a rifle cracked. The prisoner crumpled to the ground, dead. When word got around of the shooting, more than two hundred prisoners gathered at the commandant's office to protest the murder. Many of the barracks leaders considered the commandant a stern but reasonable man. But nothing was done. The Germans claimed the prisoner was trying to escape and the killing was justified.

In early June 1944, news came that shelved many escape plans. BBC radio reported that the Allies had invaded western France.

D-Day had finally come! The German Third Reich was now caught in a vise between the Western Allies and the Russian front. The intelligence officer had few details about the success of the landing, but Gene didn't care. He excitedly made guesses with Shorty and Bill when they might all be back in Wisconsin, maybe before Christmas. Prisoners who'd been planning to escape changed their minds. Why risk getting shot when liberation was so near?

The warm summer weather also improved morale around camp. After being penned up during a long winter, Gene soaked up the sun along with the other kriegies. The nice weather also brought some new entertainment. They set up a boxing ring between the American compound and the British area. Gene joined hundreds of other POWs to watch the fights. They'd only last three rounds. Living on meager rations, the boxers didn't have the energy to go much further. While watching the fights, Gene remembered Father Mathieu teaching him and the other boys in Sunday school the sweet science. He hankered to go a few rounds with some British flier, but his boxing days ended the second Luftwaffe bullets shot through his forearms.

Playing fast-pitch softball was also out of the question. When softballs and bats came to Stalag Luft 6 via donations by the YMCA, kriegies immediately set up a field. Barracks formed teams and even set up leagues that would play for the Stalag Luft 6 championship. Baseball was Gene's favorite sport in high school. He couldn't play, but he volunteered to umpire the games. Before each game, Gene would go over the foul lines with team captains and tell them he'd do the best he could calling out fair and foul balls.

The games went on all day. One kriegie who often relieved Gene was Augie Donatelli. Augie was a coal miner from Pennsylvania who'd also been a Flying Fortress tail gunner.

"Baldy, if a ball rolls to the fence, tell the captains to have everyone settle down and make sure the outfielders throw up their hands," Augie warned.

The fence was a low-slung barbed wire about a foot off the ground. Anyone crossing that line could be shot. Players were to wait for the guard in the "Goon Tower" to wave a flag, allowing the player to retrieve the ball. After a man had been gunned down a month earlier for going to the latrine too early, no one chased a fly ball over the wire, no matter how competitive the game.

One day, Gene was called in from the playing field to report to his barracks. Three men and two women dressed in Red Cross uniforms were already there. Gene was puzzled. He sat down at a table opposite the Red Cross team. They told him the Red Cross was putting together a list of POWs to be repatriated, sent home to America in exchange for German prisoners. The Luftwaffe had agreed to release twenty of the most seriously wounded Americans at Stalag Luft 6. Gene was a candidate.

This couldn't be true. The Germans releasing him from prison? Sent home during the war? From sawdust bread to Mom's fried chicken and homemade baked beans? Gene was stunned. He tried to focus as they interviewed him about his wounds. Gene told his story, the air battle above Bremen, his fall without a parachute, and his medical care at Sandbostel. One of the team members was a doctor. He walked over to Gene and carefully probed his head scar and examined his arms.

"Did you have any other injuries to report?"

"The ribs on my left side were all broken the day I was shot down."

"Do the ribs bother you now?"

"No."

"Can you walk without trouble?"

Gene's lower back still bothered him, but he told the doctor he could move around just fine.

When Gene returned to the barracks later, the chief informed him that the Red Cross team classified Gene as the first alternate on the repatriation list.

"If someone on the list dies, you get to go home," the chief explained.

Gene didn't know how to feel. The thought of going home seemed like a dream. But a comrade would have to die for that to happen. He tried to block repatriation out of his mind. A few weeks later, the barracks chief told George Fisher to pack his belongings. He said nothing to Gene. Gene wasn't too disappointed. He knew George was in rougher shape than he was. He thought back to the hospital in Sandbostel when the Belgian interpreter told Gene the shrapnel stuck in George's skull was so close to his brain. Every time Gene talked with George, his speech seemed more slurred, his mood more bizarre.

On a hot July afternoon, Gene stood behind a squatting kriegie who was playing catcher. Gene watched the pitcher go into his windup, getting ready to call "strike! or "ball!" The sound of approaching airplanes broke the ball game chatter. German planes often flew over Stalag Luft 6; those were nothing new, and players rarely bothered to pause the game. But these planes sounded different. Four planes in formation roared over the softball field.

"Look!" someone screamed. "Red stars!"

Gene broke his gaze from the pitcher and looked up. Red stars. Russian planes!

The softball game stopped. Excited men returned to their barracks. Gene and the other kriegies gathered around the chief and the intelligence leader who sat at the center table.

The leaders tried to take stock of the situation. They knew that the Soviet Red Army had launched a summer offensive against the Germans a few weeks ago, but no one knew where it was or if the attack was succeeding. But these Russian planes that had just buzzed Stalag Luft 6's ball field had given all the intelligence they needed. The Red Army's summer offensive was sweeping through East Prussia.

Their world was changing. The Russians were coming.

CHAPTER 13

The Bowels of Hell

November 2012

After ten years of nervously waiting for appointments with on-cologists to go over the latest brain scans, Carmen and I had seen our share of waiting rooms. Most were pleasant, with cushioned chairs and classical music playing overhead. My favorite was the waiting area at Mayo Clinic's Gonda Building. It had plush leather chairs set next to large windows overlooking downtown Rochester. From here I could see the Plummer Building across the street from Gonda. That architectural masterpiece with its terra-cotta trimmed tower stood out from the modern steel and glass structures that surrounded it. The way the sun hit that gold-colored brick building illuminated it like something out of Oz.

When Carmen and I were called into the examining room, the nurse went through the usual routine of checking her pulse and blood pressure. Sitting next to Carmen, I stared at the white sheet of paper stretched out over the padded examining table. At past ap-pointments, the procedure was always the same. After checking her vitals, a nurse would have Carmen put on a hospital smock. Soon after, the oncologist would arrive and go straight to the computer to show us the latest brain scans. Then Carmen would sit on the table, where the doctor would massage her back, neck, and remaining breast, looking for any unusual lumps while I stared at the floor hoping not to hear any pause or disruption from the routine.

But this time, the nurse didn't ask her to change into a hospital smock.

When the oncologist walked in, she sat down by the computer, but didn't turn it on.

"I've reviewed your latest scans, and the cancer is progressing," she stated flatly, yet holding a polite smile.

And then Carmen brought up THE question she had refused to ask in her decade of fighting breast cancer.

"How long do I have?" she asked.

"At this stage," the doctor replied, "four or five months, my dear. But these tumors started this summer, so it may be sooner."

Our battle with cancer was over. There was no reason to return to Mayo Clinic anymore. Heading out of the waiting room, I took in one more look at the Plummer Building. I didn't know if I'd ever see it again, so many things to say goodbye to. The tower glowed, reflecting the afternoon sun. It was strange how the weather was always beautiful when we came to Rochester.

We drove home without saying a word. We didn't cry. We knew. We knew before the appointment. Now the boys had to know.

I wasn't sure how much they'd already figured out. That I'd taken leave from teaching had to have given them a clue that things were serious. We met in the living room the evening we returned from Mayo Clinic. Carmen sat next to Joe, now eleven years old, on the love seat, stroking his hair. Matthew, fourteen, and I lay back on the couch.

"When are you guys going back to Rochester?" Matthew asked. A usually mundane question considering it had become a second home for us in the second half of 2012.

"We won't be going back," I replied.

That immediately got Joe's attention.

"Why aren't you going back?" Joe asked. Matthew didn't say anything, but slumped into the couch.

Carmen stayed silent too. Her speech had become so slurred that she let me do all the talking.

"There's nothing more the doctors can do, guys. The cancer is spreading," I said.

"Is Mom going to die?" Joe asked in a voice quivering with emotion.

"We've done all we can, buddy," I replied.

Joe buried his head in his mother's lap. Matthew got up and walked into the office adjacent to the living room and sat by the computer. All was silent, save for Joe's quiet sobbing. I tried to explain the unexplainable.

"Guys, I'm sorry we waited, but we wanted to do everything we could before we told you," I said. "You have every right to be sad and angry. Just let it out. If you feel you have to scream or swear, we understand."

Joe jerked his head up from Carmen's lap. He stopped crying.

"We get to swear?" he asked.

I looked through the doorway to the office. Matthew sat still in the desk chair. He stared at a blank computer, his elbow resting on the desktop with his fist propping up his chin. No tears. Stoicism was how Matthew always coped with bad news. A few minutes later, he got up and returned to the middle of the living room.

"We have a lot of work to do. Thanksgiving and Christmas are coming," he said, looking at me.

I nodded. "I'm really going to need your help this year," I replied.

We still prepared for the holidays as we always had, except this year, the boys and I went to go cut the Christmas tree without Carmen. When we returned home with the tree, she directed all the decorating and tree trimming from the living room couch. She sat up against the arm of the couch and gave orders, her legs smothered in blankets. The nativity set had to be arranged to her exact standards on the shelf inside the bay window. Then came the annual argument about what color lights to use on the tree. The boys and I preferred the multicolored tree lights.

"I wa-wa- . . . I want white this year," said Carmen, struggling to talk through the slur. "You g-g-guys had colored t-t-two years in a row."

Matthew pulled me aside. "Dad. This is her last Christmas. Let's do the white lights."

A few weeks earlier in mid-November, the Mayo Clinic oncologist had said Carmen had several months left to live, maybe less. Our family physician did everything he could to get her to live through Christmas. Carmen now received all her care from our local hospital in Viroqua, the hospital where a doctor first showed us a mammogram of that five-centimeter lump in her right breast ten years earlier. In early December, with her appetite waning, our doctor ordered that Carmen go to the infusion clinic once a week for fluids. Once a week soon became twice a week.

Hospice workers visited our living room couch to check her vitals and give her sponge baths. They also brought a wheelchair. I didn't think we needed it, not yet. During the Thanksgiving weekend, Carmen went shopping with her sister on Black Friday. For a few hours, she was able to walk through the mall crowds with very little help. But by mid-December, I was lifting Carmen out of the car and setting her in the wheelchair before pushing her to the infusion clinic.

Eight days before Christmas, her digestive tract shut down. She returned to the hospital for an enema and an overnight stay. I brought Matthew and Joe with me. I assured them that Mom's overnight stay was routine and that she'd be back home the next day. That evening, the three of us gathered around Carmen lying in her hospital bed. She was having a good day. Her speech wasn't as slurred as she spoke with the boys recounting their school day. Matthew and Joe were eighth and fifth graders now, respectively. Both were excited with just four school days left before Christmas break. They kissed their mother good night before they left, both saying they'd see her after school tomorrow.

I got up to drive the boys home. Bending over the hospital bed and kissing Carmen good night, I said, "I'm going to sleep at home tonight. Do you mind? I'll be back in the morning after I get the boys off to school."

"N-n-n-no. G-g-go home. Get sleep. See you then," she answered.

The next morning, the world had shifted. When I walked into Carmen's hospital room, she glared at me.

"You! You!" she screamed, jabbing her index finger at me.

"Honey. What's wrong? I'm sorry I'm late. I . . ."

She cut me off. "Get out! Now!"

The eyes that scowled at me were not Carmen's. My wife had vanished. I faced the eyes of an enraged animal. I backed out of the room slowly and ran to the nurses' station. I returned with a young nurse. Carmen took one look at her. "Get out! Get out! I want home!"

Carmen kept jabbing her index finger at the nurse, who went to Carmen's bedside, checked her IV tubes, and spoke to Carmen in a reassuring, monotone voice.

My wife wasn't buying it.

"Leave me alone!" she yelled. She grabbed at her IV tubes, but the nurse's hands beat her to them. In a rage, Carmen ripped her hospital smock from her chest, exposing her left breast and the scar from her mastectomy on her right side.

"You. You. Get ooouuuuuuutttttttt!" she roared at the nurse.

The nurse looked at me. I looked at her. Neither of us knew what to do. Carmen did.

"Get out . . . both . . . you . . . I want out!" she screamed, jabbing her right arm and index finger at the air.

The nurse and I hurried back to the nurses' station. She was pale and couldn't speak. At the desk, she got on a phone and called for help. We could hear Carmen still screaming from her room.

Our family physician and a team of medical personnel rushed into Carmen's room. I lingered in the hallway, my back against the wall, eyes closed, listening to Carmen rage. After about ten minutes, the room became quiet. A short time later, the doctor came out to the hallway.

"John, this caught us off guard. The best way I can explain this is that she had a car accident in her brain. The cancer has crashed into areas affecting her personality and cognition," he explained.

"I don't care what you have to do," I demanded, "see to it that she NEVER, EVER suffers like that again."

He nodded. We both knew what this meant. It was time to let Carmen die.

Carmen was sedated and sleeping when I pulled up a chair next to the right side of her bed. She lay in a state of semi-coma. I pulled up a chair and sat next to her, resting my chin and cheek on the raised metal bed railing. My hands clutched the white hospital blanket that covered her. I stared at her face. Her eyes were closed, but her mouth was open. She panted as she breathed, like a landed fish gasping for water. But aside from her labored breaths, she was still. She offered no more resistance to the advancing cancer cells completing their conquest of her brain.

In the next two days, friends came to visit. Carmen's mother and sister drove to our home to stay. The hospital staff urged everyone to keep talking to her though she would probably never respond. A group of Carmen's closest friends gathered around her bed and gasped when she raised her left arm several inches above the bedcovers and then set it back down.

Joe took Wednesday off of school to sit with me in Carmen's

hospital room. Matthew chose to go to school. Joni joined us later that morning. She'd shown up at our house often that autumn with pasta dishes and assurances that Gene was praying for us. She sat next to Carmen and took out her rosary. I listened from my chair on the other side of the bed as Joni rhythmically worked the beads dangling from her hands and prayed quietly to herself.

While Joni was there, our parish priest, Father Bill, also joined us. I introduced Joni. "You'll have some help, Father. Joni's PC, Professional Catholic."

"We can use all the help we can get," he replied.

Father Bill set his hand gently on Joe's shoulder. "I'm going to give your mother a gift."

With the lights low in the room, Father Bill slung a purple stole over his shoulders. He unlocked a padded case and took out a small glass vial filled with blessed oil. He dabbed his right thumb with the oil and leaned over Carmen's bed. He crossed her forehead. He wetted his thumbs again with the oil, opened each of her palms and crossed them, praying aloud as he worked. He'd pause periodically to explain each part of the ceremony to my eleven-year-old son. I didn't understand any part of the sacrament. I just blankly nodded my head and later crossed myself when the ritual ended.

On Wednesday evening, Matthew joined Joe and me. It was just the three of us together with Carmen in her room. The pace of her breathing had slackened. I told the boys they had to talk to their mother . . . now . . . before they left for home for the night. They understood.

I sat next to the right side of Carmen's bed. Matthew stood on the other side, his hands slung in the pockets of his winter coat.

"Well. Goodbye, Mom. Love you," he said. No tears. No hug. He turned and walked out the door.

Joe's farewell replicated his brother's, at first. But after he left the room to follow Matthew, he turned around. He rushed back into the room, went to Carmen's bedside, and buried his face into the blanket covering her stomach. His shoulders heaved. I said nothing. I did not move from my chair. My eyes did not well up. I just stared.

Alone with Carmen for the second night, I turned off the lights after the boys left and sat next to my wife. I laid my head on her hip and turned my head toward her face. I couldn't say "I love you" as the boys just did.

"I miss you. I miss us," I said.

"I miss you. I miss us. I miss you. I miss us," I repeated. I said the same words over and over until I fell asleep.

Carmen died two nights later, Friday, December 21, the longest night of the year. It was the date the Mayan calendar predicted the world would end.

My wife had always both hated and loved the winter solstice. Long wintertime nights depressed her. But the solstice also signaled the farthest advance of night's domination over day. After the twenty-first, sunlight would begin to reclaim the day from the night sky, slowly . . . very slowly. A long winter still lay ahead.

July 1944

The Russians were coming. Every kriegie at Stalag Luft 6 knew it. When planes with red stars on their wings first buzzed the prison a week earlier, the POWs dared to be optimistic. But soon their hopes soared as high as those Soviet planes that now roared over the camp each day. Men cocked their ears to the booming sound of Red Army artillery from the east. Salvation was undeniable, maybe only a few days away. Gene's sunset walks with Shorty and Bill became a must for him now. He craved to be outside, soaking in the sound of freedom.

Every evening, Gene and his friends walked the well-worn interior path of the prison. Gene and Shorty kept the pace slow for Bill, who still limped. All three of them stifled their laughter at the guards patrolling along the fence, putting on a show of normality. What a farce! The Germans could hear the same thunderclaps of Russian cannons that heralded freedom for the kriegies. Gene and the others sifted through the rumors overrunning the prison. Soon, they would be liberated. But would it be in a week or a month? Would the Germans fight or run? How would the prisoners let the Russians know they were not the enemy?

Gene speculated the route they'd take back to their air bases in England once Russian tanks crashed through the prison gates, setting them free. He wondered how long he'd remain in England before returning to Wisconsin. He could almost taste the tin cup holding the coldest, clearest water in the world scooped up from the spring-fed creek behind his home farm. Maybe he'd be back by August just in time again for harvesting oats. He smiled, thinking Dad would have the horses harnessed and waiting for him the second he arrived, just like last summer when he returned home on leave.

Back in the center of his barracks after sunset, Gene sat around the rectangular wooden table with other kriegies. Some of the prisoners did laundry, getting ready for liberation day. The single incandescent light bulb hanging above the table barely illuminated the room, but he could still see men hanging washed socks, t-shirts, and underwear from bedposts and ropes strung from the corner walls. Gene glanced at the black heating stove set against the brick chimney, the coal bucket still next to it. He smirked. Next winter, he wouldn't be sitting here enduring another winter in a cold, drafty prison barracks.

Then the door burst open. It was the barracks chief. From the doorway, the chief stared at the men around the wooden table. "The Krauts are moving us out," he said. "You've got just two hours to pack. Carry only what you need."

Moving out?! His words crushed all hopes of liberation. The German commandant had ordered an immediate evacuation of Stalag Luft 6.

Gene and the other kriegies stood like statues, dumbfounded. They could still hear the approaching roar of Red Army artillery. Gene listened bitterly to the rumbling guns. Just a few minutes earlier, the sound had him dreaming of England and so much more: the ridges and valleys of Southwest Wisconsin, the home farm, and that tin ladle lifting to his lips ice-cold creek water.

The vision of that crystal clear liquid vanished.

"Where we going, Chief?" a prisoner cried.

The barracks chief stood silently, stiff and resigned. "I have no idea," he said finally, then left to begin his own packing.

Two hours. Instantly, the barracks turned to chaos as every POW scavenged the barracks for necessities. That meant food and toilet paper. Gene spread out a long-sleeved shirt on his bunk. On top of the shirt, he set toilet paper, his diary, a toothbrush, socks, underwear, a t-shirt, and, most importantly, his empty powdered milk tin—his Klim can. That was it. No sense carrying too much in the heat. He tied up the sleeves together in a bundle. But there wasn't a morsel of food in his pack. Other men had squirreled away a few Hershey bars, crackers, or cigarettes left over from Red Cross parcels. Gene looked over at Shorty's meager stash. "Sorry, Baldy," Shorty said. "I've got about as much food as you."

"Why don't they leave us to the Russians?" one prisoner groused. "We're just going to be a burden to the Krauts guarding us."

In his mind, Gene echoed those thoughts. *Why would the Germans keep us? Where would we go? Where will I be tomorrow, next week, next month?* He wondered if they would become hostages. Or maybe the Germans would shoot them outright. He shuddered. A month earlier, a rumor got around about a whole pile of American fliers being hung from lampposts in the streets of Berlin after being shot down.

Gene took stock of his health. It had been more than seven months since he came down in *Rikki Tikki Tavi*'s tail. Except for nighttime headaches, his fractured skull didn't bother him much. He had no pain in his forearms, even the crooked right one. But his back constantly ached. He passed his hand over the left side of his chest, following the dogleg shape of some of his ribs. He could feel his ribs more easily now. Like his right forearm, they had never straightened out either. A few crooked bones, a skinny body, an aching back and headaches, but overall, he believed he was in good shape. He could march.

It was Bill he worried about. Despite the extra rations Gene and Shorty managed to smuggle to him, Bill hadn't gained any weight since spring. That day he limped into Stalag Luft 6, he'd become a gaunt shell of himself. Four months later, he wasn't any better. His broken leg had never completely healed. Gene didn't think Bill could survive a forced march on that bum limb.

On July 14, Gene assembled with nearly two thousand captured American airmen in the predawn darkness in the far corner at the prison's main gate. He watched as some of the POWs, already realizing they'd packed too much, hurled a barrage of powdered milk tins, cans of salmon, books, and cigarettes over the fence to the British prisoners, who were leaving the next day.

Then the German guards yelled, "March!" and Gene, with Shorty right next to him, filed out of Stalag Luft 6.

Gene's stomach tightened. They were passing a sentry tower. An armed soldier in the tower box leaned out and looked over the departing captives. Gene neared the main gate. He trembled. Walking past this point yesterday would have meant a bullet in the back. He fought the urge to turn around and stare back at the tower. He marched forward, but winced as he walked, expecting at any moment to hear a rifle crack. The prison gates passed by, and the

column of kriegies moved out to the open road. No gunshots . . .
for now.

A few miles beyond the camp, the prisoner column wound
along a dusty road past locals with bewildered and hostile faces.
Some of the Germans shouted, "Terrorfliegers," or "Gangsters," or
"Schwein." Others threw stones. Gene peeked at their angry stares.
He was leaving while they were being left to their own fate in the
face of the Soviet onslaught.

The men left a mess as they marched on, littering the road
with ragged coats, torn clothing, and tin cans filled with powdered
milk. Their packs had become too heavy to carry under the rising
mid-July sun. Gene was glad he'd kept his gear light. He was also
thankful he'd made himself take all those evening perimeter walks
back at Stalag Luft 6 to keep his legs strong. And he was grateful for
his American tennis shoes that Mom had sent him in a Red Cross
package. The lightweight shoes were holding up, so far.

Several hours later, sweat-soaked and stumbling, the prisoners
descended into a train yard at the town of Heydekrug. Closed cattle
cars waited for them. German guards packed the prisoners into the
train cars. They rode several hours to Memel, a city on the Baltic
Sea. When the train arrived in the seaport town, the smell of salt air
briefly lifted Gene's spirits. But his face fell when the cattle car door
scraped open. He peered out onto the bay to see two rusty ships
docked portside. All the kriegies at the open boxcar door stepped
back and recoiled in horror. Gene thought, *This is it. This is finally it.
They're gonna pack us in there, send us out to sea, and sink us. Who'd
ever know?*

The German soldiers hustled the prisoners off the train cars and
rushed them to the dock. Embarking on the old coal freighters began
immediately. But the prisoners stopped short at the entrance to the
gangplank. Fear seized the men. German soldiers screamed, "March!"
Gene and Shorty waited in the back of the group and watched as the
first POWs in front of them trudged warily up the footbridge.

Gene looked over the decrepit ship, hardly believing it could float much less sail on the open sea. Rust stains streaked its hull. It sat in the water with a slight list. Even if it did stay afloat, it would be navigating waters dotted with British-laid mines and patrolled by Russian submarines. He studied the vessel. The ship had no German markings at all, but on the hull it displayed the Soviet hammer and sickle. It was a captured ship. But it didn't matter if the Soviets were allies: American or British airplanes could never see those markings. If anything, the pilots would probably guess the ships were German supply vessels and pursue them. They'd be floating targets.

There was nothing Gene could do. He climbed the gangplank with Shorty right behind him. They were ordered to drop their packs on the deck. Armed guards prodded them down a vertical steel ladder into the ship's dark hold.

Gene clambered halfway down the ladder and stopped. The stench overwhelmed his nose. He looked back up to see a German soldier with a cocked machine gun staring right back at him. Gene swallowed. He glared back at the guard and sucked in one more breath of salt air, then stepped down the ladder into the black abyss.

Gene lowered himself slowly into a mass of men writhing like worms in a bait can. He strained his eyes to see into the darkness. The ship's hull had no windows or portholes. The only light and ventilation came from the open hatch above the ladder. Gene guessed this wreck could hold a few hundred men, tops. But through the open hatch, men kept descending the ladder.

"There's no room! Goddammit, there's no room!" men screamed around him. Still, the Germans kept sending men down into the hold. About two thousand prisoners had left Stalag Luft 6, and it appeared the Germans were intent on packing all of them into the two derelict ships.

In the noise and confusion, Gene had lost Shorty. And where was Bill?

After just minutes on the ship, the heat became unbearable.

Sweat poured off Gene's body. He gasped for air. He tried to push his way to the cool steel of the hull, but everyone else had the same idea. He could hardly shove his way from the base of the ladder. One man fell off the ladder onto Gene. The impact knocked him to the floor. He scrambled back onto his feet. Three more prisoners had filled the spot he'd just lost. Gene adjusted his stance and tried to stand upright, squeezing into a space much too small for his body. There was nothing more he could do but get ready to endure.

Finally, the last POW clambered down the ladder. The Germans left open the small hatch door above the ladder. But still, it was the only source of light for the entire hold of the ship. The ship's engines sputtered to life, but in the near darkness, Gene couldn't make out where the engine room was located.

Just then, a primal shriek erupted from the crowd. Men screamed, "Back up! Back up!" The commotion came from near the gear room, the space between the gear assembly and the drive shafts.

"Back up! Back up!"

Then more screams. Inhuman screams. Ungodly shrieks as primal as any beast in its death throes. Gene stood petrified. He went inside himself and fixated on the rivulet of sweat trickling down the recessed path of his head scar. Finally, the terrifying squeals stopped, hanging suspended in the oppressive air.

Word of what had happened soon made its way back to him. The sweaty mass of kriegies had inadvertently pressed fellow prisoners into the gear workings. One man, maybe more, had just been ground up by the unflinching steel teeth of the ship's gears.

Gene closed his eyes. *Let go. There is nothing you can do. Endure this voyage on this ship of Hell.*

The two coal freighters jammed with human cargo churned west across the Baltic Sea. Gene leaned against the man next to him. Another man rested his sweat-soaked head on Gene's shoulder. None of the prisoners had tasted water since marching out of Stalag Luft 6. Gene wondered how much longer they could last before the air ran out, before the heat suffocated their dehydrated bodies, before another man got shoved into the gear room. A day? An hour? It was hot. He'd suffered through temperatures like this before, back home in the barn haymow where he'd pitch hay in stifling heat. But on the hell ship there was no escape. He thought again about pushing his way to the coolness of the steel hull. Men there licked the condensation droplets clinging to the ship's sides. But it wasn't worth the fight. Gene figured no one would give up such a prized spot.

The stink of human waste soaked his senses. This was not the same scent that came from cows that urinated and defecated during milking time. The hold of the hell ship had no toilets. Only one prisoner at a time was allowed up the ladder to relieve himself off the deck. Gene slowly shuffled with the others, making his way toward the ladder, his bladder bursting, his bowels churning. The crowd in front of him was too thick. He'd never make it. Urine pooled under Gene's shoes as men around him gave up and gave in. Gene stood just several yards from the ladder, but the mob in front of him barely moved. Gene lost control. He pissed and soiled the only pants he possessed.

The stench got worse. Lack of ventilation and rolling seas made most of the men clutch their stomachs. Gene hardly noticed when someone vomited onto his shirt. He'd already spilled his stomach on a guy next to him. Puke and bile were now added to the stew of shit and piss merging together on the ship floor.

Gene willed himself to ignore the stench. But no one could endure the thirst. The guards didn't dare go down into the dark hold. Instead, they lowered a bucket of water through the hatch. Gene stared at it. Precious water sloshed over the sides as the Germans clumsily lowered it to thirst-crazed kriegies. Men who'd been on deck to relieve themselves said these same pails were used for toilets. The Germans cleaned them by dipping them overboard in the seawater. Gene made no attempt to fight through the horde swarming at the base of the ladder for the water bucket.

The prisoners were at their breaking point. Gene turned, distracted by sudden movement and yelling by the ladder. A particularly agitated prisoner was scrambling up the ladder for his bathroom break. The man reached the hatch and disappeared. A few moments later, Gene heard rifle and submachine gun fire erupt from above.

Other prisoners returning from bathroom breaks had witnessed the man's fate. They shared the story that filtered through the throng to Gene. The crazed POW had run straight for the ship's rail and jumped overboard. German soldiers machine-gunned him before he hit the water. The hell ship chugged on. The Germans made no attempt to recover the body.

The hours dragged for the entombed men. Gene had no sense of time other than when the open hatch above the ladder was light or dark. That first night of the voyage, he couldn't see his hand in front of his face. But daylight only brought added misery. When the summer sun shined, it baked the ship's hull, turning the hold into an oven. The kriegies of Stalag Luft 6 were stewing, literally. Waves of heat emitting from the ship's steel sides swept over Gene. A constant river of sweat flowed from the top of his scarred head onto his face. It was his second day on the hell ship. Another day with no sleep, no water, no way to lie down.

The heat and stench thickened the air. It became difficult to breathe. *Stay calm, stay calm,* Gene told himself, sucking in each putrid breath. He'd been close to death before. He wasn't afraid to die. But the thought of dying in the middle of the Baltic Sea without a trace tormented him. Mom would never know what happened to her son. She would blame Dad the rest of his life for signing those Air Corps enlistment papers.

He stood in the filth and stared into the darkness. The men around him hardly talked now. Some moaned. A few mumbled prayers. Hour after hour, a few sounds remained consistent: the expulsion of gas and diarrhea from the bowels of men near him and the retching of other prisoners.

Boom!

The hull of the ship shuddered. Startled men snapped out of their delirium in a panic. What was the noise, the thud? A mine? A torpedo? For a split second, Gene expected the hull to burst into a cascade of fire and seawater. Did a Soviet submarine patrolling the Baltic have the hell ship lined up in its periscope? Were Allied aircraft floating above, waiting for the moment to pounce? Nothing happened. Silence. What was that banging noise that had every kriegie believing they'd die like drowned rats? Maybe they'd hit a dud mine or the floating wreckage of a downed plane. Now added to the heat, the stench, the thirst, each scrape of debris against the hull set off a flurry of panicked "goddammits." Misery punctuated with terror.

The hell ship sailed on. Another wave of heat emanating from the steel hull enveloped Gene. That meant a second night had passed, two nights, three days, and no sleep. Where were they going? How long could this go on? And where was Shorty? Was Bill even alive?

Gene wavered between rage and resignation. Would more men reach their breaking point and snap today? The whole group at once? But no one talked mutiny. It was impossible. A thousand men charging up a single steel ladder would be utter madness.

Something creaked above Gene. The sound came from the large hatch cover which enclosed the main opening to the cargo hold. All the men raised their heads. The noise got louder. A crack of light appeared above, and then the sky opened up before them. The Germans had removed the main hatch cover!

Fresh air poured into the black hold. Men shot their arms up and pawed their hands toward their faces, greedily gulping in the sweet air. Gene spotted a man at the edge of the hatch opening gazing down at the grateful prisoners. The man had a clerical tab at his neck and looked surprisingly familiar. It was Father Lynch! What was he doing here? The mysterious priest who'd always arrive unannounced at Stalag Luft 6 was on the hell ship. Gene thought he was hallucinating. Yet, there he was. Gene could clearly see him. This wasn't a dream.

The priest peered down into the blackness of the hold, scrutinizing the men. He said nothing. He disappeared as quickly as he appeared, but the main hatch stayed open.

Air! The opened hatch changed everything. Gene sucked in the fresh salt air. And light! Every kriegie in the hold looked up with squinted eyes and soaked in the blue summer sky. Waste and vomit still coated their clothes, but they could breathe. Some of the men even began to talk. Gene looked around for Shorty and Bill. It was still too crowded to move around and search for them.

After more than fifty hours, the hell ship sailed into the port of Swinemünde at the mouth of the Oder River in northeastern Germany near the city of Stettin. Guards yelled out a collection of loud orders. With wobbly legs, kriegies began climbing the ladder. Gene was thrilled to finally move. Whatever came next had to be better than what he'd just endured.

As Gene shuffled toward the ladder, he noticed some men flat on the floor, not moving. Had they suffocated? Died of dehydration? Gene had no idea. A few prisoners lingered by the stilled bodies lying in the muck of human waste and vomit.

"Eyes forward. March!" a German soldier screamed in English from the opened hatch. The prisoners next to their dead comrades didn't move. Gene looked over the dead men, fearing one of them might be Bill, maybe Shorty too. The soldier yelled again, pointing his machine gun down the hatch. "March!"

Gene tore his eyes away from the corpses on the ship's floor and followed the others clambering up the ladder. His legs were as stiff as his pants, which were now caked in dried shit and piss. Sunlight blinded him when he emerged from the ship. Guards pushed and shouted to keep the prisoners moving. Just in time, Gene's eyes adjusted to the daylight and he recognized his pack piled on deck. He grabbed it, but then spotted something more important: Shorty, on the gangplank, vomit-coated, drained, but alive.

They met at the bottom of the ship's gangplank and stared. Gene looked over Shorty's clothing covered in filth, wet and dry. He was a pathetic, revolting mess, and Gene knew he looked the same. They said nothing. Gene was relieved to have emerged from hell and to have found his buddy. They both looked around for Bill. Nothing.

On the dockside, German soldiers ordered the kriegies to take off their shoes and hold them. This was unusual. Gene figured a prisoner with bare feet can't run away as fast as an escapee wearing shoes. The soldiers then moved systematically amongst the POWs, handcuffing them together in pairs. Gene had never been shackled since becoming a prisoner. Why were the Germans doing this? He tried to block out the thought that maybe he was being prepped for execution. Gene moved close to Shorty and was thankful when a soldier linked them together. They both waited dockside for the Germans to finish chaining nearly a thousand prisoners.

Gene stood quietly. Next to him, prisoners whispered estimates about how many dead were left back on the hell ship. One guessed thirty. Another believed it was more than fifty. Gene had no idea. He wondered how many had died on the other ship. A rumor rippled through the filthy men that the SS were coming to take them and parade them past the citizens of Stettin. Gene trembled. He remembered his near death by stoning on the day he was shot down when his captors wheeled him on an ox cart through a mob of enraged German villagers.

"March!" a soldier yelled. With their wrists linked together, holding their shoes, and their packs tucked under their outside arms, Gene and Shorty shuffled to boxcars waiting not more than a hundred feet away from the dock. The German soldiers stuffed each boxcar with prisoners and slammed the door shut. No windows, no ventilation.

Again, Gene struggled to breathe the thick, suffocating air. He stood, swaying, his legs rubbery after his ordeal on the hell ship. And still nothing to drink. Gene hadn't sat down or tasted a drop of water since leaving Stalag Luft 6 three days earlier.

The prison train rattled east for five hours. In the late afternoon, it stopped next to a pine forest at a small railroad junction called Kiefheide. Above the squeaking and banging of coupled boxcars coming to a halt, Gene heard a new sound: barking . . . savage barking. When the boxcar doors slid open with a bang, the snarling became even more frenzied. German shepherds and mixed breed dogs strained at the leashes held by teenaged soldiers. Gene noticed the young soldiers right away. What happened to all the older guards? He looked at the faces of these youthful men dressed in white uniforms and wielding gleaming bayonets. Some looked younger than him. They were the Kriegsmarine, cadets from the German Navy. The fierceness in their eyes matched the ferocity of the dogs they held back. Gene had never seen German soldiers like these men.

"Out!"

Shackled pairs tumbled from the boxcars to the ground. Others crawled out slowly before collapsing. The kriegies lingered near the boxcars, terrified of the dogs and the savage teenaged marines in front of them.

"Go ahead and kill us now, you Kraut shitbags!" a man yelled.

Others cried out, "Water. Water. Oh, God, give us water. We're dying!"

Gene said nothing. He wavered between cursing his tormentors or joining those begging for water. He stayed back by the boxcar. Here he was, weak and shackled, facing dogs snapping their gleaming teeth and vengeful soldiers pointing their bayonet-tipped rifles.

A German officer appeared. Gene took one look at him and hated him instantly. He was a short, chubby, red-haired man dressed in the gleaming white uniform of a Hauptmann, a German captain.

"Welcome, murderers. So, you are the child killers," he said in English.

The Hauptmann barked orders in German to his young soldiers. Gene recognized the word "schweinhunde." He hadn't heard it since the day he was captured when the German villagers tried to kill him. The officer continued screaming and gesturing wildly. Gene thought he was a crazed lunatic, like Hitler, not human. *This is it. This is where it ends. We die here when that madman orders his boy soldiers to open fire.*

Gene looked over at Shorty. "Get ready."

But death didn't come. Instead, they began to march. A column eight to ten men wide walked down the sandy road into a pine forest.

"*Raus! Raus!*" a young cadet cried out. The prisoners understood. Clutching their meager packs, the kriegies started running. Gene struggled to make his legs move. After three days of confinement on the hell ship and prison trains and no water, his muscles had seized up.

Beside them, the red-haired German Hauptmann rode a bicycle back and forth along the rows of POWs. "*Schnell! Schnell! Schnell!*" he screamed. "You are flyboys. Let's see you fly!"

The German guards and their growling dogs kept pace. The Hauptmann bellowed at the young soldiers, whipping them into a frenzy. When his bicycle neared Gene, he hollered in English, "These are the gangsters that bombed your homes and killed your families!"

Gene and Shorty ran in the middle of the column. On the edge, Gene saw several pairs of handcuffed men collapse. Immediately, the guards and their dogs pounced on them. The soldiers clubbed the fallen prisoners with the butts of their guns, their dogs tearing at their soiled, ripped clothing. Gene heard a man scream out in pain. He spotted a young Kriegsmarine soldier pull his bayonet out of the leg of a downed prisoner. "For Hamburg! For Berlin!" the young men shouted, calling out many of the cities the airmen had bombed.

A pair of handcuffed men crumpled in a cloud of dust in front of Gene and Shorty. They both yanked the two back up on their feet as quickly as they could, hoping not to draw attention to themselves. Others kept falling. The men on the edges of the column faced the full fury of the German Kriegsmarine guards, who immediately clubbed, kicked, and stabbed at any prisoner who stumbled. When a weaker man fell, the man he was handcuffed to often picked up his fallen partner and carried him.

A breaking point was coming. Talk of charging the guards and fighting back passed through the prisoners. Word came through the line that someone spotted machine guns hidden in the woods alongside the road.

The Kriegsmarine soldiers taunted the POWs. "Escape! Escape!"

"It's a trap. Don't do it," a man hollered. "If we try, they'll shoot."

Gene's mind blurred—barking dogs, falling comrades, screaming German marines. Men near him said, "Let's charge these bastards." Others warned, "Keep your cool." Gene kept running, expecting at any moment the forest on both sides of him to erupt in machine gun fire.

The prisoner column lurched forward. Gene saw stabbed legs spurting blood. He thought of Bill's injured leg. He'd never survive this. Where was he?! He swiveled his head, hoping to spot Bill amongst the running, stumbling prisoners. Still nothing. He hadn't seen him on the hell ship. Bill could have been among the dead lying on the floor in the hold for all Gene knew.

After running for two miles, Gene saw an open field. It was nearing dusk. Beyond the meadow stood two barbed-wire fences, ten feet high, which surrounded a camp cut into a forest with dense underbrush. They'd reached the gates of their new prison, Stalag Luft 4. The mad, red-haired Hauptmann yelled, "Halt!" He called off the dogs and Kriegsmarine guards.

Gene and Shorty collapsed simultaneously with hundreds of others. It was as if a giant scythe had cut through the prisoner ranks. Gene sucked in the cool night air, his legs heavy, his mind numb. Lying on the ground, he looked around and saw clothes ripped and soaked with blood. The pants of many kriegies hung in shreds around the ankles where the dogs had ripped and chewed. The chests of hundreds of prisoners heaved from exhaustion. No one spoke.

Gene lay on the evening grass with only one thought: *WATER!*

An officer came into view, leading soldiers. Gene heard a cheer. The officer drew closer. Gene gasped. He recognized the man. It was Captain Wolfe! *Here* at the gates of Stalag Luft 4. The officer who'd lived in Wisconsin before the war. The same man who'd guided Gene safely through vengeful civilians in Frankfurt on the other side of Germany five months earlier. Maybe, finally, things would start to improve. Gene gasped again. Captain Wolfe's soldiers were pulling a water wagon.

The water wagon stopped at the edge of the field. Captain Wolfe strode to the center of the prisoners. "Don't do anything foolish," Wolfe pleaded, his head swiveling back and forth to look as many prisoners in the eyes as possible. "This will all be over tomorrow. Things will be better tomorrow."

After Captain Wolfe left, Gene and Shorty, still handcuffed together, staggered to get their first drink in more than three days. Everyone was desperate for water, yet all the kriegies stood quietly in line, each waiting his turn. Gene looked at the bloody backsides of the prisoners in line in front of him. Many had been stabbed in the buttocks. Gene and Shorty had no wounds. They had not fallen once during the two-mile run.

Night fell. The temperature dropped. A few guards kept watch on the perimeter, but they maintained their distance. It was clear the Germans wouldn't process the POWs into camp until morning. They'd been rushed to their new prison for nothing.

That night, the prisoners remained in the field and slept under the sky. The cooler air and water gave the men some hope. A few talked and speculated as to what was next. The previous two nights, Gene had stewed in the heat and the filth of the hell ship. Now he looked up at the stars and breathed in the sweet, cool air of a clear summer evening. His belly growled. He hadn't eaten a morsel of food in four days. But he was no longer thirsty. He soaked in the feel of clean grass under his back.

Gene motioned to Shorty that he had to relieve himself. Still handcuffed together, the two walked to a slit trench on the edge of the field where all the prisoners were told to do their business. The two stood over the trench and urinated.

"Do you have any idea what day it is?" Gene asked Shorty.

"I don't know. July 16 or 17," Shorty guessed.

July 17?

Gene paused. His twentieth birthday. He was no longer a teenager.

CHAPTER 14

Dreams of Roast Duck

January 2013

I was okay the first month of the new year after Carmen died. I honestly felt relieved. The sword that had been hanging over my head for the last ten years had finally fallen.

The details of widower life kept me distracted: paying funeral bills, closing bank accounts, ordering new checks with my name only. I was on bereavement leave; the boys were at school. Each day, I walked my snow-covered gravel driveway to my mailbox, returning with a stack of sympathy cards sometimes stuffed with cash.

Then there were the binders: laminated pages with headstones of various rock types and designs I had to look over to pick out a monument for Carmen's grave. Carmen had ordered me to keep it simple and save the money for the boys' college funds. But I agonized over whether to choose the cheaper dull-gray stone or spend another thousand dollars on the polished red granite.

The task of closing Carmen's graphic design business filled me with dread. After sending the boys off to school, I entered her office, shut off my emotions, and started grabbing binders and folders whose contents I didn't understand. I loosely stuck all the ads, brochures, and designer business cards into scrapbooks. I'd give these to the boys someday, a record of their mother's incredible creativity. Everything else I dumped. I crushed antiquated disk drives. I opened folders and three-ring binders, held them in the air chest-high, and watched Carmen's career cascade in a storm of fluttering paper into recycling bins.

I could close her office, but I couldn't empty her closet. I rarely went into the bedroom we shared other than to grab my own clothes. In the last two months of her life, I usually slept on the living room floor next to the couch where she lay. After she died, I moved to her spot on the couch. In our bedroom, a film of dust collected on her dresser drawer, which was still filled with her folded t-shirts, socks, and undergarments.

Besides avoiding our bedroom, I was doing okay. I could do this: single dad with two boys. I tried to get them to talk about their mother. I took them to movies, restaurants, concerts. We tossed darts in the basement and played basketball in the driveway. What was a good role model for a single dad, an only parent? The only widower I knew from popular media was Atticus Finch, the regal widowed father of two children in *To Kill a Mockingbird*. Maybe I could be like him.

A counselor from our local hospice occasionally stopped by my home. He discussed the stages of grief with me, explaining how pain and heartache would come, in waves, at unexpected times. Anger would follow.

The first tsunami hit in early February.

I was baking chocolate chip cookies, a favorite treat of Carmen's. The smell of cookies emanating from the oven triggered something inside me. It came hard and fast. My eyes welled. Tears turned to crying. Crying turned to sobbing. The boys were upstairs in their rooms. I grabbed kitchen towels and buried my face in them.

Matthew and Joe hadn't shed a tear since their mother had died, and I'd be damned if they were going to see me break.

Now I wailed. Kitchen towels wouldn't contain it. I ran outside into the night air and sprinted the thirty yards to the barn. I grabbed an old aluminum softball bat sitting on a windowsill. In the unlit barn, I took aim at a support post and let go. *Wham! Wham! Wham!* I slammed the iron post and howled. Again and again, I swung the bat. My arms radiated the sting of aluminum striking solid iron. But the post held. Enraged, I slammed the bat onto the concrete floor. As it clanged across the barn floor, I screamed, "Fuck you! Goddammit, Fuuuuucccckkkk yoooooooouuuuuuuuuu!"

I vomited. Rage vomit that sprayed the concrete floor. I leaned against a post for a few minutes, panting. Moonlight streamed through the barn windows so I could see the last strings of puke slide from my mouth and pool onto the barn floor.

I wiped my mouth and headed back to the house. The oven timer pinged just as I walked into the kitchen, signaling the cookies were done.

Grief continued to pour out in rage. Someone, something would have to pay for taking away my sons' beautiful mother.

My next target was the juice machine.

I'd bought the juicer the previous summer. It was a crazy, last-ditch effort to stop Carmen's cancer. An acquaintance I'd run into during a grocery trip explained how her husband's brain cancer went into remission after he drank homemade juice mixed with ground turmeric and ginger.

I kept using the juicer after Carmen died. Who knew? It might help me. I couldn't let the boys lose their father too. I drank an herb-loaded smoothie instead of orange juice and a donut. I also squeezed fresh juice for the boys so they'd get quick nutrition before catching the bus to school. But the machine had been jamming up, delaying our hurried breakfasts. One morning, it seized up for the last time. The boys sat silently on their stools by the kitchen island, wolfing down Malt-O-Meal.

I calmly unplugged the juicer.

Then I lifted it, raised it above my head, and slammed it onto the kitchen floor.

The juicer atomized. Shards of black plastic radiated across the tiled surface.

"Whenever you're ready, John," was all Gene said when I called on the phone to ask if he was ready to get back to work.

I'd last seen him at Carmen's funeral, at the urinal in the bathroom at the Knights of Columbus Hall, to be exact. The church service had just finished. Relatives and friends then crowded into the KC Hall afterwards for a meal of ham sandwiches, scalloped potatoes, and coleslaw. I edged through the throng, glad to escape. I was startled to see Gene. The last time I'd seen him was when he'd given my family a tour of his boyhood farm back in May.

"Oh, hey," I muttered. We met at the sink. Neither of us spoke. Then as I turned to dry my hands, I felt a hand on my shoulder. Gene patted my shoulder twice and then walked out to the hubbub of the crowded dining hall.

Now it was almost a year since our last interview. I stared at Gene's front door, as familiar as my own. I walked inside and took my place at the table. Gene, clad in his bib overalls and flannel, sat finishing up a game of solitaire.

I opened my carrying bag and pulled out the voice recorder, pens, and legal pad. Gene put away his playing cards, then rose and reached in the refrigerator. The routine had returned.

"How did you feel this winter?" I asked.

"Not so good," Gene answered as he cracked open my Coors Light and placed it in the can cooler. "I've had such trouble breathing. I had to go in and get fluid drained from around my heart that was building up. I felt better this morning, but now, I'm so damn weak, John."

I'd noticed Gene's voice was softer, lacking the spunk I'd always known.

"When I called this morning, you could have said no," I replied. "All you had to do was . . ."

Gene cut me off. "No, no, no. Let's get going again," he answered, handing me my beer before taking his usual seat.

I took my first swig and soaked in my return to this familiar place. Everything was as I'd left it since our last interview ten months ago. Gene's "third eye," his magnifying glass, topped the stack of newspapers and envelopes that cluttered the end of the table. Next to that pile sat his can of Copenhagen chewing tobacco, a cribbage board, and two decks of cards: one for solitaire, the other for euchre. I glanced at the decorative glass plate with the scene from the Last Supper hanging from the wall. Over on the picture shelf sat the photo of Gene's mom and dad, the Virgin Mary statue, and the framed poem from Bridget bragging about beating her dad at euchre.

But something was new. My breathing stopped when I looked at the picture shelf again . . . a small frame with a photo of Carmen and Gene. It was taken during our visit to the farm last May. Gene stood in front of the red barn wearing his bib overalls and holding a cane. Carmen was next to him with both arms wrapped around his shoulders.

"When did you . . . I've never seen . . ." My voice trailed off.

Gene nodded. He said nothing and waited.

I sat transfixed. There she was—with Gene. She was here.

A wave was building. I grabbed my right thigh and pinched it, trying to stem the tide of rising emotion. I rocked my head back and forth. *Keep it together. Hold it in. Not here. Not now.* I glanced out the side of my eye at Gene. I wanted to grab the suspenders of his bib overalls and bury my head into that flannel shirt. I needed him. He'd known pain like no one I'd ever met. Gene would understand.

But this wasn't his fight.

I closed my eyes. *You must endure this.*

I pressed the red record button.

July 1944

Gene and Shorty stood in a long line outside the gates of Stalag Luft 4. A day after being forced to run a dirt road without shoes, the cuts on their feet ached. Sometimes, Gene massaged the bruises on his wrists left by the handcuffs the guards had finally removed that morning. The afternoon before, the Germans had brutally chased them to their new prison. Now hundreds of kriegies sweated under a scorching July sun, awaiting inspection. The line barely moved. No hurry after all. Yesterday's cruel run had been for nothing.

Just outside the prison compound, the Germans took twelve men at a time into a simple wooden building. Inside stood six guards. Finally, it was Gene's turn. He entered with Shorty, and a soldier barked at him and the others to strip naked and form a line. Gene was happy to take off his clothes inside the stuffy shed. It was a relief to be rid of, at least for the moment, the urine-soaked and vomit-caked clothes he'd been wearing for five days. He bundled the filthy wad of cloth in his arms and eyeballed the six soldiers in the room.

One stood out.

He didn't seem human. He stood about six feet, seven inches tall and looked to weigh around three hundred pounds. Everything about him was big and ugly: his broad face, his ham-sized hands, even his jagged teeth. He walked hunched over, like a caveman. Gene soon learned from the other prisoners that this guard's nickname was "Big Stoop."

Standing in a single-file line, the nude POWs approached two middle-aged uniformed men sitting on stools and wearing rubber gloves. "Arms up!" one of the seated men shouted in English. The two Germans stood up to begin their inspections. With their gloved fingers, they poked mouths, noses, and ears. "Turn around. Bend over," one of them ordered. Gene watched the inspectors sit back down and finger the anal area of each man, searching for compasses, maps, or other materials to use for an escape. He watched with dread. The Germans seemed to linger when they probed each prisoner's butt.

Gene recognized a man three spots ahead of him in line. It was Augie Donatelli, his softball umpiring buddy from Stalag Luft 6. When it was Augie's turn to be searched, he seemed unsure what to do. Big Stoop lumbered toward the confused prisoner. "Es macht wieder!" he roared.

"What the hell do ya want from me?" Augie asked.

The giant soldier answered. He raised his heavy boot and smashed down on Augie's bare foot. The former Pennsylvania coal miner twisted in pain. He said nothing. When he bent over and presented his buttocks, he let roar a pent-up reserve of gas into the inspector's face. A guard next to the seated inspector immediately smacked his rifle butt into the back of Augie's head. Gene watched him crumple to the floor. Two soldiers dragged him out of the room.

Gene was in no mood to get his own damaged skull whacked. Not even to avenge the hell ship, torture runs, sadistic guards, or anything else. He kept his butt quiet.

Outside, Gene found Augie slumped on the ground, holding his head. He was moaning, or maybe laughing. Gene couldn't tell.

"What the hell did you do that for?" Gene demanded. He raised Augie off the ground and tried to steady him.

"Baldy, I didn't care if they killed me," Augie answered. He cradled his cut head, laughing. "I just couldn't resist."

The prisoner quarters were different here. Unlike the open buildings at Stalag Luft 6, each barracks building at Stalag Luft 4 was divided into cubicles. Each room measured about fifteen by twenty feet. A small wooden table sat in the center surrounded by five sets of three-tiered bunks. In a space about the size of an average living room, the guards shoved Gene and Shorty together with thirteen other prisoners. Augie was no longer with the two. Gene guessed he'd been assigned to a different barracks.

Gene threw his pack onto the top bunk. For five days, he'd managed to hang on to his meager belongings since the evacuation of Stalag Luft 6, which now seemed like an eternity ago. He looked over the rough-cut wooden shelf that would be his bunk. The mattress was nothing more than a sack filled with wood shavings. When he lay on it, the shavings squashed flat. It felt like he was lying on a plank. The dirt barn floor back home would have been more comfortable. At least Shorty got the bunk below him. They'd be together.

Like Stalag Luft 6, almost all the kriegies at the prison were enlisted American airmen who elected a leader in each barracks building. The barracks leader gave Gene and Shorty a quick tour of their new quarters.

There wasn't much to show the new arrivals. A table sat in the middle of the hallway. There were no sinks or toilets inside. The latrine, a long board with six holes in it, was located outside the barracks. The barracks leader warned that the latrine was off-limits after lights-out. Pails sat in each cubicle room for men who couldn't hold it through the night. Stalag Luft 4 didn't have showers anywhere for the prisoners. Gene was crushed that he wouldn't get to stand under running water to wash away the filth still on him from the hell ship. The barracks leader hurried through the quick tour as roll call was coming up. Walking through the barracks, Gene brushed up against wood so roughly cut that splinters poked through his shirt.

Just before stepping out of the barracks to head to the parade ground for roll call, Gene poked his head into another cubicle. His eyes locked on one man: Bill!

"Hey, Baldy," Bill deadpanned.

Gene was stupefied. Bill was alive. How did he survive the hell ship? How did he survive the run on that gimpy leg? But here he was. Alive and in the same barracks!

"Let's go!" the barracks leader yelled at Gene.

"We'll talk later," was all Gene could sputter from his mouth before heading out the door. He felt like he could have skipped to roll call. Bill was alive and assigned to the same barracks.

The euphoria was short-lived.

Roll call was a harsh reminder that Stalag Luft 4 existed to degrade and intimidate. Gene was an American "terrorflieger," a "luftgangster." From his captors' point of view, he murdered their women and children. Guards with leashed dogs at their sides walked between the rows, shouting. Gene had no idea where to stand. He squeezed in with the nearest line when he saw the snarling hounds getting close. The dogs snapped at the buttocks of POWs who didn't stand where they were supposed to be.

A German officer appeared. "Straighten these lines. We will stand here until these lines are straight!" he shouted in English.

Gene took one look at the officer and labeled him a horse's ass. He was much more arrogant than the commandant at Stalag Luft 6. He hated the way this camp leader strutted in front of the prisoners, rubbing his freedom and power in their face.

While the officer lectured, Gene surveyed his new surroundings. The prison was divided into four square compounds. In each section, barracks surrounded open ground which Gene didn't think was big enough to hold a ball game. Stalag Luft 4 wasn't as organized as his last prison. Rough-hewn logs and boards lay piled haphazardly next to unfinished buildings. With the chaos of new construction, Gene figured more POWs were on the way. If the

Germans didn't finish the partially built barracks, his room would get very crowded.

All the barracks sat on pilings about two to three feet off the ground. This created open space between the ground and the barracks to prevent any tunneling activity. Gene looked over at the ten-foot-high double-barbed-wire fence that enclosed the camp. That barrier stood some thirty feet from a second line of barbed wire inside the prison strung out on posts raised about two feet off the ground.

"The low wire you see before the outer wire is the warning wire," the German officer explained. "Cross this wire, and you will be shot immediately."

Gene lifted his eyes to the guard towers. The towers seemed to be everywhere, and each was equipped with searchlights and manned by soldiers with machine guns. German guards had full view of the prison yard.

"You are to be in your barracks one hour before sundown," the officer shouted. "Leave your barracks after lights-out, and you will be shot!"

After the commandant finished his list of rules and threats, two German sergeants walked through each line of prisoners, jabbing their finger at every kriegie and counting to themselves. After finishing their tally, the two soldiers met to compare numbers. Gene could see they didn't agree. The count started over again. Hundreds of prisoners stood motionless and silent under the July afternoon sun. Another error. Another count. Gene was thirsty. He still hadn't eaten in almost five days. His back ached from standing what seemed like two hours. Of all his injuries from the fall, his lower back bothered him the most. Finally, the Germans seemed satisfied with the numbers.

When Gene, Shorty, and Bill returned to the barracks, they immediately sat at the wooden table in the darkened hallway and exchanged their survival stories. Gene felt bad that he'd lost track of his buddy in the darkness and confusion of the hell ship. He still couldn't believe Bill had made it. Bill admitted that he'd gotten so thirsty on the hell ship that he drank his own piss. He'd managed later to get to the side of the ship to lick the condensation drops off the hull. Bill confirmed that some men next to him died of suffocation. He added that he saw the men shoved into the gear compartment. They stopped talking about the hell ship after that story.

Gene sat in a t-shirt soaking with sweat. The breezes off the Baltic Sea that wafted over northern Germany never made it inside the barracks. It didn't help that the Germans ordered doors locked and windows shut after sunset. But Gene wouldn't let the stuffy air of the unventilated room bother him. The three Wisconsin gunners were together again. Shorty would sleep in the same room. Bill's bunk was just down the hallway.

The three men headed to their stiff beds for their first night at Stalag Luft 4. Gene lay sweltering in his wooden bunk. Looking up, he wondered how many nights he'd have to stare at this ceiling. There was nothing left to do now but gird for unknown days of humiliation, starvation, boredom, and despair.

Sleeping light had its advantages, especially during surprise inspections. The Germans would come at any time. Big Stoop often led the way, barging into the barracks, hollering his broken English into the cubicles. Many of the soldiers at Stalag Luft 4 were odd like Big Stoop. Besides being peculiar, they were often older and seemed unfit for regular army service. Gene hoped these oddballs were a sign that Germany was running out of soldiers. But these borderline crazies could melt down at any time.

The Germans clicked the safeties off on their Mauser machine guns when they stormed into the barracks for unexpected searches. The soldiers roamed through each room, tearing apart beds and flipping over tables. Some guards shouted into the prisoners' ears as they stood at attention during the raids, often kicking them in the back of the legs.

Big Stoop was the worst. His favorite tactic was to come up behind an unsuspecting prisoner and simultaneously cuff both ears with his massive hands. The victim would collapse to the floor, sometimes with ruptured eardrums. The hair stood up on the back of Gene's neck whenever Big Stoop slowly, interminably, walked behind him. He always passed Gene and Shorty without incident. Further down the hallway, Bill wasn't so lucky. On several raids, Gene had watched Bill collapse on the floor after a Big Stoop slap. The giant ogre always seemed to go after the sick and the lame.

Attacking Big Stoop during one of his rants was out of the question. He was twice the size of most of the prisoners. Gene heard rumors that before the war, "The Beast," as many called him, was a sparring partner of the great German heavyweight boxing champion Max Schmeling. That made sense. It would explain his ruddy face and broken speech. Maybe being punch drunk was what turned him into a sadist. If it rained during roll call, Big Stoop delighted in marching between the rows of prisoners and stomping on mud puddles, soaking the pants of the lined-up POWs.

Gene struggled to contain his rage and helplessness. He hated the humiliating searches and roll calls. But the "old-timers," prisoners who'd been at Stalag Luft 4 for a while, told him to just clench his fists and take it. Barracks raids became routine. The Germans claimed they were looking for knives and radios. Gene soon figured out that was a lie. When guards found a Red Cross package, they'd tear it apart, looking for food and, especially, American cigarettes. But the sergeant gunners usually had little to offer their tormentors. The Germans always left the barracks trashed.

The constant thievery of the contents of the Red Cross packages meant the only regular source of food was the bread loaves and soup pails brought to the barracks. Twice daily, the prisoners lined up with their wooden bowls to receive what they called "slop." The dark bread slapped into Gene's hand was the same sawdust-filled concoction he'd eaten at Sandbostel Prison and Stalag Luft 6. Spread with gray-colored margarine, it tasted like he was eating dirt mixed with axle grease. The bread was always the same, but Gene noticed the soup looked different each day. The thick, gray-colored broth always had potatoes, often speckled with tiny white bugs crawling on them. Sometimes, he'd spot lumps of rutabaga in his bowl. Now and then, the soup contained chunks of pale-brown meat.

Gene wondered about the source of the meat. He knew meat was a rarity, even for the German soldiers. His curiosity was answered when one day he watched a wagon roll into camp with skinned carcasses swaying from its racks. The butchered animals looked small, not that he was expecting sides of beef. Small carcasses. Four legs. Two legs would mean some type of bird. But four? With a gag in his throat, Gene realized he'd been eating dog soup that week. Later, he just shrugged when it was mealtime. Meat was meat.

Gene laughed when he saw the animals pulling the meat wagon—a horse and an ox. In all his life in rural Wisconsin, he'd never seen the two harnessed together. Back home in the barnyard, horses and cattle kept their distance from each other. The Germans were so desperate that they couldn't even find two draft horses to properly pull their equipment, much less a vehicle. And if a prisoner had to chew on the gristle stripped from the bones of a mangy mutt, the soldiers of Stalag Luft 4 couldn't be eating much better.

Dog meat. Oxen harnessed with horses. Was this hope? Just maybe the Germans were on the brink of defeat. If only he could be liberated before the winter.

As the summer turned to fall in 1944, even dog meat became scarce in the daily soup ration. The only other source of protein for the prisoners was canned salmon, a staple in Red Cross packages. The Germans stored the parcels in a warehouse just outside the prison, where they opened them and grabbed whatever cigarettes and food they could shove into their pockets. The canned salmon was withheld and dispersed only on Friday—if the kriegies had behaved the prior week. One time, the camp commandant suspended the salmon ration after a prisoner cheered when a German worker was electrocuted while working on a utility pole. When the men in Gene's barracks finally received and opened their salmon cans, the fish was green.

Nobody would touch the spoiled salmon, except Gene. He loved fish. Shorty willingly gave his buddy his salmon ration. "Don't eat it, Baldy," he warned. "I don't want you shitting in the bucket next to me all night after lights-out."

Gene ignored Shorty. He spooned his bounty into his Klim can and cooked it over the potbellied stove set in the hallway, turning it over and over until green became brown. And then he feasted. An hour later, his stomach churned. He spent the rest of the day in the latrine unloading his twisted intestines. That evening, Gene returned to his room bent over, arms wrapped around his stomach. "I told you so," said Shorty, howling with laughter.

Meat. Gene always craved meat. He'd never gone a day in his childhood without chewing on a piece of salt pork or bacon, except for Fridays. His family followed Catholic "Fish Fridays." But even on Fridays, Gene's childhood yearning for animal protein had been satisfied. Every Thursday, a man drove up from the Mississippi River in his Ford Model A, hauling buckets stuffed with fish and ice. He'd stop by the Moran farm and sell sheepshead, buffalo fish, and carp as big as a table for three cents a pound.

Gene would find a way to get his protein. It wasn't about taste anymore, but for survival.

But where to get it?

Gene noticed starlings often flew in and landed on the ground next to his barracks. He rigged a pail propped upside down with a stick that was attached to a string. After baiting the pail with a small piece of bread, Gene crouched around the corner of his barracks, waiting for a bird to wander under his trap. Sometimes it took hours to get one bird, but he usually snared at least one. Other prisoners took note of Gene's success and decided to join him. But the sight of pails set outside on the grounds caught the Germans' attention.

"There will be no more trapping of birds," the camp commandant bellowed during roll call. He strutted back and forth in front of the lined prisoners. "Anyone caught stealing the Führer's birds will be shot."

Gene didn't blink when he heard the order. He knew he'd snare birds again. He didn't have a death wish. He wanted meat. Besides, amidst the crushing monotony of prison life, trapping starlings was fun. To hell with the Führer's damn birds.

Combatting boredom and fending off "barbed-wire disease" was tougher here than at Stalag Luft 6. At least there Gene belonged to an escape committee. He missed standing watch and warning his comrades digging in the tunnels of snooping German soldiers. He longed for the thrill of carrying dirt from tunnel excavations in his pants and walking past suspicious guards on the way to dump the dirt in a pit toilet.

Tunneling was out of the question here at Stalag Luft 4. It was a long way to the tree line outside the prison. To dig tunnels several hundred yards long to reach the cover of the forest would be too much work for kriegies weakened by meager food rations. Expending precious calories chiseling out rock and dirt seemed ludicrous.

No one really talked about escape anymore. Life became an endless waiting game. Roll call, thin soup, moldy bread, night inspections . . . repeat.

On a drizzly, overcast afternoon, Bill sat at the table in Gene and Shorty's room. Gene lay in his bed and started a much-repeated conversation that began with the line, "What's the first thing ya gonna eat when you get home?" Gene's dream meal was always roast duck. He described how when he got home, the first meal he'd devour would be a golden roasted duck sopping with juice. He fantasized about taking buttered homemade rolls and circling his plate to soak up every last bit of the golden gravy Mom would make from the duck drippings. He wrote to his mother that he expected that to be his first meal when he returned home.

Sending and receiving mail was essential to treat barbed-wire disease. Stalag Luft 4 allowed the prisoners to send out one letter a week. Gene received letters from his mother, brothers, or sisters about once every ten days. But as winter approached, mail call became erratic. There were fewer vehicles driving in and out of camp.

The mail bag may have been empty, but the new prisoner roster was always full. The air war over Europe was reaching a crescendo. Newly shot-down airmen talked about thousand-plane raids pummeling Germany. The Germans had to set up tents on the parade grounds of each of the four compounds to accommodate the newcomers. In Gene's barracks, beds now lined the hallway. Some men had to sleep on the floor.

The fresh captives brought mixed emotions for Gene. The new arrivals delivered exciting news that the American and British armies were nearing the western frontier of Germany and that Allied bombers were delivering knockout blows that might soon end the war. Gene thirsted for war news as much as he anticipated mail from Mom. But more planes in the air meant more prisoners, more mouths to feed. On the orders of the barracks chief, Gene now ladled just one scoop of thin soup into his bowl instead of two. And with fewer Red Cross packages coming into Stalag Luft 4, he had nothing to add to his ever-shrinking soup and bread ration.

Gene didn't need a scale to tell him he was losing weight. The sweatshirt his mother sent from home in a Red Cross package clung loosely to his torso. The rope that held up his pants had a little extra length each week. He could see it in the gazes of the new prisoners arriving each day who stared at his gaunt face.

Gene sympathized with the new guys coming into Stalag Luft 4. Before they were shot down, they'd been fed well in England. Now they'd eat dog soup and bread made with sawdust. Many had just witnessed friends die in flaming airplanes. Other newbies suffered from busted and burned limbs that had received scant medical attention.

The shortening days of late autumn and the falling temperatures only worsened morale. Very little heat reached Gene's bunk from the single potbellied stove in the hallway. He shivered in his blankets. At night, he heard some of his roommates cry out in their bunks. Some men moaned in their sleep about exploding airplanes. Gene tried to suppress his own memories: Pee Wee screaming in his ball turret, Swedo's and Andy's bullet-ridden bodies lying on the fuselage floor of *Rikki Tikki Tavi*.

Christmas approached. The holiday made many prisoners even more depressed. The gray skies and temperatures below zero sank spirits to new lows. The barracks chief decided something had to be done to boost the men's mood. But there was no food, no decorations, not even anything to simulate a tree.

"Eugene, I was wondering if you'd say a few words on Christmas Eve. We're trying to put together a little ceremony," the chief said.

"Are you pulling my leg?" Gene replied.

"I'm serious. Some of the guys asked if you would do it. We don't have much planned other than some type of church service. Bill said he'd sing. Would you do it?" the chief asked.

On Christmas Eve, men gathered in the crowded hallway amidst the glow of flickering candles. In a holiday spirit themselves, the Germans allowed lights-out time to extend to 1:00 a.m. Earlier in the day, the POWs had unexpectedly received extra Red Cross parcels. The packages included nuts, candy, sausages, hams, and cheese. Gene overindulged his shrunken stomach. He spent a large portion of the day sitting and shivering in the latrine.

Bill started singing "Hark the Herald Angels Sing." Other prisoners joined in when he followed with "O Little Town of Bethlehem." Gene had heard Bill whistle and hum a few popular tunes before, but the carols showcased his beautiful voice. When Bill finished, it was Gene's turn. He really didn't want to speak at first. His innards still churned. He worried about another dash to the latrine. But the body heat from all the men packed in the room and the sound of Bill's voice soothed his stomach a bit.

The packed hallway was eerily still. Gene had no script. He simply talked about what made Christmas special. He shared his own stories from home: the cedar boughs tied together that made the Moran Christmas tree, walking with his family in the snow to Christmas Mass at St. Philip's, the bag of treats Dad put together for each of his children—peanuts, chocolate drops, hard candies. Gene looked up from recalling the contents of his candy bag and saw a few tear-stained cheeks glistening in the yellow-orange light from the candles.

He stopped talking about Christmas.

"Hang in there, guys. This war can't go on forever," he said. He wanted to say that this would be their last Christmas away from home, but he didn't dare make that promise.

Gene just stood there. He had nothing else to say. He looked out at the assembled men. Some stood looking down at the floor. Others sat up against the barracks walls with pale, drawn faces. They'd also eaten too many rich food items from their Red Cross packages. Standing or sitting, no one moved. No one said a word. But a few tears had become many.

Bill jumped in and started singing "Silent Night." All of the prisoners tried to sing along amidst muffled sobbing. The ceremony ended, the final notes of "Silent Night" still lingering. Gene helped some of the other men blow out the candles, then he returned to the darkness and cold of his bunk.

Gene lay in his bunk, recounting his second Christmas as a POW. A year earlier, French prisoners had gotten him stone-cold drunk on homemade cognac. He thought of home and wondered if Dad had packed a candy sack for him. He figured he should have two bags waiting for him when he returned to Wisconsin.

The warm spirit of the holidays faded quickly. One day during the first week of January, prisoners stood outside stomping their feet and blowing into their hands, trying to stay warm during roll call. An airplane engine growled in the distance. Gene's neck craned to the sky. The plane sounded like a single-engine fighter. When it first came into view, all the prisoners guessed it to be a German fighter plane. Soon, they knew they were correct: it had the black cross emblazoned on its wings. This was January 1945, and it had become a scarce sight to see a German airplane fly above the prison yard. Back at Stalag Luft 6, Nazi aircraft had roared over the prison almost daily, but here it was rare.

The Luftwaffe fighter plane executed a barrel roll over the camp. But the hot-dogging pilot lost control and crashed into the forest outside the prison. A cheer went up from some of the prisoners when they heard the crash. Tower guards let loose with machine gun fire into the compound. The POWs scrambled for cover. No one was hurt, but the message was clear. Christmas was over.

January temperatures plunged way below zero, unusual even for northern Germany. Like many of the prisoners, Gene had no winter coat. He wore the same sweatshirt every day that Mom had sent from home. He wrapped himself with his blanket wherever he went. The influx of new prisoners did provide extra body heat in the barracks. But the coal scuttle, a steel pail with a spout on it, came only once a day. In the early morning, after the rationed charcoal had burned out in the potbellied stove, Gene simply wrapped himself in his blanket and stayed in bed.

Morale plummeted when dysentery hit. Prisoners became filthy from so many visits to the latrine. And many had stopped bathing because of the extreme cold. This was shocking for airmen trained to look impeccable in uniform. Mom had sent Gene new clothes in his Red Cross packages, but he missed the feel and look of an Army Air Force uniform: the olive drab tie, leather bomber jacket, crisp garrison cap.

Barbed-wire disease infected Gene. Lying in his bunk, he had nothing to do. It was too cold to trap starlings. Running to the latrine had become the main activity of his day. He fought off despair by drawing sketches in his logbook or writing down the addresses of roommates he promised to visit after the war. But on many days, he'd just stare blankly out the window at the same gray sky, the same guard towers, the same fences, the same barracks, the same everything.

The one bright spot was reports from new prisoners, but the news wasn't always good. Recently, they'd shared stories of a German offensive on the Western Front. The news put Gene into a tailspin. To him, it didn't matter who won the battle. The fact that the Germans could launch any kind of large attack could only mean the Krauts were not on the brink of defeat. *Just how long can the war go on?*

Spirits rose a bit when Father Lynch appeared. As he did at Stalag Luft 6, he just seemed to come from out of nowhere. When he stopped by Gene's barracks, not many of the prisoners were in the mood to hear scripture. Gene, Shorty, and Bill didn't mind stepping out into the cold with him to walk the perimeter of the camp. Tromping in the snow, the three Wisconsin Catholics shared their confessions together with the mysterious priest.

Also arriving in January were British POWs. This was unusual, but welcome. Anything new helped break the monotony of wintertime prison life. Gene learned that these new arrivals came from camps in the east that had evacuated just in front of the advancing Soviet Army. The news brightened the mood of some of the kriegies. Despite the massive German attack in the west, could the war finally be coming to an end?

The booming sound of artillery from the Eastern Front rolled over Stalag Luft 4 at the end of January. The Russians were coming, again. The rumor mill started churning, just as it had the previous summer. Gene, Shorty, and Bill sat in their cold barracks and listened to the gossip.

"The SS won't shoot us. Or we'll take their pilots and do the same," one kriegie blurted out, more with hope than conviction.

"What if the Germans force us to fight the Soviets?" asked another prisoner.

"Maybe the Krauts will take off and let us go to the Russians," another added.

Gene rejected that possibility. He remembered his dashed hopes of liberation from the previous summer when the Red Army got close to Stalag Luft 6. One thought tormented him, a topic most of the prisoners would not discuss: What if Hitler had all the POWs executed?

Gene's refusal to be optimistic was correct.

On January 29, the camp commandant ordered every prisoner into the compound. This wasn't roll call. Something was happening. Gene noticed a little less strut in the German officer's walk. He announced that the most seriously wounded and sick prisoners would be marching out to the train station a few miles from the camp.

Why just the lame and the sick?

German sergeants started screaming out, in English, prisoner identification numbers. Those whose numbers were called fell out of formation and lined up at the main gate of the camp. One of the numbers hollered was Bill's.

Bill, who still limped when he walked, stepped out of his row and shuffled past Gene. "Take care, Baldy. I'll see you back in Soldiers Grove," he said.

Gene turned and nodded toward Bill. He watched him hobble away on that still unhealed leg. Gene was glad his injured farmhand friend would get to ride a train to wherever the Germans were taking him. But where? Why?

The soldiers continued shouting out numbers.

"108629," a guard barked.

Gene recognized his number bellowed out in rough English. He didn't expect to be called. He couldn't move.

"108629!" the soldier yelled again.

Gene looked over at Shorty. The two had almost never been apart since they first met at the Dulag Luft interrogation center nearly a year ago. They'd survived bombings stuck in jammed cattle cars, the hell ship, the torture run to Stalag Luft 4, starvation, deprivation, sickness, despair . . . always together.

"108629?" the soldier yelled for the last time. With Russian artillery rumbling in the distance, Gene's mind spun. Should he join the wounded? But were the Germans protecting the feeble or planning to execute them? Would the relatively healthy be leaving soon too, or forced to stay behind and face the Red Army?

Gene said nothing. The soldier called out another number.

Gene and Shorty watched Bill march out of Stalag Luft 4 with about a thousand more of the sick and the lame.

The commandant addressed the remaining kriegies. "The rest of you will be leaving by a different conveyance later."

What does he mean by "different conveyance"? Gene thought.

On the evening of February 5, German soldiers entered Gene's barracks to announce that all prisoners were to be ready to evacuate the camp early the next morning. As soon as the Germans left, kriegies scrambled through the barracks to find any morsel of food and any shred of toilet paper. But this time, the top priority was blankets, towels, any piece of cloth to wrap their heads and torsos from the cold. Gene desperately searched for anything made of cloth. He had no coat. Gene could withstand an hour of standing and shivering outside during roll call without a coat. But he had no idea when he'd see a roof over his head again. He needed more than his sweatshirt and blanket if he was going to survive.

The Germans let the kriegies outside the prison gates to enter the warehouse where they stored the Red Cross parcels. With armed guards surrounding them, every prisoner stuffed packages with powdered milk, canned salmon, and crackers into their pockets. The Germans let the Americans grab as many of the parcels as they could carry; better for the prisoners to have the food than to give it up to the Russians. Gene was grateful to get at the bounty. But then he wondered why the Germans were letting them load up on food. Nothing had been said about marching to a train station. Were they simply going to walk ahead of the oncoming Soviets? To where? And how long was the food in his pockets supposed to feed him?

In the dim early-morning light, Gene looked out on the more than a foot of snow that carpeted the ground outside of the camp. He listened to other men cough and sniffle as they awaited the order to march. *A lot of these guys aren't going to make it.*

Gene stood in sub-zero temperatures with a blanket wrapped around his sweatshirt and a cap on his head. He wore tennis shoes. With two thousand other POWs, he waited before a fenced-in corridor that would lead them all out of Stalag Luft 4. When the wind was right, he could hear artillery booming from the battlefront. Some kriegies were guessing the Russians couldn't be more than thirty miles away. Gene tried to suppress thoughts of what had followed his evacuation last summer: the hell ship, the torture run.

More than six months had passed, and here Gene was again: standing before a prison gate exit, listening to the booming guns of deliverance denied, and waiting to begin a march to nowhere, or worse.

CHAPTER 15

Death March

January 2013

God gave me that girl to lean on. Then he put me on my own.
Heaven help me be a man and have the strength to stand alone.

Johnny Cash crooned these lyrics in his bass-baritone voice
from my car music player. I punched repeat. Then repeat again.

Matthew had given me this CD of Johnny Cash hits as a Christmas present. The CD sat in my glove compartment shrouded in its
cellophane wrapper for weeks. Christmas. It had arrived only four
days after Carmen's death. On Christmas Eve, I'd wrapped presents
alone while watching Midnight Mass on a television broadcast from
the Vatican. The Mass had always been the backdrop for Carmen's
and my Christmas Eve routine: drink hot chocolate, wait for Matthew and Joe to fall asleep, and then wrap presents while watching
Midnight Mass. That evening, I heard the interpreter translate the
pope's words to English as I fumbled with transparent tape, trying
to gift wrap two fishing poles.

Now here I was, facing another day. Carmen had been gone

for weeks now, and it wasn't getting any easier. I'd lie in bed for hours after waking. Food tasted flat. I punched repeat on the car CD player for the same song. Then repeat again. Johnny Cash sang:

I don't like it, but I guess things happen that way.

I was on my way to Rockton, Illinois, to visit Wayne Orrison. Wayne, the son of *Rikki Tikki Tavi*'s navigator, Jesse Orrison. Forcing myself to do book work, I wasn't sure I could focus. What would Wayne be like? Orrison was the only other survivor of Gene's bomber crew, so this was important. What had Orrison shared with his son about that final mission that Gene didn't or wouldn't tell me?

I pulled into the driveway of a ranch house, and there he was in real life: the son of the navigator that Gene so revered. I studied this man. He was in his mid-sixties, of medium height like his dad, but bald with a gray, short-stubbed goatee and mustache. His father had been thin and dark-haired in the photo of *Rikki Tikki Tavi*'s crew. I didn't see any resemblance in Wayne, but of course the picture in my mind of his father had been taken almost seventy years earlier.

Wayne didn't look like his dad, but he acted like him. His warm greeting, his gentle way of ushering me to his dining room table reminded me of the same temperament Gene always described in Orrison. Kindness. Humility. Gene said Orrison was the officer the enlisted guys could go to if there was a problem. He was their leader. Though I'd just met Wayne, I felt the same big-brother assurance.

"I don't know how much I'm going to be able to help you, John. My dad just never talked about the war. But I'll give you what I know."

We sat at his small, round dining room table. Wayne's wife, Phyllis, stood nearby.

I'd be grateful for whatever he shared with me. Gene sat in the tail of *Rikki Tikki Tavi*, Orrison in the nose. Gene had told me what Orrison shared with him about the day they were shot down, but those were difficult interviews for Gene. Details were missing.

Perhaps Wayne had new puzzle pieces to complete the story of that fateful day. Even if he didn't have new information, it was good to get out of my house and think about something other than cancer, death, and grief.

"My father loved Uncle Mo," Wayne said. "Dad talked about him so much. There was always a lot of communication between those two throughout their lives."

Uncle Mo? Mo. That was one of Gene's nicknames from the war, that and Baldy. Mo came from Moran. But "Uncle"? Wayne obviously wasn't a blood relative. His bond with Gene startled me. Wayne explained how every three years, his parents packed the kids into the car to visit relatives in the Midwest.

"The first stop was always to see Uncle Mo and Aunt Peg in Wisconsin," Wayne said. "Uncle Mo always had fresh corn on the cob ready for us."

Wayne didn't know much about his father's war. He'd been born a year after his dad was liberated from the prisoner-of-war camp. He'd seen the shrapnel scars on his dad's back, but he never asked about them. His father also carried shrapnel embedded in his eye his whole life. He died at age 80 in 1997.

Orrison had only discussed the war with Wayne twice. He knew nothing of his father's prisoner-of-war experience.

"I wish I could be of more help to you," Wayne said. "I think Dad talked to my daughter about the war more than he talked to me about it."

"Do you have any pictures of your dad from the war?"

Wayne shook his head. Then, after a pause, he rose from the table and disappeared into another room. He returned clutching a 1950s photo of his father bending down to a pigeon on a sidewalk. Orrison was dressed in a light-colored fedora and a dark, long coat. His right arm was stretched out just under the beak of a pigeon, his hand cupped as he made his offering to the bird. Wayne's eyes welled with tears.

"I'm sorry, John, I didn't think this would be so emotional. He was just a gentle, gentle man."

February 1945

Panic invaded the camp. Officers yelled. Guards scurried. Gene watched the Germans' drawn faces. Instead of droning lectures accompanied by sneers and strutting, the camp commandant barked terse orders to the prisoners. There was only one mission now: get away from the Russians.

In the dark, gray morning, Gene and Shorty waited by the main gates of Stalag Luft 4 for the order to march. Wisps of condensation blew out of Gene's mouth and clouded around, mixing with the whitish puffs coming from thousands of POWs all stamping their feet and trying to stay warm in the twenty-below-zero air.

Gene's feelings stirred in a mass of anxiety and confusion. He couldn't wait to get out of a camp he loathed. He'd been staring at the same gray buildings and barbed-wire fence for seven months. His eyes hungered to see a new road, forest, people, *anything*.

But where were they going? Why did the Germans seem so hell-bent on keeping them prisoners? It was the same as last summer when the Germans evacuated Stalag Luft 6 in the face of the advancing Soviet Army. If they feared Russian revenge, why didn't the Germans take off instead of wasting time herding kriegies? Rumors persisted that Hitler wanted the prisoners as bargaining chips for a negotiated surrender. Maybe. Many POWs assumed they'd simply be shot. The kriegies knew the Germans harbored no pity for malnourished, lice-infested sergeant gunners. Gene knew he and the rest were still *terrorfliegers* and *luftgangsters* in German eyes, men who'd once bombed German women and children.

The guards divided the prisoners into groups of about three hundred and ordered them to space themselves at arm's length from one another. Last summer, Gene had stumbled through the gates of Stalag Luft 4 chained by his wrist to Shorty. But with Russian artillery booming in the east, there was no time for handcuffs.

"March!"

The gate loomed. Gene scrunched his shoulders, involuntarily expecting a rifle shot. But nothing happened when he walked out the gate. The nearest guard tower stayed silent, witness only to a motley collection of blanket-wrapped men. Gene eased up, recalling the same instinct that he'd had to duck bullets when he exited Stalag Luft 6.

The prisoners trudged through the snow-covered road, forests stretching out on both sides in this remote land in eastern Germany. Gene looked down at his canvas, rubber-soled tennis shoes. It was the same pair his mother had sent to him months ago back at Stalag Luft 6. How long would they last sloshing through slush and ice?

Guards with rifles and machine pistols patrolled both sides of the prisoner column. The kriegies marched three to four men wide.

"*Laufen schneller!* Walk faster!" the guards yelled.

The sound of Klim cans clanging and striking other Klim cans echoed as Gene and the prisoners picked up the pace. Gene's Klim can, slung from his belt, constantly banged into Shorty's. Just minutes into the march, Gene's shoes were already soaked with slush.

The prisoners got their first scrap of news that day: Expect a three- or four-day hike. So, they'd likely have something to eat in a few days. Based on this information, some of the men tossed their Red Cross parcels into the snow, freeing themselves of the seven-pound packages. Soon, all kinds of foodstuff littered the ground. Gene kept his. It made no sense that starving men were throwing away food. No one knew for sure when they'd eat again. Gene tightened the blanket he cinched around his torso. He'd stuffed several Red Cross packages inside that blanket, and he wasn't going to let one drop, despite the cumbersome weight.

There were no rest breaks that first day of the march. The guards allowed only a few five-minute toilet breaks. Kriegies whose hands weren't frostbitten helped unbutton the pants fly of a friend fumbling with cold, numb fingers.

Some men vomited while marching. After months of eating meager rations of bread bulked up with sawdust and soup dotted with swimming lice, they couldn't resist gorging on the sudden bounty of Red Cross food parcels. For others, the rich food only worsened their dysentery. With all the frequent defecating, the kriegies grew dangerously dehydrated. The Germans provided no water. Many men scooped up snow as they walked. As the day wore on, Gene found it difficult to find snow that wasn't stained with urine or bloody feces.

At dusk, the guards halted the prison column in a frozen swamp. Here they were supposed to camp in the snow and ice without shelter. The Red Army was only twenty miles behind, so the Germans forbade any fires that might be spotted by Russian scouts advancing ahead of their armies.

In the waning light, Gene and Shorty scrambled around the swamp reeds and grasses, looking for some high ground that would be slightly drier for sleeping. A few other kriegies joined their spot. They huddled next to each other, sharing body heat and blankets.

The next morning, the march started up again. Gene saw they weren't the only ones fleeing the Russians. Up ahead, coming out of the forest, he watched roughly a thousand people of all ages cramming the main road, Polish and German civilians. Dressed in ragged and mud-splattered clothing, families staggered along the road, pulling push-bikes and farm carts. The carts were loaded with clothing, farm tools, framed pictures, and even pieces of furniture. Children and the elderly rode in the backs of some of the carts, faces as gaunt as the prisoners' staring back at them.

Kriegies who could speak Polish or German picked up stories from the refugees as they moved. Gruesome accounts of Red Army soldiers raping women. Even slaughtering children. Mutilated bodies were said to be strewn everywhere in eastern Germany.

The refugees seized the marching prisoners' arms, begging for food. Gene spotted one bent-over elderly woman wrapped in a brightly colored shawl. He pulled out two packages of dried prunes from one of his Red Cross parcels and handed them to her. She grabbed Gene's hand and kissed it over and over.

"*Dziekuje. Dziekuje.* God bless. God bless," she said.

The German guards pushed the refugees aside and ordered the prisoners to keep moving. Gene handed out a few more precious food items from his Red Cross parcels to outstretched hands as he walked. He could spare some. At least he hoped he could. If only the rumors of the march lasting a few days turned out to be true.

The second night found the kriegies of Stalag Luft 4 stumbling over tree stumps in another frozen swamp looking for a dry spot to sleep. The weather had warmed a bit, and with hundreds of men milling over the same area, the slightly thawed field turned into a quagmire. Wet, icy slush mixed with bog water, and worse. The Germans gave no orders about a toilet area, so feces soon littered the rest stop and became indistinguishable from the mud in the dark of night.

Gene and Shorty found a group to bunch with for the evening. Lying on the cold ground and gazing at the night sky, Gene worried about Bill as he'd done on the hell ship a summer ago. Where was Bill? Had the Germans forced him to march on that wounded leg? Was he also sleeping on cold ground somewhere? Since meeting Bill at Stalag Luft 6, Gene and Shorty had shared their food rations with him to try to nurse him back to health, but no matter how much food they slipped him, Bill never put on weight. He'd never survive days, maybe weeks, of forced marching and constant winter exposure.

Day after day, they marched. The march was well beyond a week. No new food supplies. The men who'd thrown away their Red Cross packages to relieve weight cursed their foolish decision. With wet feet and aching bodies, the kriegies pushed forward ten to fifteen miles each day. The prisoner column shuffled in a westerly direction, but on clear days, Gene could tell they were moving south as well. Even the approaching spring brought no relief. As the late-winter days became longer, with more daylight, the Germans forced the men to walk more and sleep less. Move west, move west.

Though it wasn't always west. Sometimes they'd march across a bridge only to march back over it the next day. Gene raged at the aimless wandering. There was only one goal: keep ahead of the Russians.

Refugees continued to cram the roads with the prisoner column. The pathetic people he saw reminded him of the unemployed and homeless men that walked the back roads of the Kickapoo Valley when he was a kid during the Depression. Those men often stopped by the Moran farm, begging to clean calf pens or pitch hay for a meal. But this time, Gene didn't share his food packages with any of these hungry souls. His supply was waning. He watched their wretched faces and trudged on.

The prison column now moved through small villages, towns not touched by the air war that had targeted larger cities and pounded them to rubble. Many of them were packing up to escape the advancing Soviet armies, but these villagers had food and seemed friendly. Some prisoners approached the civilians and traded what few valuables they had for food. Fraternizing with German civilians was strictly forbidden, but the guards looked the other way as the starving kriegies gave up the last of their cigarettes and chocolate from their Red Cross packages. Some traded class rings and wedding bands for a chunk of bread. Gene kept his distance. He remembered German civilians nearly lynching him the day he was shot down. Did these Germans know they were airmen?

Sometimes the guards halted the column near farms where prisoners could shelter in a barn or a shed. One night, the hayloft and calf pens filled up before Gene and Shorty could find a spot to sleep. Gene was determined not to sleep out in the snowy field. He had an idea. He told Shorty to follow him outside to the back of the barn. They stopped at a mound of steaming manure.

"Baldy, I ain't sleeping on a shit pile," Shorty said, glaring at Gene.

"What difference does it make?" Gene asked. "We're already full of shit, and I'll guarantee you this will be the warmest bed here."

Shorty relented. The two Wisconsin boys clambered up the heap of livestock dung. They used their arms to push and grade the pile into a reasonable bed shape, at least one with a horizontal surface. Gene fetched some straw from the barn and sprinkled it over the top. Sleeping next to Shorty, Gene soaked in the warmth that radiated up through the manure. It was the warmest he'd been in months.

February turned to March. They'd been marching for more than a month, and Gene still didn't have a clue where he was headed. The guards didn't even know. They seemed almost as miserable as the kriegies themselves. Most of the guards were older men, many in their sixties, men unfit for battle. They yelled less now—acting more like guides than guards. As the march grew from days to weeks, they allowed more rest breaks. Sometimes a command car would pull up next to the prisoner column. A German officer would step out, yell at the guards, and then get back in the car and drive away.

However, one guard's demeanor had not changed: Big Stoop. Stoop had patrolled near Gene's group ever since they'd left Stalag Luft 4. Gene marveled at his good fortune that Stoop had never come after him. The sadistic guard had slapped Shorty and Bill a few times back at the prison. On the march, Stoop didn't tire like the older guards, and he went out of his way to make life miserable. Big Stoop would purposefully stomp through puddles of melted snow to splash mud and slush on the prisoners. He frequently picked on a group of kriegies a few rows back from Gene and Shorty. Once, they heard his rifle butt slam into a prisoner's back, and the man crumpled to the ground. Gene dared not look back. Stoop screamed and kicked the man writhing in the mud.

"Baldy, that son of a bitch is gonna get his soon," Shorty muttered under his breath.

Big Stoop was a beast, but at least he was a known beast. Fear of the unknown plagued the kriegies. Would they be ambushed at the next turn in the road? Or executed? Gene thought back to last summer after the hell ship voyage when he and the other filthy sergeant gunners from Stalag Luft 6 stumbled off boxcars. He remembered the sight of young German Kriegsmarine soldiers waiting for them, machine guns pointed. He remembered the torturous run to Stalag Luft 4 and the warning from fellow prisoners that the Germans had machine gun crews hidden in the woods. Now Gene's stomach tightened every time he walked into a forest. It was the one time he wanted German guards near him. He figured hidden machine gun nests wouldn't open up on their own soldiers.

The march without end continued. The men became less human. They were already filthy from sleeping in barns and on open ground every night, and they'd worn the same clothes for months. Now many prisoners didn't wait for rest stops to defecate. Besides, they couldn't. Dysentery was rampant, and they couldn't control their bowels. The prisoner column was a mess of unwashed hands and soiled clothes. They'd been drinking from roadside ditches. Up and down the column, Gene heard bowels erupt. Just like the farm animals pulling refugee wagons. Gene did the same. He washed out his pants with melted snow at the end of the day.

One day, the haggard column reached a larger town. They passed a cemetery and saw a train station up ahead. A steaming locomotive was waiting in the marshalling yard.

Just then, Gene heard a faint whine coming from the sky. The whine became a snarl, then a roar. Gene spotted the silhouette of two airplanes.

"Mustangs!" someone screamed.

Suddenly, geysers of dirt exploded from the ground, heading right for Gene. He and Shorty shot from the prisoner column and sprinted for the cemetery. Kriegies and guards scattered in every direction. Gene had never seen Mustang fighter planes, but he spotted the American markings on their fuselages when they streaked overhead. *Goddammit! I'm gonna get killed by my own countrymen.*

Gene was shocked at the speed of the older guards. He ran with them and dove behind a headstone. A guard was already there. The old man kicked hard, catching Gene full in the thigh.

"My place! My place!" the guard screamed, giving Gene a few more kicks.

Gene rolled over and sprang up. He looked in the sky. The two fighter planes were turning back toward the prisoners. His head snapped back and forth, looking for any type of cover. He ran and jumped behind another gravestone that was unoccupied. He looked up, searching the sky.

American Mustang fighter planes arrived in England after Gene was shot down. He knew they were sleek and fast; other prisoners always talked about them. Gene peeked over the headstone and spotted the planes again. They were streaking in his direction. He couldn't look away. They were beautiful and terrifying. But this time, the Mustangs flew in a line heading toward the train station a few hundred yards away from the cemetery. Gene stared in awe as dirt geysers burst from the ground straight at the parked locomotive. The bullets found their mark.

Ka-Whoom!

The locomotive erupted in a cloud of steam that shot hundreds of feet into the air. The Mustangs roared overhead, banked in unison, and flew away, disappearing as quickly as they'd arrived. Gene watched the enormous steam cloud rise into the blue sky. The locomotive hissed like a dying beast. It was the most spectacular sight he'd ever seen.

Slowly, prisoners and guards stuck their heads out from around the gravestones. German soldiers ran from the train yard toward prostrate bodies lying on the ground. Gene could hear men crying and moaning. The guards screamed at the kriegies, waving their rifles and machine pistols for them to get back into a line. Shorty ran at Gene, and together they jogged back to the column of prisoners forming up.

"Eyes front!" a guard yelled while running along the side of the prisoners.

"*Schnell! Schnell!*" another guard ordered, waving the kriegies forward.

Gene and Shorty tried to make sense of what they'd just witnessed. Hustling away from the train yard, they had no idea how many prisoners or Germans had just been killed or wounded. Were the German guards hustling them away from the carnage so the German yard workers wouldn't exact their revenge? Was this a protective measure, or was there no thought at all, just run?

Gene had seen no Luftwaffe planes come out to duel the Mustangs. Actually, he couldn't remember the last time he'd seen a German plane in the air. Was this a sign that the war was coming to an end? After surviving all that he had, now a new concern weighed on Gene: Would he be killed by unopposed friendly fighter planes who mistook the POWs for German soldiers?

Marauding Mustangs were dangerous, but they weren't the daily danger to the prisoners. Starvation and fatigue were ever present, and much more likely to kill. Kriegies dropped in their tracks or fell asleep on frozen ground during the night, never to wake to their pleading buddies shaking their emaciated shoulders.

Each day, Gene cinched the rope that held up his shit-stained pants a little tighter. The prisoners walking ahead of him looked thinner too. The Red Cross food had long since disappeared. Sometimes, a horse pulling a small wagon would show up with something resembling bread. The kriegies maintained discipline amongst themselves when splitting up the bread. But even though every loaf was shared, Gene was lucky if he got a small piece.

For the most part, the prisoners were left to fend for themselves for their food. They had nothing to eat during the day as they marched. The Germans did try to end each day at a farm, where they let the starving men scrounge for a meal. Despite the chaos of war, German farmers continued to raise food. Some farms even had a few vegetables stored from the fall harvest.

At the end of another day's marching, Gene spotted a farmer stirring a large cast-iron kettle over a fire. The man was probably preparing evening slop for his hogs. Gene grabbed his Klim can, stepped out of line, and walked toward the kettle. He thrust the can down into the concoction of grain and water.

"*Schweinhund*," the farmer said, laughing at him.

Pig slop? Gene didn't mind. He smiled and walked away, chugging down the liquid. Other kriegies followed his lead. One by one, they scooped a share of the kettle slop for themselves.

"*Nein! Nein! Nein!*" the farmer yelled. He thrust his stirring stick out at them, but the starving prisoners kept coming. Soon, the kettle was empty.

They spent the night at the farm. The angry farmer lodged complaints with the guards, but they ignored him.

"Let's go scrounging," Gene told Shorty.

Gene understood the secret to finding hidden food. He knew some farmers buried vegetables in mounds for the winter, so he looked for slightly raised ground. With bare hands, he and Shorty clawed at a cold dirt mound. Jackpot! They found a few abandoned potatoes and rutabagas.

Other prisoners quickly realized Gene was a food magnet. Each night, an entourage of fellow kriegies followed him as he went scrounging. If they did find some potatoes, they roasted them. The

Germans allowed small cooking fires inside barns or under shed roofs. The kriegies skewered the potatoes on small tree branches and blackened them over the fire. They'd learned that charcoaled potatoes slowed diarrhea. They also used the charcoal to rub over toothaches. One evening, an American doctor who'd been imprisoned with the sergeant gunners at Stalag Luft 4 walked up to the fire where Gene and other kriegies were roasting potatoes on sticks.

"You boys make sure you eat the skins before you blacken those too much," the doctor advised. "The skin is where all the vitamins are."

That made sense. From then on, Gene made sure to never waste a potato skin.

On another nighttime stop, Gene saw a two-story shed that he thought might be a granary. He and Shorty ran straight for it, and several other prisoners followed. The door to the main room was locked, so Gene raced up the stairs to the second floor. Empty. Or was it? Gene pried up the floorboards and looked down to the first floor. Below them was a mound of barley.

Gene and Shorty squeezed through the hole of the floor and dropped onto the pile of food, scooping up handfuls of grain and chowing down great fistfuls. After eating, they filled the inside of their filthy pants with as much grain as they could carry. When Gene tried to climb back through the hole, he got stuck. His comrades above him on the second floor yanked his arms, but couldn't pull him up. Gene sighed. He dropped his pants and unloaded some of the barley until he could fit through the hole. Gene and Shorty waddled around outside with grain spilling from the cuffs of their pants, pointing at the granary so the other prisoners could get their share.

It was rare to find such a bounty, however, especially as the march dragged on. Each farm seemed to have less food than the one the night before. They were allowed only to scrounge for vegetables and grain. The guards strictly forbade prisoners from stealing chickens or eggs. That food was for Germans only. But some men became desperate. One night at dusk, the prisoner column had just halted when Gene watched a prisoner break from the line and sneak into a chicken coop. He ran back out with two eggs in his hands and disappeared over a small rise, out of Gene's sight. A guard followed him.

Crack!

The rifle shot echoed in Gene's ears. Word was passed down the line: *Don't go near chicken coops.*

Drinking water also became scarce. The melting snows of winter had long since disappeared. They could march for hours without even getting the respite of a roadside ditch.

But again, Gene's childhood on a farm gave him knowledge the other prisoners didn't have. In the morning after they'd sheltered at a farm, Gene got up early and went looking for a cow pasture. He knew the morning dew pooled in deep cow tracks that he'd find in the mud. It wasn't long before other kriegies joined Gene lying flat on their bellies, lapping at the water in the tracks.

Men began to die of starvation and dehydration. Many dropped as they marched. Sometimes they were conscious, sometimes not. The guards picked up a collapsed prisoner and tossed him onto a horse-drawn wagon. Sometimes, after the column moved ahead, a rifle shot rang out. Then the name of the man who fell would pass down the line, identifying the latest victim.

Gene couldn't guess how many fellow POWs were dying or what happened to the bodies. He and Shorty figured the Germans probably just tossed them in the woods or dumped them in a nearby ditch. The guards certainly wasted no time getting rid of fallen prisoners. The column had to keep moving.

The prisoners trudged forward in silence. They had no energy to talk. The only sound was the shuffling of feet on the dirt road and the scraping of pants legs encrusted with dried urine and feces. Occasionally, a rare cigarette passed down the line for prisoners to share. Once, Gene got a nub so small that he puckered his lips to inhale the last drag. He accidentally sucked the butt into his mouth and swallowed it.

Many kriegies walked without shoes. Gene was almost barefoot. Two months of marching through all types of weather and terrain had shredded his canvas tennis shoes. A horse-drawn cart traveled up and down the column, picking up limping men. Gene prided himself on never having to sit on the cart. But large blisters and cuts now covered his feet. When the horse cart came by, he swallowed his pride and hobbled over to it. One day off his feet, that's all he needed. Yet he felt ashamed when the cart passed other prisoners limping.

The next day, he was back in the line. Somebody tapped Gene's shoulder as he walked. He looked over at a man wearing a clerical collar.

"Father Lynch!" Gene blurted out. He couldn't believe his eyes. The mysterious priest had shown up again just as he had in the prison camps and on the hell ship.

"Hello, Sergeant Moran," the priest answered.

Gene was flattered that Father Lynch knew his name. Perhaps the priest remembered Gene from all those confessions while walking around Stalag Luft 6 and Stalag Luft 4 with Shorty and Bill. Father Lynch reached into his coat pocket and handed Gene a three-inch by five-inch book with a black paper cover.

"I want you to have this," the priest said. It was a copy of the New Testament. "The war will be over soon. Keep your faith and hang in there."

Still marching, Gene shook the priest's hand, grasping it for a few seconds.

"Thank you, Father."

Father Lynch disappeared as quickly as he'd arrived that day. Gene looked over at Shorty.

"He's like John the Baptist. He just shows up anywhere."

Gene had a chance to read his gift that night. He hadn't seen a printed word for more than two months, and with the April daylight hours getting longer, the German guards often stopped the march an hour before dark. Each evening, he took out the small book and read a few passages that gave him some comfort. But what he really needed was food. Anything.

His nightly scrounging had turned up nothing. Like many of the kriegies, Gene pulled new grass shoots from the warm spring ground and ate them. Other prisoners turned over dead wood on the ground, looking for grubs which they swallowed whole.

Most of the farms they stopped at now were stripped bare of food, often raided by starving refugees. The refugees weren't just Polish or German now. They spoke a mix of languages, and they filled the roads alongside the kriegies. Some rode in overcrowded buses or on the backs of trucks over roads too damaged to handle such traffic after six years of war. Most refugees traveled in small groups. Some begged the prisoners for food. But Gene had none to give. The refugees shared more horror stories of the Red Army's raping and pillaging back at the battlefront. The accounts didn't surprise Gene. The Russians had been despised by the Germans, and now they were taking their revenge. He thought back to Sandbostel Prison where he'd seen, at a distance, massed Russians staring from behind a fence. He remembered the starvation and cholera outbreaks that had killed so many malnourished Soviet soldiers. So many dead Russians . . . he paused and rubbed his fingers over his scar. He would never know for sure if the flesh sewn into his scalp was Russian or not.

Gene started seeing bodies of all ages lying in the ditch. Refugees, kriegies. More and more prisoners were falling out.

Gene willed himself not to fall. He knew he was getting weaker. He clutched the New Testament in his pocket and kept putting one foot in front of the other.

CHAPTER 16

Liberation

April 2013

My stages of grief: shock, denial, anger, acceptance. Despite living with Carmen's cancer for ten years, her death had still come as a shock to me. I'd blindly believed we would beat it. Then I headed straight to the anger stage, where I planned to remain.

Interviewing Gene again helped. At least it distracted me. I'd survived my first interview since Carmen's death, even with her photo gazing down at me over Gene's kitchen table. But Thursdays with Gene only took care of Thursdays. On the other six days, my anger and loss threatened to consume me.

I had just two reasons for getting out of bed in the morning: to take care of the boys and to write Gene's story. All else was meaningless. I let friendships wane. I had no desire to visit family. Dating was out of the question. Raise Matthew and Joe and write the story of a man who fell four miles without a parachute. Once those two tasks were done, I would build a secluded cabin on a lake and tell the rest of the world to go to hell.

Matthew and Joe immersed themselves in school and sports.

Parenting came down to the basics: just add food and water, keep the electric bill paid, and clean the toilets occasionally. My task to write Gene's story, on the other hand, needed a jump start. I was not a writer. I had no idea how to find an agent or a publisher. I still felt I had no business taking on one of the greatest survival stories I'd ever heard. But I remembered Ben Logan's words three years earlier: "Gene's story deserves a book." And the same thought haunted me: *If I don't write it, who will?*

It was clear I needed help. But how? The answer appeared in my UW–Madison alumni magazine, where I saw an advertisement for a writers' workshop. The workshop promised meeting agents, authors, and editors, and was open to writers of all abilities and at any stage of their current writing project. This was what I needed. Writing was not my world. This would be the place to start.

Prospective writers attending the conference had to submit a writing sample, which would be reviewed by a professional. I typed my first draft of chapter one. I wrote it as a history teacher, not a writer, and loaded it with too many facts, background, and big-picture analysis. It lacked a human connection. How could I take such an incredible story and make it mundane? But still, I had the required sample ready to send to Madison.

At the conference, I met author and editor Heather Shumaker. Heather read that first draft and asked what my plans were for Gene's story. I told her I was going to write it and that Gene's children would front the costs to self-publish the story for a local audience. But Heather saw more. She wanted to meet again.

Yes! The first good news I'd had since Carmen died. This is what I hoped for. Guidance through a world I didn't understand. Now was the time to begin. I'd been working part-time at school because of bereavement leave, but I'd return full-time in the fall. Returning to teaching amidst raising sons and fruit, there would be no time for writing conferences. I needed Heather now.

We arranged to have dinner that evening with three other

writers attending the conference. Our group crowded into a booth at a small Nepalese restaurant. After ordering wine, everyone shared their writing projects. I said nothing. *Why am I here? I can't do this. It's spring. I should be hitting fly balls to the boys in the big yard in front of the barn.* Heather sensed my insecurity.

"John is going to write a beautiful book about a remarkable World War II survivor story," she said.

I looked at Heather and said to myself, *You're a hundred pounds soaking wet, and your wine glass is empty.* I didn't share her confidence in me. I was dining with real writers. I didn't belong.

Heather and I met in the hotel lobby after dinner to map out a plan. She believed Gene's story had the potential for a bigger audience than the Kickapoo Valley. She advised me to submit my writing to thorough editing and to seek a publisher. She agreed to be my editor, but told me that writing a good nonfiction book could take years, maybe five years, what with the research, writing, and revising. And with me now being a single dad with a full-time job, it might be longer.

"I'm going to warn you," Heather said. "This will not be easy. Good books take time."

Gene didn't have that kind of time.

The very next day, Joni called me in my hotel room. Gene had had a heart attack. He was alive, but recovering in the VA hospital in Madison just over a mile from my hotel.

A heart attack? No. This was not the end. Not three months after losing Carmen, and not after Heather's news that his story had so much promise. Gene needed to get better. He simply had to. We had so much work to do.

I was so desperate to see him right away, but Joni suggested later in the day. When I arrived, Gene's son, Mike, was there. Mike sat in one of those plastic chairs for patient room visitors that I knew so well. But I was surprised to see Gene himself standing next to his bed. He was supposed to be the patient—he'd just had a heart attack!

Gene was dressed in a canary-yellow gown, open at the chest. A blue-and-white adhesive patch was stuck near his heart, and he leaned on a wooden cane. But Gene was still Gene. Wearing his signature black Army Air Corps baseball cap, he grinned and handed me a photograph.

"Here, check this out," Gene rasped in his gravelly voice.

The picture was Gene standing in his hospital robe holding his cane. He was flanked by two young women topped with tiaras and wearing sashes that read "Miss Wisconsin" and "Miss Teen Wisconsin." Both beauty queens had long, blonde hair and sported radiant smiles.

"What do you think of that?" Gene said, chuckling. He looked better already.

I laughed and shook my head. Joni's phone call had startled me into thinking Gene might be dying. Then when I get to the hospital, here's this married man who's twice my age hanging out with beauty queens. I just couldn't compete when it came to a decorated World War II veteran.

Gene had survived again. Even at eighty-eight years old, it seemed nothing could kill him. He looked well enough for me to share my news about the writing conference. How an editor liked it. How she thought people outside southwestern Wisconsin might read it. How it could even be a real book, published and sitting in bookstores.

"Wow," Mike said, leaning back in his chair. "What do you think, Dad?"

I jumped in before Gene could answer. "If we do this, look for a publisher . . ." I paused, carefully reviewing the next sentence in my head. "If we do this, it's going to take time, five years, maybe more."

Sitting on the side of his bed, Gene nodded. He needed no further explanation. He knew what I was getting at.

"This is your call, Gene," I said. Did he just want me to get the story down on paper for his family and friends? Or was he willing to take the time with me and craft his story into a compelling read for a larger audience?

He didn't hesitate.

"John. If I don't read it down here," Gene said, then pointed at the ceiling, "I'll read it up there."

April 1945

Gene and Shorty shuffled forward with the rest of the prisoners. They rarely spoke. There was nothing to say. Conversation consumed energy that starving bodies couldn't spare.

Some prisoners walked barefoot. When their shoes shredded beyond use, they kicked away the remnants. Gene's shoes were at their end. Shreds of cloth barely clung to the rubber soles of his tennis shoes, but he wouldn't toss them to the roadside—not yet. They didn't help much against the muddy roads. Now that it was April, spring rains soaked the dirt roads, turning them into cold slop. The ragged fragments of Gene's shoes didn't keep the mud out, but they did provide some cover on his feet when evenings turned chilly.

Kriegies with no shoes or coats tried to steal clothes from fallen prisoners or dead refugees, but only if the Germans didn't grab the clothes first. By now, the guards looked almost as miserable as the prisoners. They didn't have anything to eat, either. By spring, all the farms had been ransacked by the thousands of prisoners, refugees, and German soldiers that came before them. The yelling had stopped. Like the kriegies, the guards hardly spoke at all. They just plodded forward. If a prisoner asked where they were going, the Germans answered, "Next town, next town."

Things improved a bit when the spring sun appeared and warmed Gene's lice-ridden sweatshirt. The constant diarrhea had slowed since he learned to charcoal his potatoes before eating them. But two plagues never left him: hunger and lice. There were also fewer potatoes every night. Some kriegies ate burnt wood to stop the "runs."

The prisoner column thinned each day. Frostbite had taken its toll in February and March. Now pneumonia swept the ranks of haggard prisoners. Packed into wooden barns for the night, Gene and Shorty listened to the coughing of sick men lying on damp dirt or straw, often filthy with manure. The ill usually died at night. After another day of toughing it out, striving to keep up on the march and not fall into a roadside ditch, the sick men sank into the sodden straw of their barn beds and never woke up.

The next day, the march to nowhere continued. Men too weak to walk clung to a buddy to assist them. Gene leaned on Shorty when his lower back ached, and Shorty put his arm on Gene's shoulder when he grew weak from hunger. When prisoners lagged, the guards half-heartedly prodded them with rifles. Carts still traveled up and down the prisoner column packed with the most lame and sick, but because of the shortage of horses, kriegies pulled some of the carts. Gene was as weak and sore as the prisoners on the "sick wagons," but he refused to hop on. He remembered the judgmental stares he'd seen the one day he'd ridden the wagon, his blistered feet so sore he couldn't walk. He slogged on. Others fell back to the end of the column where they collapsed by the roadside. Gene had no idea how many men had died since the kriegies evacuated Stalag Luft 4 two months ago. But he knew it was bad when the Germans stopped taking roll call. The march to nowhere had become a death march.

But it was also fatal to stop.

One morning, Gene heard a whine in the sky. It was a plane with that unique snarl. By now, he knew better than to wait to identify the sound.

Mustangs. American Mustang fighter planes. *Again.*

Gene cursed. How bitter it was to dodge machine gun fire from Americans. He'd been strafed by planes several times since the day he'd seen Mustangs blow up that German locomotive. *Here we go again.*

Gaunt men wearily scattered from the road. Gene and Shorty hobbled to a ditch and collapsed onto the wet grass. The drone above them grew to a roar. They hugged the ground and waited for machine gun bullets to strike. Nothing. Gene raised his head. No sprays of dirt fountains. Gene looked up again. Above him, one Mustang fighter plane roared past, waggling his wing tips as he flew. The pilot flew so low, Gene could see his face. Another Mustang raced by, repeating the wing rocking. This pilot was waving wildly from his cockpit.

The pilots knew! They knew these were POWs!

Gene stood up, elated. He shielded his eyes from the sun and watched the Mustangs disappear in the distance. Just maybe this was a sign that the march to nowhere had an end. The pilots were waving, not killing. How did the American pilots know? And no enemy aircraft either. Gene's spirits rose even further. It had happened before, but now again: no German planes in sight, no enemies challenging these American fighter planes. Germany *had* to be close to surrender.

A few days later, another American plane flew by. This time, it was a twin-engine attack bomber with its bomb doors open. Paper pamphlets, not bombs, fluttered from its bomb bay. The pamphlets were in German, instructions on where and how the German soldiers were to surrender.

Kriegie spirits soared, and soon more hints emerged that their ordeal was nearly over. The prisoners passed through towns where white flags and white bedsheets hung from upper windowsills. Every day, American Mustang and Thunderbolt fighter planes shot over the prisoner column. Occasionally, Gene spotted a British plane, but never any airplanes with black crosses and swastikas. They no longer ran from the road when they heard planes approaching, but instead waved at the pilots.

The guards changed too. They smiled at the kriegies now and chatted. Even Big Stoop walked up near Gene and Shorty and cracked a joke. Shorty didn't laugh.

"It's too late for that bastard," Shorty muttered to Gene.

At nighttime stops, the guards relaxed their strict boundaries. When Gene and Shorty scrounged for food in the evening, it seemed they could walk a little further away from the guards.

Liberation was in the air. Gene could smell it, breathe it. But would it come soon enough? Kriegies continued to drop on the march.

Dysentery and malnutrition slowed the column to a crawl. The guards suffered too, and no longer yelled at anyone to walk faster. There were no more bathroom breaks. The road was the toilet, and the sound of defecating bowels was as common as shuffling feet.

With the Germans loosening their guard, kriegies with any strength left began to escape. Gene and Shorty discussed making a break for it. They weighed their options. They'd go in the middle of the night, when the sky was darkest and there were fewer guards awake. They'd run and find a meal somewhere. But did they have the strength to roam about the German countryside scrounging for food? Maybe instead they could hide out in a house basement in some town until the American lines arrived. There might be food in that basement. But if civilians found them first, would they turn escapees over to the German military? Would the civilians kill them outright? Or with the end of the war so close, maybe German citizens would be kind and curry favor with Americans.

Both men were barefoot. Gene had tossed away the last shreds of his tennis shoes days ago. He'd torn cloth from his blanket to wrap his feet. What if they ran into German soldiers? Would they be able to run away on calloused feet wrapped in blanket shreds?

The trouble was they had no idea how close the Allied armies were. They might waste the last of their precious energy if they took off on their own, perhaps wandering just as aimlessly as they did now in the prisoner column.

Gene and Shorty lay on the ground and huddled next to other kriegies. They decided to wait to escape, at least until they heard the booming of Allied guns.

The next day, the prisoners marched to the Elbe River in central Germany. Gene and Shorty met other groups of POWs equally miserable also marching west. They all crossed a bridge to the western side of the Elbe. The following morning, they crossed back over the same bridge and returned to the east bank. Gene seethed. They were starving and wasting precious energy walking on a bridge only to cross back over it. Thousands of panicky refugees stumbled along with them. No one seemed to know where they were going, not even the Germans.

On the morning of April 26, German guards rounded up the kriegies for another day of pointless marching. While forming up, Gene recognized his old barracks chief from Stalag Luft 4 walking back through the prisoner column. The chief had a bounce in his step. Gene, Shorty, and others gathered around him.

"The Germans are saying the American line is at the next river, about ten miles away," the chief said. "So just look straight and march. Don't cause any trouble or make any foolish moves."

Even to men on the brink of death, the news was electric. But Gene was cautious with his optimism. He'd believe it when he saw white stars on American tanks and jeeps.

The prisoners walked faster than they had in weeks. This road was jammed with refugees and German soldiers also moving west as fast as they could. *Maybe the American troops are close.* Gene had trouble keeping up with the mass of human beings suddenly surging forward. Infected sores covered his bare feet. The lack of food was finally catching up to him. He'd never felt so weak.

The prisoner column reached the east bank of the Mulde River by afternoon. About a ten-mile trek, just as the barracks chief had said. On the other side sat the town of Bitterfeld. Gene saw military vehicles moving amidst the trees on the opposite bank. He held his breath. The trucks and tanks were not the dull-gray color of the German military. They looked olive-green, but from a distance and with the trees in the way, he couldn't be sure.

The bridge across the Mulde had been bombed. It was largely intact, but a section near the west bank sat partially submerged in the water. At the end of the bridge, the metal structure stuck out of the water at a steep angle. People crowded the bridge. Gene looked around and estimated ten thousand refugees gesturing, shouting, and clamoring to get across. They shouted in multiple languages, but the meaning was the same: should they cross the damaged structure?

The German soldiers didn't wait. Suddenly, the guards threw down their rifles and stepped on the angled surface of the bridge. The prisoners followed. They didn't advance all at once, instead venturing out in groups of five to ten. At first, everyone walked over the largely undamaged east end of the bridge. But when they reached the bent section, they lowered themselves onto their hands and knees and clambered like crabs.

It was Gene and Shorty's turn to cross. They leaned back when reaching the first bent portion and then dropped to all fours. Gene inched forward on his knees, limbs shaking. Below him, the current swirled. The river was swollen with the spring snowmelt. He knew he didn't have the energy to swim if he fell into the current. One slip and almost three months of starvation and marching would end with him drowning. He crawled forward, again, his skinny body struggling. Halfway across the bridge, he stopped and gasped for air. Shorty waited next to him.

"Go on," Gene told Shorty. "I'll catch up. Go."

Shorty dutifully crawled forward. He had to, with the bridge loaded with prisoners pressing behind. Gene gulped in a few more breaths of air and gazed up. Soldiers milled on the west bank. Soldiers dressed in olive drab uniforms. There was no doubt now.

American soldiers!

The sight gave him a burst of energy. He crawled forward again, ignoring the water below. Up ahead was a broken section. Gene dropped down, clinging to bent struts, fighting gravity. Now he faced the last section of the bridge which rose out of the water at a sharp incline. He gauged the distance. Would his wounded forearms and weakened legs fail him? He was just yards from freedom. On his hands and knees, breathing heavily, he clawed his way up the steep surface. It was like climbing up a wet silo ladder back at the farm. Slick, steep, but now nearly impossible with his diminished body.

He was fifty feet from the end of the bridge. Gene's muscles had nothing left. He collapsed. Gene lay facedown on the last section. He tried to raise his body, he pushed against the bridge with his bent forearms—but it was no use. He couldn't get up. His body had finally quit.

For eighty days, Gene had walked six hundred miles through ice, snow, and mud to an unknown destination where many of his comrades thought they'd all be shot. Now he couldn't crawl the last fifty feet to freedom on a warm late-April day.

He was barefoot, his feet covered with infected cuts and seeping abscesses. The same pants he'd worn for months were caked in dried feces and urine. He hadn't eaten in days. He couldn't move. He was done.

Then Gene felt two hands grab his shoulders. Two hands that guided him and lifted him on his feet. He was looking into the smiling, youthful face of a soldier wearing an American infantry helmet.

"Come up out of there, buddy. I got ya," the soldier said.

The American soldier heaved Gene onto his shoulder as if he were a feed bag and climbed the last fifty feet to the end of the bridge. More hands reached from the riverbank to grab Gene. They carried him to a spot under a tree and set him down on his feet. Gene steadied himself. A soldier handed him a canteen, and Gene gulped down most of the water. Then he collapsed.

"Jesus Christ, they said there'd be a thousand of them, not ten thousand."

Gene opened his eyes and stared at the trunk of a tree. He didn't know how long he'd been out. All about him was chaos. Filthy kriegies milled about, not knowing what to do. Refugees begged for food. The bridge over the Mulde still crawled with humans.

The American soldiers wore shoulder patches with the image of a timber wolf. It was the 104th Infantry Division, part of General George Patton's army. Some prisoners hugged the American liberators as they stepped off the bridge. Gene didn't hug anyone. He and many other POWs simply stared, too tired to move, unable to comprehend their sudden freedom.

Liberation became a little more real when Gene watched American soldiers round up the German guards and march them away. Their turn to be prisoners. Gene sighed and shuffled over to a kriegie who was piling up twigs and broken furniture pieces. The man started a fire and set his Klim can near the blaze.

"What are you doing?" Gene asked.

"I'm going to warm up some coffee," the prisoner answered. "And there ain't nobody that's gonna stop me."

Gene nodded and went to find Shorty. It was near dusk when American officers and sergeants managed to restore some order on the riverbank. Gene and Shorty were both sent to the rear of the American lines where there was a compound of trucks and tents. They were directed to the largest tent.

The tent teemed with arriving prisoners. Soldiers ran in and out of the doorway. Inside was chaos. Some American GIs handed their K-rations to the starving prisoners. An officer hurried up. "Stop! Stop!" he cried. "Stop feeding the prisoners."

A group of eight POWs had already died when they overindulged on fresh bread, which their shrunken stomachs couldn't digest. No bread. No rich food. They'd receive some soup in the evening and more food in the morning after a night's rest.

Gene and Shorty gratefully sipped a small cup of broth. Then they lay down, not on the high spot of an icy bog or on a manure pile—but on actual cots. Hundreds of other kriegies crammed the tent with the same coughs and stench, but in one afternoon, the world had changed. Staring up at the tent's canvas ceiling, Gene tried to comprehend it all. For the first time in seventeen months, he was not a prisoner. He didn't feel free. He couldn't eat what he wanted. Officers still told him what to do and where to stand. But after months of marching to nowhere, he'd slurped warm soup and now lay on a dry bed under real blankets. Gene drifted off to sleep, the occasional *rat-a-tat-tat* of machine gun fire from the front lines punctuating the night.

The next day, the prisoners received food. Gene was given a small bowl of oatmeal and a thin slice of bread, no butter. After the light meal, it was time to travel. They were herded onto the backs of trucks for a long ride to Halle, Germany, site of an American Army base. On the truck, Shorty sidled up next to Gene.

"They killed Big Stoop," Shorty said. "They cut him up good."

Gene was stunned. He'd never given another thought to the giant beast-man since he'd been out from under his clutches. Miraculously, Big Stoop had never touched him, but he'd seen the sadist guard slap up Shorty and Bill a few times back at Stalag Luft 4. In chilling detail, Shorty described how several men jumped on Big Stoop at a roadside and one former prisoner slammed a pickaxe into his head. They cut off his head and tossed it into a ditch and left the body on the road. The American soldiers who were supposed to be guarding Big Stoop and the other captured Germans did nothing to stop them.

Gene glanced at his buddy. So many vivid details about that roadside scene. Then he knew. Shorty must have been there, per- haps even joined in on the killing. *Had he done it? Had Shorty been one of the killers?* Gene wanted to know, wanted to ask, but he fought the urge. It didn't matter. Big Stoop was dead.

Looking out of the back of the truck, Gene saw the beauty of the German countryside in the spring daylight. There was no war here. Just quaint houses surrounded by green, leafy trees and rolling farm fields. Big Stoop was gone. There were spring flowers and new grass in the country. It was beginning to feel like freedom.

The cities were different. The convoy stopped near a German city for a short break. Urinating on the side of the road, Gene stared at the great heaps of rubble everywhere. City? It was the corpse of a city. Silence enveloped the ruins. No dogs barked. No children called. Thin wisps of smoke still rose from some of the gutted buildings.

The Americans scrambled back to the trucks in silence. The war had returned to them. This is what Allied bombers had done. What had it looked like before? How many mothers and children had been killed?

The back-jarring ride continued for twelve hours over mud-rutted roads. Finally, the convoy pulled into an American Army base outside the city of Halle in late evening. The compound was a former Luftwaffe base, but now it teemed with American soldiers. Olive drab jeeps and trucks were parked everywhere. After one day of freedom, a treat awaited the former prisoners. A luxury they couldn't have fathomed two days before: a hot shower.

Gene peeled off his filthy rags and strode into the shower room. Hot, clean water splashed on his skin for the first time in seventeen months. The first time since his last hot shower back at Snetterton Heath Air Base in England. Gene stood still under the showerhead, soaking in the water's warmth. The simple bliss of clean, hot water. It was the greatest sensation he'd ever felt.

After showering, Army privates handed Gene a fresh set of clean clothes. He slid on the Army underwear. *Clean underwear!* He couldn't believe it. For nearly three months, he'd walked in clothes soaked in his own waste. Gene stood, dressed only in his underwear, and smiled. He was in no hurry to put on his pants. Clean underwear. A clean rear end. This was freedom.

Gene soon realized that freedom came in stages. Advancing to the mess hall after getting dressed, Gene and Shorty were disappointed at the menu: oatmeal, jello, and mashed potatoes with no butter. Doctor's orders. Soft food was all the prisoners could digest. Loading his tray, Gene thought of the story of the eight POWs back at Bitterfeld who'd enjoyed only a few hours of freedom before dying an agonizing death from eating too much fresh bread. At the end of the food line, Gene and Shorty did spot angel food cake. Was it off-limits? They each took a piece. Sitting at the table, Shorty ate dessert first.

"Baldy, that is the best cake I've ever had."

A brief physical examination came next. Gene stepped on a scale: 128 pounds. He'd weighed about 170 pounds before he was shot down. Some of the other prisoners in the examination room with Gene had fared worse, weighing in between 90 and 100 pounds. Gene had starved too, but his country boy skills at finding food managed to keep a few more pounds on his body.

Once they'd been cleaned, clothed, fed, and examined, all the former POWs were assigned to barracks. Since the Halle headquarters was a former German air base, Gene mused at the irony of sleeping in beds once occupied by enemy airmen.

"We're going to leave you guys alone," an officer said, speaking in soft, friendly tones. "Check the bulletin board in the morning for any assignments, but if you see nothing, you're free to do as you please. Just make sure you're back here for evening roll call. You are restricted to the base."

The POWs were allowed to check out bicycles to cruise around the base.

After a couple of days on the base at Halle, meatless meals and short bike rides grew dull for Gene. He and Shorty stared glumly at the morning message board: no assignments.

"What do you say about doing some scrounging today?" Gene asked.

Shorty needed no convincing to sneak off the base with Gene. On their bicycle rides, they'd noticed a hole in the barbed wire that ringed the perimeter. But when they pedaled up to the opening, they saw an armed soldier standing guard next to it.

Gene and Shorty were not dismayed. They set their bikes on the grass and approached the soldier. It didn't take long for the guard to figure out what Gene and Shorty wanted.

"Here's how I see it," the soldier explained. "I've been assigned to guard this hole, and I'm not letting you through. But there are a few other holes further down which I hold no responsibility for."

Gene and Shorty took off where the guard pointed, and, sure enough, there was another hole in the barbed-wire fence. The two friends slipped through the hole and sauntered outside. Soon, they came upon a parked U.S. Army car. No one was in it. Gene spotted the keys in the ignition.

"Get in," he ordered Shorty.

Now this was freedom! Gene drove away from the ruins of Halle and headed out to the countryside. It was a sunny May day. They passed a few picturesque villages that had not been destroyed by the war. The joy ride was like a dream. Gene hadn't driven a car since his last leave back home in Wisconsin almost two years earlier.

They stopped at a village in front of what looked to be the most beautiful house in the small town. A nice house might have some food. Who knows? Gene and Shorty approached the door and knocked. A well-dressed man appeared who spoke some English. The man explained that he was the burgermeister of the town, and Gene and Shorty were welcome to dine with them.

"We do not have much food here, but you're welcome to what we have," he said.

Gene was startled. Such a friendly reception in enemy territory! He accepted. He and Shorty entered the house and sat down at a table draped in linen cloth. The burgermeister's wife set boiled eggs in porcelain cups before them. Two teenage daughters, both beauties, joined their American guests at the table. Gene looked past the girls. He had no interest in women or romance; all his senses were fixed on what food the burgermeister's wife would bring to the table next. She brought out bread and some sliced meat. The burgermeister encouraged Gene and Shorty to eat as much as they desired.

The glow of the evening sun entered the dining room when Gene and Shorty realized they needed to get back to their base. They politely excused themselves and drove back to Halle, leaving the car near enough to where they'd found it. Then they ran back through the hole in the fence and hustled back to their barracks . . . too late. They'd missed roll call. The officer in charge of the prisoners found Gene and Shorty just before lights-out.

"Where the hell have you two been?" the officer asked in a voice that seemed disgruntled, but not angry. Gene wasn't going to lie.

"We were hungry. We just went looking for something to eat."

Gene explained the general direction and location where he and Shorty traveled. He said nothing about stealing the car.

"You guys were several miles beyond our front lines," the officer explained. "There are still bands of German soldiers running around, especially young die-hards looking for revenge. Don't travel outside secured areas."

The officer paused and looked Gene and Shorty squarely in the eyes.

"And next time, make sure you use the bikes."

Gene and Shorty got the message. The next few days, with the morning message board showing no responsibilities, they hopped on bikes and traveled the outskirts of Halle. As they gained strength each day, they rode out a little further from the main city. They learned that the little hamlets not touched by war had friendlier people who shared their food.

The news of Germany's surrender came on May 8, 1945. Gene

and Shorty didn't celebrate or pay much attention to the announcement. For them, the war was over on April 26, 1945. The day they'd crossed the bridge at Bitterfeld.

Shortly after Germany's capitulation, Gene and Shorty waited in line with other former prisoners to board one of the C-47 transport planes parked nose to tail on a runway. The men were headed to Camp Lucky Strike, a giant tent city located near the English Channel in northwestern France. The U.S. Army set up the camp specifically as a gathering post for ex-POWs.

Gene sat in the plane, this time as a passenger. He listened to the engines rev up before takeoff. Then the wheels pounded down the runway, and he was airborne.

Airborne!

The sensation of being in the air overwhelmed Gene. The liftoff from the runway, the rush of flight brought him back to *Rikki Tikki Tavi*. All those times he'd taken off, his buddies beside him.

He looked out the window. He'd left the air war a year and a half ago, but the bombing had continued long after he was shot down. Any German town of any size was a splotch of gray ash against the green of the fields and forests that surrounded it. Devastation. Flying over France, Gene witnessed the same scene. Town after town smashed to gray rubble. They landed briefly in Rheims, France. Gene spotted the towers and spire of the famous cathedral from the airfield. Still standing. At least some of Europe's beautiful landmarks had survived the war.

Gene's transport plane set down on a temporary airstrip near the French city of Le Havre. They were taken to a sprawling tent city crammed with ex-POWs: Camp Lucky Strike. At Camp Lucky Strike, Gene learned that he was no longer a POW; the Army had relabeled him as a RAMP: Recovered Allied Military Personnel.

What followed was a whirlwind of activity: showers, a full medical examination, and new uniforms. Gene liked dressing in an Army Air Corps uniform again. He also received new wool shirts, underwear, socks, and overseas caps with the insignia of rank pinned to the cap.

RAMPs who were aerial gunners ended with a thorough debriefing by an Army Air Corps intelligence officer. The interrogating officer pressed Gene about his time as a prisoner.

"How was the Baltic cruise?" he asked. "Or the run up the road?"

Gene bristled when the officer called the hell ship a cruise. The stench, the suffocating heat, his desperate search for water, men licking drops off the steel hull between the rivets . . . or the tortuous run afterward on the way to Stalag Luft 4, German guard dogs biting at his heels, rabid young German soldiers stabbing with their bayonets, kriegies in torn, bloody pants falling . . . Gene pushed away the nightmare images. He kept his answers brief.

It was the first time Gene talked about the hell ship and the torture run on the route to Stalag Luft 4. The intelligence officer let him go, realizing Gene wasn't going to divulge much.

Why should he? He'd be going home soon. Back to Mom's home cooking. Back to drinking from the creek with Wisconsin's best water. Reliving the hell of being a prisoner would only consume him. He'd bury those memories. It was time to be free.

At Lucky Strike, the liberated prisoners had two duties: eat and relax. The menu was still soft food, but had expanded a bit. Gene got to eat creamed chicken and potatoes. Later, American young women from the Red Cross served doughnuts and milkshakes made with real ice cream. Now that his belly was full, the sight of young women in skirts turned Gene's mind to thoughts he hadn't had in a long time. He remembered his last date almost three years ago with Peg. Peg Finley. Gene had promised her a second meeting after their first blind date. Was she still waiting for him? Did she ever think about him? Gene made up his mind that he'd ask Peg out as soon as he got home. Suddenly, Gene became very anxious to leave Europe.

The ex-POWs had no duties other than to stay on the base and stay out of trouble. Now there was no need to sneak off the base in search of food. Gene had plenty to eat, and the milkshakes and chicken were good. Besides, he didn't want to miss his first opportunity for the plane ride home.

The officers at Lucky Strike were exceedingly polite to the former prisoners. There were no marching, drilling, or kitchen duties. Instead, the Army set up movie theaters in some of the tents, though the lines to see them were long.

At dusk each evening, Gene joined hundreds of others who stood by the gate to watch trucks drop off new loads of liberated prisoners. Most of the ex-POWs at Camp Lucky Strike were enlisted men, but one night, truckloads of Air Corps officers arrived. Gene headed out immediately to look for Orrison, his "big brother." Was it possible that he might see him? Gene had last heard Orrison was alive back at Dulag Luft from the lips of the Luftwaffe interrogator. Had the man been telling the truth? Besides, that was more than fifteen months ago. More than a year. Anything could have happened to him since then. Killed in an air raid, died of wounds, died in a prison bunk of dysentery. He had no idea if Orrison had been injured when *Rikki Tikki Tavi* went down. Did he survive prison? Maybe he was liberated but sent to England or a different camp. Or maybe the Dulag Luft interrogator had been lying to get Gene to talk. He might never know, and certainly might never find him at Camp Lucky Strike amongst tens of thousands of prisoners.

The odds of reuniting with his Orrison were slim, but each night, Gene stood in line by the main gate until the last ex-prisoners jumped off the trucks. Hundreds arrived each night. Some of the skinny frames wore new Army clothing. Gene wondered if they were enjoying the new underwear as much as he did.

On the fifth night of his vigil, a thin, dark-haired man clambered off the back of a truck, carrying a bag. Gene leaned forward. Right height, same hair. The dark-haired man followed the line of ex-POWs heading toward the tent city. *Maybe.* Just maybe. The man grew closer.

That's him! Orrison!

Orrison spied Gene in the crowd. He stopped walking. Dropped his bag. Gene burst out from the line of onlookers. Orrison ran toward him. The sole survivors of *Rikki Tikki Tavi* met and embraced. Neither man would let go. They held each other and rocked, rooted in place. A place no one in the world could go.

Gene finally slapped Orrison on the back. The hug could have lasted ten seconds or ten minutes.

The next morning, Gene waited for Orrison outside the tent that processed new arrivals. The two walked to the mess tent. They grabbed coffee and breakfast.

For a moment, neither talked. There was simply too much to say. Gene plunged in first. He couldn't wait any longer.

"Why did we fall back?"

It was the question that had haunted Gene during all his hellish months in captivity. *Why did we fall back?* A question only one person in the world could now answer. And here he was, drinking coffee in front of him.

"I don't know, Mo."

Gene bowed his head. Orrison didn't know. They would never know.

"Langley said nothing," Orrison went on. "Could you see anything?"

"Me? I couldn't see anything in the back."

They analyzed every detail they could remember from those last, dreadful minutes. What could have gone wrong with any of *Rikki Tikki Tavi*'s four engines before the final air battle? No smoke. No fire. Nothing. No explanation.

Mo. It was nice to hear Orrison calling him Mo again after a year of being called Baldy. Mo, the name given to him by his bomber crew. Orrison had never known Gene as Baldy. Mo and Baldy. He'd be both forever now.

"I'm pretty sure Benny was hit badly right away," Orrison added. "Soon everyone was screaming. I'm not sure about Langley. He yelled something about trouble with the plane. I later crawled back and saw Reed hanging from his turret."

Gene nodded. It was no secret that Langley had not been liked by the crew. But if their pilot was hurt, he'd still flown the plane. He'd kept flying *Rikki Tikki Tavi* and for precious moments kept her level, allowing the crew to fight or bail out.

Gene shared what he knew about Pee Wee. About Swedo and Andy sprawled out on the fuselage floor. About his own desperate crawl for the spare parachute. But he was more interested to hear from Orrison about what was going on in the nose of *Rikki Tikki Tavi*.

In the nose, everything had been chaos. Curtis was wounded, and his body kept falling into Orrison. Three times he fell, until Orrison strapped a parachute on him and pushed him out the nose hatch door, hoping someone on the ground would care for him after he landed.

"He was pretty much gone by the time I pushed him to the door," Orrison said.

As for himself, an explosion blasted Orrison out the plane's nose. His legs and groin were slashed by Plexiglas shards. His parachute came down on the edge of a German city, where he landed in a tree. Blood covered his leather flight pants. He couldn't untangle himself from his parachute straps. Local Germans got there right away, many screaming to kill him.

Gene shuddered. He remembered the thrown rocks, the screams from shrieking women, the spittle dripping down his face after he was captured.

Someone shoved a ladder against the tree, and then another cut Orrison away from his parachute. After he was lowered to the ground, he was taken to stay with a group of nuns for two days before the German military picked him up. He'd spent most of the rest of the war at Stalag Luft 1, a camp for Allied air officers located in northern Germany.

At last, Gene told his own story about his fall when the tail tore from the plane.

"I know your story, Mo," Orrison said. "I heard about it later."

How far had Gene's story gone? Had it reached every prison camp? Had it reached America? Would his mom know despite his careful shielding?

For the next week, Gene and Orrison met every morning in the mess tent for breakfast. Sometimes Shorty joined them. They'd been trained in a military that frowned on fraternization between officers and enlisted men. But what did that matter? Gene and Shorty were gunners, and Orrison was a navigator. Among the ex-POWs at Camp Lucky Strike, there was only one rank: freed men.

Conversation about the war faded. They talked more and more of home. Orrison was anxious to get back to Michigan to see his wife, Margaret, the young bride he'd married just before setting out for war. Margaret had been living with Orrison's parents there. She'd lost their first baby, a girl, in childbirth. They talked about marriage and starting families. Gene's thoughts drifted to Peg. Would she mind a man called Baldy with a skull scar? Gene listened in as the talk turned to possible careers. He had trouble contemplating a future after the war. Life's only goal had been to survive. Now, talking about jobs seemed trivial, mundane.

Longing for home intensified. But still they waited, stranded at Camp Lucky Strike. Some men grew tired of the long waiting and took off for Paris. The officers running Camp Lucky Strike warned men to stay in camp and not sneak out. The moment of departure to America could come any day. But when the ex-prisoners asked when, no one had an answer.

One morning in the mess tent just before lunch, Gene noticed high-ranking officers in resplendent uniforms milling about. Someone screamed, "Attention!" Gene stood up and straightened himself. The room fell silent.

A man wearing a cut-down officer's jacket, buttoned sharply at the waist, walked to the center of the tent. On the shoulders of his jacket were four silver stars. It was General Dwight Eisenhower.

Gene and the others stood in shock. No one expected the Supreme Commander of Allied Forces to show up for lunch. Eisenhower didn't waste any time. "At ease," he said. "Take a seat."

Eisenhower looked over the silent men before him. "We are trying to get you men home as soon as possible. You will be the first Americans to leave."

Gene listened as the general explained that planes were being ferried across the ocean to pick them up, but it might be six weeks before there were enough aircraft available to return all the ex-POWs to the United States. The other option was to ride a "Liberty" boat, a transport ship, back home across the Atlantic. The voyage would be longer than a plane ride, and the vessels would be packed. But Eisenhower believed the ships could arrive in the port of Le Havre in about a week. The choice to leave by ship or wait for the planes was up to each man.

Eisenhower ate lunch with the ex-prisoners. Gene was only about one table away and could hear him speak to the men around him. Most said they'd prefer to take the ship ride. The general was keenly interested to hear stories of how the Germans treated American POWs.

When Eisenhower rose to leave, Gene got in a line to shake the general's hand.

After Eisenhower's visit, there was a buzz in camp. Finally, definitive news about going home. Gene opted for the ship ride. He wanted to leave as soon as possible. Shorty did too. Cramped quarters and seasickness be damned!

Gene scribbled off some quick letters home to say he'd be home in a few weeks, by early June. Then, less than a week after Eisenhower's visit, word came to pack up and leave. Enlisted men had to travel separately from the officers, so Gene said goodbye to Orrison, promising to see him stateside soon.

In the port city of Le Havre, Gene and Shorty walked up the gangplank onto a ship teeming with ex-POWs. Eisenhower was right. The ride home would be crowded. The captain of the ship called for order.

"Nobody push and shove. We won't leave anyone behind," the captain said over a loudspeaker. "Be orderly, and we'll get you home quickly."

Milling about the deck, waiting for the ship to head out of Le Havre harbor, Gene and Shorty spotted a face they recognized.

Bill Dorgan!

Gene and Shorty pushed and shoved their way forward. It had been four months since they'd seen Bill, back when he'd left on a truck for severely wounded prisoners from Stalag Luft 4. And who knew how well the severely wounded would fare? The three Wisconsin aerial gunners were back together.

When the Liberty ship steamed out of the harbor, it tooted its horn over and over. Gene, Shorty, and Bill stood at the deck railing among a press of ex-POWs, all hooting and hollering until they were hoarse. It was over! It was *over*! Gene had never felt such elation. Bill and Shorty were by his side, and the European continent was slowly fading away,

But as he stood at the rail looking back at the disappearing coastline, his joy faded. Gene was leaving a land where he'd dueled Nazi Germany's best fighter pilots and survived a four-mile fall without a parachute. He'd survived brain surgery in a POW camp, braved through bombings by his own comrades, ridden the hell ship, and endured interrogation, starvation, and disease. He'd suffered a death march in the dead of winter. Against all odds, he had lived.

But eight of the crew from *Rikki Tikki Tavi* weren't going home with him. Pee Wee, Swedo, Andy, Sparky, Reed, Benny, Langley, and Curtis.

Somewhere in Europe, his brothers' bodies remained.

CHAPTER 17

Homecoming

May 2013

Gene knew nothing of what happened to his dead buddies after *Rikki Tikki Tavi* went down.

But I did.

I learned the story thanks to a case worker from Wisconsin Senator Tammy Baldwin's office and the Freedom of Information Act. All the information came from Individual Deceased Personnel Files for each of the eight crew members who died on *Rikki Tikki Tavi*. In two years of researching Gene's World War II story, I'd learned a long list of Army acronyms. But no military jargon moved me like the IDPF documents did.

There, stuffed in my roadside mailbox, was an "official business" mailer from U.S. Army Human Resources Command in Fort Knox, Kentucky. Yes! The Army came through for me. In my hands lay the end story of *Rikki Tikki Tavi*'s crew.

The package arrived not long after Gene and I resumed interviews. Inside the mailer was a CD containing all the files of Gene's dead crewmates. I shoved the CD into my laptop, and a list of IDPF files appeared in alphabetical order, starting with Amatulli and ending with Swedo. There was so much information. Seventy pages on Pee Wee. One hundred forty-three on Curtis.

I became dizzy sifting through the nearly nine hundred pages of documents. As I sorted through them, details began to emerge.

And there, among the official typed reports, were handwritten letters from mothers and fathers begging the Army for information about their missing sons. What had happened to them? Where were they buried? None of the families had any idea where their sons' bodies were when the war ended.

Answers began to trickle in by 1946, a year after the war ended. The International Red Cross discovered information on the burial site of Second Lieutenant Linwood Langley and Second Lieutenant Donald Curtis. The Germans had buried both of them in a civilian cemetery in the town of Vechta, Germany, about twenty-five miles from the forest where Gene had crashed. After investigating the lead, the U.S. Army issued a follow-up letter from the Headquarters American Graves Registration Command–European Theater Area, which said six "unknowns" with crosses dated November 29, 1943, were also buried next to Langley and Curtis.

In the spring of 1946, almost one year after the European war ended, the U.S. Army dug up the eight graves. Another body, Joseph R. Sawicki, was buried with the dead of *Rikki Tikki Tavi*, the Germans perhaps believing he was part of the same crew.

Sawicki? There was obviously no Sawicki on Gene's plane. But I knew that name! He was the tail gunner who'd had an arm shot off but managed to push two wounded waist gunners out of his Flying Fortress *Dark Horse* before he went down with his flaming plane. One of those waist gunners was George Fisher, the man who'd witnessed Gene's fall.

The Army was meticulous. A second lieutenant at the exhumation site filled out a four-page "Check List of the Unknown" for each body disinterred. Each checklist stated that all the corpses had multiple broken bones. The bottom half of Sparky's head was missing. Benny's corpse did not include most of his skull, his left pelvis, left hand, and right collarbone. Langley's sideburns were charred.

Of the eight, only Reed was immediately identified, since he was the only one wearing his metal identification necklace, "dog tags." The others were marked "body unidentified, but the examiner went to great lengths to find any identification." In Swedo's file, the examiner said he searched the lining of Swedo's underwear and found "S-7541," the numbers being the last four digits of Swedo's serial number. But even with the underwear, it wasn't enough for positive confirmation. What if he'd swapped clothes with another gunner in the Nissen hut at his air base in England?

Final confirmation took dental records. Except for Reed's file, all of the other seven IDPFs had a dental record called "Tooth Chart," which positively identified the entire crew of *Rikki Tikki Tavi*.

All eight reports told the same story of how the bodies ended up in Vechta, Germany: *Rikki Tikki Tavi* went down near the city of Syke, Germany, at 2:30 p.m. The plane was "scrapped by German Air Police." And most telling, standard questions such as "Did the plane explode in the air?" "Did the plane burn in the air?" "Were parachutists seen?" were all answered "unknown." No one would truly know the final moments of *Rikki Tikki Tavi* and its dead crew.

Each man was buried in a plain wooden box. Most of the graves were marked by a plain wooden cross with the words "*unbekannter Flieger*"—unknown flier. Curtis' grave was correctly labeled "Donald M. Curtis, Nov. 29, 1943," but Benny's grave was mistakenly labeled "Linwood Langley."

The wooden caskets and crosses gave me pause. Just a day or so after Gene was nearly lynched by German civilians after he was captured, other Germans took the time to give each of his dead comrades their own coffin and grave marker. They could have just dumped the corpses in an unmarked mass grave. I was perplexed that the dead of *Rikki Tikki Tavi* received a dignified burial from a nation that called them *terrorfliegers* and *luftgangsters.*

All the bodies were buried in their electric flight suits, but the leather jackets, pants, and flight boots were missing. Did the Germans take these items out of necessity or for souvenirs? Did they find the Hershey bars? Most of the usable stuff was gone, except Langley's corpse, which still had fur-lined flight boots on his feet.

The U.S. Army reburied the bodies in the United States Military Cemetery near Neuville-en-Condroz, Belgium. More than five thousand American dead from World War II lie in this manicured shrine now known as Ardennes American Cemetery. A few years later, the Army asked the families if they wanted their sons' remains shipped home. The parents of Sparky, Reed, and Curtis requested the bodies be transported to the United States for private burial. Langley, Swedo, Benny, Andy, and Pee Wee are still buried at Ardennes.

When I first received the IDPF information from the Army, I couldn't wait to share my research bonanza with Gene. But after reading about crushed skulls and missing limbs, I decided not to show Gene diagrams and notes about his buddies' bodies. By the time the examiner had gotten to them, much of their bodies had decomposed. The file explained it all in heartbreaking detail. There was no need to torture Gene with this graphic information.

On my next "Thursdays with Gene," I explained that all eight of the bodies had been found. Gene nodded. He knew some of the story. After the U.S. Army shipped Curtis' remains to his Michigan home, Gene attended the funeral. He spent several days afterwards with Curtis' parents and went perch fishing with them in Saginaw Bay.

"I may as well have been their son," Gene said. "They were just wonderful people. We had a big fish fry when we got back."

That's what mattered. Gene didn't need to know the intimate details described in the 143 pages of Curtis' death file. He'd lived the most important part of the story. During the funeral service, Gene sat right next to Curtis' parents in the front pew.

May 1945

Leaning on the railing of the Liberty ship, Gene soaked in the warm, late-spring weather on the North Atlantic. Just one month before, he'd trudged barefoot through mud and rain, shivered through cold nights on the bare ground, and inhaled the sick scent of death everywhere. Shorty and Bill joined Gene by the rail, all three staring at the ocean as the ship steamed to the United States and New York harbor. They were long past their liquid diet now. A month after nearly starving to death, the three Wisconsin boys had just feasted on steak, mashed potatoes, fresh vegetables, pies, and ice cream served down in the ship's mess hall. The deck was packed with ex-POWs enjoying the beautiful day. But the mood was soon spoiled: the scent of salt air overtaken by the stench of vomit. None of the ex-prisoners had sea legs; feasting on steak and ice cream only made their seasickness worse.

Below deck, Gene was lucky to find a hammock to sleep in at night. The ship was so packed that many of the ex-POWS had to sleep on the deck. Patrolling marines politely asked their passengers to spread out so the ship wouldn't list. But despite the crowded conditions, the mood was mostly joyful: joy mixed with the burning impatience to get home. When they weren't resting, the men played poker and shot crap games. There was no gambling. No one had any money.

And there was absolutely no talking about the war. The men buried their memories of burning airplanes and screaming wounded. They suppressed thoughts of constant hunger, lice-infested blankets, and feces-caked pants. They filled their minds with the heady anticipation of seeing mothers, girlfriends, wives, and children. For now.

The American coastline came into view after a week of sailing. New York harbor. It was June now. On the deck, Gene, Shorty, and Bill pushed their way through other men to the ship's railing to catch their first glimpses of America. The captain's voice came on the loudspeaker, warning everyone not to crowd one side of the ship. His order was ignored. How could anyone possibly leave the railing when the Statue of Liberty came into view?

The entire deck erupted with cheering when the men spotted Lady Liberty. Then suddenly, the yelling fell into an eerie silence. The silence turned to muffled crying. Gene couldn't hold back his tears. All around him, men wept. A month ago, he'd first jumped into a hot shower and slid on clean underwear. That had felt like freedom. But now, seeing the Statue of Liberty, that felt like home.

With a shipload of hundreds of crying men, the Liberty ship docked at New York harbor. Gene picked up his scant possessions and walked down the gangplank and off the ship. That's when it truly hit him: the war was over.

An Army bus took him to a base in New Jersey. They gathered in a huge building for welcome back messages and processing. Gene received money and tickets for trains leaving that very day. General Eisenhower had kept his promise. Prisoners would be the first to get home.

Gene, Shorty, and Bill sat together on a packed train filled mostly with ex-prisoners heading for Fort Sheridan, Illinois. Fort Sheridan. That's where Gene's life in the Army had begun almost three years earlier. It seemed like a lifetime ago. So much had happened to him since he first put on a military uniform: training that molded him into an aerial warrior, meeting the men who'd become his brothers, and losing those brothers. Gene had to push those thoughts out of his mind. The war was over. A new life awaited him back home in Wisconsin.

At every train station stop, volunteer groups served coffee, soda, and doughnuts. At a layover in Chicago, officers told the men not to leave the station. Gene stayed near the train, but many ignored the order. For the first time in months, even years, the former kriegies had spending money burning holes in their pockets and a big city in front of them. The temptation was overwhelming. Soldier after soldier stole away from the train station. The military police near the trains did nothing to stop them. When the train chugged out of Chicago, about one hundred men were missing.

"They'll all return to the station once they run out of money," an officer quipped.

They arrived at Fort Sheridan and bunked for the night in the barracks, just yards away from where Gene first learned to march nearly three years ago. The next day, he and all the men received a fresh uniform and three hundred dollars. Gene learned he'd be getting more back pay from his time served as a POW. The money would be waiting for him at the Gays Mills Post Office near his home. The payment for being a prisoner was odd. How could the Army put a wage on all that he'd endured as a kriegie? Who could put a price on being so thirsty and having to lick the droplets off the rusty hull of the hell ship or slurp water from the muddy holes of cattle footprints on the death march?

Gene was about to depart from the only people who understood that thirst, and all the other suffering. It was time to say goodbye. He couldn't wait to get home, but it also meant separating from his tight-knit group of Wisconsin kriegies. All the former prisoners were heading home on different trains.

Shorty was going home to Chippewa Falls in northwestern Wisconsin. Gene and Shorty hadn't been apart since they met at Dulag Luft. That was in Germany sixteen months ago. They'd starved together, slept together to preserve body heat, survived together. Now at a Chicago train station, neither could find the right way to say goodbye. It wouldn't be forever. Shorty was going home to propose to his girlfriend in Chippewa Falls. He'd already asked Gene to be his best man. Amidst the hustle and noise of throngs of people heading to their trains, the two embraced quickly, awkwardly, before Shorty walked away to board his ride home.

The break between Gene and Bill was easier. Bill's home farm was only twenty-five miles away from the Moran farm. They both made plans to meet for beer after seeing their families.

"Baldy, I promised you I'd come up to see you in Soldiers Grove," Bill said.

Gene remembered that promise murmured to him back at Stalag Luft 4 when Bill stepped out of the roll call line to board the truck evacuating wounded prisoners.

Then Gene was whisked away from his fellow kriegies on a train to Milwaukee. He stared out the window. Northern Illinois rolled past. In a couple of hours, he'd actually be in Wisconsin. In Milwaukee, he'd stay at a cousin's home for the night, then take a train ride to Madison the next day where relatives would pick him up and drive him to the farm. Home!

That afternoon at his cousin's home, a reporter from a Wisconsin newspaper showed up. He pulled out a notepad and asked Gene about his fall and survival.

His fall? Gene was stunned. How did the reporter know? How did anyone in America know his story? He'd never told his parents. The short notes he'd sent home from prison camp only mentioned that his health was good and please send shoes and sweatshirts. His parents never said anything about it in their letters to him. Did they know?

The next day, Saturday, June 16, Gene hopped aboard a train headed to Madison. When he arrived at the station there, four of his aunts and uncles and a half dozen cousins met him. With his relatives was Rosemary, Gene's sister. When he'd left for war, she was still in high school. Now she was about to enter nursing school in Madison, a young woman on her own. Such changes!

Gene slid into a car with his aunts and uncles, and the five of them headed for Soldiers Grove, the last leg of Gene's journey home. Rosemary returned to her clerical job at the Army-Navy Institute. Soon, Gene saw dairy cows grazing in pastures, bright green, untouched by tank treads or scavenging refugees. When they passed through towns along the highway, he pushed away thoughts of the gutted German cities he'd witnessed just weeks before. Home. It was getting close.

Up the road at the Rolling Ground Store and Tavern, a dozen cars waited to escort Gene the final two miles to the Moran farm. Uncle Nick, who was driving Gene home, was unaware of the entourage. He took a different route to the home farm through the Kickapoo Valley, driving up from the south on a back road, and missed the escort.

So, the car was alone when it pulled into the Moran yard. The engine stilled. Gene heard a scream. His mother came running at the car. Gene leaped out just in time to catch her bear hug. Mom buried her face into his shoulder and bawled. Then his father was there, and he wrapped his arms around both of them.

Home. Little Revy was home.

There were his three younger siblings too. JoAnn, Michael, and little Marty, all stretched tall. Gene smiled and gave them quick hugs, but he didn't go into the house. He couldn't go inside yet.

He was thirsty.

Gene was drawn to the creek. He separated from his family and walked the sandy trail alone and smiled when he saw the tin cup hanging on a bush. It was the same cup he'd latched to a branch the last time he'd been home two years ago. Two years of bombing runs, flak, Nazi fighter planes, prison guard towers, and barbed wire. Gene plunged the cup into the cold, clear water and sat on the bank. Here it was, the finest water in all of Wisconsin. He drank heavily, the cool elixir soothing every fiber of his body.

Gene heard the sound of honking coming all the way from Highway 61, two miles away. A few minutes later, a dozen cars paraded toward the Moran farm, kicking up gravel and blasting their horns. Gene wiped his mouth and hung the cup back on its branch before heading back to the house. It was nice by the creek, but a party was about to start in his honor.

The Moran house was packed with a crowd that spilled out the door and onto the lawn. It seemed like a dream. More cars pulled in, looking for space to park. In the kitchen, the table was crammed with canned beef, baloney, liverwurst, and a line of desserts made with sugar purchased with ration stamps donated to the family. Beer was everywhere.

Gene sat on a chair in the middle of the living room crowded by a parade of friends and relatives all slapping him on the back and hugging him. He spotted Byron, his older brother, coming toward him with a young woman he didn't recognize at first. That's right, Byron's *wife,* Florence. They'd gotten married just a month after Gene was shot down. Some people pressed ration stamps into his hand for gas and cigarettes. Gene had a beer, but then his mother snatched it away from him and carried the bottle out to the kitchen. What? No beer for a combat veteran? His father approached. Taking side glances toward the kitchen, he placed another cold beer in his son's hand.

A few minutes later, Gene's dad appeared again with two paper bags. He quieted the room and set the paper sacks in Gene's hands. Gene looked up, perplexed.

"Merry Christmas, son," his father said. There was a mischievous twinkle in his eye.

Gene peered into the sacks. They were the candy bags his dad had always made for each child at Christmas. He'd saved them all the time Gene was at war. Two sacks for the two Christmases Gene had spent as a prisoner. Gene opened one of the bags and pulled out a glob of candy and peanuts that had all melded together. He held up the messy lump and grinned, and the room erupted in laughter.

The party went on well past midnight. The next day was Sunday, and Gene joined his family for Mass at St. Philip's. Like the Sunday before he'd left for war, Gene was dressed in his Army Air Force uniform. Before the service, Father Mathieu stepped down from the altar and walked to the pew where the Moran family sat. He leaned over the pew in front of Gene.

"I'd be honored if you'd serve Mass with me," he said.

It had been several years since Gene's days as an altar boy. When the time for Mass came, he rose and stood beside the priest in his Army Air Force uniform. He remembered all his duties: holding the liturgical book open for the priest to read aloud, ringing the bell at the consecration of the bread, holding the Communion plate under the chins of his relatives and neighbors as they received the sacrament.

Gene's homecoming was front-page news in the *Kickapoo Scout* newspaper. The headline read: "S. Sgt. Eugene Moran Arrived Home Saturday After 17 months In German Prison." More visitors came to the farm in the following days, including a middle-aged woman who handed Gene a carton of cigarettes and introduced him to her daughter. Gene shook his head. He had Peg Finley on his mind and planned to meet her in Madison soon. When he politely declined the match-making attempt, the woman snatched back her cigarettes and left.

The Army granted Gene a generous sixty-day leave, and although the European war was over, the war with Japan still raged in the Pacific. Gene was still an Army Air Force sergeant, and he'd have to return to service soon.

Before reporting to duty, Gene saw a lot of Bill Dorgan. Bill lived close by, and he stayed over at the Moran house for several nights. Gene was happy that his parents both liked Bill, but it irritated him when he felt his mother's disapproval every time he and Bill headed over to the Rolling Ground Store and Tavern for the evening. After all they'd been through in prison, Gene saw nothing wrong with two ex-POWs having a few beers together.

Gene did stay home some nights. One evening, he sat with Mom in the kitchen after she brought out all the newspaper clippings she'd saved about Gene's war record. A headline from a St. Paul, Minnesota, newspaper read: "Trapped Yank Airman Falls 4 Miles—Lives." The Associated Press reported the story. Gene glanced at clippings from New York and Baltimore newspapers sent to the Moran family. Mom also had cut out articles from local papers in La Crosse and Crawford County.

Gene had still said nothing of his miraculous survival. He'd written to his mother that he'd parachuted safely and suffered only minor injuries. Gene read the newspaper clippings. He saw George Fisher's name. George, the wounded waist gunner who parachuted from his plane and watched *Rikki Tikki Tavi*'s tail section hurtle through the sky. When George arrived in New York in the summer of 1944 after a prisoner exchange, he spilled to the Associated Press the story Gene had kept from his family. George was quoted in many of the articles laid out on the table. Gene's mother also told him about the letters the family received from anonymous citizens who'd picked up German reports on shortwave radio about Gene's fall.

Gene scowled. Why did George blab about his fall and worry his parents like that? He had no right. Gene suppressed his anger. It didn't matter. He was home. The war was over.

Toward the end of his leave, Gene used his savings and back pay to buy a '42 Ford sedan. After he'd made sergeant two years ago, he'd always sent home sixty dollars a month, and his parents put every dollar into Gene's bank account. Gene heard that some parents spent their sons' military pay. He appreciated that his mother and father never spent a dime of his money.

Gene traveled to Madison and Milwaukee to visit friends, but most of his trips took him to Madison to visit Peg. He'd kept his promise to ask Peg out again as soon as he got home. Gene had written her just a few times in the three years since he'd taken her out to dinner. He was delighted when he called Peg and learned that she hadn't married someone else. She was still Peg Finley. She hadn't dated much since she'd last seen Gene. She'd focused on getting through nursing school.

They had a flurry of dates. Sometimes Gene helped his dad with barn chores or the summer hay crop, but mostly his family left him at peace. And where he wanted to be was with Peg. He never forgot her dark hair and those hazel-green eyes set in her porcelain face. During the summer, Peg graduated from nursing school. Gene's graduation gift to her was an engagement ring.

In mid-August, Gene traveled up to Chippewa Falls to stand as best man for Shorty's wedding. His mind was distracted, worried. His leave would be up soon, and the war with Japan was still going on. America had been girding up for a final assault on the main Japanese islands, preparing servicemen who'd just returned from Europe to fight again. Gene figured his injuries would keep him out of combat, but who knew where the Army would send him next.

On Shorty's wedding day, radios blasted the news that Japan had surrendered. Joyous news! Shorty's wedding turned into a wild celebration. No one was happier than Gene and Shorty. Japan's surrender confirmed that neither would be going overseas again.

Summer was almost over. Gene had reconnected with his family and was engaged to Peg. He still had a short stint with the Army, but soon he'd be home again. No more war. It was finally all over. When he returned from his last days of military service, he'd be starting his new life with Peg, away from the dairy barn at the Moran farm.

About that time, a neighboring couple invited Gene for dinner. Clara and Tom Malone lived just a couple miles down the road, and they'd waited their turn to spend time with their famous neighbor. Clara prepared a huge meal with roast duck since she'd heard that was Gene's favorite meal.

Gene stared at the golden-skinned bird on the platter. Thoughts of prison rushed into his mind. The sawdust-laced bread, the lice-infested soup. The watchtowers. The barbed wire. The guards. The lifeless body on the dirt compound of the man who left for the bathroom too early before the barracks restriction was lifted. There at the Stalag Luft compounds, he'd dreamed of roast duck, a food fantasy he shared with his prison mates. Now that dream was a reality sitting before him, swimming in juices.

Gene froze. His stomach was queasy. He couldn't do this. He pushed back his chair.

"Excuse me," Gene said.

Then, without a word, he walked outside and drove away.

The war was not over. It would never be over for him.

CHAPTER 18

The Family's War

June 2013

"I found something for you, John."

Gene handed me a framed black-and-white photograph of the Soldiers Grove High School class of 1941. I looked over the youthful faces in the group picture, trying to see if I could identify Gene without his help. There he was. I spotted his always mischievous grin.

"Did any of the other boys join the military after Pearl Harbor?" I asked.

"Oh, God. We pretty much all did," Gene answered.

"Thursdays with Gene" were back on that summer. We met every other week. Today, looking at old photos was a nice icebreaker before getting to the difficult topic I wanted to talk about: how the war affected his fifty-seven-year marriage to Peg.

I hadn't brought up Peg since last summer when our conversation caused Gene to break down into a sobbing mess. That meltdown ended further discussion. I knew he'd suffered spasms, flashbacks, and worse. The war he carried in his mind had never really ended. It plagued him and his family. A year had gone by now.

Maybe today we could return to those struggles. Together, we'd gotten through the loss of his *Rikki Tikki Tavi* buddies. He'd shared excruciating details from his prisoner-of-war time with me. Maybe now he'd talk to me about his nightmares. After all, I was a man reeling from my own family nightmare.

Six months after Carmen's death, I was still sullen. I rarely spoke to my friends. I stayed up late sprawled out on the couch watching reruns of *Seinfeld* and *The Office*, episodes I'd seen countless times. If the moon was out, I'd go jogging at midnight, absorbing the blackness of the silhouetted trees I passed as I counted the rhythmic pounding of my footsteps on the blacktop side roads.

Matthew and Joe rarely talked about their mother. They continued their routines of playing summer baseball, mowing the apple orchard, and selling raspberries and cherries at the local farmers' market. We agreed to leave Carmen's cheerful voice on our answering machine. *Hello, you've reached the Armbrusters. We can't come to the phone right now . . .* We wouldn't change the message. To push that button and erase her voice would seem like another death.

The orchard was struggling without her. She wasn't there to help pick fruit. She wasn't there to create the graphic work for our business: product labels, t-shirts, business cards, signage. I canceled an order for a hundred apple trees I'd intended to plant this spring. Those hundred trees were part of my grand plan to put our entire five acres into orchard production. But with driving the boys to basketball tournaments, scrubbing grass stains from their football pants, and rescheduling missed dentist appointments, there was no time for my farm fantasy. The realities of being an only parent were setting in.

I was bitter about having to downsize my orchard dreams. Bitter about everything. About all the boys' ball games and their band concerts Carmen wouldn't see, about being a confused, half-assed parent to sons who deserved better, about staring at an empty chair every meal.

I canceled the apple tree order. Besides single parenting, teaching, coaching football, and running an orchard, I had to make time for Gene's story. We'd done more than two years of interviews. We'd come too far. Gene was counting on me. His kids were counting on me. I remembered Joni's words when I agreed to take on Gene's story: *He'll only do it if you write it.*

I cleared my throat. Time to open up Gene's memory vault again. Time to dig into the difficult times that happened after the war seventy years ago.

"What was the first thing you did after you returned from the war?" I asked.

"Finding Peg was the first item on my list," said Gene. I remembered he'd only seen Peg once on a blind date. Peg had tagged along with Gene's cousin, Ruth, when Gene invited Ruth to dinner celebrating his joining the Army Air Force. He'd been so excited to finally get the chance to fly in airplanes and then became smitten by Peg all in the same day.

"Though I did check out a lot of other girls when I got home," he chuckled.

Gene returned to American soil in June 1945, looked up Peg, who was finishing nursing school in Madison, and proposed to her just over a month later. This was not unusual for the times. World War II compressed romance. Jesse Orrison proposed to Margaret just a few weeks after a blind date. During training at Dyersburg Air Base, Benny Cipresso was desperate for leave so that he could get home to marry his girl.

Hurry up and marry now, you might not get a tomorrow. Even though the European war had ended, Gene was still in service. The war with Japan still raged in the Pacific.

"I proposed to Peg soon after her graduation," said Gene. He shook his head. "She always said that was her downfall."

Downfall? That sounded harsh. Their marriage lasted fifty-seven years, and she considered it her downfall from the beginning?

"She didn't pass her state boards nursing examinations to

become a registered nurse," Gene explained. "She had two more subjects she had to write to pass her state boards, but she never went back to finish them. Then the kids started to come."

Gene and Peg were planning their wedding when the Army sent him to a psychiatric ward at an Illinois hospital. Japan had surrendered two months earlier, and Gene was due to be discharged. But the Army delayed that discharge after he attacked a sergeant who'd been interviewing Gene about his POW experience. Gene was anxious to get back to Peg, to his friends, to his Wisconsin life. But the Army wasn't going to let him go until he completed a full mental evaluation.

Just two months before his wedding date with Peg, an old Army doctor came into Gene's room one day with a dire assessment. The doctor said Gene's head wound and POW ordeal were so severe that they'd probably shorten his life, maybe even damage people around him.

"Son, I just can't say what's going to happen to you, but I wouldn't get married or start a family if I were you," the doctor said. "I'll pray for you, but you only got about ten years. You'll be in an asylum or dead. I hate to tell you this."

Peg and Gene married in February 1946 at a Catholic church near the farm where Peg grew up, about a half-hour drive north of the Moran farm. Bill Dorgan was Gene's best man.

When I asked Gene when his kids started coming, he suddenly turned around in his chair and leaned over to open a drawer in the bureau behind the kitchen table.

"I've got that list right here," he said proudly.

He opened a notebook and started reading. Tim was born first in November 1946. Tom followed two years later. The first girl, Margo, came in 1950. Then Joni in 1951, Laurie 1954, Mike 1957, Liz 1960, Bridget 1961, and Pat in 1964.

I'd come that day to discuss how the war affected Peg, but now Gene's list of his children changed my focus. What did the kids see?

I didn't want to pry into that dark space. A year ago, I hated myself for bringing such pain to Gene when I asked how his post-traumatic stress affected Peg. To ask how it distressed the kids might trigger terrible memories they'd suppressed. Maybe I should keep my nose out of family business.

But I knew the Moran children revered and loved their father. So, it had come out all right in the end. Right? But how? How did Gene survive his second war? The never-ending war inside his mind? Post-traumatic stress wasn't even a term in the 1940s and 1950s. How did Gene, Peg, and their nine children cope?

"My physical problems after the war . . ." Gene began, haltingly. We were on treacherous ground. This could be worse than the hell ship or the death march. This was his family, his legacy. "The headaches were bad," he said. He took a deep breath and went on. "There was a wind noise always blowing in my ears. That was the worst part. The wind blew in my ears all the time for a long time, and it would just drive you crazy."

The war in Europe had come home with Gene. I said nothing, nodded, waited for him to continue.

He didn't. He just stared at the table and said nothing.

I stopped too. I couldn't do it. I'd seen Gene blow up in a restaurant when we first started this project. I'd witnessed inconsolable grief and regret when I dared ask him how his head wound affected Peg. I'd brought pain to this man before at his own kitchen table. I would not, could not, do it again.

If I was going to know how World War II infiltrated the Moran home, terrified Gene's children, angered his brothers and sisters, tormented family dinners, ruined holidays, I couldn't ask Gene.

I'd have to ask his siblings. I'd have to ask his kids.

1945

Gene rarely missed a party after returning from the war. He drove up to the Auditorium, the all-purpose town hall, ready to celebrate. The Auditorium hosted everything from Soldiers Grove High School basketball games to school plays and proms. Tonight, it was full of girls, guys, and live dance music, including Gene's sister, Rosemary, who had a break from nursing school and was there with her date.

Gene dragged every girl he talked to out onto the wooden dance floor. He slammed a beer after every song and went scouting for another dance partner. The life of the party! Gene drank and danced with abandon. Rosemary stayed off the dance floor. He caught her look of scorn. He was drunk, very drunk, and he knew it. Gene grabbed another beer and collapsed in the middle of the dance floor. There he lay in his Army Air Force uniform, passed out drunk at the Auditorium.

Everyone stared at Rosemary. She began to cry and asked her date to drive her home. They left as Gene's friends dragged him from the dance floor.

1945

Cochran Field. Gene called the Georgia air base "the asshole of creation." Nothing but bugs, heat, and humidity. It was a far cry from his last post: Miami Beach. When Gene's leave ended in August, the Army sent him and other POWs to southern Florida for two weeks of rest and relaxation at a beachfront hotel. What an assignment! Drink beer. Wade in the surf. Lie on the beach and share stories with fellow POWs.

But an oncoming hurricane cut the vacation short by a week, so the Army moved Gene up to Cochran Field for the next step of his discharge from the military. Now he sat across from an Army sergeant who shuffled endless papers and peppered him with a barrage of questions about his time in the POW camps. Trapped in his chair, Gene stewed at the pace of the processing. Where was this sergeant during the war? Riding it out behind a desk? Why was he making Gene relive his worst memories? He was at the end of his rope when the sergeant changed his tactics and asked a blunt question.

"Sergeant Moran, most of the POWs I've talked to are pretty skinny. Seems to me you're in pretty good shape."

What?! Was the sergeant insinuating that he was a traitor? He'd starved! He'd eaten bugs and grass and drunk from cow pastures. Good shape? He couldn't even crawl the last few feet to freedom. Sure, he knew some of the prisoners had weighed in at 90 pounds at their liberation, while he'd weighed 128. But those extra pounds on his frame came from good scavenging, from his farm boy know-how. And he'd shared, always shared with his comrades. How *dare* this smug desk jockey accuse him of collaborating with the enemy for food!

In a bolt of rage, Gene launched forward and punched the sergeant full in the face. The sergeant flipped back over his chair. His head slammed against the wall, and he fell unconscious to the floor behind his desk.

A week later, the Army put Gene on a train bound for a psychiatric hospital in Illinois.

1945

Gene lay in a deep slumber, sleeping off the effects of a sedative. He was resting in the psychiatric ward in a Galesburg, Illinois, hospital run by Mayo Clinic. It was Gene's last stop before being discharged from the military. After he laid out the sergeant at Cochran Field in Georgia, the doctors had issued him a bottle of

Southern Comfort wrapped in a brown bag. His "prescription" for war trauma was a doctor-signed permission slip allowing him to discreetly sip whiskey on the train ride to Illinois.

But now that he was here in the Illinois hospital, the psychiatric treatment involved more than a bottle of booze. Doctors there told Gene he wasn't leaving until "the truth came out." He had to verbalize his combat and prison stories. All of them. He had to relive his nightmarish memories.

A doctor told Gene he'd be receiving a sedative. They injected a hypodermic needle filled with what was known as the "truth serum" into Gene's lower spine. Once the drug took effect, the psychiatrists would interview him. Try as he might, Gene couldn't suppress images of the hell ship and death march.

Things became foggy. Gene talked, but afterwards didn't recall much of the conversation. They wheeled him out to sleep off the sedative. He remembered only that the doctors and nurses promised that he'd be left alone to rest. They meant it too: a sign hung above Gene's bed warning all staff not to touch the patient or wake him.

Gene drifted into a blissful sleep. Empty of dreams. Then a young nurse approached. She didn't see the posted message and gently shook his arm. The touch startled Gene from his drug-induced haze. He'd been lying half-awake with his eyes closed, but now he swung his right fist at the "intruder." The blow landed full on her mouth and knocked her to the floor. The nurse lay unconscious. Two of her front teeth lay scattered beside her.

A flurry of activity followed. Hospital staff wheeled Gene's bed into a room with barred windows. They locked the door. Gene was confused when he saw the barricaded windows. What had he done? Then he saw tooth marks on his right knuckles. Tooth marks from the nurse's face. Five months after being freed from German guards, Gene was a prisoner again.

For two days, Gene lay in a locked cage. A hospital orderly slid his food tray through a small opening on the bottom of his room door, exactly how the Germans had delivered his meager rations to him back at the Dulag Luft interrogation center. Gene sat, trapped. Again. Finally, a doctor unlocked the door and entered the room warily.

"Sergeant Moran, why did you attack the nurse?" the doctor asked.

"She woke me up," Gene pleaded. "I never meant to hit her."

The doctor's demeanor changed. A few hours later, Gene was escorted to a regular patient room, no bars. The doctor returned. In a deeply apologetic voice, he explained that Gene had been locked up because the hospital staff thought he'd had a nervous breakdown. He'd questioned the nurse Gene hit, and she said it was her fault and that Gene had done nothing wrong. She'd forgotten the strict order not to touch or wake the ex-POWs.

The next day, the nurse herself entered Gene's room and sat by his bedside. She began to cry.

"I'm so sorry. It was all my fault they locked you up," she sobbed.

When the nurse opened her mouth to speak, Gene could see that she was missing two front teeth. He never felt so bad in all his life. He sat up, and tears rolled off his cheeks as he held her.

Early 1950s

Another late-summer afternoon melted away at the Rolling Ground Store and Tavern located just off Highway 61. Gene sat at a barstool sipping beer from a bottle. He looked through a window behind the bar and stared at the roadside where a decade earlier he'd started his hitchhiking trips to Madison to join the Army Air Corps.

What came next was always the same. A scene would jog a memory. A memory would morph into a flashback from the war. It happened again. Gene started shaking. The convulsions grew so violent that he toppled off his barstool and fell to the floor. Men playing cards at a table nearby shoved back their chairs and rushed over to Gene. They gathered around him, not sure what to do other than keep him away from sharp edges.

The bartender always knew what to do. He rushed over to the wall phone, picked up the receiver, and toggled the L-shaped handle on the side of the phone.

"Operator? Get me Doc Sannes at six-six!" he yelled into the mouthpiece.

Having to drive five miles from Soldiers Grove, it seemed like an eternity before Doc Sannes finally burst through the entrance doorway. He knelt beside Gene, who moaned and thrashed on the floor. Then Doc pulled a hypodermic needle from his bag and plunged the cold steel into Gene. In just moments, Gene's limbs slowed and stilled. His face relaxed. The men standing around Gene waited before picking him up to drive him back to Peg and the children.

1960

Heavy rains sent the Kickapoo River spilling over its bank and into downtown Soldiers Grove. Gene raced downtown to get the mail for his route before the muddy water flooded the post office.

For more than a decade, Gene had worked as a rural mail carrier for the Soldiers Grove Post Office. It was work that didn't require too much from his mended forearms and sore lower back. His bones still bothered him seventeen years after he was shot down. A steady job, it provided for Gene's growing family, now at seven children after the birth of his daughter Liz in February.

Once he finished his mail route, Gene went back to town to help a tavern owner friend shift his inventory to higher ground. Later, Gene stumbled home, drunk. Staggering into the kitchen with him was a fellow mail carrier and his wife who lived down the street. They were as sloshed as Gene.

Peg waited next to the table. She had just warmed a bottle and had baby Liz balanced in her arms. She glared at the husband and wife slouched against the kitchen wall. All this flooding and she was home alone with the kids while her husband partied with the neighbors.

Gene stood in the middle of the room, staring glassy-eyed at Peg. They fought. The quarrel turned to screaming. The four oldest children stood immobile on the far side of the kitchen, watching their parents' rage. Peg still held baby Liz clutched in her arms, the milk growing cold.

Gene abruptly left the room and lurched back to the kitchen, grasping a deer rifle. He fumbled to load the gun. His shaky fingers bungled the job, and bullets fell from his hands and tumbled onto the table, where they rolled off and skittered across the linoleum floor. He managed to chamber a bullet. The gun was loaded now. Gene pointed the gun at his wife's head, the rifle barrel aimed just inches from her skull.

The fluorescent kitchen light cast a pale glow on Peg's face. She stared at Gene and set the baby bottle on the kitchen table. Still holding Liz, she squared her face with Gene's.

"Go ahead," she growled. "I dare you to shoot me."

Nine-year-old Joni screamed. Her brother Tim slapped her face.

"Relax!" whispered Margo, age ten. *"Quiet down!"*

The children gaped at the scene, all eyes on their mother and father. Peg stared down the rifle muzzle. Liz pressed up against her chest. *I dare you. I dare you to shoot.*

"Now, Eugene. You know you're not going to pull the trigger," the drunken neighbor woman slurred. "Now put that gun down!"

Gene lowered the rifle. Margo escorted all the kids out of the kitchen and into the living room. They watched their father walk by, carrying the rifle on his way to his bedroom. He closed the bedroom door and passed out on the bed.

1964

It was a summer evening when Peg was about to call the kids in for supper. But she had to wait. Gene was late, again. The table was all set, but the roast beef and mashed potatoes now sat cold in their serving dishes. Gene finally walked through the kitchen door.

"Where the hell have you been?" Peg snapped.

Gene had an answer. He grabbed the edge of the table and flipped it on its side. Plates, cutlery, and drinking glasses cascaded onto the linoleum kitchen floor. But Gene wasn't done. He knocked over each chair. Then he stared at his wife.

At that moment, Laurie walked into the kitchen. She'd been down the street playing at a friend's house. She saw the roast beef scattered across the floor. Mashed potatoes clung to the ceiling. Her parents glared at one another. Peg then turned her head toward Laurie.

"Call the police!"

Laurie ignored her mother's command. She backed away and ran out the kitchen door. As fast as her ten-year-old legs could carry her, she sprinted down the sidewalk toward her friend's home. Peg hollered out the kitchen door at her daughter disappearing down the street.

"You chickenshit!"

1965

Yelling and staggering, Gene burst into the house. He'd been barhopping in Soldiers Grove, and Peg met him, stone-faced.

"You may as well go back to the tavern for all I care," she said.

Gene froze. Her indifference startled him. He backed away from her and collapsed in the corner of the kitchen. There he curled up in a fetal position and began to weep.

Margo came into the room with some of the other kids. She

was fifteen now and had seen many of her father's fits. The other children began to cry at the sight of their father curled up on the floor weeping, but Margo yelled at everyone to be quiet. She took her father by the hand and led him to his bedroom. Gene curled up on the bed. He choked out names of men dying in faraway places.

Peg entered the bedroom. She sat down on the bed next to Margo. As Gene moaned, she stroked his head.

"What do you need, dear?" Peg asked. "You're home. It's over. You're safe now."

1970

"Call your father and tell him to get home. I'm hungry!" Peg said.

Even as a young boy, Pat knew when his father was drunk. He was the youngest Moran child, and every child in the house knew that when Dad came home from the bars, anything could happen. How many times had he stomped upstairs to wake the kids and order them to the kitchen to do dishes at 2:00 a.m.? The girls dressed in oversized t-shirts and the boys in their underwear would all tromp sleepily to the kitchen sink while their father sat at the kitchen table to supervise.

Now, Peg was pushing the rotary phone receiver at Pat, urging her five-year-old son to talk to his daddy and tell him to come home from the bar. It was suppertime.

But Gene didn't come home for supper. The dishes were washed. Pat and the older children were already in their pajamas, upstairs in bed, when Gene finally rolled in late from the tavern.

The door slammed shut. Peg screamed. Gene cursed and shouted back. Young Pat slipped out of bed and ventured out into the hallway. He slid his legs under the hallway railing and grasped the twisted wrought iron spindles with his hands, peering down. His older brother Mike rocketed out of his bedroom and raced downstairs, vainly trying to outshout his parents. Liz and Bridget joined Pat at the railing, dangling their legs from the upstairs landing and yelling, a chorus of children's voices all shouting, "Leave her alone, you damn drunk!"

1974

It was after supper. Bridget squirted dishwashing liquid into the deep, white, porcelain-coated kitchen sink and filled it with hot water. Peg cleared the table, then paused, seeing Gene's plate. She'd made steak and baked potatoes for that Saturday night meal. For the first time Peg could remember, Gene's plate was clean.

"I thought you said you'd never eat potato skins again," said Peg.

1977

It was late November, the weekend after Thanksgiving. Laurie was back home, showing off her firstborn. Matt was only a month-old baby, and she'd just finished feeding him. Sitting on the floor, she leaned back against the couch and rocked her baby boy as Peg sat across the living room in the recliner.

Gene walked in. He went behind the couch and braced his arms on its backside. Dad was drunk again. Laurie didn't need to turn her head to confirm it. She could smell the stench of cigarette smoke and stale beer. But she didn't tense up the way she had when she was a kid and he came home from the taverns. It was always bad then when he did that, but Thanksgiving time was the worst. Gene could stay drunk for four to five days around Thanksgiving, whenever the date edged toward November 29.

November 29, 1943. The day *Rikki Tikki Tavi* fell back to waiting German fighter planes.

Today was Saturday, November 26, 1977.

But this time, Gene breathed slowly and looked at his new grandson. He didn't yell. Then he turned to Peg.

"You know, Mom. For the first time in thirty-two years, I didn't get the headaches." Gene turned and walked quietly to the kitchen. He grabbed a box of crackers and went to the fridge to pull out some liverwurst.

1988

Joni and her husband prepared a bedroom in their home to host a foreign exchange student. She would attend North Crawford Schools just a few miles down the highway.

Her name was Sylvia Thun. She was from Germany.

Before Joni introduced Sylvia to Gene, she warned her to never speak German around her father. Sylvia followed that order, but it didn't matter to Gene. He couldn't believe that his own daughter was hosting a citizen from a country that killed his buddies. His daughter Bridget tried to soothe Gene after he met Sylvia. After all, it had been more than forty years since the war.

"Times are different now, Dad. Let it go," she said.

Let it go?

"Don't tell me I don't know what I'm talking about!" Gene roared. "I watched kids in Germany that age stab my friends to death with a pitchfork."

2002

Gene sat at the kitchen table playing solitaire. It was Christmas Eve, and it was snowing outside. Peg lay sleeping on the twin bed set in the living room. Gene had the bed set up right next to the anteroom that he built for the wood stove. He'd just given Peg her medication. She was in the final stage of her battle with liver cancer. She'd swallowed her pills with homemade applesauce that Gene had made for her. He left the living room with the television on. From the adjacent dining room, lights twinkled from the Christmas tree.

It was just after 8:00 p.m. As Gene silently flipped cards onto the table, Joni burst through the back kitchen door. Following her on that dark, snowy evening was a woman in her early thirties. The woman saw Gene. Not stopping to brush the snow off her coat, she ran to him. Gene stood up to receive her embrace.

"Merry Christmas, Eugene!" the woman said. She kissed him on the cheek and then hugged him again.

It was Silvia Rojek, Joni's second foreign exchange student from Germany. Gene loved *"Mein Schatz"* (My Treasure). When she'd lived with Joni as a student, she'd baked German cookies for Gene and Peg and made them a snowman cake for Christmas. Silvia always shared her care packages from Germany. Peg loved German chocolate. Gene's favorite was the small crumble cakes. Silvia had called Gene and Peg her "Opa" and her "Oma."

Thirteen years after being an exchange student at North Crawford, Silvia returned to her host family, this time bringing her husband Thorstan and their five-year-old son, Sascha. Gene offered Thorstan a can of Blatz.

"Excuse me, Eugene," said Silvia, translating. "My husband said to tell you most American beers are weak. But this is good, thick beer."

Gene raised his beer can and smiled at Thorstan. Then Silvia guided her shy son to meet Gene.

"Das ist Joni's papa," Silvia said.

Silvia wanted her son to show off some of the English he'd learned. Standing next to his mother, still clinging to her knee, he slowly, bashfully counted, "One . . . two . . . three . . ."

"*Eins, zwei, drei*," Gene said after Sascha.

Sascha's eyes popped open. Gene could speak German!

Silvia explained to her son that Gene learned a long time ago how to count in Germany. Sascha moved closer toward Gene.

"Should we do it again?" Gene asked Sascha.

Sascha nodded, and they counted in German in unison. Sascha giggled when Gene mispronounced "sieben."

February 10, 2003

Nineteen-year-old Tim Moran hadn't been home for more than a few minutes when the phone rang.

"Grandma is fading fast," said his aunt Margo. "Go get Grandpa."

Tim, one of Gene's eleven grandchildren, had just returned from dropping off Gene at his home in Soldiers Grove. Gene had spent the morning at his wife's bedside at Vernon Memorial Hospital in Viroqua, but had come home for a nap. Peg wanted to die at home after battling liver cancer for five years, but now that she was in hospice care at the hospital, it was clear she wouldn't be returning home.

The next day would be their fifty-seventh wedding anniversary. The last five years of their marriage had been good ones for Gene and Peg. All the kids noticed. Gene had found peace. His drinking subsided. Doc Sannes had been dead for years, but Gene didn't need that hypodermic needle loaded with a sedative anymore. The fits and rages were a distant memory.

On top of that, the doctors seemed to have finally gotten the right medication for Peg, which greatly improved her mood. These days, she'd get so excited when she saw Gene drive into the yard. Gene would get out of his car and embrace his wife, giggling and kissing her. When Gene's children visited, they thought, *Who are these sweet strangers, and what have they done to our parents?*

For much of their fifty-seven-year marriage, Peg suffered when Gene suffered. She was there for seizures, nightmares, flashbacks, and drunken arguments. But in their final years together, Gene cared for his wife the way she had taken care of him for decades. He washed dishes and cooked all the meals, including making home-made applesauce to aid Peg in swallowing her medication. He also did the laundry.

"Mom, I just can't get these sheets without the corners folded as good as you do," Gene said. They both smiled. They'd settled into a comfortable role reversal, and Gene took pride in taking care of Peg. These were good years, indeed. But would the two get to celebrate one more anniversary together?

Now Gene sat in the passenger seat of Tim's pickup truck as his grandson pushed the speed up to seventy miles an hour. Gene reached over and grabbed his grandson's shoulder.

"It's going to be okay," Gene said. "We'll get there."

Tim wasn't so sure. They rushed to the hospital. There was already a crowd of Morans in the hospital room, and one look at their faces confirmed they were too late. Gene leaned over Peg's bed and spoke to his dead wife.

"We didn't quite make our anniversary, did we, Mom," Gene said. "But that's okay."

Gene buried his wife in the cemetery across the road from St. Philip's church, just two miles north of his childhood farm. The left side of the gravestone read: *Margaret V. Moran (Finley) 1923-2003.* The right side read: *Eugene P. Moran 1924- . . .*

CHAPTER 19

The Toughest to Ever Draw Breath

September 2013

"Thursdays with Gene" were put on hiatus again. But this time, I wasn't the one who called off the interviews. Our two-beer talks at Gene's kitchen table were dredging up war memories he'd once buried. Late in his life, Gene had achieved a tenuous peace, but at odd hours, grief and terror crept back out of the dark recesses of his mind. The war had returned to Gene.

Joni called me.

"Dad said he needs a break. He's been having nightmares."

I could only imagine the demons I'd awakened. Was he dreaming about flaming bombers cartwheeling through the air? In the middle of the night, did he hear Pee Wee screaming in his ball turret? Was he crawling toward Swedo's and Andy's shot-up bodies intertwined on the fuselage floor? In our summer interviews, we'd reviewed his POW days and the death march. Did he wake up at night scratching for lice? Did he see the gaunt face of the old Polish woman, the refugee who begged him for food on the death march? Did he witness again emaciated kriegies collapsing and rolling into a ditch?

I was actually glad for the break. I was due to return to teaching full-time in September, and this school year was my first as a widower and single dad. On top of that, the apple tree branches in my orchard bent heavy with fruit. I was also coaching Joe's youth football team and attending Matthew's freshman games. I certainly didn't mind putting World War II aside for a few months.

That winter, the editor I'd met at the writers' workshop the previous spring began pushing me to finish the interviews.

"Before anything else," she told me, "make a list of all your final questions, any holes in the story, and talk to Gene. Now. Eighty-nine-year-old men who've just had a heart attack don't live forever."

At first, I resented her prodding. In my three years working with Gene, I'd caused him to blow up at a restaurant and sob in his kitchen. I was the one who brought back his nightmares. The man said he needed a break. I should respect that. Besides, my editor didn't have to sit at that aluminum table wracked with guilt while tears streamed down Gene's cheeks.

Gene was indestructible. For Chrissakes, he fell four miles in airplane wreckage and lived! He'd survived decades of flashbacks and seizures. He remarried at age eighty-four. He'd live forever. There'd be time.

Then I thought about the frail man in the yellow smock that I'd visited nearly a year ago at the VA hospital. Gene said then if he didn't read his story down here, he'd read it in the next life. Did he sense his end was near? Nearer than I wanted to accept? Gene was my last living witness to an era I'd been enthralled with since third grade. What was I clinging to?

After Christmas, I asked Joni if she could check if her father was ready to get back to work. It wasn't until late February 2014 that I sat at Gene's kitchen table again. Gene had just returned from a vacation with friends. Vacation for him at this time of year was snowmobiling through the frosty pine forests of northern Wisconsin. He and his buddies were already planning their annual summer fishing trip to Canada. Gene couldn't wait for another week of walleye shore lunches alongside an Ontario lake. They'd already set a date. Gene laughed. He was feeling great. The chest cold and cough that had plagued him the previous two winters were gone thanks to a tabletop respirator. He demonstrated the gadget for me.

"I'm even getting out for short walks, John."

I imagined Gene walking with his cane down to the creek and back to his mobile home in sub-zero weather. Venturing out in Wisconsin in the dead of winter was impressive for anyone at any age.

Gene was in high spirits, but I didn't want to risk bringing up topics that would trigger nightmares again. In three years of on-again, off-again interviews, I'd gathered most of the information on Gene's air war and POW days. Now I had questions about Gene's post-war life, how he made a living and raised a family. I was stunned when he told me he wanted to re-enlist a few years after the war.

"It was somewhere around '47," Gene said. "Things had gotten tough around here, and I was looking for a job. An Army official wrote back and said due to my injuries and disabilities, I was unfit for service."

Gene still had the rejection letter from the Army. The government did help him get on his feet by approving a loan through the GI Bill to purchase a freight truck. He hauled everything from apples to milk. He trucked bottled beer for a distribution business run by a local boy, Beauford Anderson. Anderson had won the Medal of Honor at the Battle of Okinawa and had grown up on a dairy farm just a few miles from the Moran farm.

"We were great friends, Beauford and me. I had to haul empties back from Janesville one time, and I told him I wasn't contracted to haul empties. He said he'd give me eighty bucks if I brought them back. He died a few years ago still owing me that eighty bucks."

But Gene's war injuries couldn't handle the constant lifting involved with hauling freight. He sold his truck and turned to his job with the post office as a rural mail carrier, a job that paid the bills until he retired in 1981.

Gene's life of service to his country continued on the local level.

"I joined the fire department in December of '45 right after I got out of the service," Gene said. He served as a volunteer firefighter in his rural community of Soldiers Grove. "When I was first on the fire department, we had a '38 GMC pickup with two water tanks. That was our little fire truck. That was it. We once had a fire at the creamery, and everyone showed up, but nobody brought the truck."

Everywhere he went in Crawford County, Gene served. He served on the Soldiers Grove Fire Department for fifty-one years, including twenty years as fire chief. He also volunteered as an emergency responder, driving an ambulance on the twisting roads of the Kickapoo Valley to every kind of accident and emergency. Back then, the EMT crew was separate from the fire department. Gene helped pioneer the first emergency medical transit crew for Soldiers Grove.

He was a member of the Soldiers Grove American Legion for sixty-six years. He served his community by playing Santa at the Legion's Christmas charity that gave out toys to poor families. He served as a trustee on the Crawford County Board for twelve years.

Despite his battle wounds, Gene played for the local baseball team, the Soldiers Grove Cardinals, after the war. His injuries limited his playing time to pinch-hitting and an occasional start in right field. One time, an Army team came down from Camp McCoy. An African American ballplayer from the opposing team came trotting from the outfield and asked Gene if he would share his glove. It was Elston Howard, who later became the first African American player for the New York Yankees.

I loved leaning back in my chair at Gene's kitchen table and talking baseball with him. This was happy talk. No war. It was an easygoing Thursday afternoon with Gene. Just conversation about baseball, civic life, and fighting fires. It was the perfect restart after seven months of no interviews. But my editor's advice gnawed at me. We'd have to return to the war, soon. I had a few gaps to fill in, a couple of areas where I wanted to ask more questions. I had to return to the memories that had brought nightmares to a man now eighty-nine years old.

We met again in early March. Gene was still in a good mood, full of plans for his ninetieth birthday party. Maybe this was the time to get back to the war.

"I got the Legion Hall reserved for the weekend after my birthday in July," said Gene in a cheerful, raspy voice. "Make sure you tell your boys."

Tell your boys. No Carmen. It had been more than a year since she died on that dark, snowy night. I was still getting used to the fact that she was gone. The routine of all those hospital visits was gone, replaced by the endless details of child-rearing as an only parent. Now that I was back teaching full-time, I couldn't keep up. Something had to give. I'd have to give up coaching. Reduce the orchard. Buy more wrinkle-free clothes. Maybe Joe could take on more work now that he was twelve. I focused back on Gene. Of course we'd be at his birthday party. But today, all thoughts of being a single parent and teacher had to be set aside. With Gene in a good mood, I had to make this interview count.

I decided to chance it. I'd bring up a touchy topic: George Fisher. Fisher was the Flying Fortress waist gunner who'd been shot down and witnessed *Rikki Tikki Tavi*'s tail hurtling through the air. Gene was furious when he found out that George had blabbed the story of his free fall to the newspapers in New York City. It was late in the war, in 1944, after George had been repatriated, but Gene didn't want his mother knowing anything about his ordeal or the wounds it caused.

"But George said in the Associated Press article that you wanted people to know," I said. "He said you asked him to back your story when he returned to . . ."

"I never told him that!" Gene shot back. He pounded his index finger on the table. "I'm not sure why he said that when he got home. He maybe wanted to make a big name for himself."

Suddenly, Gene closed his eyes and held up his hand. Was he still mad at George? Then I realized he was chuckling. His chuckling turned to giggling. Tears streamed from his eyes as Gene erupted into uncontrolled laughter.

"I never told you about the turd contest," Gene choked out, barely able to mouth the words between gasps of laughter.

"Turd contest? What are you talking about?"

"Back at Heydekrug . . . Stalag Luft 6 . . ." Gene was still laughing. He stopped his story to catch his breath. "We couldn't use the latrine at night, so we had to use the buckets in the barracks. We had a contest to see who could crap the longest turd. George was the all-time champion, twelve and a half inches."

"How do you know the exact length?"

"I'm the one who measured it!"

Gene slammed the table with his hand and burst out laughing again. We laughed together between swigs from our beer cans. Then he exhaled. It was time to get serious. Gene reminded me that George was the man he'd held down for the doctors at the Sandbostel prison hospital while the Serbian prison doctors removed shrapnel from his head without using anesthesia.

"He visited me a couple of times after the war," Gene added. "Even then, he never seemed quite right in the head."

I drove away from Gene's home looking forward to sharing the turd contest story with my boys. It had been our best interview. Well, at least our most entertaining. I didn't ask all my questions about war and death that day, but I did get some more answers, a few more details to fill the gaps. Maybe it didn't matter. Gene was feeling good and loving life. I certainly had most of the information I needed to write Gene's story by now, and I sensed that Gene wanted to wrap up the interviews. Keep the nightmares at bay.

Focus on fishing in Canada, the birthday party, and jokes about a turd contest.

We both knew "Thursdays with Gene" were coming to an end.

Friday, March 21, 2014

"Dad had another heart attack."

Joni was on the phone.

"He's resting and seems to be doing okay. I'm at the hospital now."

I was startled, but not scared. He'd make it. He had survived a heart attack a year earlier, and he would do it again. Pretty soon we'd be together again, talking about fishing. Joni didn't seem as confident. She and her sister Margo had already called their siblings, urging them to come to the La Crosse hospital immediately. Liz flew in from her home in California and Pat from Washington, D.C. By Friday night, all of Gene's nine children were at his bedside.

Saturday morning, Joni called again.

"His vitals are good. He's awake and talking."

"Can I bring the boys up to see him?" I asked.

"Let's wait," said Joni. "He's pretty tired."

The worst of the heart attack aftermath passed, and Gene settled into recovery mode. Pat prepared for his return flight for Sunday night. A few of the siblings discussed who was going to tell their father that maybe it was time for him to move to an assisted living home, or at least allow a home health nurse to stop by his mobile home.

Then Gene stopped talking. His pulse weakened, and his heart rate slipped. It was Saturday afternoon, almost two days since his heart attack. Pat canceled his flight back. Liz extended her stay. Gene's kids remained at the hospital and took turns at his bedside.

Gene was in and out of sleep, but he stirred when Pat put on a baseball game between the Milwaukee Brewers and Atlanta Braves. The Braves were Wisconsin's team in the '50s and '60s before they moved from Milwaukee to Atlanta. It was a close game, and Gene was a fan of both teams.

Gene could barely talk, but he lifted his hand and displayed five fingers. Then he showed four fingers. Gene repeated the motion, five fingers followed by four. Nine.

"Do you want us all?" asked Pat, who was the sibling on bedside duty. "I don't understand."

Nine kids. Yes, all nine Moran kids were there. For the last two days, they'd taken turns by his bedside. Their spouses were there too, out in the waiting room, with the grandchildren nearby playing cards.

Gene made the hand motion for a third time, then lifted his oxygen mask.

"Is it the fourth or fifth inning?" he whispered.

Joni called again Sunday morning. In my twenty years of knowing her as a friend and colleague, Joni had always been a talker. Her gift for gab was constant and voluminous. Now she spoke in a quiet, breathy voice.

"Dad has taken a turn for the worse. I'm sorry, John. He's not taking any visitors. I think this is it."

It can't be. Gene and I had just talked two weeks ago. He'd been as spry as a beaver. The man had fallen four miles and lived. He'd survived *everything*. Nazi bullets. A split skull. Starvation. Seizures. Grief. Nightmares. This couldn't be it. He's got the Legion Hall reserved for his ninetieth birthday bash this summer. Gene never missed a party. He's got reservations!

I couldn't sleep that night. Joni called just before midnight. A doctor had gone over options. There were some interventions they could try for Gene's failing heart. Did they want to try? Gene didn't hesitate. In front of his nine children and their spouses who filled the room, he replied, "Nope. We're done."

Early Sunday morning, Gene held Pauline's hand as she sat next to him. He lifted his oxygen mask and looked at Margo sitting on the opposite side of the bed.

"I'm ready."

Margo needed no further explanation.

"Are you sure, Dad?"

Gene nodded. Margo fetched a nurse. Two nurses came into the room to detach the oxygen mask and remove the intravenous needles from his arm. Gene leaned over and waved a goodbye to Pauline.

"Do you want a priest?" Margo asked.

Gene nodded again. Margo checked on getting a priest to Gene's room, but since it was Sunday morning, the priests were away at church services. He'd have to wait a few hours.

"Dad, no priests are available. Do you care if we say a few prayers?"

Margo recited The Lord's Prayer and Angel of God. Then she looked at her dad and smirked.

"With all the powers vested in me, I absolve you . . ." She paused. ". . . of MOST of your sins."

Gene smiled through closed eyes and shook his head.

He held on until the priest from St. Philip's arrived midafternoon. St. Philip's, his very own church an hour away just south of Soldiers Grove. Gene had been baptized there as a baby, taken Communion as a gap-toothed seven-year-old, and learned to box with Father Mathieu. He baptized his own children and married Pauline there. Now Father Zacharie was by his side to perform last rites. This priest looked nothing like the priests from Gene's childhood. Those men had been white, many of them old. This priest was thin and dark-skinned, a man who'd moved his life from the Democratic Republic of the Congo to rural Wisconsin.

"Hello, Father," mouthed Gene. The two men knew each other well since Gene attended daily Mass.

Father Zacharie kissed the cloth around his neck and set out small bottles of anointing oils. He recited prayers of forgiveness as he dabbed oil on Gene's forehead and rubbed it into each palm. As he completed the ritual of last rites, Gene's shoulders dropped and he fell asleep.

"We should probably do a toast." The priest had gone. It was Gene's oldest son, Tim, who spoke.

Pat drove to the nearest liquor store and picked out a bottle of Grand Marnier cognac. They filled paper medicine cups with the cognac and passed them around to all the Moran relatives who crowded around the bed.

"To our dad, Eugene P. Moran: veteran, hero, father," said Pat.

"Rest in peace, Dad."

"We love you, Grandpa."

"Say hi to Mom."

Laurie, the middle child, gave the last toast before everyone lifted their paper cups.

"To Eugene Moran. The toughest son of a bitch to ever draw breath."

Thursday, March 27, 2014

The school day at North Crawford had just finished. The normal sounds of students slamming lockers and yelling after-school plans echoed in my ears as I drove straight to St. Philip's for Gene's wake. A soft rain peppered my windshield under gray skies. I stepped into the church and crossed myself, dipping my hand in the holy water font.

Up at the altar, Pauline and all nine of Gene's children, lined up in order from Tim to Pat, took in hugs and condolences. Men I knew from around the area were looking at a photo of the crew of *Rikki Tikki Tavi* mounted on white poster board along with other pictures from Gene's life. There they were, Gene's crew, all ten of them at rest now.

Talk swirled around me, plain talk:

"We simply didn't talk about his war days. Ever. We knew better."

"No one has a goddamned clue what it's like when these guys get back. Nobody."

"Damned politicians have no idea how these guys suffer."

I paused when I saw a card with the name "Wayne Orrison" among the bouquets of flowers.

And then I saw Gene. His body lay in an open casket dressed in his blue-and-white-striped bib overalls, a red flannel shirt underneath. I swallowed hard and pushed back tears. Just three weeks ago, we'd both been in tears the day we'd laughed so hard about the turd contest.

I looked down at Gene's face covered with makeup. That didn't look right. The Gene I knew would never put anything on his face but a mischievous grin. At least they dressed him in his overalls, and one of the grandchildren had sneaked a can of Blatz beer into the casket.

The funeral was the next day. Joni told me to get there early. She was right. An hour before the service, the parking lot was jammed. The funeral was scheduled for 11:00 a.m. at St. Philip's, but by 10:00 a.m., every pew was packed. The balcony overflowed with mourners. People lined the side walls, and many more streamed out the door. Fire trucks arrived, then turned back because of the crowd. They were there to lead a parade in honor of Gene after the service, but there was simply no room with parked cars lining both sides of the road and stretching for a quarter mile.

The service began with an older man wearing an American Legion garrison cap walking up the aisle to salute the flag-draped casket. Twenty-five more veterans followed and saluted Gene. They all wore black garrison caps with the names of towns from across Wisconsin embroidered in yellow letters. The first veteran to approach the casket was elderly; the last was a young Navy sailor, Ryan Donner, the husband of Kelly, Gene's granddaughter.

Next came five firemen in dress uniform. They each wore white gloves and carried a chrome-coated axe. This was the honor guard sent from the Middleton Fire Department, just outside Madison. *Middleton.* That's where Gene had taken Peg to dinner on their first date. An image of Gene sitting at his aluminum kitchen table flashed in my mind, his magnifying glass, Copenhagen tin, and can coolers at his side. I pushed the memories away. Did they leave that can of Blatz in the casket after they closed it?

We were saying goodbye to Eugene P. Moran. A man whose own children knew only a fraction of what I knew about their father's past. I promised Gene I wouldn't share his story with his family until the book was done. Now he was gone. It was my story now.

The church rang with Gene's favorite hymns, "The Old Rugged Cross" and "My Wild Irish Rose." Eight grandsons and two great-grandsons rose to be pallbearers. I pinched my leg hard to fight back tears.

As the crowd spilled out onto the rain-soaked church lawn, the leader of the American Legion honor guard shouted orders to the rifle squad. There was a crack of rifle shots, then a buzz of voices as the crowd headed to the basement for ham sandwiches, hamburger casseroles, and lemon bars. It was a Lenten Friday, but Father Zacharie had given his blessing to eat meat.

After an hour or so of picking at tater tot casserole, I left the crowd at St. Philip's. I had someplace I had to be, and that someplace was Gene's home farm.

I hadn't been there since I'd snapped that picture of Carmen hugging Gene by the barn nearly two years ago. Now both of them were gone. I knocked on the house door where the renters lived, grateful when no one answered. I was alone with the land and its history.

I walked over to the white, wood-sided milk house attached to the red barn. The barn where Gene had milked so many cows was still in good shape. The line of the roof was level and the side walls plumb. The red paint on the barn paneling was weathered, but none of the boards were missing. I looked back across the ridge where Gene had complained to me about the woods. The woods that had grown in over land he'd worked so hard to clear. I was standing right where Carmen and Gene had stood for their picture. I crouched and touched the grass, looking out over the ridgetop at the sky.

Carmen . . . and now Gene.

He'd survived a four-mile fall, the hell ship, a death march, nightmares, flashbacks, post-traumatic stress, too much drinking. The bare logic that an eighty-nine-year-old man with a weakening heart would likely die didn't matter to me. Of course Gene would survive. That's what he did. And I needed him. We had work left to do.

I don't know how long I stood there by the milk house until it hit me. Here I was feeling sorry for myself at the childhood home of the most resilient human being I'd ever met. Gene had suffered unimaginable pain, yet in three years of interviews, he'd never complained about his fate. Once, I asked him what secret, what motivation, had helped him survive. He answered with a chuckle. "John, we were tougher than boiled owl shit."

The toughest son of a bitch to draw breath was at rest. He'd done his part. Now it was my turn.

CHAPTER 20

A Place in a Woods

November 28-29, 2018

"Tomorrow, you be like Mick Jagger," said a German-accented voice. Ulf Kaack slapped me on the shoulder. Ulf was my host here in Syke, Germany, the very city where in a nearby woods, Eugene Moran had crawled from plane wreckage.

Tomorrow was November 29, 2018. Seventy-five years to the day Gene fell from the sky. And here was Ulf, standing in a lodge dining room, asking me to make a speech tomorrow on national German television to commemorate Gene's fall.

I was shocked. I wasn't prepared for a speech. When it came to that, I still couldn't believe that I was even a guest in this German lodge. It was late November, and here I was playing hooky in the middle of the school year. And I wasn't alone. With me were twenty-five family members and friends of Gene Moran, Jesse Orrison, and Edmund Swedo—all of us hosted by the Germans as honored guests.

The citizens of Syke never forgot the day *Rikki Tikki Tavi* exploded in the sky. The city of 25,000 sat about a dozen miles south of Bremen, the target of Gene's last mission.

When *Rikki Tikki Tavi* blew up after its air battle over Syke, the bomber left a debris field stretching four kilometers. The falling wreckage ignited fires and a thousand stories. We were here to learn those stories during the next four days. We were here—unbelievably—to take part in Syke's commemoration to honor the American airmen who bombed them.

Ulf was a German writer who'd co-authored the book *Luftkrieg in der Region* (*Air War in the Region*). It was a coffee-table book filled with photos and stories of thirty famous plane crashes in Germany during World War II, with one chapter featuring the downing of *Rikki Tikki Tavi*.

Ulf had contacted me in the summer of 2017 while researching his book. I gladly gave him and his co-author, Jürgen Kuhlmann, permission to use my photographs and information. They sent me a copy of the finished book.

Six months later, Ulf told me that Syke was planning a commemoration of the crash and Gene's famous fall. All family and friends of the crew of *Rikki Tikki Tavi* would be guests of the city. All meals. All lodging. All ceremonies and tours. All we had to do was pay for the plane tickets to Europe.

I couldn't believe it. Was Gene really being honored by the nation that almost killed him? I had to be there. But then I hesitated. November? I'd have to leave my students. Matthew would be a sophomore at the University of Wisconsin–Madison. I couldn't afford a European vacation. And I wasn't comfortable leaving Joe, a high school junior, alone at home for two weeks. I shared my concerns with my editor.

"You're going," she replied.

Easy for her to say. She didn't have my bills. Or schedule. Teachers just don't pick up and leave in November to drink beer in Germany. But . . . should I? Could I?

"This is a once-in-a-lifetime opportunity," she said. "You'll regret it if you don't."

Ridiculous. There was no way I could go. Of course, I'd reacted the same way eight years earlier when Joni asked me to write her dad's story. There was no hesitation on Joni's part about going to Germany.

"I wanted to do cartwheels down my stairs when I heard about the trip!" she said.

Joni contacted all her siblings and Gene's grandchildren. She understood if the grandchildren with their young families and new careers couldn't make it, but in the end, fifteen members of the Moran family said yes, including Gene's grandson Joe, who said, "I wouldn't dream of missing this."

Neither would I. I told Joni to buy two airline tickets.

Greg Swedo and Wayne Orrison also said yes right away. Wayne was astounded . . . and perplexed. Why would Germans honor men who dropped bombs on them?

Why would they? We'd have to find out together.

That summer, I met the Moran family at Laurie's lakeside home to discuss final trip details. We sat on lawn chairs in a circle on the driveway. Gene's youngest son issued a warning.

"We have to remember, we'll be representing our family and our country," Pat said.

"Look who's talking!" chided his brothers and sisters in a chorus of hoots and hollers. But Pat knew the family fondness for good drink and long nights.

"I'm being serious," said Pat. "I'm wondering what they will think of us. We're the children of a man who bombed their country. There might still be some hard feelings over there."

The first day of the commemoration event started when Joni and I toured the Sandbostel Prisoner-of-War Camp Museum and Memorial. Sandbostel, the first POW camp where the two Serb doctors had stitched Gene's head back together. The camp where

Gene met George Fisher, the downed gunner who'd witnessed his incredible fall.

Joni and I had arrived in Europe a few days before the rest of our group, and on a frosty day, Ulf and Jürgen drove us to Sandbostel. We pulled into the camp entrance next to a modern, single-story building that served as the museum headquarters. I stared at a row of a half-dozen dilapidated buildings in the distance. The unremarkable structures were nothing more than sheds made of weathered barn boards with a few windows and several chimneys. Prisoner barracks. Maybe one of those barracks was where Gene teetered on the edge of life recovering from his fractured skull.

I was startled by the sound of barking dogs. Was it a sound effect? A recording of snarling German shepherds meant to enhance the museum tour experience? I recoiled. Ulf steadied my nerves.

"No, not sound effects," Ulf said, laughing. "There is an animal shelter across the road."

I relaxed. I remembered Gene telling me about the vicious dogs that howled at him and Shorty after disembarking from the hell ship. The dogs from the animal shelter didn't stop barking. It seemed a bit too real.

A museum archivist led Joni and me across the grounds of about a dozen barracks. He explained that just twenty-three of the one hundred fifty buildings from the original camp still stood. A few steps behind us trailed a reporter and his cameraman from a German national news program. Sunlight streamed in through windows as we poked our heads into the barracks rooms. Our condensed breath hung in the air. The bunk bed frames were stacked three high. Some rooms had nothing but wooden center posts and busted floorboards crisscrossed over a cement base. Maybe in one of these buildings was where Gene got drunk when the French POWs carried his cot to their Christmas party.

"The wounded did not stay in these quarters," the archivist explained. "Gene would have stayed in the medical area about a kilometer away. But those buildings are no longer here."

The archivist motioned in the direction where the wounded were housed. It was just a line of trees and bushes now. Such a simple scene compared to the complexity of barbed wire, high fences, and guard towers that existed when Gene was brought in lying in the back of that German truck with the wood-burning engine.

We walked quietly from one building to the next. In one barracks, portraits of Russian prisoners hung from the walls of crumbling plaster. Families still made the trek from Russia for any information of lost Soviet Army relatives who died by the thousands at the prison. Gene had told me how the French POWs made fun of the flesh plate that covered his head wound, muscle and skin they told him had probably been torn from a Russian corpse. How many grieving Russian mothers had no idea they had sons buried here?

By evening, Joni and I were back at the lodge. We were all staying at two large guest homes, compliments of a German newspaper publisher who footed the bill. Tomorrow was the actual seventy-fifth anniversary of Gene's fall, and suddenly I was expected to give a speech at the crash site. The German television crew would be with us again, recording my every word.

I didn't even know we'd be stopping at the actual woods where Gene landed. We'd also be meeting citizens who'd witnessed Gene's plane come down when they were schoolchildren. It all seemed incomprehensible. After once being told by Joni, "We don't go there," about her father's story, I was actually going to be "there," at the very spot that made Gene a legend.

I didn't sleep a wink that night. Late-autumn rain pelted the tiled roof. My open suitcase sat on a couch near my narrow twin bed. And there in the hazy light of early dawn on top of a stack of unpacked clothes rested a brown leather bomber jacket. Not a whole one—a torn section of a World War II bomber jacket newly etched with the words "Gene Moran" and also my initials, "JMA."

I smiled. It was a gift from Kris. She had folded it around a leather-bound notebook that I'd use for note-taking and tucked both gifts away in my luggage.

Kris and I had been dating for ten months.

It had been nearly six years since Carmen's death, and here I was unexpectedly dating an old friend of hers. Carmen and I were freshmen in college when we first dated, and she introduced me to a friend in her painting class. Now, thirty years later, Kris herself was in my life: blonde, striking, a mom with three boys of her own about the ages of Matthew and Joe. Kris had attended Carmen's funeral and often spoke of her. She loved theater and was a renowned actor in central Wisconsin.

I'd had a few bad first dates before Kris. A year-long relationship ended when the woman told me, "You're still in love with your dead wife." I felt awful, but she was right. After that breakup, I had no interest in dating. Kris came from out of nowhere. This was different. Something had shifted in me. I was ready to share my life again.

I got up and grabbed the brown leather. Sitting back on the edge of the bed, I stroked it. Tomorrow I would take this torn leather with me to the woods where Gene fell.

November 29—the big day. The entire American party along with several of our German hosts boarded a tour bus in drizzling rain. The windshield wiper flicked back and forth over a sign in the front window, a sign with large black letters that read: "Rikki Tikki Tavi." Next to those words was a colorful emblem of a Flying Fortress, the flags of Germany and the United States crisscrossed above the plane. The words *Im Gedenken* circled the image of the plane. *In Memory*.

The bus pulled up by a woods at the edge of Syke. We crossed a busy road to a grove of tall trees located only yards from a row of houses. Ulf pointed out two large beech trees. That was where Jesse

Orrison had fallen, entangled in his parachute straps, bleeding and moaning. Now, three generations of Orrisons stared up at the trees, from Jesse's son Wayne to his great-grandson Dane Jesse.

We gathered by a brand-new historical marker mounted on a pole in front of the beech trees. It was covered with a white cloth, and Ulf invited Wayne to unveil the plaque. Underneath was a picture of the crew of *Rikki Tikki Tavi*, along with the story of the bomber's demise, Gene's fall, and Orrison's landing. I was stunned, yet again. What an effort the people of Syke made to commemorate a former enemy! I gazed at the historical sign, the familiar picture of *Rikki Tikki Tavi*'s crew grinning back at me. Gene's story was no longer hidden. It was here, in Germany, out in the open air for all to see.

Ulf tapped me on the shoulder and drew me over to meet an elderly woman standing nearby under an umbrella.

"This is Annelore Franke," said Ulf. "I interviewed her for my book. She saw *Rikki Tikki Tavi* come down when she was a child."

Annelore nodded and smiled. She'd been eight years old in 1943 and witnessed Orrison float down in his parachute and fall into these trees. In slow, halting English, Annelore told me her story.

"When the air raid sirens began . . ."

When the air raid sirens began wailing that day, Annelore ran to the basement. Later, back outside, she heard a "loud, terrible noise" when *Rikki Tikki Tavi* exploded above her.

Airplane debris fell from the sky, and amidst the tumbling wreckage, a single parachute floated down. Orrison. She and other kids ran to the woods where the parachute landed. There was a bleeding man dangling from his parachute straps entangled in a large beech tree.

"He was yelling and crying, 'Doctor, doctor!'" she said. "A crowd gathered, and some people cried, 'Kill him! Kill him!' But others said no."

Someone shoved a ladder up into the tree and climbed up to

cut Orrison from his parachute straps. Several men lowered him to a waiting ox cart that wheeled him away from the scene. I was shocked when Annelore said Orrison came back years later to thank the people of Syke for sparing his life. He had? Wayne had never mentioned the trip, never heard of it himself. It must have been his father's private reconciliation. But the story made sense; Orrison was stationed in Germany when he rejoined the military in the 1950s.

After posing for pictures next to the new historical marker, we headed to city hall for the formal part of the commemoration. On the way, Ulf pointed out a subdivision of houses that had once been a farm field. One of the crew of *Rikki Tikki Tavi* had been found dead in that field, lying near a searchlight. Two more corpses were found on the street the tour bus now drove over. Who were they?

We entered city hall. The large dining room was filled with local politicians and dignitaries. A few tables were filled with elderly people who had been living in Syke the day *Rikki Tikki Tavi* came down. The schoolchildren! Witnesses like Annelore. They were all in their eighties now, but they'd seen the explosion firsthand. I twisted in my seat, eager to talk to them, but I knew I had to wait.

First, Syke's mayor spoke, offering us a warm welcome in German. Next to the mayor stood Silvia Rojek, Joni's former exchange student. She was volunteering as our unofficial interpreter. The girl Gene called "*Mein Schatz*," who at seventeen had won over his heart, was here with us now. After the mayor's welcome, Joni presented the mayor with a glass art piece, a gift from the Moran family to the city of Syke.

But it was Dr. Henning Scherf who stole the show. He was a former mayor of Bremen and a nationally known politician.

Scherf was a spellbinding speaker. He spoke in English, then German, about how as a six-year-old boy living in Bremen during the war, he would sit in a bomb shelter, holding his grandmother's hand. As explosions shook the earth around him, his grandmother told him to be grateful for the Allied bombing because it was the only way that Nazism would be destroyed.

I was stunned. I'd never heard such a sentiment. Gene and Orrison were almost lynched when the Germans captured them seventy-five years ago. And this man, who could have very likely been bombed by Gene's plane, spoke of the bombing as a blessing?

"No German of today carries any grudges toward any Allied airmen or soldiers, because they were needed to achieve peace," Scherf said.

Scherf spoke about the refugee crisis currently facing Germany and how any problem must be faced with love. The room sat riveted. Tears streamed down a nearby man's cheeks, trickling past his handlebar mustache. All around me were nods and sighs.

"We will solve this crisis," Scherf said. "But we must not choose hate. We did that once, and it almost destroyed us."

Lunch was served. I gulped my food. I should have savored the mouthwatering finger sandwiches and delicate cakes. But I was itching to get to the table filled with elderly eyewitnesses who were in Syke seventy-five years ago. Finally, it was time. A man from those tables pointed out people I could interview. Then he quietly and firmly warned me not to go near one man seated nearby.

"That man lost his mother when he was five. A bomb hit his home. He saw his mother cut in two halves. He also lost three siblings in that explosion. He will not talk to you."

I nodded, grateful to know. I needed no further instructions to avoid the man. But why had he chosen to attend the ceremony? Was he still searching for closure?

Many others wanted to talk to me. Too many at once. People lined up, impatient to tell their stories, and a small crowd pressed me in. Some knew English and spoke for themselves. Others used a translator. I stood there in their midst, overjoyed at their enthusiasm, yet overwhelmed by all the voices and languages. I furiously scribbled notes into my leather-bound notebook from Kris. I was enthralled with their childlike wonderment as they talked. They were all in their eighties, but the eyes looking back at me were the eyes of excited schoolchildren.

Annelore Franke returned with two of her grandsons to serve as interpreters. I learned more about her story. After seeing Orrison cut out of the tree, Annelore said she ran with the other kids to a sheared airplane wing lying in the street. A pair of legs stuck out from under the wing, legs with a good pair of boots on them. The children stared at the boots.

"The shoes looked very good," said Annelore. "We wanted them. But we became scared and ran away."

A body under a wing. Another man lying dead in a field. Two corpses on the street. Who were they? Which one was Pee Wee, Swedo, Andy, Sparky, Langley, Benny, Reed, or Curtis?

One man said he was ten years old when he emerged from a bomb shelter. He ran down the street, where a bakery was ablaze. Wreckage from *Rikki Tikki Tavi* had crashed into the bakery, igniting it. He described firemen trying to rescue a fat lady trapped in the bakery who was too large to pull through an escape door.

Another very animated man told me through an interpreter how he witnessed *Rikki Tikki Tavi* blow up over the city. One flier came down in a parachute and crashed through a neighbor's tile roof and fell dead onto a kitchen table. He said the body cut a perfect silhouette in the tile roof, describing it as something seen in a cartoon.

That could have been Curtis. Orrison threw a parachute on the dying man and pushed him out the nose hatch. He was the only man besides Orrison that I knew for sure left the plane with a parachute. Pee Wee was killed in the ball turret. Gene saw Swedo and

Andy dead at the waist position. Orrison's post-war combat report said Benny, Reed, and Sparky had all been wounded and were
screaming. Orrison didn't know about Langley. Maybe Langley got
out of the plane. The more I heard, the more questions I had that
would never be answered.

Under a steady rain, our tour bus pulled to the side of the road
across from another woods. But not just any woods. This was the
place. We were finally at the site where Gene had crashed in 1943.

The windshield wipers squeaked. I stared out the window, peering at the leafless, spindly trees. Then the tour guide tapped me on
the shoulder.

"You will need to make your speech here on the bus. It is raining, and we are behind schedule."

I looked back at Greg Swedo sitting a few seats behind and
mouthed, *We need to go outside.* He nodded. I got up and informed
our tour guide. I'd come half a world away. I was mere yards from
the woods where Gene came down. That forest pulled me irresist-
ibly down the bus steps.

Dashing across the road, light rain splashed my face, and I tried
to remember the weather Gene once described to me when he was
shot down. That day was dry and cold. When Gene lay in these
woods, exactly seventy-five years ago, he couldn't see the sky above
him. His own blood had filled his eyes and blinded him during his
fall in the tail section.

Greg followed me off the bus. We stood together in a field adjacent to the woods, our shoes and socks soaked from the wet grass.
But the rain was fading. Soon, our entire group followed us across
the road, every move recorded by the German television camera
crew. Together, German and American, we gathered silently, staring
at the leafless forest.

The simplicity of the scene surprised me. I'd envisioned a large forest with ranks of tall pine trees covering a sloping hillside, soft, swaying branches that would have cushioned Gene's fall. But the terrain here was flat, and the woods were small, filled with young trees and brush. Maybe it looked different seventy-five years ago. But still, I couldn't envision a soft landing for Gene.

Here I'd give my speech. Out here next to the woods and the fading drizzle. I called out Gene's great-grandson, fourteen-year-old Jackson Moran, to step forward.

"Look around you, Jack," I said, putting my hand on his shoulder. "Seventy-five years ago, your great-grandfather fell into these woods. In another seventy-five years, you will be eighty-nine, the same age when your great-grandfather died. You may be the last living witness who knew Gene. Remember what you learn here today."

I looked at the rest of the family and talked about Gene, his comrades. Then I turned my head toward the trees.

"What happened in these woods was only the beginning of Gene's story."

After my speech, we were supposed to get back on the bus, but Jürgen pointed toward the woods. His English was heavily accented, but he kept pointing, and I gathered he was describing where Gene fell.

"Wait. You know the *exact* spot?" I asked.

"*Ja.* One hundred meters, straight," Jürgen answered. He flattened his hand and motioned his arm perpendicular to the tree line. "Then twenty meters into woods."

I had to be there. I left the crowd and walked toward where Jürgen pointed. First, I paced off a hundred meters along the edge of the woods, then turned and entered the wet brush, pushing away tree branches for twenty meters before stopping. I was *here*. Here at the very spot. My mind raced. Which tree? Which tree did Gene crash into? The trees stared back, their bark dark with moisture, each bearing their silent testimony.

My hands reached for the torn piece of a leather bomber jacket Kris had given me. My fingers ran over the letters of Gene's name stamped on the replica cloth. Seventy-five years earlier, Gene's actual jacket had been torn by Luftwaffe bullets. I draped the brown leather over a tree branch and stepped back. I was standing on the actual ground where Gene crawled out of the mangled tail of *Rikki Tikki Tavi* . . . seventy-five years ago to the day!

Almost eight years ago over a fish fry dinner, I had told Gene we didn't have to write his story. Not if it was too painful. Who was I to make a man at the end of his life revisit anguished memories? It was his choice, his story. His raspy voice came back to me: *John, if we don't do it now, it will never happen.*

Over three years of Thursday afternoons and cold beer, I helped Gene tell the story he'd suppressed so long. In these very woods, near the spot where I stood, Gene had split his skull wide open. Decades later, I'd split his memories open and brought him more pain. Despite unleashing new bouts of nightmares and flashbacks, I desperately hoped Gene had gained some comfort and relief.

Gene had told his story. And because he did, generations of his family and the families of Orrison and Swedo stood in a quiet, damp forest with our German hosts, building bonds of friendship. There was Gene's granddaughter Kelly stepping over slick, rotting logs in her high heels and skirt, her husband, a Navy sailor, beside her. There was Gene's son Tom with Dr. Henning Scherf. Together, they climbed up a homemade hunting stand perched in a nearby opening. It was like any other Wisconsin deer stand, but here it was in this German woods. What a pair they made: Henning, dapper and stylish in black, Tom in a large, green jacket, wearing a Green Bay Packers cap. They acted like two kids playing: one the son of an American bomber boy and the other a man who once sat underneath falling American bombs, holding his grandmother's hand.

I stood alone, staring at the bomber jacket leather hanging from the tree branch. The leather hung motionless, but my memory was awash with the kaleidoscope of characters connected to this place: Gene's mom who'd forbidden him to go to war, his sister JoAnn who'd watched the MIA telegram arrive, his brothers on *Rikki Tikki Tavi*, the Serb doctors, George Fisher, Captain Wolfe, Shorty, Bill, Father Lynch, Peg, Joni and her brothers and sisters, Carmen, Matthew, Joe, Ulf, Jürgen, and Kris. Their stories were now one, a story Gene would never read. But I heard his gravelly voice: *If I don't read it down here, I'll read it up there.*

Leaning my back against the damp bark of a tree, I opened my leather-bound notebook. Then closed it. It was enough to be here, in these woods, with these people, with Gene.

EPILOGUE

July 2019

Gene and I had an agreement: no one would read his story until it was published. For years, I'd kept that promise.

"You're killing me, Armbruster," Joni would complain after I'd rebuff her latest attempt to get details on *Rikki Tikki Tavi* or Stalag Luft prison camps. But was I being stubborn? Gene himself had died five years earlier. How long would Joni and the rest of the Moran family have to wait? Gene's three surviving siblings were in their eighties and nineties. Gene's children weren't children. The oldest was approaching seventy.

The story was finally written, though not yet published. I'd carried this story by myself for so long. All those Thursdays with Gene. All his searing memories of war, interrupted by Carmen's war with cancer. And then after her death, after Gene's death, soldiering on alone. Squeezing time to complete Gene's story between grading history exams, sitting alone at youth basketball tournaments, and tending the apple orchard with two motherless boys. All those years of trading chapters across cyberspace with my editor Heather, who sent back the first drafts of each chapter flooded with electronic red ink.

"Looks like a goat exploded again," I'd tell my boys after opening her comments. Then I'd open a beer, trudge down to my basement office, and pound out another draft of a chapter.

Now the Moran summer reunion was inching up on the calendar. It was an annual backyard affair where we all joked and feasted on fried catfish. Each time, I'd share an update on the book's progress without giving too much away. But it was getting harder and harder to hold back story lines from the inquiring minds of Gene's children and grandchildren. Maybe this time I'd give a little more, show them a sneak peek of *Tailspin*. They'd waited. The book was ready. I printed out two sample chapters, a copy of both for each Moran sibling and grown child.

The Moran reunion was at Bridget's house. We gathered in her backyard amid webbed lawn chairs and tiki torches a few miles east of the Mississippi River, a half-hour drive from Soldiers Grove. Kris was by my side. She smiled at me over her fried catfish as I endured ribbing from Gene's daughters.

"I don't know what she sees in you," quipped Laurie. "She's out of your league," said Joni. Typical. I was family now, and it was their way of welcoming Kris. But I wasn't there to trade barbs with Gene's sassy daughters. It was time to pass out the sample chapters.

What would they think? Gene had trusted me. This whole family had trusted me. Would my writing be worthy of Gene's incredible survival story?

Marty, Gene's brother, avoided eye contact. But Gene's son, Tom, stood up from his chair, waving the rolled-up chapters, and gave a loud shout. "I'm finally going to find out who my dad really was!"

Amid shouts of joy and tearful hugs, I realized I'd cracked a dam holding a reservoir of sixty years of pent-up desire. There was no holding back anymore. It was time to give the family the entire story, twenty-five years after Joni first told me, "We don't go there."

I shared the whole manuscript with Gene's children in 2020, the year of the pandemic. With fried catfish gatherings on hold, we gathered by phone to talk about *Tailspin*. I was irritable and hardly ate that day. What would they think now that they'd read the whole story? How would they react to the terrors their father had suffered on the hell ship and death march? My greatest fear was the brutal truth I'd exposed about the horrors Gene suffered *after* the war. Once that chaos was laid bare for all to see, would people tear down street signs that bore Gene's name and strip him of his honors?

I could have ended the book with Gene sailing away from France with a boatload of Greatest Generation warriors cheering their victory over fascism. End of story. The good guys won. But the truth was the war never ended for Gene. The war came home. And if I didn't tell *that* part of the story, then this book would be a work of fiction.

Down in my basement office, I sat back for the phone call and braced myself for whatever might come. From the oldest, Tom, to the youngest, Pat, the Moran children told me what they thought.

"A tremendous weight has been lifted off my chest," said Margo.

"Our father was one tough son of a bitch," said Tom. "I was in Vietnam, and it was a mess. But what Dad went through was worse."

I listened in disbelief as each of Gene's children embraced their father's story, even the painful memories of PTSD rages, drunken meltdowns, and thrashing seizures.

"This book is a gift," Liz said. "A gift to our family."

When she said that, I was on the verge of dissolving into tears. Gene's secret story had finally been told. And his children approved.

I hung up the phone, exhausted. I couldn't wait to call Kris. She was the one who'd kept me on a tight writing schedule. She was the one who'd always buoyed me up when the task seemed overwhelming. Soon, Kris and I would be empty nesters. We'd spent the summer setting up graduation parties for our two youngest sons. Joe was entering his freshman year at the University of Wisconsin–Madison, joining his brother Matthew there, now a senior finishing a degree in criminal justice. Eight years after Carmen's death, our boys were grown and in college. The book was written. And against all odds, I'd stumbled into happiness with Kris.

As I stood up to call Kris, one of the hastily scrawled sentences in my notebook caught my eye. It was something Joni said during the group phone call.

"When Dad is crawling across that bombed-out bridge," Joni said, "I'm telling him, 'C'mon, Dad. Keep going. You can make it.'"

He made it, Joni. We all made it.

Gene riding the pet sheep "Buck" in front of his house on the farm. His older brother Byron and sister Rosemary stand next to Buck.

Gene in the back row on the left next to Byron. In the front are his brother Michael and sisters JoAnn and Rosemary.

Gene standing next to his first car: a used Model T Ford. He rigged up a battery and wires to create an electrical ignition.

Gene dancing with his cousin Imogene Cummings in a jitterbug contest. They won first place.

Gene's senior picture. Soldiers Grove High School, Class of 1941.

Gene home on leave in his summer uniform.

The final picture taken of Gene and his family before he left for war. Standing in the back row from left to right is Gene, Byron, JoAnn, and Rosemary. In the front row left to right are Dad (Joe), Michael, and Mom (Ethel) holding new brother, Marty.

Gene (right) with Wilbert "Pee Wee" Provost at "Camp Rattlesnake" in Pyote, Texas.

Eugene Moran
Tail Gunner

Sam Amatulli
Radio Operator

Edmund Swedo
Waist Gunner

Wilbert "Pee Wee" Provost
Ball Turret Gunner

Anderson King
Waist Gunner

Walter Reed
Top Turret Gunner

Berline "Benny" Cipresso
Co-pilot

Donald Curtis
Bombardier

Jesse Orrison
Navigator

Linwood Langley
Pilot

WWII B-17 Crew
Shot Down on November 29, 1943
96th Bomb Group

The crew of Rikki Tikki Tavi *at Grand Island, Nebraska, Army Air Force Base before flying to England.*

Bombardier Donald Curtis from Alma, Michigan.

Navigator Jesse Orrison from Marshall, Michigan.

Pilot Linwood "Woody" Langley from Pittsfield, Massachusetts, kneeling with dog. Standing is Woody's brother, Llewellyn, who would become a Navy pilot during the war.

Top turret gunner/flight engineer Walter Reed's senior class picture. Reed, of Broken Bow, Nebraska, is seated in the front row, far left.

Gene's wife Margaret "Peg" Finley
while a nursing student in Madison,
Wisconsin.

Gene's photograph for his phony
identification papers as part of his
escape kit.

The only known picture of Gene's Flying Fortress, Rikki Tikki Tavi.

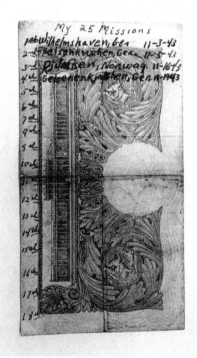

A British one-pound note which waist gunner Edmund Swedo used to keep track of his first four completed missions. The note was one of Swedo's effects returned to his parents after he was declared missing-in-action.

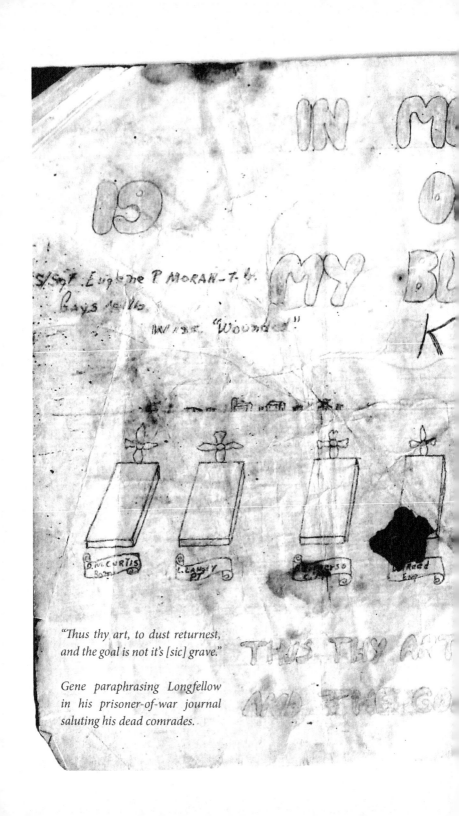

IN M...

19

S/Sgt. Eugene P MORAN-7-4...
Says hello

Was "Wounded"

MY BL

K

"Thus thy art, to dust returnest,
and the goal is not it's [sic] grave."

Gene paraphrasing Longfellow
in his prisoner-of-war journal
saluting his dead comrades.

THIS THY ART

AND THE GO

ORY

ES

IN ACTION

CREW No. 50 -B-
"RICCI TICCI TAUI"

43

2ed Lt. Jess F. ORBISON

Mich. WA

| S. AMATO | W. PROUO | A. KING | E. SWEDE |
| R.O. | RB | R.W. | |

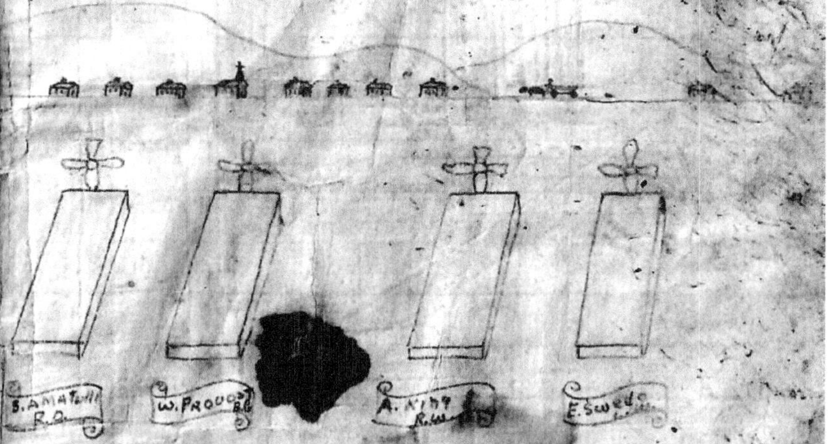

ST RETURNST

T IT'S GRAVE

(LONG FELLOW)

Soldiers Grove Gunner Falls 4 Miles In Plane Tail—And Lives!

NEW YORK—(AP)—Trapped in the severed tail of a Flying Fortress, S. Sgt. Eugene Moran of Gays Mills, Wis., fell four miles into a tree top in Germany and lived, to become a German prisoner of war, an eyewitness relates. (Moran's home is near Soldiers Grove, the Tribune was told today.)

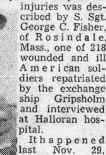

Moran's escape with only minor injuries was described by S. Sgt. George C. Fisher, of Rosindale, Mass., one of 218 wounded and ill American soldiers repatriated by the exchange ship Gripsholm and interviewed at Halloran hospital.

It happened last Nov. 29, Fisher said, after

MORAN flak had cut off the plane tail, with Moran, the tail gunner, caught inside. Moran couldn't jump because his parachute had been shot full of holes, so he folded the chute around him and waited for the inevitable.

Stabilizer Hits Tree

As the tail dropped earthward, the damaged vertical fin and horizontal stabilizers fluttered and flapped, Fisher said, breaking the speed of the fall. Then, one of the stabilizers stabbed into the tree—and held.

Fisher said that he saw the plane tail fall and lodge in the tree as he floated to earth after bailing out of a plane which had been hit on a bombing mission over Bremen. After he was captured, Fisher said, he heard the Germans talk about "a soldier found in the tail of the plane," and later heard Moran's story when the two men became friends in the prison camp.

Moran's one request, Fisher said, was for backing when he returned to the United States with the almost unbelievable story, similar to the experience last April of another tail gunner, Sgt. James A. Raiey of Henderson, Ky., who fell more than three and one-half miles in a Fortress tail section and landed in a tree top in the Italian area.

Fisher said he promised to vouch for Moran's story.

Sgt. Moran is the son of Mr. and Mrs. Joseph Moran, who live in the West Fork community about five miles from Soldiers Grove. His parents received word that he was missing in December, 1943. Notification that he was a prisoner came Jan. 21, 1944.

Sgt. Moran entered service Oct. 18, 1942 and trained at Jefferson Barracks, Mo., Las Vegas, Nev., and Lowrey Field, Colo. He landed in England Oct. 19, 1943.

One of several newspaper clippings from around the country mailed to the Moran family during the war.

Gene (far right) standing as best man at Harold "Shorty" Cyr's wedding.

Gene and Peg's wedding day. From left to right: Ruth McDonald, who introduced Peg to Gene, best man Bill Dorgan, Peg, and Gene.

Gene (front row, second from left) after the war with the Soldiers Grove baseball team. Gene's war injuries limited him to managing the team and serving as the occasional pinch hitter or outfielder.

Jesse Orrison sometime in the 1950s. Wayne Orrison said it was his favorite picture of his father.

Peg, Gene, Jesse's wife Margaret 'Nel,' and Jesse during a visit by Gene and Peg to Jesse and Nel's home in Arizona in the 1970s.

Gene and Peg surrounded by their nine children.

The author's sons, Joe and Matthew, with Gene.

The author's wife, Carmen, in 2009.

Carmen and Gene while touring Gene's childhood farm. Carmen died six months later.

The grave of Rikki Tikki Tavi waist gunner Edmund Swedo at the Ardennes American Cemetery in Belgium.

Eugene P. Moran at the time our interviews began for Tailspin.

Ulf Kaack, Joni Moran Peterson, and the author during a tour of Sandbostel POW Camp Memorial.

Greg Swedo, Wayne Orrison, and the author after unveiling of historical marker in the woods near Syke, Germany, where Jesse Orrison landed in his parachute.

Gene's granddaughter Kelly touches the image of her grandfather on the newly unveiled historical marker in the woods near Syke, Germany, where Jesse Orrison landed in his parachute.

Syke resident Annelore Franke points to where she saw Jesse Orrison land in his parachute. Annelore was eight years old when she witnessed Rikki Tikki Tavi *explode over Syke.*

A shredded bomber jacket hanging near the spot where Gene crashed.

Gene's family and friends gather near the spot in the woods where Gene crashed.

Kris and the author in the cockpit of a Flying Fortress at the EAA Air Show in July 2021 after the author completed a ride on the plane.

ACKNOWLEDGMENTS

It's strange to thank a dead man. But *Tailspin* wouldn't exist had Gene Moran not made the courageous decision late in his life to tell his story, which he'd suppressed for so long. During our three years working together, Gene opened the vault of his darkest memories so that we'd learn one of the most astonishing survival stories of World War II. Inside his mobile home at that aluminum kitchen table, Gene and I laughed, cried, and sometimes just stared blankly at the tabletop. My gratitude to this man cannot be quantified.

I also want to thank Gene's siblings and his children, who contributed their own stories. The ripple effect of November 29, 1943 washed over your lives as well, staining your memories of home and family. Courage and resilience are woven into the DNA of the Moran clan.

I want to thank another rural Wisconsin bomber boy who is no longer with us: Jim Millin. Jim, who died in 2019 at the age of ninety-seven, was a Flying Fortress ball turret gunner who served in the 94th Bomb Group. Jim bailed out from his burning plane over France and was captured by the Germans a month before Gene was shot down. When I first called, Jim refused to talk to me, explaining that he'd rebuffed others who wanted to write his story. When I explained that I was writing about Gene Moran, he invited me to visit his condo in La Crosse, Wisconsin. I was shocked to learn that

Jim also stewed on the hell ship and starved on the death march of '45, but like Gene, he too was reticent when recounting those nightmares. I sat with Jim for five visits talking about the air war over Europe, and each time, he'd lift his right pants leg to show me the ghastly scar where a bullet from a German fighter plane ripped through his lower leg.

Another special mention goes to Bill Thoftne, who worked tirelessly to get Gene the Distinguished Flying Cross. The passage of time and the death of witnesses proved too much for the award to happen, but I know Gene was flattered by Bill's effort.

It was a privilege to get to know the families of Gene's comrades. Thank you for your stories, documents, and pictures. Greg Swedo, nephew of Edmund Swedo, got the ball rolling for this group when, from out of the blue, he wrote to Gene just as we were beginning our interviews together. Wayne Orrison, son of Jesse Orrison, and Tim Dorgan, son of Bill Dorgan, both provided priceless photos and background information. And thank you, Leslie Feldman, niece of Walter Reed, for sending me the correspondence between your grandmother and the other mothers of the crew of *Rikki Tikki Tavi*. Those letters between grieving mothers desperately seeking information about their missing sons are all one has to see to know the true cost of war.

Many of the friends and family of Gene and some of his bomber crew enjoyed the journey to Syke, Germany, for the seventy-fifth anniversary commemoration of the crash of *Rikki Tikki Tavi*. We are indebted to our German friends Ulf Kaack, Jürgen Kuhlmann, Barbara Frerker, and Edgar Fischer, who made that poignant four-day event possible. Thank you to Silvia Rojek-Zierau for hosting me in your home and serving as the unofficial translator during that entire trip. We extend a special note of gratitude to Dirk Ippen, who financed much of the commemoration.

Thank you to the administration and school board of the Westby Area School District, who gave me the time to take that trip to Europe and a semester off to finish the manuscript. And for all of the test readers—teaching colleagues, former students, veterans, friends, and family—your insight and critiques hopefully made this a better read than the first drafts I gave you.

To my family, starting with my late wife, Carmen, who loved Gene and selflessly supported this project all while battling the cancer which would take her life. To my six-foot-plus sons, Matthew and Joe, who heard me shout time and again from my basement office, "Pick up your feet! I'm writing!"

Kristin Zieher-Hughes came into my life in the middle of writing *Tailspin*. It was Kris who pushed me across the finish line. She listened to my endless complaints about rewrites and publisher rejections. Kris hid that bomber jacket leather in my luggage before the trip to Germany. In the summer of 2021, she put me in the air in a Flying Fortress during the annual EAA air show in Oshkosh, Wisconsin, a gift for finally finishing the book. I hope for a long life to thank her. Carpe diem, my dear friend.

Thank you to Shannon Ishizaki of Ten16 Press for taking a chance on a first-time author. I was told by other Ten16 writers that I'd have a blast working with your staff of Lauren Blue, Sean Malone, and Kaeley Dunteman. They were right.

Finally, there is my editor, Heather Shumaker. During a break at a writing workshop, the director of the event sidled up to me and told me, "You're lucky. You got a good one. Heather is a true professional." With a mixture of patience and class, Heather guided this novice to create a book I never could have created on my own. Now that *Tailspin* is complete, I hope I can call her my friend.

NOTES

Information not noted on these pages came from twenty-eight recorded personal interviews with Gene Moran and many brief telephone interviews. All interviews were conducted by the author between January 2011 and March 2014.

Abbreviations

AFHRA – Air Force Historical Research Agency, Maxwell Air Force Base, Alabama.

IDPF – Individual Deceased Personnel File, U.S. Army Human Resources Command, Fort Knox, Kentucky.

MACR – Missing Air Crew Report, National Archives and Records Administration, College Park, Maryland.

NARA – National Archives and Records Administration, College Park, Maryland.

Chapter 1: The Secret Story

1 – *Outside, the air temperature measured nearly forty-five degrees below zero:* Thirteen aircraft from 96th A Group bombed Bremen "at 1441 hours from altitude of 29,000 feet." Report of Bremen Mission,

29 November 1943. Headquarters Ninety-Sixth Bombardment Group (H), Army Air Forces, Office of the Operations Officer, A.P.O. 634, 30 November 1943, NARA, p.1. Temperature: 25,000 FT at -41 degrees, 30,000 at -45 degrees, "Operational Route Forecast," Operations Report, Nov. 29, 1943, Headquarters of 96th Bombardment Group, NARA.

2 – *Gene watched strings of five-hundred-pound bombs fall:* aircraft loaded with eight 500 lb. bombs. Narrative Report of Operations of the 96th "A" Bombardment Group (H), AAF, Bremen, Germany, November 29, 1943. Headquarters Ninety-Sixth Bombardment Group (H), Army Air Forces, Office of the Operations Officer, A.P.O. 634, 29 November 1943, NARA, p.1.

3 – *from more than a hundred Flying Fortresses:* 8th Air Force VIII BC Mission #140: 154 of 360 1st and 3rd BD B-17s bomb Bremen. Donald Caldwell, *Day Fighters in Defense of the Reich: A War Diary, 1942-45* (South Yorkshire, Great Britain: Frontline Books, 2011), p. 154.

4 – *Bombardier Donald Curtis flicked the bomb door switch to close the bomb bay doors:* B-17 Bomber - Pilot's Flight Operating Instructions, originally published by United States Army Air Forces December 25, 1942: republished in Lexington, KY by Periscopefilm.com: 2013, p. 105.

5 – *Messerschmitt 109s, Focke-Wulf 190 and Messershmitt 410s:* Attacking German fighters that day included Me 109s, FW 190s, ME-410s. Narrative Report of Operations of the 96th "A" Bombardment Group (H), AAF, Bremen, Germany, November 29, 1943. Headquarters Ninety-Sixth Bombardment Group (H), Army Air Forces, Office of the Operations Officer, A.P.O. 634, 29 November 1943, NARA, p. 2.

6 – *"Two o'clock high":* Individual Casualty Questionnaire of Jesse E. Orrison for Berline Cipresso, MACR #1392, printed Nov. 2, 2014, NARA.

7 – *"Jesus! They're everywhere!":* S/E aircraft attacked in trail two to four A/C from all clock positions. Report of Bremen Mission, 29 November 1943. Headquarters Ninety-Sixth Bombardment Group (H), Army Air Forces, Office of the Operations Officer, A.P.O. 634, 30 November 1943, NARA, p.2.

8 – *Some screamed out in pain*: Individual Casualty Questionnaire of Jesse E. Orrison for Anderson King, MACR #1392, printed Nov. 2, 2014, NARA.

9 – *He also spotted Swedo and Andy*: copy of handwritten note by Eugene P. Moran, MACR #1392, printed Nov. 2, 2014, NARA.

10 – *The severed tail of Rikki Tikki Tavi began its four-mile free fall toward enemy soil*: Mission report stated that bombs were away at 1441 from 29,000 feet. Report of Bremen Mission, 29 November 1943. Headquarters Ninety-Sixth Bombardment Group (H), Army Air Forces, Office of the Operations Officer, A.P.O. 634, 30 November 1943, NARA, p.1.

11 – *Gene had suffered a skull fracture*: "Bombers bring back memories of tail gunner's four-mile free fall," *La Crosse Tribune, July 1, 1992* (La Crosse, WI).

12 – *Wearing his black U.S. Army Air Force cap*: Interview conducted with U.S. Congressman Ron Kind, Mike Herro, Rotary Club-North, La Crosse, WI, Major William E. Bruring, U.S. Civil Air Patrol-U.S. Air Force (aux) and the American Legion. *Veterans History Project – Eugene P. Moran, U.S. Army Air Corps, World War II, July 2, 2007* (La Crosse, WI). Interview recorded onto a CD and provided by U.S. Representative Ron Kind's office.

13 – *"This time, there will be no one shooting at us."*: "One Last Time, Former POW takes another ride in a B-17 . . . 64 years later," *La Crosse Tribune, July 3, 2007* (La Crosse, WI).

14 – *Gene held hands with his new bride*: "Soldiers Grove names street after 85-year-old newlywed," *La Crosse Tribune, Oct. 19, 2008* (La Crosse, WI).

15 – *First published in 1975*: Ben Logan, *The Land Remembers* (Blue Mounds, WI: Itchy Cat Press, 2006, first published by Viking Press, Inc., 1975).

16 – *"I told Dad about your visit with Ben"*: telephone interview with Joni Moran Peterson, Dec. 27, 2016.

Chapter 2: Fibbing Flyboy

1 – *an area of Wisconsin unlike any land in the Midwest:* Curt Meine and Keefe Keeley, *The Driftless Reader* (Madison, WI: The University of Wisconsin Press, 2017), p. 1.

2 – *Bill was a few years older than Gene:* Tim Dorgan, telephone interview, Feb. 5, 2013.

3 – *Dad . . . held the first draft number in Crawford County:* undated newspaper clipping saved by Gene's mother, Ethel. Clipping provided by the Moran family.

4 – *"You know you just signed his death warrant!":* telephone interview with JoAnn Moran, July 18, 2017.

Chapter 3: Gunner Gene

1 – *"hazel-green eyes that speckled with gold flecks":* telephone interview with Joni Moran Peterson, Feb. 6, 2019.

2 – *The baby was found dead in a tree:* Ibid.

3 – *checking hearts and hernias:* Dale VanBlair, *Looking Back: A Tail Gunner's View of WWII* (Bloomington, IN: self-published, 2003), p. 23.

4 – *"Bend over and spread your cheeks":* John C. McManus, *Deadly Sky: The American Combat Airman in World War II* (New York: Penguin Random House LLC, 2000), p. 19-20.

5 – *Low ranking non-commissioned officers:* Lt. Col. Eugene T. Carson USA (Ret), *Wing Ding: Memories of a Tail Gunner* (self-published, 2000), p. 30.

6 – *a series of demanding physical and mental tests:* Donald L. Miller, *Masters of the Air: America's Bomber Boys Who Fought the Air War Against Nazi Germany* (New York: Simon & Schuster, Inc., 2006), p. 165. And . . . "The History of Fort Sheridan, Illinois January 1, 1944 - John T. Rhett, Colonel, Infantry, Commanding" Prepared by Robert Schall, 2nd Lt. AUS For the Public Relations Office Published by The Clerical

School and the Visual Training Aids Section 1672nd Service Unit (Illinois State Library General Collection, Illinois Digital Archive), p. 65.

7 – *Now he was enlistee #16132701*: Eugene P. Moran's military serial number is listed in the "Report of Personnel Missing in Action, November 29, 1943, Bremen, Germany", Office of Operations Officer, Headquarters Ninety-Sixth Bombardment Group (H), Army Air Forces (NARA).

8 – *mow down small plane silhouettes*: "Aerial Gunners," *Life Magazine*, July 13, 1942, p. 43-44.

9 – *developed the skill of leading a target*: VanBlair, *Looking Back*, p. 41.

10 – *"super skeet"*: "Aerial Gunners," *Life Magazine*, July 13, 1942, p. 43-44.

11 – *"hanger without its hook"*: "World War II Left Its Mark on Las Vegas," *Las Vegas Review-Journal, Dec. 29, 2014* (Las Vegas, NV).

12 – *"The Texan"*: Enzo Angelucci & Paolo Matricardi, *World War II Airplanes: Volume 2* (Chicago: Rand McNally & Company, 1978), 40-41.

13 – *America's four-engine bombers . . . flew as high as thirty thousand feet*: Ibid, p. 57 & 79.

14 – *He had graduated with "scholastic honors . . ."*: from two undated newspaper articles saved by Ethel Moran. Articles provided by Moran family.

15 – *It snowed and rained often that early March*: telephone interview with JoAnn Moran, July 18, 2017.

16 – *1928 green Chevy sedan*: telephone interview with JoAnn Moran, March 2, 2019.

17 – *Gene pulled into the Rolling Ground Store and Tavern*: Ibid.

18 – *B-24 had greater range and carried a heavier bomb load*: Miller, *Masters of the Air*, p. 45.

19 – *durability in combat:* Lauren Hillenbrand, *Unbroken: A World War II Story of Survival, Resilience, and Redemption* (New York: Random House, 2010), p. 59.

Chapter 4: Closer Than Brothers

1 – *"Asshole of the Universe"*: Robert E. Doherty and Geoffrey D. Ward, *Snetterton Falcons II – The 96th Bomb Group In World War II* (Dallas, TX: Taylor Publishing Company, 1989), p. 15.

2 – *"Rattlesnake Army Air Base"*: website of the 96th Bomb Group Association, http://96bg.org. History section.

3 – *The PX store*: Doherty and Ward, *Snetterton Falcons II: The 96th Bomb Group In World War II*), p. 15.

4 – *carried .45 caliber pistols*: Ibid.

5 – *covered in tarpaper*: Ibid.

6 – *tents of all sizes and color*: Tommy LaMore and Dan A. Baker, *One Man's War: The WWII Saga of Tommy LaMore* (Lanham, MD: Taylor Trade Publishing, 2002), p. 37.

7 – *Sending and understanding complex radio codes*: McManus, *Deadly Sky*, p. 38-39.

8 – *Reed raised and sold chickens*: telephone interview with Tim, Jerry, and Jeff Mayo, nephews of Walter Reed, June 7, 2020.

9 – *His father suffered from severe arthritis*: email from Leslie Feldman, niece of Walter Reed, June 3, 2021.

10 – *Kept a close eye on every dial and gauge*: McManus, *Deadly Sky*, p. 37.

11 – *getting out was next to impossible*: Ibid, p. 40.

12 – *Enemy fighter pilots knew*: Ibid, p. 41.

13 – *It was Jim Winters, their pilot*: Gene was not sure of his pilot's first name as he could only remember calling him by his surname. Research failed to confirm Lieutenant Winters' first name. 'Jim' is used because Gene believed that to be his first name.

14 – *he preferred that his crew not salute him*: letter from Walter Reed to his mother, Julia, June 18, 1943. Letter provided by Leslie Feldman, niece of Walter Reed.

15 – *A soon-to-be father:* personal interview with Wayne Orrison, son of Jesse Orrison, January 28, 2013.

16 – *Swung and tilted on their own*: LaMore, *One Man's War*, p. 39.

17 – *ring and bead sighting system*: Graeme Douglas, *Boeing B-17 Flying Fortress Owners' Workshop Manual* (Minneapolis, MN: Zenith Press, 2011), p. 81.

18 – *some 15,000 airmen died*: Miller, *Masters of the Air*, p. 166.

19 – *two-block town*: Doherty and Ward, *Snetterton Falcons II*, p. 15.

20 – *"We'll never see him again"*: telephone interview with JoAnn Moran, July 18, 2017.

21 – *sometimes as far as over the Gulf of Mexico:* letter from Walter Reed to his mother, Julia, Aug. 13, 1943. Letter provided by Leslie Feldman, niece of Walter Reed.

22 – *oxygen regulator*: B-17 Bomber Pilot's Flight Operating Instructions, p. 136 & 137.

23 – *hidden killer*: Miller, *Masters of the Air*, p. 93.

24 – *pilot leaning off first base eyeing up a chance to steal second*: letter from Walter Reed to his mother, Julia, Aug. 27, 1943. Letter provided by Leslie Feldman, niece of Walter Reed.

25 – *Six hundred men lost in a single mission*: Martin W. Bowman, *The Mighty Eighth at War* (South Yorkshire, England: Pen and Sword Books, 2010), p. 68.

26 – *Another sixty bombers lost to the Germans*: Philip Kaplan and Rex Alan Smith, *One Last Look: A Sentimental Journey to the Eighth Air Force Heavy Bomber Bases of World War II in England* (New York: Abbeyville Press, 1983), p. 21.

27 – *sliding doors behind the gunner:* VanBlair, *Looking Back,* p. 61.

28 – *air base on east coast of Greenland:* "The Ghost Air Force Bases of Greenland" by Paula Froelich, *The Daily Beast*, 7-29-17

29 – *cockpit heater:* Ray Matheny, *Rite of Passage: A Teenager's Chronicle of Combat and Captivity in Nazi Germany* (Clearfield, Utah: American Legacy Media, 2009), p. 83.

30 – *one-way landing strip*: Ibid, p. 86.

31 – *"go-around"*: Ibid, p. 87.

32 – *Several wrecked airplanes that had not made successful landings:*

Ibid. Matheny landed at the Greenland air base on Oct. 8, 1943, just days before Gene landed in Greenland.

33 – *across glaciers and rocky stream beds*: Ibid, p. 88-89. Matheny also went hunting for ptarmigan while waiting for the next leg of his flight to England.

34 – *average airman survived fewer than ten missions*: John R. Bruning, *Bombs Away: The World War II Bombing Campaigns Over Europe* (New York: Zenith Press), 2011.

Chapter 5: "It's Just a Job."

1 – *yellow-brick terrace houses and stucco cottages*: Thomas Childers, *Wings of Morning: The Story of the Last American Bomber Shot Down Over Germany in World War II* (Lebanon, Indiana: Da Capo Press, 1995), p. 127.

2 – *the Germans had bombed Norwich*: Doherty and Ward, *Snetterton Falcons II*, p. 78.

3 – *Airmen listened to the attack:* Ibid.

4 – *forty bomb groups*: Miller, *Masters of the Air*, prefix map in front of book.

5 – *own airport maintained roughly forty bombers.* Ibid. Organization Chart 8th Air Force, p. 61.

6 – *grazing cows and farmhouses surrounded by lush green fields*: Jack Novey, *The Cold Blue Sky: A B-17 Gunner in World War Two* (Charlottesville, Virginia: Howell Press, 1997), p. 39.

7 – *practically ceded the entire region*: Miller, *Masters of the Air*, p. 58.

8 – *Nissen huts*: https://www.facebook.com/96thBombGroupAssociation/posts/nissen-huts-at-snetterton-heath-

9 – *blackout curtains shaded the window*: VanBlair, *Looking Back*, p. 112.

10 – *two light bulbs strung from the ceiling*: Ibid.

11 – *renounced her citizenship*: "Mildred Gillars, 87, of Nazi radio, Axis Sally to an Allied Audience," *New York Times-Obituaries*, July 2, 1988.

12 – *Rikki Tikki Tavi*: Doherty and Ward, *Snetterton Falcons II*, p. 294 & 302. Lists 42-30359 to 2/Lt. Linwood D. Langley (QJ-D), but with no nickname, p. 294. The book does list two other planes with similar names: Rikki Tikki Tavi II, 42-29747 and Rikki Tikki Tavi (Georgia Peach), 42-3324 p. 302. Gene was certain to his plane's name and immediately recognized the nose art when shown a picture of the plane.

13 – *Airmen on alert were restricted to base*: Juliet Gardiner, "*Overpaid, Oversexed & Over Here*" (New York, Canopy Books, 1992), p. 160.

14 – *flew practice missions over England*: Novey, *The Cold Blue Sky*, p. 39-40.

15 – *hand-operated winches*: Miller, *Masters of the Air*, p. 176.

16 – *German planes still roared across the English Channel at night*: Doherty and Ward, *Snetterton Falcons II*, p. 78.

17 – "*You will have P-47 escort*": "Narrative Report of Operations of the 96th Bombardment Group (H), AAF, Wilhelmshaven, Germany, 3 November 1943, (A, B, & C Group reports), Office of the Operations Officer, Headquarters Ninety- Bombardment Group (H) Army Air Forces, AFHRA, p. 2, 4, 6.

18 – *number fifty for the 96th*: Doherty and Ward, *Snetterton Falcons II*, p. 77.

19 – *only see anti-aircraft from the ground around the target*: Carson, *Wing Ding*, p. 99.

20 – *flak jackets and mats, and yellow "Mae West" life jackets*: Gardiner, "*Overpaid, Oversexed & Over Here*," p. 165.

21 – *gave the ball turret a final power check*: Carson, *Wing Ding*, p. 59.

22 – *five thousand pounds of bombs*: All planes that day were loaded with four 500 lb. G.P. and 31 M-47A1 incendiaries (100 lb. each), Narrative Report of Operations of the 96th Bombardment Group (H), AAF, Wilhelmshaven, Germany, 3 November 1943, (A, B, & C Group reports), Office of the Operations Officer, Headquarters Ninety-Sixth Bombardment Group (H) Army Air Forces, AFHRA, p. 1, 3, 5.

23 – "*Tail wheel locked, light on, light out*": Donald E. Casey, *To Fight For My Country, Sir!: Memoirs of a 19 Year Old B-17 Navigator Shot*

Down in Nazi Germany and Imprisoned in the WWII "Great Escape" Prison Camp (Chicago: Sterling Cooper Publishing, Inc., 2009), p.73.

24 – *would have to wait a full minute*: Gardiner, *"Overpaid, Oversexed & Over Here"*, p. 169.

25 – *110 mph. It lifted into the air*: Douglas, *Boeing B-17 Flying Fortress Owners' Workshop Manual*, p. 127.

26 – *divided into groups of three planes*: James Lee Hutchinson, *B-17 Memories: Memphis Belle to Victory* (Bloomington, Indiana: Author-House, 2014), p. 32.

27 – *better protection against fighter attacks*: Ibid.

28 – *more than five hundred*: Miller, *Masters of the Air,* p. 234.

29 – *Flying Fortresses and Liberators*: Caldwell, *Day Fighters in Defense of the Reich*, p. 144.

30 – *twenty-three thousand feet:* Narrative Report of Operations of the 96th Bombardment Group (H), AAF, Wilhelmshaven, Germany, 3 November 1943, ("A" Group), Office of the Operations Officer, Headquarters Ninety-Sixth Bombardment Group (H) Army Air Forces, AFHRA, p. 1.

31 – *more than three hundred American fighter planes*: Miller, *Masters of the Air,* p. 234.

32 – *that would detonate as high as thirty-five thousand feet*: Hutchinson, *B-17 Memories: From Memphis Belle to Victory*, p 40.

33 – *This time they did*: operations report stated the first flak observed ranged from light and inaccurate to light but fairly accurate. Narrative Report of Operations of the 96th Bombardment Group (H), AAF, Wilhelmshaven, Germany, 3 November 1943, (A, B, & C Group reports), Office of the Operations Officer, Headquarters Ninety-Sixth Bombardment Group (H) Army Air Forces, AFHRA, p. 1, 3, 5.

34 – *Famous for its mud baths*: Robert Morgan with Ron Powers. *The Man Who Flew Memphis Belle: Memoir of a WWII Bomber Pilot.* (New York: New American Library, a division of Penguin Group, 2001), p. 177.

35 – *Submarine and ship construction centers*: Narrative Report of Operations of the 96th Bombardment Group (H), AAF, Wilhelmshaven, Germany, 3 November 1943, (A, B, & C Group reports), Office of the

Operations Officer, Headquarters Ninety-Sixth Bombardment Group (H) Army Air Forces, AFHRA, p. 7.

36 – *mechanical gyroscope system*: Douglas, *Boeing B-17 Flying Fortress: Owners' Workshop Manual*, p. 47.

37 – *auto pilot*: Ibid.

38 – *guided the plane using the controls of his aiming device*: McManus, *Deadly Sky*, p. 36.

39 – *More flak bursts lit up the sky*: Narrative Report of Operations of the 96th Bombardment Group (H), AAF, Wilhelmshaven, Germany, 3 November 1943, (A, B, & C Group reports), Office of the Operations Officer, Headquarters Ninety-Sixth Bombardment Group (H) Army Air Forces, AFHRA, p. 5.

40 – *locate targets through an overcast sky*: Miller, *Masters of the Air*, p. 235.

41 – *release his bombs soon when the lead planes dropped theirs*: Ibid.

42 – *Four general purpose bombs and thirty-one fire-igniting incendiaries*: Narrative Report of Operations of the 96th Bombardment Group (H), AAF, Wilhelmshaven, Germany, 3 November 1943, (A, B, & C Group reports), Office of the Operations Officer, Headquarters Ninety-Sixth Bombardment Group (H) Army Air Forces, AFHRA, p. 1, 3, 5.

43 – *German fighters taking their revenge*: Narrative Report of Operations of the 96th Bombardment Group (H), AAF, Wilhelmshaven, Germany, 3 November 1943, (C Group report), Office of the Operations Officer, Headquarters Ninety-Sixth Bombardment Group (H) Army Air Forces, AFHRA, p. 6.

44 – *It seemed everybody made it back*: Doherty and Ward, *Snetterton Falcons II*, p. 77.

45 – *twenty-eight thousand and joined the other thirty two*: Narrative Report of Operations of the 96th Bombardment Group (H), AAF, Gelsenkirchen, Germany, 5 November 1943, Office of the Operations Officer, Headquarters Ninety-Sixth Bombardment Group (H) Army Air Forces. A.P.O.634, 5 November 1943, (A & B Group report), AFHRA, p. 8 & 10.

46 – *five hundred bomber raid*: Caldwell, *Day Fighters in Defense of the Reich*, p. 145.

47 – *Messerschmitt 109 fighter planes*: Narrative Report of Operations of the 96th Bombardment Group (H), AAF, Gelsenkirchen, Germany, 5 November 1943, Office of the Operations Officer, Headquarters Ninety-Sixth Bombardment Group (H) Army Air Forces, A.P.O.634, 5 November 1943, (A & B Group report), AFHRA, p. 8.

48 – *German gunners found their range*: Ibid, p. 9.

49 – *Cloudless day*: Caldwell, *Day Fighters in Defense of the Reich*, p. 145

50 – *Fifteen Flying Fortresses lost:* Ibid.

51 – *All thirty-two planes returned, many had holes in them*: Narrative Report of Operations of the 96th Bombardment Group (H), AAF, Gelsenkirchen, Germany, 5 November 1943, AFHRA, p.12.

52 – *Plane crashed on landing*: Doherty and Ward, *Snetterton Falcons II*, p. 78.

53 – *Died from lack of oxygen*: Ibid.

Chapter 6: A Thousand Ways to Die

1 – *It was only 3:00 a.m.*: Narrative Report of Operations of the 96th Bombardment Group (H), AAF, Rjukan, Norway, 16 November 1943, Office of the Operations Officer, Headquarters Ninety-Sixth Bombardment Group (H) Army Air Forces, A.P.O.634, 16 November 1943, AFHRA, p.22.

2 – *1:30 a.m.*: Doherty and Ward, *Snetterton Falcons*, p. 79.

3 – *He lectured about . . . "heavy water"*: Novey, *The Cold Blue Sky*, p. 132.

4 – *bomb a molybdenum mine in Knaben*: Narrative Report of Operations of the 96th Bombardment Group (H), AAF, Rjukan, Norway, 16 November 1943. Headquarters Ninety-Sixth Bombardment Group (H) Army Air Forces, Office of the Operations Officer, A.P.O.634, 16 November 1943, AFHRA, p. 26. Gene also stated in his interviews that his plane attacked Knaben, not Rjukan.

5 – *the mine was also connected to the effort to build a super bomb*: Theo Boiten & Martin Bowman, *Battles with the Luftwaffe: The Bomber Campaign Against Germany 1942-1945* (London: HarperCollins Publishers, 2001), p. 77.

6 – *Thick wooly fog*: Ibid.

7 – *Fire broke out on lead plane*: Narrative Report of the Operations of the 96th Bombardment Group (H), AAF, Munster, Germany, 11 November, 1943. Headquarters Ninety-Sixth Bombardment Group (H) Army Air Forces, Office of the Operations Officer, A.P.O.634, 11 November 1943, NARA, p.2.

8 – *Langley and four other bomber pilots got lost*: Separate aborted missions list for November 13, 1943, NARA, p. 2. And Narrative Report of the Operations of the 96th Bombardment Group (H), AAF, Bremen, Germany, 13 November, 1943. Headquarters Ninety-Sixth Bombardment Group (H) Army Air Forces, Office of the Operations Officer, A.P.O.634, 13 November 1943, NARA, p.1.

9 – *21,500 ft*: Narrative Report of the Operations of the 96th Bombardment Group (H), AAF, Rjukan, Norway, 16 November, 1943. Headquarters Ninety-Sixth Bombardment Group (H) Army Air Forces, Office of the Operations Officer, A.P.O.634, 16 November 1943, AFHRA, p. 24.

10 – *Clear, intensely blue skies*: Matheny, *Rite of Passage,* p. 109.

11 – *friendly fighter planes were not expected to escort*: Narrative Report of the Operations of the 96th Bombardment Group (H), AAF, Rjukan, Norway, 16 November, 1943. Headquarters Ninety-Sixth Bombardment Group (H) Army Air Forces, Office of the Operations Officer, A.P.O.634, 16 November 1943, AFHRA, p. 24.

12 – *dropped the plane down to 13,000 feet*: Ibid.

13 – *snow-capped, jagged mountains*: Brian O'Neill, *Half a Wing, Three Engines and a Prayer* (McGraw-Hill Companies, New York, 1999), p. 185.

14 – *enemy fighters. None. No flak either*: Narrative Report of the Operations of the 96th Bombardment Group (H), AAF, Rjukan, Norway, 16 November, 1943. Headquarters Ninety-Sixth Bombardment Group

(H) Army Air Forces, Office of the Operations Officer, A.P.O.634, 16 November 1943, AFHRA, p.23 & 24.

15 – *let the bombs go just before noon:* Ibid. p. 22 &24.

16 – *flew loosely apart from one another:* Matheny, *Rite of Passage,* p. 109.

17 – *maximum load of incendiary bombs:* Narrative Report of the Operations of the 96th Bombardment Group (H), AAF, Gelsenkirchen, Germany, 19 November, Headquarters Ninety-Sixth Bombardment Group (H) Army Air Forces, Office of the Operations Officer, A.P.O.634, 19 November 1943, AFHRA, p. 27.

18 – *Seven other bomb groups:* Roger Freeman, *Mighty Eighth War Diary* (Jane's Publishing, London, 1981), p. 140.

19 – . . . *German fighters. But none appeared:* Narrative Report of the Operations of the 96th Bombardment Group (H), AAF, Gelsenkirchen, Germany, 19 November, Headquarters Ninety-Sixth Bombardment Group (H) Army Air Forces, Office of the Operations Officer, A.P.O.634, 19 November 1943, AFHRA, p. 28 & 30.

20 – *Three of the 130 bombers . . . equipped with Pathfinder radar:* Freeman, *Mighty Eighth War Diary,* p. 140.

21 – *the Pathfinder equipment failed:* Doherty and Ward, *Snetterton Falcons,* p. 79.

22 – *With an ungloved hand . . . stopped the spinning primer:* Ibid. NOTE: Doherty and Ward's book mention two 96th Bomb Group bombers, *G-String and Ramblin' Wreck,* having similar problems with bomb hang up, although Gene's plane was not mentioned in the account. This account came from Gene.

23 – *The height was correct, but the range was off:* Narrative Report of the Operations of the 96th Bombardment Group (H), AAF, Gelsenkirchen, Germany, 19 November, Headquarters Ninety-Sixth Bombardment Group (H) Army Air Forces, Office of the Operations Officer, A.P.O.634, 19 November 1943, AFHRA, p. 30.

24 – *at 5:00 a.m.:* Narrative Report of the Operations of the 96th Bombardment Group (H), AAF, Bremen, Germany, 26 November, Head-

quarters Ninety-Sixth Bombardment Group (H) Army Air Forces, Office of the Operations Officer, A.P.O.634, 26 November 1943, AFHRA, p. 32.

25 – *This was the target they were to hit the day they got lost:* Aborted missions list Oct. 14, 1943-Dec. 20, 1943 NARA, p. 2 and Narrative Report of the Operations of the 96th Bombardment Group (H), AAF, Bremen, Germany, 13 November, 1943, Headquarters Ninety-Sixth Bombardment Group (H) Army Air Forces, Office of the Operations Officer, A.P.O.634, 13 November 1943, AFHRA, p. 17.

26 – *its largest formation ever sent into battle:* Bowman, *The Mighty Eighth at War*, p. 84.

27 – *Pee Wee, Reed, Sparky to fill in:* "Individual Casualty Questionnaire" - Missing Air Crew Report (MACR) #1392, NARA. NOTE: Gene couldn't remember exactly who had to go. Jesse Orrison and Gene Moran's MACR Individual Casualty Questionnaires list Provost, Reed, Amatulli, Curtis, and Cipresso with six missions to their credit. One more than the rest of the crew noted with five missions in the same questionnaires.

28 – *Benny and Curtis were going to Bremen:* Ibid.

29 – *Forty-three Flying Fortresses:* Freeman, *Mighty Eighth War Diary*, p. 142.

Chapter 7: Bremen

1 – *My research on the internet:* letter from Greg Swedo, March 17, 2012.

2 – *"Do you think that's the pilot you saw?":* telephone interview with Greg Swedo, May 21, 2019.

3 – *"You wrote that you remembered the two waist gunners lying on the floor":* audio recording from May 2012, provided by Greg Swedo, May 22, 2019.

4 – *"He has to face his demons":* telephone interview with Joni Moran Peterson, March 12, 2019.

5 – *mission briefing a.m.*: Narrative report of the Operations of the 96th Bombardment Group, (H), AAF, Bremen, Germany, 29 November 1943, Headquarters Ninety-Sixth Bombardment Group (H) Army Air Forces, Office of the Operations Officer, A.P.O.634, 29 November 1943, AFHRA, p. 39.

6 – *third time that month*: Doherty and Ward, *Snetterton Falcons*, p. 80.

7 – *planes would take off at 9:45*: Narrative report of the Operations of the 96th Bombardment Group, (H), AAF, Bremen, Germany, 29 November 1943, Headquarters Ninety-Sixth Bombardment Group (H) Army Air Forces, Office of the Operations Officer, A.P.O.634, 29 November 1943, AFHRA, p. 39.

8 – *overcast sky*: Ibid.

9 – *forty-five Flying Fortresses*: Ibid, p. 37 & 39.

10 – *Five aborted*: Ibid.

11 – *28,000 feet*: Ibid.

12 – *More than 300 Flying Fortresses*: Freeman, *Mighty Eighth War Diary*. p. 143.

13 – *No enemy fighters, no flak*: Narrative report of the Operations of the 96th "A" Bombardment Group, (H), AAF, Bremen, Germany, 29 November 1943, Headquarters Ninety-Sixth Bombardment Group (H) Army Air Forces, Office of the Operations Officer, A.P.O.634, 29 November 1943, NARA p. 2. Stated "enemy fighters first seen about ten minutes from target." Also, "A" Bombardment Group records used as Langley's plane, #359, listed in "A" Group according to SUBJECT: Gas Consumption Report, Bremen, 29 November, 1943 Headquarters Ninety-Sixth Bombardment Group (H) Army Air Forces, Office of the Operations Officer, A.P.O.634, 29 November 1943, NARA.

14 – *The fighters should have been here by now*: Ibid. Stated "fighter rendezvous would be about 15 minutes late."

15 – *"I'm showing nearly fifty below up here."*: Thirteen aircraft from 96th A Group bombed Bremen "at 1441 hours from altitude of 29,000 feet." Report of Bremen Mission, 29 November 1943. Headquarters Ninety-Sixth Bombardment Group (H), Army Air Forces, Office of the

Operations Officer, A.P.O. 634, 29 November 1943, NARA, p.1. Temperature: 25,000 FT at -41 degrees, 30,000 at -45 degrees, "Operational Route Forecast," Operations Report, Nov. 29, 1943, Headquarters of 96th Bombardment Group, NARA.

16 – *They left a few minutes before:* Narrative report of the Operations of the 96th "A" Bombardment Group, (H), AAF, Bremen, Germany, 29 November 1943, Headquarters Ninety-Sixth Bombardment Group (H), Army Air Forces, Office of the Operations Officer, A.P.O. 634, 29 November 1943, NARA, p. 2. Stated "Friendly fighter support was met as German coast in and continued to the turn toward I.P. route in. No friendly support was afforded from that time until 20 miles west of Oldenburg."

17 – *More than a dozen twin-engine fighters:* Mission summary "Bremen 29 November 1943" from Narrative report of the Operations of the 96th Bombardment Group, (H), AAF, Bremen, Germany, 29 November 1943, Headquarters Ninety-Sixth Bombardment Group (H), Army Air Forces, Office of the Operations Officer, A.P.O. 634, 29 November 1943, AFHRA, p. 41.

18 – *Firing rockets:* Ibid.

19 – *A hundred German fighters:* Ibid.

20 – *Twin-engine planes that looked more like bombers than fighter planes:* SUBJECT: Report of Bremen Mission, 29 November 1943. CONFIDENTIAL, Headquarters Ninety-Sixth Bombardment Group (H) Army Air Forces, Office of Combat Intelligence, A.P.O. 634, 30 November 1943, NARA. p. 1.

21 – *Ju 87 Stuka:* Ibid.

22 – *Below him were clouds:* Ibid.

23 – *It was almost 3:00 p.m.:* Narrative report of the Operations of the 96th "A" Bombardment Group, (H), AAF, Bremen, Germany, 29 November 1943, Headquarters Ninety-Sixth Bombardment Group (H), Army Air Forces, Office of the Operations Officer, A.P.O. 634, 29 November 1943, NARA p. 2. Stated "bombs were away at 1441 . . ."

24 – *"Fighters, two o' clock high":* Individual Casualty Questionnaire of Jesse E. Orrison for Berline Cipresso, MACR #1392, printed Nov. 2,

2014, NARA. Orrison stated on Cipresso "He called planes coming at us from 2 o'clock high."

25 – *Andy still calling out fighters and shooting back:* Individual Casualty Questionnaire of Jesse E. Orrison for Anderson King, MACR #1392, printed Nov. 2, 2014, NARA.

26 – *It was Sparky crying out:* Individual Casualty Questionnaire of Eugene P. Moran for Samuel Amatulli, MACR #1392, printed Nov. 2, 2014, NARA.

27 – *Curtis slumped into Orrison a third time:* Individual Casualty Questionnaire of Jesse E. Orrison for Donald Curtis, printed Nov. 2, 2014, NARA.

28 – *wrestled onto Curtis' back:* interview with Wayne Orrison, Jan. 28, 2013.

29 – *tore through his flight pants:* Ibid.

30 – *He spotted the severed tail:* Casualty Questionnaire of Jesse E. Orrison, MACR #1392, printed Nov. 2, 2014, NARA, p.1.

Chapter 8: Gangster

1 – *highly sophisticated escape routes*: Miller, *Masters of the Air,* p. 99.

2 – *German and French money*: McManus, *Deadly Sky,* p. 219.

3 – *its military generally followed those guidelines: Ibid.*, p. 221.

4 – *the Allies would protect its captured fliers*: Miller, *Masters of the Air,* p. 385.

5 – *German women were the most vicious*: David Foy, *For You The War Is Over: American Prisoners of War in Nazi* Germany, (Stein and Day, New York, 1984), p. 39.

6 – *"Hang the scoundrels!"*: McManus, *Deadly Sky,* p. 225.

7 – *toward an open field about twenty-five yards away*: author visit to Gene's crash site, Nov. 29, 2018.

8 – *dark, concrete room*: Carl Fyler, *Staying Alive*, (Leavenworth, Kansas: J.H. Johnston, 1995), p. 85.

9 – *twenty-fifth mission*, Ibid, p. 81.

10 – *two flak bursts*: Ibid.

11 – *German fighter planes finished off*: Ibid, p. 82.

12 – *along with other men*: Ibid

13 – *All of them were sergeant gunners*: Ibid, p. 85.

14 – *"Calm down . . . or things are going to get bad."*: Ibid.

15 – *squashed watermelon*: Ibid, p. 86.

16 – *"rode a tail section all the way to the ground"*: Ibid.

17 – *two years of high school German*: Ibid, p. 87.

18 – *ordering Fyler to get up and leave the room*: Ibid, p. 86.

Chapter 9: Celebrity

1 – *"strange roommate"*: Kaplan and Smith, *One Last Look*, p. 163.

2 – *"wild screaming delirium"*: Ibid.

3 – *one kilometer from the main compound*: author visit to Sandbostel Prisoner-of-War Camp Museum and Memorial. Tour given by Ronald Sperling, museum archivist and documentarian, Nov. 28, 2018.

4 – *The camp held 20,000*: Ibid.

5 – *a typhus outbreak killed three thousand*: Ibid.

6 – *performed an average of forty operations a week*: visit by Joni Moran Peterson to Sandbostel Prisoner-of-War Camp Museum and Memorial. Information given by Ronald Sperling. October 2016.

7 – *thin man with dark, short hair*: physical description taken from photo provided by Ronald Sperling and given to Joni Moran Peterson, October 2016.

8 – *several other Americans and three British prisoners*: Kaplan and Smith, *One Last Look*, p. 163.

9 – *rows of wooden, half-foot wide boards*: Andreas Ehresmann, *Das Stalag XB Sandbostel-Geschichte und Nachgeschichte eines Kriegsgefangenenlagers*, (Hamburg, Germany: Dolling and Galitz Verlag, 2015), photograph, p. 274-275.

10 – *Vermin lurked everywhere*: Ibid, p. 94.

11 – *interrupted by nightmares:* Kaplan and Smith, *One Last Look,* p. 163.

12 – *Shortage of nurses:* Ehresmann, *Das Stalag XB Sandbostel,* p. 94.

13 – *just two camp kitchens:* Ibid. p. 82.

14 – *very little medical equipment.* Kaplan and Smith, *One Last Look,* p. 163.

15 – *lay bleeding . . . each with a broken arm*: Fyler, Staying Alive, p. 84

16 – *managed to buckle a parachute on both Fisher and the other waist gunner:* Ibid.

17 – *The tail gunner himself never got out*: Ibid.

18 – *The Germans gave the Russians even fewer rations:* author interview with Ronald Sperling, Sandbostel Prisoner-of-War Camp Museum and Memorial archivist and documentarian, Nov. 28, 2018.

19 – *systemic malnutrition:* Ehresmann, *Das Stalag XB Sandbostel,* p. 82.

20 – *Germans were very good at extracting information*: Miller, *Masters of the Air,* p. 385-386.

Chapter 10: The Telegram

1 – *"There's good news tonight.":* telephone interview with JoAnn Moran, June 21, 2016.

2 – *Father Matheiu drove down from St. Philips:* author interview with JoAnn Moran, Aug. 13, 2018.

3 – *in pink taffeta:* clipped article from the *Kickapoo Scout,* undated newspaper clipping saved by Gene's mother, Ethel. Clipping provided by the Moran family.

4 – *Dad's migraine headaches came back*: recorded interview of Rosemary Moran Koerber by Joni Moran Peterson, April 6, 2013.

5 – *letter arrived from Sen. Robert LaFollette Jr.*: Robert M. Lafollette Jr., United States Senate, January 4, 1944. Letter provided by Moran family.

6 – *"Eugene is suffering from a skull fracture"*: clipped article from the

Kickapoo Scout, saved by Gene's mother, Ethel. Clipping provided by the Moran family.

7 – *she'd rather have her son dead than be taken prisoner*: recorded interview of JoAnn Moran by Joni Moran Peterson, April 6, 2013.

8 – *"Postkarte" and "Kriegsgefangenenpost"*: prisoner-of-war postcard written by Eugene Moran, Dec. 2, 1943. Postcard provided by family.

Chapter 11: Solitary

1 – *Shards of broken glass framed blown-out window openings*: Matheny, *Rite of Passage*, p. 196.

2 – sign that read *Frankfurt am* Main: Ibid.

3 – *Welcome to Dulag Luft*: Ibid. p. 197.

4 – *checked pockets and seams for compasses or other contraband*: Carol F. Dillon, *A Domain of Heroes*, (Palm Island Press, Sarasota, Florida, 1995), p. 39.

5 – *130 degrees*: Miller, *Masters of the Air*, p. 387.

6 – *mice scurry under his bed*: Ibid.

7 – *moaning, screaming, singing*: Fyler, *Staying Alive*, p. 87.

8 – *Sawdust made up more than half the slice*: Dillon, *A Domain of Heroes*, p. 45.

9 – *tree leaves, tulip bulbs, acorns and even coal*: Ibid.

10 – *small cup of potato water with boiled* cabbage: Matheny. *Rite of Passage*, p. 198.

11 – *plain-looking room with a table and a chair*: John Bacchia, *Augie: Stalag Luft VI to the Major Leagues*, (iUniverse, Inc., Bloomington, Indiana, 2011), p. 54.

12 – *draped window*: Matheny, *Rite of Passage*, p. 203.

13 – *the bond between the bomber boys*: Dillon, *A Domain of Heroes*, p. 48.

14 – *not far from a train station in Frankfurt*: Matheny, *Rite of Passage*, p. 205.

15 – *Kriegsgefangenen*: Miller, *Masters of the Air*, p. 390.

Chapter 12: Kriegie

1 – *on the old Prussian-Lithuanian border*: Dillon, *A Domain of Heroes,* p. 127.

2 – *three large compounds*: Ibid.

3 – *red Nazi flag*: Bacchia, *Augie,* p. 59.

4 – *a small room housed several buckets that the prisoners used for toilets at night*: Ibid.

5 – *MOC, Man of Confidence*: Dillon, *A Domain of Heroes.* p. 128.

6 – *built specifically for non-commissioned Allied airmen*: Ibid. p. 127.

7 – *played college basketball at Kentucky University*: "Cliff Barker, 77, a Kentucky Basketball Star." *New York Times-obituaries*, March 21, 1998.

8 – *Prisoners fantasized about food far more often than they talked about women or sex*: Rob Morris, *Untold Valor: Forgotten Stories of American Bomber Crews over Europe in World War II* (Potomac Books, Washington, D.C., 2006), p. 113.

9 – *the Swiss Red Cross*: Miller, *Masters of the Air,* p. 399.

10 – *Germans distributed the food parcels about once a week*: Ibid.

11 – *condensed milk, canned salmon, Spam, crackers, jam and raisins*: Ibid.

12 – *"air raid hero"*: "Air Medal Given Eugene Moran at Traux Ceremony," undated newspaper clipping saved by Gene's mother, Ethel. Clipping provided by the Moran family.

13 – *"THUS THY ART . . .":* Gene's journal notebook from Stalag Luft 6. Notebook provided by Moran family.

14 – *truck batteries and parts from German Army field radios*: LaMore and Baker, *One Man's War,* p. 153.

15 – *equipment from German soldiers in exchange for cigarettes*: Ibid.

16 – *scribbled notes on to scrap paper*: Ibid.

17 – *landed on a warehouse roof*: telephone interview with Bill Dorgan's son, Tim, July 24, 2016.

18 – *wrapped his leg with their shirts*: Sworn statement by Bill Dorgan to a notary public, Richland County, Wisconsin, October 8, 1946, p. 1.

The two-page letter was to prove Bill's war-related injuries to the Veterans' Administration. Typed copy provided by Tim Dorgan.

19 – *to pick up all the body parts:* telephone interview with Tim Dorgan, July 24, 2016.

20 – *solitary confinement for fifteen days:* Bill Dorgan's sworn statement, p. 1.

21 – *farthest north and east Allied POW camp:* Bacchia, *Augie,* p. 58.

22 – *makeshift basketball court:* Ibid. p. 65.

23 – *From a guard tower:* author interview with Jim Millin of La Crosse, Wisconsin, ball turret gunner on the Flying Fortress *Ten Knights in a Bar Room* of the 94th Bomb Group. Millin was shot down October 4, 1943 during a raid on a German airfield in France. Interview took place July 5, 2015.

24 – *without warning or an order to halt:* Dillon, *A Domain of Heroes,* p. 131.

25 – *more than two hundred prisoners gathered:* interview with Jim Millen, July 5, 2015.

26 – *reasonable man:* Dillon, *A Domain of Heroes,* p. 129.

27 – *the killing was justified*: Ibid. p. 131.

28 – *maybe before Christmas:* Ibid. p. 133.

29 – *between the British and American area:* Bacchia, *Augie,* p. 61.

30 – *only last three rounds:* Ibid.

31 – *donations by the YMCA:* Ibid.

32 – *Stalag Luft 6 championship:* Ibid, p. 62.

33 – *sweeping through East Prussia*: Ibid, p. 67.

Chapter 13: The Bowels of Hell

1 – *"We can use all the help we can get"*: telephone interview with Joni Moran Peterson, June 18, 2018.

2 – *the black heating stove set against the brick chimney*: Parrent, Eric (editor), *Stalag Luft IV, 1944-1945 - 50th Anniversary,* (Turner Publish-

ing Company, Paducah, Kentucky, 1996), description of barracks room taken from illustration, p. 24-25.

3 – *The German commandant had ordered an immediate evacuation*: John Nichol and Tony Rennell, *The Last Escape: The Untold Story of Allied Prisoners of War in Europe 1944-45*, (Viking-Penguin Group, New York, 2003), p. 19.

4 – *On July 14, Gene assembled with nearly two thousand American captured airmen*: Miller, *Masters of the Air*, p. 400-401.

5 – *powdered milk tins, cans of salmon, books, and cigarettes over the fence to the British prisoners*: Nichol and Rennell, *The Last Escape*, p. 19-20.

6 – *dusty road past locals with bewildered and hostile faces*: Bacchia, *Augie*, p. 68.

7 – *Others threw stones*: Nichol and Rennell, *The Last Escape*, p. 21.

8 – *littering the road with ragged coats, torn clothing, and tin cans filled with powdered milk*: Ibid, p. 20.

9 – *Closed cattle cars waited for them*: Miller, *Masters of the Air*, p. 401.

10 – *They rode several hours to Memel*: Bacchia, *Augie*, p. 68 said five-hour train ride. Dillon, *Domain of Heroes*, p. 136 said a one-hour ride.

11 – *coal freighters*: Miller, *Masters of the Air*, p. 401.

12 – *waters dotted with British-laid mines and patrolled by Russian submarines*: Nichol and Rennell, *The Last Escape*, p. 24.

13 – *on the hull it displayed the Soviet hammer and sickle*: Bacchia, *Augie*, p. 69.

14 – *ordered to drop their packs on the deck*: Nichol and Rennell, *The Last Escape*, p. 23.

15 – *cocked machine gun*: Ibid.

16 – *ground up by the unflinching steel teeth of the ship's gears*: newspaper interview with Bill Dorgan's son, Tim, "Catholic World War II vet keeps faith in God, friends," *The Catholic Times*, May 14, 2009, p. 12.

17 – *Men there licked the condensation droplets*: telephone interview with Tim Dorgan, February 5, 2013.

18 – *Lack of ventilation and rolling seas*: Dillon, *A Domain of Heroes*, p. 137.

19 – *these same pails were used for toilets*: Nichol and Rennell, *The Last Escape*, p. 24.

20 – *German soldiers machine gunned him*: author interview with Jim Millin, July 5, 2015.

21 – *The Germans made no attempt to recover the body*: Dillon, *A Domain of Heroes*, p. 138.

22 – *turning the hold into an oven*: Nichol and Rennell, *The Last Escape*, p. 24.

23 – *port of Swinemunde at the mouth of the Oder River*: Miller, *Masters of the Air*, p. 401.

24 – *take off their shoes and hold them*: Nichol and Rennell, *The Last Escape*, p. 25.

25 – *A rumor rippled through the filthy men that the SS were coming to take them and parade them*: Ibid.

26 – *stopped next to a pine forest at a small railroad junction called Kiefheide*: Ibid, p. 26.

27 – *Kriegsmarines, cadets from the German Navy*: Miller, *Masters of the Air*, p. 401.

28 – *"Go ahead and kill us now, you Kraut shitbags!"*: LaMore and Baker, *One Man's War*, p.167.

29 – *"Water. Water. Oh, God, give us water. We're dying!"*: Ibid.

30 – *a short, chubby, red-haired man dressed in the gleaming white uniform*: Dillon, *A Domain of Heroes*, p. 139.

31 – *sandy road into a pine forest*: Nichol and Rennell, *The Last Escape*, p. 27.

32 – *"You are flyboys. Let's see you fly."*: Dillon, *Domain of Heroes*, p. 140.

33 – *"Escape, escape!"*: Ibid. p. 141.

34 – *stood two barbed wire fences, ten feet high, which surrounded a camp*: Parrent, *Stalag Luft IV*, p. 15.

35 – *pants of many Kriegies hung in shreds around the ankles where the dogs had ripped and chewed*: Dillon, *Domain of Heroes*, p. 142.

36 – *two-mile run*: Miller, *Masters of the Air*, p. 402.

Chapter 14: Dreams of Roast Duck

1 – *simple wooden building*: Parrent, "Imprisoned Flyer" by Michael Pappas, *Stalag Luft IV*, p. 27.

2 – *Inside stood six guards*: Bacchia, *Augie*, p. 72.

3 – *six foot seven inches tall and looked to weigh around three hundred pounds*: Miller, *Masters of the Air*, p. 396.

4 – *jagged teeth*: Dillon, *Domain of Heroes*, p. 139.

5 – *two middle-aged uniformed men sitting on stools and wearing rubber gloves*: Parrent, "Imprisoned Flyer" by Michael Pappas, *Stalag Luft IV*, p. 27.

6 – *mouths, noses, and ears*: Dillon, *Domain of Heroes*, p. 147.

7 – *seemed to linger*: Parrent, "Imprisoned Flyer" by Michael Pappas, *Stalag Luft IV*, p. 27.

8 – *"Es macht wieder"*: Bacchia, *Augie*, p. 72.

9 – *"What the hell do ya' want from me?"*: Ibid. p. 73.

10 – *fifteen by twenty feet*: Dillon, *Domain of Heroes*, p. 148.

11 – *sack filled with wood shavings*: Ibid. p. 149.

12 – *The latrine, a long board with six holes in it*: LaMore and Baker, *One Man's War*, p.150.

13 – *didn't have showers anywhere for the prisoners*: Dillon, *Domain of Heroes*, p. 175.

14 – *wood so rough cut that splinters poked through*: LaMore and Baker, *One Man's War*, p.150.

15 – *"Straighten these lines. We will stand here until these lines are straight"*: Ibid, p. 149.

16 – *The prison was divided into four square compounds*: Dillon, *Domain of Heroes*, p. 148.

17 – *pilings about two to three feet off the ground*: Ibid.

18 – *barrier stood some thirty feet from a second line of barbed wire*: Bacchia, *Augie*, p. 74.

19 – *"Cross this wire and you will be shot immediately"*: LaMore and Baker, *One Man's War*, p. 149.

20 – *"Be in your barracks one hour before sundown"*: Dillon, *Domain of Heroes*, p. 173.

21 – *"Leave your barracks after lights out, and you will be shot!"*: LaMore and Baker, *One Man's War*, p.149.

22 – *jabbing their finger at every kriegie and counting*: Parrent, "Imprisoned Flyer" by Michael Pappas, *Stalag Luft IV*, p. 27.

23 – *drank own piss*: telephone interview with Tim Dorgan, Feb. 5, 2013.

24 – *some men next to him died of suffocation*: telephone interview with Tim Dorgan, July 31, 2016.

25 – *older and seemed unfit for regular army service*: LaMore and Baker, *One Man's War*, p.151.

26 - *clicked the safeties off on their Mauser machine guns*: Ibid.

27 – *sometimes with ruptured eardrums*: Parrent, "The Testimony of Dr. Leslie Caplan," *Stalag Luft IV*, p. 22.

28 – *just clench his fists and take it*: LaMore and Baker, *One Man's War*, p. 151.

29 – *often speckled with tiny white bugs crawling on them*: Miller, *Masters of the Air*, p. 399.

30 – *Germans stored the parcels in a warehouse just outside the prison*: author interview with Jim Millin interview, July 3, 2018.

31 – *moaned in their sleep about exploding airplanes*: Miller, *Masters of the Air*, p. 403.

32 – *gray skies and temperatures below zero*: Dillon, *Domain of Heroes*, p. 187.

33 – *allowed lights out time to extend to 1 a.m.*: Ibid, p. 188.

34 – *packages included nuts, candy, sausages, hams, and cheese*: Ibid.

35 – *Luftwaffe fighter plane executed a barrel roll over the camp*: Ibid, p. 157.

36 – *January temperatures plunged way below zero*: Ibid, p. 174.

37 – *many had stopped bathing because of the extreme cold*: Bacchia, *Augie*, p. 75.

38 – *new arrivals came from camps in the East*: Nichol and Rennell, *The Last Escape*, p. 118.

39 – *"What if the Germans force us to fight the Soviets?"*: Dillon, *Domain of Heroes,* p. 194.

40 – *On January 29, the camp commandant ordered every prisoner into the compound*: Richard Bing, *You're 19 . . . Welcome Home: A Story of the Air War Over Europe and its After-Effects,* (Privately printed, 1992), p. 96.

41 – *wounded and sick prisoners would be marching out to the train station a few miles from the camp*: Ibid.

42 – *On the evening of February 5 . . . evacuate the camp early the next morning*: Harold Cyr, handwritten notes *The Walk Home,* copies provided by Paul Cyr and given to *Catholic Times* correspondent Joseph O'Brien. O'Brien provided copies to Joni Moran Peterson, p. 1.

43 – *better for the prisoners to have the food than to give it up to the Russians*: Dillon, *Domain of Heroes,* p. 202.

44 – *two thousand other POWs*: Parrent, "Liberation " by Clarence Odegard, *Stalag Luft IV,* p. 38.

45 – *the Russians couldn't be more than thirty miles away*: Joseph P. O'Donnell, *The Shoe Leather Express: The Evacuation of Kriegsgefangenen Lager Stalag Luft IV Deutschland Germany,* (privately printed, 1982), p. 2.

Chapter 15: Death March

1 – *dark, gray morning*: Harold Cyr, handwritten notes *The Walk Home,* p.1.

2 – *twenty-below-zero air*: Parrent, "Liberation " by Clarence Odegard, *Stalag Luft IV,* p. 38.

3 – *Hitler wanted the prisoners as bargaining chips for a negotiated surrender*: Bacchia, *Augie,* p. 79.

4 – *Many POWs assumed they'd simply be shot:* author interview with Jim Millin, July 5, 2015.

5 – *groups of about three hundred*: Bacchia, *Augie.* p. 76.

6 – *spaced themselves at arms length:* Ibid, p. 77.

7 – *The kriegies marched three to four men wide:* Parrent, "Evacuation" by Rudolf Vidmar, *Stalag Luft IV,* p. 19.

8 – *"Laufen schneller":* Bacchia, *Augie,* p. 79.

9 – *The sound of Klim cans clanging and striking other Klim cans echoed:* O'Donnell, *The Shoe Leather Express,* p. 2.

10 – *Three or four-day hike:* Parrent, "Evacuation" by Rudolf Vidmar, *Stalag Luft IV,* p. 19.

11 – *seven-pound packages:* Nichol, & Rennell, *The Last Escape,* p. 126.

12 – *allowed a few five-minute toilet breads:* Parrent, "Evacuation" by Rudolf Vidmar, *Stalag Luft IV,* p. 19.

13 – *unbuttoning the pants fly of a friend:* Ibid.

14 – *only worsened their dysentery:* Parrent, "Bail-Out to Prison Camp" by Richard H. Hamilton, *Stalag Luft IV,* p. 31.

15 – *stained with urine or bloody feces:* Miller, *Masters of the Air,* p. 501.

16 – *Red Army was only twenty miles behind:* Ibid.

17 – *pulling push-bikes and farm carts:* Keith Lowe, *Savage Continent: Europe in the Aftermath of World War II,* (St. Martin's Press, New York, 2012), p. 28.

18 – *Mutilated bodies were said to be strewn everywhere in eastern Germany:* Ibid, p. 75.

19 – *feces soon littered the rest stop:* Dillon, *Domain of Heroes,* p. 204.

20 – *villagers seemed friendly:* Foy, *For You The War is Over,* p. 142.

21 – *the guards looked the other way:* Dillon, *Domain of Heroes,* p. 205.

22 – *traded class rings and wedding bands:* Ibid, p. 206.

23 – *worn the same clothes for months:* Bacchia, *Augie.* p. 79.

24 – *German farmers continued to raise food:* Earl R. Beck, *Under the Bombs: The German Home Front, 1942-1945,* (The University of Kentucky Press, Lexington, Kentucky, 1986), p. 185-186.

25 – *used the charcoal to rub over tooth aches:* Jim Millin, "*Death March in Germany in World War II.*" type-written personal account by Jim Millin provided to author, p. 2.

26 – *a rifle shot rang out:* author interview with Jim Millin, July 5, 2015.

27 – *grubs which the swallowed whole:* Parrent, "Fleeing the Death March" by Harold Scott, *Stalag Luft IV,* p. 18.

28 – *They spoke a mix of languages:* Lowe, *Savage Continent,* p. 32.

29 – *rode in overcrowded buses or the backs of trucks:* Ibid, p. 28.

Chapter 16: Liberation

1 – *only if the Germans didn't grab the clothes first:* Mitchell Bard, *Forgotten Victims: The Abandonment of Americans in Hitler's Camps,* (Westview Press, Boulder, Colorado, 1994), p. 97.

2 – *they didn't have anything to eat, either:* Morris, *Untold Valor,* p. 115.

3 – *"Next town, next town.":* Bard, *Forgotten Victims,* p. 98.

4 – *ate burnt wood:* Dillon, *Domain of Heroes,* p. 212.

5 – *pneumonia swept the rank:* Morris, *Untold Valor,* p. 115.

6 – *lying on damp dirt or straw, often filthy with manure:* Bacchia, *Augie,* p. 83.

7 – *sick men sank into the sodden straw of their barn beds and never woke up:* Bard, *Forgotten Victim,* p. 99.

8 – *clung to a buddy to assist them:* Ibid, p. 100.

9 – *kriegies pulled some of the carts:* Dillon, *Domain of Heroes,* p. 211.

10 – *"sick wagons":* Ibid.

11 – *collapsed by the side of the road:* Ibid.

12 – *where and how German soldiers were to surrender:* Harold Cyr, handwritten notes *Highlights,* p. 2.

13 – *white bed sheets hung from upper windowsills:* Ibid.

14 – *Dysentery and malnutrition slowed the column to a crawl:* Kaplan and Smith, *One Last Look, p.* 181.

15 – *curry favor with Americans:* Bard, *Forgotten Victims,* p. 101.

16 – *April 26:* Harold Cyr, handwritten notes *Highlights,* p. 3.

17 – *six hundred miles:* Allen L. Griggs, *Flying Flak Alley: Personal Accounts of World War II Bomber Crew Combat,* (McFarland & Company, Inc., 2008), p. 217.

18 – *104th Infantry Division*: Parrent, "Bail-Out to Prison Camp" by Richard Hamilton, *Stalag Luft IV*, p. 31.

19 – *GIs handed their K-rations to the starving prisoners*: Harold Cyr, handwritten notes *Highlights*, p. 2.

20 – *slammed a pickaxe into his head*: Dillon, *Domain of Heroes*, p. 255. Also, Nichol and Rennell, *The Last Escape*, p. 376, which parenthetically notes that there are varying accounts of the killing of Big Stoop.

21 – *former Luftwaffe base*: Harold Cyr, handwritten notes *Highlights*, p. 3.

22 – *"best cake I've ever had"*: Harold Cyr, handwritten notes *Highlights*, p. 5.

23 – *set up the camp specifically as a gathering post for ex-POWs*: Matheny, *Rites of Passage*, p. 296.

24 – *spotted the towers and spire of the famous cathedral from the* airfield: Harold Cyr, handwritten notes *Highlights*, p. 5.

25 – *temporary airstrip*: Casey, *To Fight for My Country, Sir!*, p. 251.

26 – *Recovered Allied Military Personnel*: Matheny, *Rites of Passage*, p. 296.

27 – *new wool shirts, underwear, socks and overseas caps with the insignia of rank pinned to the cap*: Casey, *To Fight for My Country, Sir!*, p. 251-252.

28 – *"Baltic cruise" and "run up the road"*: Nichol and Rennell, *The Last Escape*, p. 398.

29 – *creamed chicken and potatoes*: Casey, *To Fight for My Country, Sir!*, p. 252.

30 – *American young women from the Red Cross served doughnuts and milkshakes made with real ice cream*: Matheny, *Rites of Passage*, p. 296.

31 – *the lines to seem them were long*: Dillon, *Domain of Heroes*, p. 70.

32 – *"Soon everyone was screaming"*: Jesse Orrison, "Casualty Questionnaire – King, Anderson M.," Missing Air Crew Report, NARA, printed Nov. 2, 2014. Orrison reported "several crew members called out that they were wounded seriously."

33 – *"He yelled something about trouble with the plane"*: Jesse Orrison, "Casualty Questionnaire – Langley, Linwood D.," Missing Air Crew Report, NARA, printed Nov. 2, 2014. Orrison reported Langley "called trouble with plane."

34 – *"Reed hanging from his turret"*: Jesse Orrison, "Casualty Questionnaire – Reed, Walter F.," Missing Air Crew Report, NARA, printed Nov. 2, 2014. Orrison reported on Walter Reed "I saw him in his position before I left the ship . . . standing in his position."

35 – *many screaming to kill him*: author interview with Annelore Franke, Nov. 29, 2018 in Syke, Germany. At age eight, Annelore witnessed Jesse Orrison hanging from his parachute in a tree.

36 – *he was taken to stay with a group of nuns*: author interview with Wayne Orrison, January 28, 2013.

37 – *Margaret had been living with Orrison's parents in Michigan*: Ibid.

38 – *Some men grew tired of the long waiting and took off for Paris*: Dillon, *Domain of Heroes*, p. 270.

39 – *cut-down officer's jacket, buttoned sharply at the waist*: Matheny, *Rites of Passage*, p. 297.

Chapter 17: Homecoming

1 – *The International Red Cross discovered information on the burial*: SUBJECT: Reports of Burial, Second Lieutenant Arnold L. Robinson, GRS officer, March, 8, 1946. IDPF for Donald Curtis, U.S. Army Human Resources Command, Fort Knox, KY, p. 84.

2 – *civilian cemetery in the town of Vechta, Germany*: REPORT OF BURIAL, Office of the American Graves Registration Command, Oct. 16, 1946. IDPF for Linwood Langley, U.S. Army Human Resources Command, Fort Knox, p. 68.

3 – *"unknowns"*: SUBJECT: Isolated Burials, Headquarters American Graves Registration Command-European Theater Area, March 29, 1946. Donald Curtis IDPF, U.S. Army Human Resources Command, Fort Knox, KY, p. 83.

4 – *Joseph R. Sawicki was buried with the dead*: CHECK LIST OF UNKNOWN, Second Lieutenant Arnold L. Robinson, GRS officer, May

14, 1946, p. 4. IDPF for Donald Curtis, U.S. Army Human Resources Command, Fort Knox, KY, p. 27.

5 – *went down with his flaming plane:* Fyler, *Staying Alive, p.* 84.

6 – *The bottom half of Sparky's head was missing:* CHECK LIST OF UN-KNOWN, Second Lieutenant Arnold L. Robinson, GRS officer, May 14, 1946, p. 4. IDPF for Samuel Amatulli, U.S. Army Human Resources Command, Fort Knox, KY, p. 87.

7 – *corpse did not include most of his skull, his left pelvis, left hand and right collar bone:* SKELETAL CHART, March 3, 1948. IDPF for Berline Cipresso, U.S. Army Human Resources Command, Fort Knox, KY, p. 63.

8 – *Langley's sideburns were charred:* CHECK LIST OF UNKNOWN, Second Lieutenant Arnold L. Robinson, GRS officer, May 14, 1946, p. 3. IDPF for Linwood Langley, U.S. Army Human Resources Command, Fort Knox, KY, p. 13.

9 – *the only one wearing his metal identification necklace, "dog tags".:* "REPORT OF INVESTIGATION AREA SEARCH," April 18, 1946. IDPF for Walter Reed, U.S. Army Human Resources Command, Fort Knox, KY, p. 12.

10 – *S-7541:* REPORT OF INTERNMENT, April 27, 1946, p. 2. Edmund Swedo IDPF, U.S. Army Human Resources Command, Fort Knox, KY, p. 36 & 37.

11 – *Curtis' grave was correctly labeled:* REPORT OF INVESTIGATION AREA SEARCH," April 16, 1946, p. 1. IDPF for Donald Curtis, U.S. Army Human Resources Command, Fort Knox, KY, p. 19.

12 – *but Benny's grave was mistakenly labeled "Linwood Langley":* REPORT OF INVESTIGATION AREA SEARCH," April 16, 1946, p. 1. IDPF for Berline Cipresso, U.S. Army Human Resources Command, Fort Knox, KY, p. 37.

13 – *Langley's corpse which still had fur-lined flight boots on his feet:* CHECK LIST OF UNKNOWN, May 14, 1946, p. 2. IDPF for Linwood Langley, U.S. Army Human Resources Command, Fort Knox, p. 12.

14 – *feasted on steak, mashed potatoes, fresh vegetables, pies and ice cream:* Nichol and Rennell, *The Last Escape,* p. 399.

15 – *captain's voice came on the loudspeaker warning everyone not to crowd one side of the ship*: Ibid, 399.

16 – *received money and tickets for trains leaving that day*: Matheny, *Rites of Passage*, p. 298.

17 – *volunteer groups served coffee, soda and doughnuts*: Ibid, 299.

18 – *Saturday, June 16*: "S. Sgt. Eugene Moran Arrived Home Saturday After 17 Months in German Prison," *Kickapoo Scout*, June 21, 1945.

19 – *four of his aunts and uncles and a half dozen cousins met him*: "Man Who Fell 4 Miles Back Home to Tell It," *Wisconsin State Journal*. Newspaper clipping provided by Moran family. No date listed on clipped article.

20 – *Gene's homecoming was front-page news*: "S. Sgt. Eugene Moran Arrived Home Saturday After 17 Months in German Prison," *Kickapoo Scout*, June 21, 1945.

21 – *"Trapped Yank Airman Falls 4 Mile -- Lives."* Newspaper clipping marked "St. Paul" provided by Moran family. No date on article clipping.

Chapter 18: The Family's War

1 – *Rosemary, who had a break from nursing school and was there with her date*: interview conducted by Joni Moran Peterson with Rosemary Moran Koerber, April 6, 2013. Notes and audio recording provided to author.

2 – *"Sergeant Moran, most of the POWs I've talked to are pretty skinny"*: telephone interview with Mike Moran, April 23, 2019.

3 – *"Doc Sannes at six-six"*: telephone interview with Joni Moran Peterson, August 9, 2019.

4 – *"Go ahead . . . I dare you to shoot me"*: telephone interview with Joni Moran Peterson, April 23, 2019.

5 – *"Relax . . . quiet down"*: telephone interview with Margo Moran Murphy, April 24, 2019.

6 – *"Where the hell have you been?"*: author interview with Laurie Moran Hackman, May 20, 2019.

7 – *"You may as well go back to the tavern for all I care"*: telephone interview with Margo Moran Murphy, April 24, 2019.

8 – *"Call your father and tell him to get home. I'm hungry!"*: telephone interview with Patrick Moran, May 21, 2019.

9 – *"I thought you said you'd never eat potato skins again"*: telephone interview with Bridget Moran Trussoni, April 24, 2019.

10 – *"You know, Mom. For the first time in thirty-two years, I didn't get the headaches"*: telephone interview with Laurie Moran Hackman. June 28, 2019.

11 – *"Times are different now, Dad. Let it go"*: telephone interview with Bridget Moran Trussoni, April 24, 2019.

12 – *"Don't tell me I don't know what I'm talking about"*: typed document emailed from Bridget Moran Trussoni, July 12, 2017.

13 – *"Merry Christmas, Eugene!"*: telephone interview with Joni Moran Peterson, April 17, 2019.

14 – *"Grandma is fading fast . . . Go get Grandpa"*: telephone interview with Tim Moran, Aug. 29, 2019.

15 – *Peg wanted to die at home*: email from Laurie Moran Hackman, Aug. 7, 2019.

16 – *the doctors seemed to have finally got the right medication for Peg which greatly improved her mood*: email from Bridget Moran Trussoni, Aug. 8, 2019.

17 – *Gene would get out of his car and embrace his wife*: email from Margo Moran Murphy, Aug. 8, 2019.

18 – *Who are these sweet strangers, and what have they done to our parents?*: email from Joni Moran Peterson, Aug. 8, 2019.

19 – *making homemade applesauce to aid Peg in swallowing her medication*: Ibid.

20 – *"Mom, I just can't get these sheets without the corners folded as good as you do"*: email from Patrick Moran, Aug. 8, 2019.

21 – *pushing his Ford Ranger up to seventy miles an hour*: telephone interview with Tim Moran, Aug. 29, 2019.

22 – *"It's going to be okay . . . We'll get there"*: Ibid.

23 – *"We didn't quite make our anniversary, did we Mom? . . . But that's okay*: Ibid.

Chapter 19: The Toughest to Ever Draw Breath

1 – *Pat prepared for his return flight for Sunday night*: telephone interview with Patrick Moran, May 21, 2019.

2 – *tell their father that maybe it was time for him to move to an assisted living home*: telephone interview with Joni Moran Peterson, June 28, 2019.

3 – *His pulse weakened and his heart rate slipped*: Joni Moran Peterson, August 9, 2019.

4 – *Gene was in and out of sleep, but he stirred when Pat put on a baseball game between the Milwaukee Brewers and Atlanta Braves*: telephone interview with Patrick Moran, May 21, 2019.

5 – *"I'm ready"*: telephone interview with Margo Moran Murphy, April 24, 2019.

6 – *"Hello, Father"*: telephone interview with Joni Moran Peterson, June 28, 2019.

7 – *"We should probably do a toast"*: telephone interview with Patrick Moran, May 21, 2019.

8 – *"To Eugene Moran. The toughest son of a bitch to ever draw breath"*: author interview with Laurie Moran Hackman, May 20, 2019.

9 – *one of the grandchildren had sneaked a can of Blatz beer into the casket*: Ibid.

10 – *honor guard sent from the Middleton Fire Department*: telephone interview with Mike Moran, April 23, 2019.

SELECTED BIBLIOGRAPHY

Manuscript Collections

Air Force Historical Research Agency, Maxwell Air Force Base, Alabama

Narrative Reports of Operations of the 96th Bombardment Group (H), AAF, (A, B, & C group reports), Office of the Operations Officer, Headquarters Ninety-Sixth Bombardment Group (H) Army Air Forces for the following missions:

- Wilhelmshaven, Germany, 3 November 1943
- Gelsenkirchen, Germany, 5 November 1943
- Munster, Germany, 11 November 1943
- Bremen, Germany, 13 November 1943
- Rjukan, Norway, 16 November 1943
- Gelsenkirchen, Germany, 19 November 1943
- Bremen, Germany, 26 November 1943
- Bremen, Germany, 29 November 1943

National Archives and Records Administration, College Park, Maryland

"Individual Casualty Questionnaire" – Missing Air Crew Report (MACR) #1392.
"Operational Route Forecast." Operations Report, Nov. 29, 1943, Headquarters of 96th Bombardment Group.

"Narrative Report of Operations of the 96th "A" Bombardment Group (H), AAF, Bremen, Germany, November 29, 1943." Office of the Operations Officer, Headquarters Ninety-Sixth Bombardment Group (H) Army Air Forces.

"Report of Personnel Missing in Action, November 29, 1943, Bremen, Germany." Office of Operations Officer, Headquarters Ninety-Sixth Bombardment Group (H), Army Air Forces.

Department of the Army: US Army Human Resources Command, Fort Knox, Kentucky

Individual Deceased Personnel File for:
* Amatulli, Samuel
* Cipresso, Berline
* Curtis, Donald
* King, Anderson
* Langley, Linwood
* Provost, Wilbert
* Reed, Walter
* Swedo, Edmund

Illinois State Library General Collection, Illinois Digital Archive

"The History of Fort Sheridan, Illinois January 1, 1944 John T Rhett, Colonel, Infantry, Commanding" Prepared by Robert Schall, 2nd Lt. AUS For the Public Relations Office Published by The Clerical School and the Visual Training Aids Section 1672nd Service Unit).

Oral Histories

Veterans History Project "Eugene P. Moran, U.S. Army Air Corps World War II," interview conducted with U.S. Congressman Ron Kind,

Mike Herro of Rotary Club–North, La Crosse, WI, Major William E. Bruring of U.S. Civil Air Patrol–US. Air Force (aux) and the American Legion, July 2, 2007.

Personal Recordings

Cyr, Harold "Shorty"
- "Highlights"
- "The Walk Home"
  Copies provided by Paul Cyr, and given to *Catholic Times* correspondent Joseph O'Brien. O'Brien provided copies to Joni Moran Peterson.

Dorgan, Bill
- Sworn statement to a notary public, Richland County, Wisconsin, October 8, 1946
  Copy provided by Bill's son, Tim

Millin, Jim
- "Death March in Germany in World War II"
  Typewritten personal account provided to author

Books

B-17 Bomber Pilot's Flight Operating Instructions (originally published by United States Army Air Force, Dec. 25, 1942: republished in Lexington, Kentucky by Periscopefilm.com: 2013).

Angelucci, Enzo & Matricardi, Paolo. *World War II Airplanes: Volume 2*. Chicago: Rand McNally & Company, 1978.

Bacchia, John. *Augie: Stalag Luft VI to the Major Leagues*. Bloomington, Indiana. iUniverse, Inc. 2011.

Bard, Mitchell. *Forgotten Victims: The Abandonment of Americans in Hitler's Camps*. Boulder, CO: Westview Press, 1994.

Beck, Earl. R. *Under the Bombs: The German Home Front, 1942-1945*. Lexington, Kentucky. The University Press of Kentucky, 1986.

Bing, Richard L. *You're 19 . . . Welcome Home: A Story of the Air War Over Europe and its After-Effects*. Privately printed, 1992.

Boiten, Theo & Bowman, Martin. *Battles with the Luftwaffe: The Bomber Campaign Against Germany 1942-1945*. London: HarperCollins Publishers, 2001.

Bowman, Martin W., *The Mighty Eighth at War: US 8th Air Force Bombers Versus the Luftwaffe 1943-1945*. South Yorkshire, Great Britain: Pen & Sword Books Ltd, 2010.

Bruning, John R., *Bombs Away: The World War II Bombing Campaigns Over Europe*. New York: Zenith Press, 2011.

Caldwell, Donald. *Day Fighters in Defense of the Reich: A War Diary, 1942-45*. South Yorkshire, Great Britain: Frontline Books, 2011.

Carson, Lt. Col. Eugene T. Carson USA (Ret), *Wing Ding: Memories of a Tail Gunner*. Privately printed, 2000.

Casey, Donald E., *To Fight For My Country, Sir!: Memoirs of a 19 Year Old B-17 Navigator Shot Down in Nazi Germany and Imprisoned in the WWII "Great Escape" Prison Camp*. Chicago: Sterling Cooper Publishing, Inc., 2009.

Childers, Thomas. *Wings of Morning: The Story of the Last American Bomber Shot Down Over Germany in World War II*. Lebanon, Indiana: Da Capo Press. A Member of the Perseus Books Group, 1995.

Dillon, Carol F., *A Domain of Heroes: An Airman's Life Behind Barbed Wire in Germany in World War II*. Sarasota, Florida: Palm Island Press, 1995.

Doherty, Robert E. and Ward, Geoffrey D., *Snetterton Falcons II: The 96th Bomb Group In World War II*. Dallas, Texas: Taylor Publishing Company, 1989.

Douglas, Graeme. *Boeing B-17 Flying Fortress Owners' Workshop Manual*. Minneapolis, Minnesota: Zenith Press, 2011.

Ehresmann, Andreas. *Das Stalag XB Sandbostel-Geschichte und Nachgeschichte eines Kriegsgefangenenlagers,* Hamburg, Germany: Dolling and Galitz Verlag, 2015.

Foy, David A. *For You the War is Over: American Prisoners of War in Nazi Germany.* New York: Stein and Day, 1984.

Freeman, Roger A. *Mighty Eighth War Diary.* London: Jane's Publishing, 1981.

Fyler, Carl. *Staying Alive: A B-17 Pilot's Experience Flying Unescorted Bomber Missions by 8th Air Force Elements During World War II.* Leavenworth, KS: J.H. Johnston, 1995.

Gardiner, Juliet. *"Overpaid, Oversexed & Over Here."* New York: Canopy Books, 1992.

Griggs, Allen L. *Flying Flak Alley: Personal Accounts of World War II Bomber Crew Combat.* Jefferson, North Carolina: Edited by McFarland & Company, Inc., 2008.

Hillenbrand, Laura. *Unbroken: A World War II Story of Survival, Resilience, and Redemption.* New York: Random House, 2010.

Hutchinson, James Lee. *B-17 Memories: From Memphis Belle to Victory.* Bloomington, Indiana: AuthorHouse, 2014.

Kaplan, Philip and Smith, Rex Allen. *One Last Look: A Sentimental Journey to the Eighth Air Force Heavy Bomber Bases of World War II in England.* New York: Abbeyville Press, 1983.

LaMore, Tommy and Baker, Dan A. *One Man's War: The WWII Saga of Tommy LaMore.* Lanham, MD: Taylor Trade Publishing, 2002.

Logan, Ben. *The Land Remembers.* Blue Mounds, WI: Itchy Cat Press, 2006 (first published Minocqua, WI: Heartland Press, 1975).

Lowe, Keith. *Savage Continent: Europe in the Aftermath of World War II.* New York: St. Martin's Press, 2012.

Matheny, Ray. *Rite of Passage: A Teenager's Chronicle of Combat and Captivity in Nazi Germany.* Clearfield, Utah: American Legacy Media, 2009.

McManus, John C. *Deadly Sky: The American Combat Airman in World War II.* New York: Penguin Random House LLC, 2000.

Meine, Curt and Keeley, Keefe. *The Driftless Reader*. Madison, WI: The University of Wisconsin Press, 2017.

Miller, Donald. *Masters of the Air: America's Bomber Boys Who Fought the Air War Against Nazi Germany*. New York: Simon & Schuster, Inc., 2006.

Morgan, Robert with Ron Powers. *The Man Who Flew Memphis Belle: Memoir of a WWII Bomber Pilot*. New York: New American Library, a division of Penguin Group, 2001.

Morris, Rob. *Untold Valor: Forgotten Stories of American Bomber Crews over Europe in World War II*. Washington, D.C.: Potomac Books, Inc., 2006.

Nichol, John & Rennell, Tony. *The Last Escape: The Untold Story of Allied Prisoners of War in Europe 1944-45*. New York, Penguin Group, 2002.

Novey, Jack. *The Cold Blue Sky: A B-17 Gunner in World War Two*. Charlottesville, Virginia: Howell Press, 1997.

O'Donnell, Joseph P. *The Shoe Leather Express: The Evacuation of Kriegsgefangenen Lager Stalag Luft IV Deutschland Germany*, Privately printed, 1982.

O'Neill, Brian D. *Half a Wing, Three Engines and a Prayer*. New York: McGraw-Hill Companies, 1999.

Parrent, Eric (editor). *Stalag Luft IV, 1944-1945: 50th Anniversary*. Paducah, Kentucky: Turner Publishing Company, 1996.

VanBlair, Dale. *Looking Back: A Tail Gunner's View of World War II*. Bloomington, IN: Privately printed, 2003.

Newspapers

The Catholic Times
Gays Mills Independent
Kickapoo Scout
La Crosse Tribune

Las Vegas Review-Journal
New York Times
Wisconsin State Journal

Articles

"Aerial Gunners," *Life Magazine*, July 13, 1942, p. 43-44.
"The Ghost Air Force Bases of Greenland" by Paula Froelich, *The Daily Beast*, 7-29-17.

Author Interviews

Much of this book is based on twenty-eight recorded personal interviews conducted with Gene Moran in his home from Jan. 11, 2011 through March 8, 2014.

Personal, telephone, and email interviews were conducted with the following:

- JoAnn Moran – sister of Gene Moran
- Rosemary Moran Koerber – sister of Gene Moran
- Bridget Moran Trussoni – daughter of Gene Moran
- Elizabeth Moran – daughter of Gene Moran
- Joni Moran Peterson – daughter of Gene Moran
- Laura Moran Hackman – daughter of Gene Moran
- Margo Moran Murphy – daughter of Gene Moran
- Mike Moran – son of Gene Moran
- Patrick Moran – son of Gene Moran
- Tom Moran – son of Gene Moran
- Wayne Orrison – son of Jesse Orrison
- Greg Swedo – nephew of Edmund Swedo
- Tim Dorgan – son of Bill Dorgan

- Charles Cyr – nephew of Harold "Shorty" Cyr
- Paul Cyr – son of Harold "Shorty" Cyr
- Jim Millin – former Flying Fortress ball turret gunner and POW, 94th Bomb Group
- Ulf Kaack – co-author of *Luftkrieg in Der Region*
- Jürgen Kuhlmann – co-author of *Luftkrieg in Der Region*
- Ronald Sperlman – museum archivist and documentarian of Sandbostel Prisoner-of-War Museum
- Annelore Franke – eyewitness to *Rikki Tikki Tavi* coming down over Syke, Germany
- Jeff, Tim, and Jerry Mayo – nephews of Walter Reed
- Leslie Feldman – niece of Walter Reed

Printed in Great Britain
by Amazon

58318608R00235